He's A Rebel

He's A
REBEL

PHIL SPECTOR
ROCK AND ROLL'S LEGENDARY PRODUCER

Mark Ribowsky

Da Capo Press
A Member of the Perseus Books Group

For my own little rebel, my son Jake Ribowsky,
and in loving memory of my mother, Frances Ribowsky

Cataloging-in-Publication data for this book is available from the Library of Congress.

First Da Capo Press edition 2006
ISBN-10 0–306–81471–4
ISBN-13 978–0–306–81471–6

Published by Da Capo Press
A Member of the Perseus Books Group
www.dacapopress.com

Da Capo Press books are available at special discounts for bulk purchases in the U.S. by corporations, institutions, and other organizations. For more information, please contact the Special Markets Department at the Perseus Books Group, 11 Cambridge Center, Cambridge, MA 02142, or call (800) 255-1514 or (617) 252-5298, or e-mail special.markets@perseusbooks.com.

1 2 3 4 5 6 7 8 9—09 08 07 06

ACKNOWLEDGMENTS

The sources that made this book come alive number over one hundred. Of these, almost all spoke on the record freely and thoughtfully, and their contributions are self-evident in the pages of history that follow. My deepest thanks to all of them, as well as to those few sources who chose anonymity rather than risk Phil Spector's wrath but still kindly provided crucial information.

I would like to especially acknowledge the aid of Annette Merar Spector and Marshall Lieb. There simply could not have been a definitive Phil Spector book without the vivid memories of both of these wonderful people. Though Annette had to relive the pain and anxiety of a crumbled marriage, she repaid my constant intrusions with grace, understanding, and complete cooperation. A busy man in Hollywood movie circles these days, Marshall knew how important it was for me to speak with one who had traveled with Spector from childhood to manhood. With the patience of a schoolteacher conducting a history lesson, he acted both as tour guide of their old West Hollywood neighborhood and chief interpreter of Spector's psyche.

I would like to single out a number of others who offered invaluable recollections in long, sometimes tedious interviews. My sincere appreciation goes to Carol Connors, Donna Kass, Michael Spencer, Steve Douglas, Harvey Goldstein, Stan Ross, Don Kartoon, Lew Bedell, Lester Sill, Elliott Ingber, Russ Titelman, Beverly Ross, Doc Pomus, Terry Phillips, Ray Peterson, Gene Pitney, Gerry Goffin, Snuff Garrett, Bobby Sheen, Fanita James, Arnold Goland, Larry Levine, Sonny Bono, La La Brooks, Mary Thomas, Nedra Talley, Vinnie Poncia, Danny Davis, Irwin Levine, Dan and David Kessel, and Joey Ramone.

One can't begin to describe the feeling a rock-and-roll devotee and scholar gets by spending time with the legendary studio musicians of rock's age of romance. For the thrill of a lifetime and for enriching my music education, I particularly want to thank Howard Roberts, Barney Kessel, Hal Blaine, Earl Palmer, Ray Pohlman, Gary Chester, Artie Kaplan, Artie Butler, and Charlie Macey.

I would also like to acknowledge with gratitude the hardy souls who dutifully culled archives for precious details of the early rock terrain now covered by two decades of dust and neglect. Buried deep in file cabinets and basement catacombs, the recording contracts, ledgers of fabled studio sessions, and long out-of-print record labels were reclaimed through the time and efforts of Bob Rafkin of the American Federation of Musicians Local 47, the House of Oldies in Greenwich Village, and Bob Merlis and Meryl Zukowsky of Warner Brothers Records.

Special thanks to Bob Shannon, Arnie Kay, Marsha Vance, Kenny Vance, Jack Jackson, Barry Goldberg, and Rodney Bingenheimer for vital contacts and telephone numbers; and to Harvey Kubernik for the use of his interview material with Jack Nitzsche.

For reasons of logistics, time, and the fact that some, sadly, had passed on, it was not possible to revisit all of these valuable assets for the updated edition of this book. Some others, not knowing what they should say about Spector's status as a charged and indicted murderer, simply opted to say nothing. Michael Spencer, for example, asked to be spared from commenting until after the trial. Carol Connors, who seemed especially distraught and eager to vent about Spector being involved in the death of a friend—"I *knew* her!" she said of Lana Clarkson—nonetheless begged off until after the trial as well. Nino Tempo, who's been joined at the hip with Spector for decades, always seemed to have something on the stove that required his immediate attention. The Kessel brothers' phone numbers were disconnected.

Thus, I would like to reprise my gratitude for five longtime Spector allies who didn't hide in the face of saying something Phil might not appreciate, and indeed offered some extraordinary insights and anecdotes—Larry Levine, Hal Blaine, Don Peake, Mike Lang, and Jimmie Haskell. Triple thanks are due to Levine, Lang, and Haskell for also providing important studio documentation from Spector's mysterious studio sessions with Céline Dion, as did Chris Ogrodowski, the archivist of Professional Musicians Local 47 in L.A. By contrast, no thanks are extended to the Rock and Roll Hall of Fame Foundation, who refused to allow a viewing of Spector's induction ceremony in 1989 or even a look at a transcript of his remarks, with the remarkably flip explanation that such archived material "is not available to the public or the media"—at once laying to rest any doubts that rock and roll's brain waves are today all but dead. Indeed, in no small part due to the self-important buffoonery of its Hall of Fame, rock's long and magnificently noble history of populist rebellion is merely a historic curio, a frame of reference, allegedly cherished but in fact desecrated by the very corporate elitism and conventionality that bred its original mission—and, in the end, took its revenge by buying out the rock industry for no other reason than that it *could.*

Finally, many thanks to Michael Dorr, who purchased the book for its second printing in 2000 as an editor and ushered it into its third printing as a literary agent; and to Ben Schafer, Alexis Rizzuto, and everyone else at Da Capo Press for maintaining their enthusiasm for the book and for bringing it out on schedule despite several trial postponements. I am eternally grateful.

INTRODUCTION

A single shot from a blue steel Colt Cobra .38 made it necessary to revisit and revise a story that seemed to have been told to the bursting point in the first edition of this book published in 1989. At the time, all assumptions were that Phil Spector, having been inducted into the Rock and Roll Hall of Fame, would slip back into the endless exile he seemed so comfortable with. But a cautionary note was sounded by the estimable rock critic Greil Marcus in a February 1989 review of *He's a Rebel* in *California* magazine. "The tale Ribowsky tells is good enough, and likely finished," he wrote. "But don't touch that dial."

Greil was right. Spector was an antsy sort of hermit, popping up over the ensuing decade just long enough to receive fleeting mention on "Entertainment Tonight" or in *Entertainment Weekly*. He could be seen here and there, giving speeches and parties at the Rock and Roll Hall of Fame; working on an ill-fated album project with Céline Dion; sitting in a high-profile courtside seat at Lakers games; hosting bowling parties in Montrose; giving the eulogy at his old arranger Jack Nitzsche's funeral in 2000; schmoozing with some old studio session men at a Sunset

Boulevard club; trying to stay hip upon turning sixty by producing a couple of tracks for the British pop band Starsailor.

However, all that changed on February 3, 2003, when in the wee hours of the morning outside Spector's palatial hilltop "castle" in Alhambra, California—this is no exaggeration; the place is known as the Pyrenes Castle—a limo driver parked in the driveway heard a bang, then saw Phil open the door and say something that freaked him out: "I think I killed somebody."

That "somebody" turned out to be a forty-year-old former B movie actress, Lana Clarkson. Phil had used his awkward, rich-nerd charm to pick her up at the House of Blues in West Hollywood during a wild night on the prowl. When cops responded to the limo driver's 911 call, they ran into a maniacal Spector, mumbling about an "accident" and saying, "I didn't mean to shoot her." Typically, he got in their faces, mouthing off. And when he refused to take his hands out of his pockets, a cop blasted him with 50,000 volts from a Taser, breaking his nose, blackening both eyes, and laying him flat on the cold tile floor.

Spector was placed under arrest and put in a police cruiser—the moment preserved for posterity when a news photographer snapped him in the back of the car looking like a vagrant who had been caught prowling the grounds. He was disheveled—hair matted against his face, eyes bleary, white nightshirt wrinkled and dirty—and he stared like an elk about to become roadkill into a sea of popping flashbulbs as photographers snapped away deliriously.

He would eventually face indictment for murder on September 27, 2004. By then, his big problem had morphed into merely another challenge, another chance to marshal the energy he had once put into his masterpiece studio productions for his looming courtroom showdown. Only now the price for failure would not be a self-imposed exile in a mansion on a hill but incarceration in an eight-by-eight-foot cell. Given his age, if convicted he would likely spend the rest of his life in prison.

Within hours after making his initial statements to police, after he had sobered up and could think clearly, he switched gears, swearing that Clarkson had killed herself. Apparently believing that he could help make his case by eschewing grief and remorse and instead feigning outrage over what *she* had done to *him*, he launched into a bizarre tirade in front of police interrogators. "I don't know what her fucking problem was," he said at one point, "but she certainly had no right to come to my fucking castle [and] blow her fucking head open."

• • •

As the fabled, faded, elderly incarnation of the "First Tycoon of Teen," Spector had been unable to score up much attention in the media in the 1990s. Now, in the wake of Clarkson's death, he was suddenly everywhere, in newspaper headlines and on televisions tuned to cable news, MTV, VH1, and Court TV. The story was a perfect tabloid saturnalia: a retrograde *Hollywood Babylon* hash with all the mandatory elements—fame, money, sex, psychosis, and a beautiful but aging actress who turned up dead by a gunshot to the mouth. There was even a castle thrown in reminiscent of William Randolph Hearst's sprawling San Simeon manse where he carried on with his mistress Marion Davies. It was Hearst, of course, who also pumped the life out of the Fatty Arbuckle sex scandal after the silent film actor went on trial in 1921 for raping Virginia Rappe with a Coke bottle in a San Francisco hotel room. That Arbuckle's acquittal was secondary to the sensational charges that cost him his career was an ominous echo for Spector: guilty or not, he stood to be tarred forever with the seamy nature of the crime.

But Spector would not let that happen without a fight. In the months following his arrest, the man famous for delivering unto rock and roll the Wall of Sound erected a wall of smoke and mirrors. He even adopted a catchphrase to explain what had gone down at his house. "She kissed the gun," he declared, now infamously, in an interview with *Esquire.* Intended or not, those words, which sound like something Humphrey Bogart could have said in *The Big Sleep,* and which in the modern vernacular are a euphemism for fellatio, cast Clarkson's "suicide" as a metaphor for the latter. The lasting image was of her sliding a steel shaft into her mouth and performing a manual release. In fact, Spector's choice of *Esquire* as a platform to try out this theme was no accident. Phil intended to remake himself into a man's man, a babe magnet who'd given the time of day to a crazy, fucked-up broad who'd had the nerve to kill herself—in his castle, for chrissakes! How could anyone fail to see that Lana Clarkson—who (unlike Spector) possessed no history of psychotic or suicidal behavior—was the psycho, not him?

Why Clarkson had kissed the gun he never said, but those four simple words became the cornerstone of his defense. The fatuous gossip media pitched in, dishing up dirt on Clarkson as well. Even the usually high-minded *Vanity Fair* published a piece about the case that included a preposterous inference that Clarkson was a high-priced Hollywood call girl. Spector was no doubt pleased by the credulous nature of the media and was more than happy to let aberrant rumors about Clarkson play out in public. When he waived his right to a speedy trial, few expected that it would be four years before the trial began. Meanwhile, Spector and his ever-revolving team of high-powered lawyers played the system. Although the "she kissed the gun" strategy seemed to most observers to carry enormous risks, perhaps he thought otherwise. He may have bought into the prevailing wisdom that in the post-OJ Hollywood legal system, fame, money, and power would trump overworked prosecutors.

Even as this book was redrafted in the endless months before the trial, the question hung heavy in the air: how will Spector's legacy be rewritten in rock history? The short answer is, that's anyone's guess. Will he be condemned to perdition, the Wall of Sound closing in on him as he goes progressively insane? Or will he soon be making the rounds of the TV talk show circuit? It may be instructive to recall the precedent of Spade Cooley. Faintly echoing the Spector story line, Cooley, an exceedingly popular cowboy bandleader of the 1940s and 1950s famous for the "Yodeling Polka," had receded into semi-oblivion when in 1961 he made headlines by beating his estranged wife to death in front of their fourteen-year-old daughter. After a sensational trial, Cooley was convicted of murder and sentenced to life in prison. In 1969, he was granted a parole so he could play at a benefit concert in Oakland, California. The show sold out, raising the prospect that Cooley had actually gained in popularity because of his crime. He might have gone on to greater fame as a real-life desperado had he not dropped dead from a heart attack backstage after the concert.

As always with the risky business of legacies, only time will tell how Phil Spector will be remembered. What we do know is that, notwithstanding February 3, the year 2003 brought Spector a measure of vindication in an artistic sense when in November Paul McCartney finally delivered on his long-threatened desire to release the Beatles' *Let It Be* album shorn of the tracks he insisted Spector had "ruined" with his signature stentorian embellishments. To great fanfare, the pointedly re-titled *Let It Be . . . Naked* tanked, its sapless, nearly unlistenable grooves only reinforcing why Spector had been brought in to salvage the album in the first place. Spector, who has never lost touch with industry doings, no doubt savored McCartney's defeat as much as he did the Grammy he won for *Let It Be* in 1970.

⊙

As for his own catalogue of songs, the rights to which he's held fast for four decades, God knows how many megabytes Spector's work fills on iPods from Kansas to Kuala Lumpur. Cruel as it sounds, the death of an innocent woman completely peripheral to Spector's orbit has only enhanced the immortality of his art, further embedding him in the rock-and-roll ethos of restless, reckless rebellion. Never mind that a dispassionate look reveals a little man with a Napoleon complex who stamped music by filling it with overcompensating layers of excess, then slunk away not knowing quite what to do with himself after the thrill was gone. But Spector always has lived on the fault line between myth and reality.

Rereading the original edition of this book in the glaring light of February 3, 2003, is, correspondingly, a more intense experience as well, amplifying the real and the unreal—with the surreal intrusion of a woman's death. In a strong sense, the original pages allow one to connect the dots between Phil Spector's life and Lana Clarkson's death. And if Spector's musical genius seems an innocent bystander in his later years, maybe it's not so innocent, given the impulses that created it and then caused its maker to fear it. To crib a line from a song by another tortured soul, Spector, living off The Wall, let the madness in the music get to him. Life was so bad, after all. And yet he continued to have an odd sort of currency, and no doubt always will.

More than a cult figure, Spector is a never-fading musical influence. Bruce Springsteen's rumbling saxophone arrangements and histrionic tableau of noise is a straight cop of the Wall of Sound, as Springsteen has himself attested. Every musician today, regardless of his age and context, knows that rock and roll was not taken as serious music before Spector put his mark on it. Spector's Wall covers some of the most definitive music of the sixties: the Crystals' "He's a Rebel," "Da Doo Ron Ron," and "Then He Kissed Me"; Bob B. Soxx and the Blue Jeans' "Zip-A-Dee-Doo-Dah" and "Not Too Young to Get Married"; Darlene Love's "(Today I Met) The Boy I'm Gonna Marry"; the Ronettes' "Be My Baby," "Walking in the Rain," and "Baby, I Love You"; the Righteous Brothers' "You've Lost That Lovin' Feelin'" and "Unchained Melody"; and Ike and Tina Turner's magnum opus of Valkyries-driven pop and soul, "River Deep—Mountain High."

The failure of the last, a song in which Spector shot his wad, sent him into a river deep with self-doubt and neuroses. Yet even in periodic, then long-term, exile, he remained a prodigious force in pop music—for where he had been, not where he was going. From 1961 to 1965, his records made the charts twenty-seven times; seventeen of those nestled inside the Top 40. As a body of work, they were a cultural seed. Spector's work as whole has a peculiar kind of relevancy even now. Because we never really come of age, or long not to, the teen ethos he rhapsodized has a visceral hold on the subconscious of anyone born early enough to take the *bom, bom-bom* intro riff of "Be My Baby" as an immediately identifiable heartbeat. This also holds true for anyone young enough to hear it sampled, as it has been, a thousand times since the sixties. Indeed, the Wall of Sound doesn't reflect the sixties motif as much as it is the era's apotheosis by lionizing the sentimentality in all humans. Spector's 1963 Christmas album—an astounding portrait of shimmering, maudlin beauty—is this generation's "White Christmas."

The real flip side of Spector's crusade was that when the music changed too radically for him to keep his brilliant but soon to be obsolete monophonic Wall of Sound process intact, he was a genius lost. Although Phil could provide almost any act in rock with a viable hit, his price was too high. That price was subjugation, and the distance people kept from his as a result had an uncomfortable spillover effect on his life outside the studio as well. His longtime seclusion, interrupted by sporadic and fleeting bursts of work—most productively, a quarter century ago with the Ramones—have led many to compare Spector with Howard Hughes. A better parallel might be Orson Welles, a genius in his twenties who later withdrew in resignation, unwilling or unable to compete with his own legacy.

If Spector's "recluse" persona was designed to prop up a proud and noble sense of isolation, surely February 3, 2003, led to the inescapable conclusion that the man never really let go of the outside world and its grimy seductions. The events of that date ripped away the shroud not of a lofty iconoclast but of a smarmy night crawler who couldn't keep his gun out of Lana Clarkson's mouth.

In the first edition, I conveyed that on a hazy stratum above the petty cruelties and deceits of a man *Vanity Fair*'s James Wolcott has dubbed a "malignant munchkin," I admired Spector for apparently not craving or needing attention and for mastering the art of the dropout. I was wrong—dead wrong, as it turned out. As will be seen in the new chapters of this book, Lana Clarkson wasn't an aberration. Given that no one in Spector's immediate orbit ever intervened to stop what they knew to be criminally insane behavior—which at times extended to the sexual corruption of his own young sons—the wonder is that it didn't happen sooner. The women who testified at Spector's grand jury about incidents of physical abuse, imprisonment, and gunplay never reported any of it to authorities. Therefore, one can imagine how invincible he believed he was when he hit on Clarkson. And yet one also suspects that Spector knew how loathsome he was, and how unenviable his seclusion really was.

Nevertheless, from my place in the legion of baby boomers who reached adolescence in time to appreciate and be affected by Spector's music in real time, it is impossible not to regard the man who made all that music as a stately, heroic figure. The other Phil Spector—the scaly, night-crawling pod—deserves not a word of praise. But since I can't separate the two, I must try to live, however uneasily, with him as a whole.

Whether Phil Spector is good or bad, divine or disordered, towering or cowering, murderer or dupe in the matter of Lana Clarkson's death, it is my hope that history will be able to delineate the legendary producer from the disoriented sluggard in the back of that police cruiser. Let's not forget that America once had its own Mozart and that his name was Phil Spector.

1

JOCASTA: *Put this trouble from you.*

OEDIPUS: *Those bold words would sound better, were not my mother living. But as it is—I have some grounds for fear; yet you have said it well.*

JOCASTA: *Yet your father's death is a sign that all is well.*

OEDIPUS: *I know that: but I fear because of her who lives.*

—SOPHOCLES' *King Oedipus*, in the translation by W. B. Yeats

In 1956, when Phil Spector was fifteen years old, he lugged his second-hand guitar to Studio City in the San Fernando Valley once a week for a month to take instruction from a jazz guitarist named Howard Roberts. The young Spector, who was smitten by jazz, had specifically sought out Roberts in the directory of the musicians' union, and when he got to the jazzman's house he listened hard as Roberts explained about chord structure and the theory of rhythm guitar.

⊙

8

But Roberts thought there was something strange about the kid. After each lesson, Spector would leave and go home to West Hollywood without having taken his guitar out of its case. After the final tutoring session, the young man said a polite thank you, shook Roberts's hand, and was out the door.

"I never saw a guitar in Phil's hands, and he never played a note for me," Roberts would remember over three decades later. "I waited and waited, because that's the thing kids do when they take lessons: they play for approval and advice. But he never did."

Howard Roberts never did know if Spector was skittish about playing in the presence of an expert musician, or if the boy thought he could do whatever was required. Actually, it could have been either, or both, or neither. Spector was a shy boy but also one with rare talent. More crucially, however, in 1956 Spector *couldn't* play his guitar for approval. Not yet. This was something that was deep in his gut, playing the guitar. It may have been the only part of his identity that made him feel good, and he wanted it to be real. So Spector wouldn't play for Howard Roberts. He would play only for the darkness.

At fifteen, Phil Spector stood barely over five feet tall, not counting the bird's nest of reedy brown hair he kept piled high atop his forehead. Thin as a matchstick, and with bones as brittle, Spector was sallow and pale, hollow around the eyes and under the cheekbones. When he spoke it was in a high nasal whine and with a lisp. He was also a chronic asthmatic, and when the Santa Ana wind blew in off the Pacific Ocean it carried pollen into his wide nostrils that sent him into great coughing jags that would double him over and frighten his friends. Spector was not popular in the corridors of Fairfax High School, and most of his time was spent by himself. He was fatherless and his mother, Bertha, worked, so Spector had to make do as a latchkey kid, letting himself in after school. He appreciated this web of seclusion, since when his mother and his older sister, Shirley, were at home, they treated him like precious china. Phil's fragility was a constant worry to them both. If they didn't know where he was, or if he was out of their line of sight too long, they would flood phone lines to his friends' homes, trying to track him down. Finding him, they would spew tirades at him. They were hennish, to be sure, but they adored the male of the house, and took his poor health as a sign that he was special and in need of protection from a cruel world.

Small and stocky, standing under five feet tall in her orthopedic shoes, her salt-and-pepper hair pulled into a bun and her smile exuding warmth, Bertha Spector was the prototype of a Jewish mother. But kind and gracious as she was, she was also an angry hornet of a woman. Her energy and resolve were her son's lifeline; whatever strength he had was transfused from her. On his own, Phil had a hard time. He hated the way he looked. He hated his long nose and his big ears, and he silently brooded about being a teenage nerd. Though his mother and sister offered him support and encouragement, that he was dominated by two strong and willful women checked his independence. His name was a symbol of his desire to stand on his own. Given the names Harvey Phillip, Spector loathed his real first name and called himself Phil. Bertha wouldn't go along. Pointedly, acridly at times, she called him by the name she had given him. "Harvey!" her voice would crack the air, embarrassing him when he was with friends.

Phil Spector was a nervous, hyperactive teenager, for whom the line between day and night had long since vanished. In fact, he welcomed the darkness descending over West Hollywood, because in its calm isolation he could believe that the night belonged only to him. Spector's guitar-playing filled those hours, stretching sometimes to daybreak inside the family's top-floor apartment in a two-story, woodframe fourplex located at 602½ Spaulding Avenue. Knowing how much his guitar meant to him, Bertha rarely put her foot down about it, and so Phil would enter a nightly ritual knowing he would not be interrupted. Sitting cross-legged on his bed, he cradled the guitar and played it to the sound of a transistor radio, tuned to a jazz or black music station. Spector didn't often bother with the rock-and-roll stations. To him, white rock was pimple-cream ads separated by two-minute retreads of black music with half the vitality. The reward for tuning in the low-watt stations was great. On KFOX, for example, Johnny Otis—the bandleader who founded much of the black music scene in Los Angeles—had a show, acquainting a pale Jewish boy with acts like Little Willie John, Jackie Wilson, Hank Ballard, Big Mama Thornton, and Redd Lyte. Spector's trips to the music shops led to the bargain bins in the back, to the jazz and rhythm and blues, even to the classical music albums. He craved the vicarious feeling of brute force and naked emotion in music. He played his guitar in solitude, and the passion and conviction of jazz, soul music, and the ornate majesty of Bach and Beethoven were his real teachers.

Seen in the prism of a generation of teenagers discovering rock and roll, Spector was one of scores of kids who were picking up guitars and jiggling like Elvis. But Spector was way ahead of most of the other lemmings in understanding the pain and alienation of rock. *Real* rock was the state of mind and soul that bled from open wounds. Spector understood. He had his own open wounds.

A year after taking lessons from Howard Roberts, Spector was ready to play for approval, having learned the rudiments and the essence of the guitar like few others his age. By 1957 he found that his talent had even made people like and gather around him—which had been his original intention when he first considered playing guitar. Confident and ambitious, he was now composing words and music in the new rock language. In the spring, Spector was seasoned in the art of making a record. But it wasn't until months later, in his room on a late spring night, that he discovered musical truth—in his most painful wound.

Spector was on the edge of sleep, his eyes shut, his guitar at his side, when a harsh memory cut through his subconscious. He saw the blue shale tombstone of his father's grave, which was three thousand miles to the east in a Long Island cemetery. In his haze, Spector thought he was at the foot of Ben Spector's grave, and the epitaph on the stone—"To Know Him Was to Love Him"—was staring at him, assaulting him, taunting him.

It was a vision that the sixteen-year-old Phil Spector didn't want to see and never would have consented to seeing had he been fully awake. To recall the father who had died—the only figure of male authority he could have had but didn't—was almost self-mutilation. Spector hardly ever spoke about his father because that might ease the pain. He was repelled by the apparition of that godforsaken grave, and it jolted him awake. But as in any other time of pain, there was a pacifier. The guitar.

Spector reached for it, to hit the strings hard. He thought about the terrible dirge of loss and grief—"To Know Him Was to Love Him"—as he played. Hours passed, and the black night and the grief faded. What was left was poetry and the renaissance of Ben Spector in the guise of a song that Phil Spector knew was perfect.

It was around 7 A.M. The sun was shining into his room. Spector picked up the telephone and dialed the number of Marshall Lieb, his best friend and singing partner. "Marsh!" he whispered breathily into the phone. "I got a new song. You gotta hear it."

On the other end, Lieb yawned and rubbed his eyes as Spector sang his new lyric. Used to Spector's apoplectic ways, Lieb humored him. "Yeah, Phillip. Sounds real good," he mumbled, then hung up and went back to bed.

For Phil Spector, there would be no sleep; there rarely was. There were plans to be made for this song. That afternoon he and Marshall Lieb were working on it, putting an arrangement together. At that moment, Spector was probably too busy to think that his father had not died in vain, after all.

Benjamin Spector was swept to America in the great Russian immigration of the early 1900s. Born on January 10, 1903, he was ten years old when his parents, George and Bessie, and their six sons and one daughter stepped onto U.S. soil on Ellis Island, in the shadow of the Statue of Liberty. There, an immigration officer Americanized their Russian name by spelling it with a c, not a k. The family's migration ended in the Bronx, in the Soundview section, a district typical of the low- and middle-class Jewish society that dominated the borough. Ben Spector was young enough to adopt his new homeland, and went about trying to realize the American Dream. He studied hard, became a citizen, and fought in World War I as a teenager.

Bertha Spector's parents traced almost the same path from Russia to the U.S. Eerily enough, her father was also named George, and his surname was Spektor, the correct Russian spelling of Ben's family name. George Spektor and his wife, Clara, however, detoured first to France in the early 1900s, and it was there, in Paris, that Bertha Spektor was born in 1911. A few years later, George and Clara came to America, arriving at the same Ellis Island pier, with Bertha and her sister, Doraine, who had also been born in Paris. After they settled on the same Grand Concourse turf as the Spectors, they had a son, Sam, on Armistice Day, November 11, 1918.

Meeting Bertha Spektor in the middle of this ethnic broth, Ben Spector knew she was meant to be his wife. After a brief courtship,

⊙   12

they married in 1934, then had a daughter, Shirley. Five years later, they had a son, Harvey Phillip, on December 26, 1940, a baby with the promise of a bright future.

The country went to war soon after, but at age thirty-eight, Ben Spector had a wife and family,which he housed in a two-family brick house at 1024 Manor Avenue in the heart of the Soundview section, and he had a secure union job as an ironworker in Brooklyn. Ruddy-faced and handsome—the jovial, fun-loving "Uncle Ben" as his swarm of nieces and nephews knew him—Ben was the picture of American stability. What's more, his legacy, his children, were two of the most beautiful babies the Spector and Spektor clans had ever seen. Blond and almost WASP-looking, Shirley grew by the yard, sprouting up a head taller than Ben and Bertha, both of whom were built low to the ground. Ben and Bertha's nieces thought their cousin Shirley was the most gorgeous lady they could imagine, and no one in the family was surprised when Shirley landed some teenage modeling work.

Then there was Harvey Phillip: a round-faced, wavy-haired infant with searching eyes. Bertha, Doraine, and Sam Spektor had all been musically inclined in their youth, and it seemed that Harvey was the recipient of that bloodline. At family enclaves, Harvey would sing loudly and without a care. Except for bouts of asthma, Harvey was a happy child, and he loved his father with all his being. It was, in fact, a loving, close-knit family, envied by the relatives on both sides as ideal.

But something went wrong for Ben Spector. He grew dispirited, estranged. The money just wasn't enough to keep his family as comfortable as he wanted them to be. Sensing his depression, a friend and co-worker of Ben's named Bernie Weiss became concerned about him. But Bernie knew Ben to be a hardy, proud man. Ben was optimistic, and he bragged about his children and his family, all of whom loved him dearly. At 5 foot 7 inches and 225 pounds, he was a broad chunk of granite, a man who could surely take care of himself. He would work it out, in time.

But there wasn't enough time for Ben Spector.

On the morning of April 20, 1949, Ben awoke as usual at daybreak. He said good-bye to his wife and drove to the steelworks plant. When he was a few blocks away, he pulled up to the curb in front of a deserted building at 1042 Myrtle Avenue. It was a warm, sunny day in New York, but Ben Spector probably felt a chill as he got out of the car and opened the trunk. Methodically, he drew out a water hose and attached one end to the exhaust pipe, then dangled the other end through the open front window.

Ben got back in the car, rolled up the windows tightly, and restarted the engine as he reclined against the headrest. It must have been a kind of relief when the deadly gas fumes began to drain the air inside the car.

Half an hour later, at 8:40 A.M., passersby saw the lifeless hulk of Ben Spector slumped in the front seat, the engine still running. They called the police, and within a few minutes officers from Brooklyn's 79th Precinct arrived, much too late. They took the body to the morgue, where Bernie Weiss, called from the factory, came to identify the body of the friend he had worried about.

The Brooklyn coroner set the time of death at 8:05 A.M. and noted the cause of death as "Carbon Monoxide Poisoning—Asphyxia; Suicidal." When Ben Spector died, his blood contained 65 percent carbon monoxide. He had left no chance that he would not die on this day.

On April 22, 1949, Bertha Spector buried her husband in Beth David Cemetery in Elmont, New York. A year later, according to Jewish law, a headstone was unveiled at the grave site. It was magnificent, marked with a Star of David and the heart-rending epitaph of personal loss. If Ben had terrible mental anguish and considered himself a failure, it was to be forgotten, buried with him.

On both sides of the extended family, the trauma of Ben's suicide was regarded as a horribly ugly stigma, a perversion and aberration of the hope and promise that the Spector and Spektor families had brought to America. Bertha certainly didn't deserve to be held as a cause of her husband's anguished death, and the family heads were protective of propriety and her feelings. They didn't tell their children how their cherished Uncle Ben had died, only that he'd met with an accident. Some of them wouldn't find out the truth until they were adults. It is possible that Bertha kept the truth even from her son.

For now, and hopefully into eternity, Bertha wanted it to be known and accepted that anyone who truly knew her troubled husband would have loved him.

⊙

It fell to Sam Spektor, Bertha's younger brother, to try to alleviate her sense of loss. An aeronautical engineer, he was now living on 164th Street and Broadway in upper Manhattan, right near the George Washington Bridge, and he made it his business to drop by at 1024 Manor Avenue frequently to provide a male presence, especially for Harvey. Shirley was less of a concern: beautiful and independent as she was, by the time she was fifteen she boldly saw herself as a future movie star.

Harvey, though, was devastated by the death of the father he revered; he needed a male to lean on, and spent much time with his uncle. The trauma of Ben's death was so hard for him to bear that when people asked what his father's name was, he replied "Sam"—as if hiding behind an effigy rather than having to confront the pain of his father's name. But while Harvey could push the memory of Ben out of his conscious mind, he allowed no one to replace him.

Neither did the pain ease for Bertha. She did not and would not remarry, such was her fealty to Ben's gripping memory, and living in the Bronx made it impossible for the memory to fade. Reminders of Ben were everywhere along Manor Avenue. This was Ben's kingdom, and that he was so unhappy here made the area a monument to despair. As if living in a dark cloud, Harvey's asthma became worse as he grew into a teenager, and his plump cheeks had sunk into a general pallor.

Four bleak years after Ben's death, Bertha realized she had to start a new life for herself and her children a long way from the Bronx. Her uncle, George Spektor's brother, was living in Los Angeles, and he had begged her to come out there; other relatives there made the same plea. The Hollywood of the early 1950s had become a bright, sunny beacon for a human wave of East Coast Jews, and finally Bertha gave in. Her relatives secured an apartment, and her brother Sam drove her, Harvey, and Shirley to the airport. After touching down in Los Angeles, they were taken to their new digs on Spaulding Avenue, in one of West Hollywood's long rows of squat, turn-of-the-century houses, sequestered by leafy palm trees. With no office skills, Bertha took a job as a seamstress in a stifling back room sweatshop in downtown L.A. Because she couldn't afford a car, she waited every morning and night for the long bus ride to and from her sewing machine.

Phil Spector, as he began to insist he be called, went to school first at Laurel Elementary School, then to John Burroughs Junior High. He entered Fairfax High School in 1954. The outgoing child was an introvert now, a voracious reader of books—next to the guitar, which he had taken up while in junior high school, works about American history were his personal refuge. His room was lined with books about Abraham Lincoln, whose life fascinated him to no end.

Phil was a splendid student. There was an American history teacher at Fairfax High, a Mr. Goetze, a chops-buster who sprang surprise quizzes on the first day of class. Most students dreaded Goetze, but Spector worshipped him and passed all his exams effortlessly. Phil was more than smart; he was clever, keen-witted, sharp as a whip, but it was all undirected, loose wheels looking for a direction. His guitar seemed to be the only funnel to consolidate his intellectual and artistic impulses.

Spector met Marshall Lieb at John Burroughs. Lieb was the son of an automobile dealer named Leonard Lieb and his wife, Belle, and he could not have been more dissimilar to Phil. Marshall was tall, muscular, and swarthy, as outgoing and popular as Phil was meek and insulated. But both boys were artistically inclined, they liked the same music, and they took their first guitar lessons together, from a session guitarist named Burdell Mathis across the street from a huge music emporium in Hollywood called Herb Wallach's Music City. Unlike many parents in the neighborhood who thought Spector was weird, Leonard and Belle Lieb more than abided him, and even thought he could be a positive influence on their son.

"My parents liked him. They didn't feel he was any kind of threat," Lieb explained. "In those days, most of the kids in the neighborhood wanted to be bad guys, gangster types, as opposed to collegiate types. There were certain looks that we liked emulating that were less than Ivy League. So then Phillip comes along and he's not real macho he-man, not visibly the troublemaker type, whereas I had more of that look."

But Spector did have a problem with his mouth, and it could get him into trouble, Lieb mentioned. "Someone would say something to Phillip and he'd mouth right back. That would instigate a problem, and then it would be, 'Marsh!' and I'd have to turn around from what I was doing and go bail him out. I had a history of having a few little tussles from time to time, but I didn't carry a chip on my shoulder like he did. He had a way about his answers that antagonized people. One time this guy in school was going to kick his butt, no matter what. A big ring of people got in there, Phil's in the middle with this guy, and this guy's gonna beat him to shreds, and he just sort of gave me his little kitten eyes, to help him, so I came to his rescue and got the thing broken up. I was really his first bodyguard, when you think about it."

Family strife intensified in the Spector household during Phil's high school years, when Bertha moved with her son to a smaller flat seven blocks away at 726 N. Hayworth Avenue—Shirley having moved out on her own, was in an apartment nearby—just north of Melrose Avenue and a block from Fairfax High School. It was there that an older, somewhat emboldened Phil became embroiled in arguments with his mother.

"As I remember, Phillip would have trouble with whatever her suggestions would be," Lieb said. "It would be opposite of what he'd think. It was like 'Can I go out?' 'No, you gotta stay home!' And as soon as she'd leave, he'd be gone. A couple of times she hit him with her purse. He'd open a mouth on her and she would answer that and they would go back and forth. And she'd have some answer that he'd *never* agree with. I can remember times when she'd be chasing him around the apartment and he'd be hiding in places, like under his bed. I got phone calls in the middle of the night— 'Come over and help!' And I would go over and sort of break the mood that was going on. Someone had to answer the door and stop shouting."

But even when peace was restored, it was an uneasy truce. "The most vivid memories I have of them was just a lot of bitterness, a lot of intolerant conversation," Lieb said. "I didn't see a lot of endearment. I never really had a feeling of any kind of togetherness among the three of them."

Spector never told anyone of his inner suffering. Unfamiliar with the feel of human warmth—the Spectors were not the hugging kind of family since Ben's death—he shied away when he thought someone would touch him. But Spector was not a shut-in. He was drawn to the crowds of teenagers who cruised the wide strip of Fairfax Avenue, and the aromatic corridor of ethnic food shops along the avenue had a romantic appeal for him. He and Lieb were regular denizens at Canter's Delicatessen—Spector could inhale a truly astonishing cartload of hot pastrami, though none of it ever padded his bony frame. They also belonged to a Fairfax High social club called the Chapparals and bowled at the Pan Pacific, an indoor mall.

Spector dated a few times, but to most girls he was spooky. His glaring eyes and ashen complexion kept them at a distance. It wasn't until a pretty blonde girl named Donna Kass sidled up to him that he found himself in a relationship. Bright and chirpy, Donna was fifteen, a year younger, but where the other girls saw only Spector's exterior, she saw much more.

"Phil was not a handsome guy, not at all. He was very pale and had no chin. Not real masculine," Kass acknowledged. "My mother used to say he was sick, but he wasn't, he just looked like he was. But there was something so funny-looking about him that he was cute to me. My mother thought he was vile looking, but there was something very captivating there. He had these delicate hands, small, not stubby but very pretty. His hands looked like they would never have worked in a field. They were very white, with callouses from the guitar.

"My mother always felt Phil was crazy. She thought that some-day he would wind up committing suicide. I didn't see that then. He was a normal kid, he didn't drink or use drugs, although he might have smoked a cigarette once or twice. Phil turned to music to show the world he could compete, but he was doing all right. He was the town crier in school, he danced, he was a cheerleader—but there was a genius about him that went beyond all that. Sometimes geniuses step one step beyond what the rest of us can understand. That's what I saw in him."

As her father had died recently, Donna was receptive to an older boy with the kind of quiet maturity Phil had. "I was crazy about him," she said. "I had never really had a boyfriend before, and he was a very brilliant guy. God, he was brilliant. He was a great historian—he knew *everything* about Lincoln. He was intense and very inward, but he had a great personality, he was charming. Phil was just so different from everybody else. He was not the run-of-the-mill kid."

But there was another side to him, a despair and an estrange-ment that became obvious to Donna whenever his family would en-ter his life. Their dates would always be at her house, where they'd play Ping-Pong and Phil would sit at the piano in the living room and play for her. "In the artistic sense, you sensed there was a soul of an artistic genius there. I mean, he could hear a song and play it right away, on the piano or the guitar. He was amazing." Donna knew little about his family, and she could tell he was keeping her away from it. Unfortunately, that was impossible.

"I think he was very frustrated," Kass recalled. "They watched over his every move. If he would come to my house, they would call fifteen times: 'Come home, come home.' He was very, very angry about it. He was an angry person.

"We'd be on the phone talking for the longest time and his mother would come in and he'd want to hang up."

It was as if the Spector women believed that little cherry-cheeked Donna Kass was trying to "steal" Phil from them. "I always felt they were in love with him or something. They treated him like he was a god. They protected him, and they wanted to protect him from me." What hurt Bertha and Shirley the most, and likely intensified the arguments, was that Phil seemed not to return their idea of adoration. Indeed, Phil's misery could be measured by his contrasting mood in the rare moments when he spoke of his father.

"Phil was very insecure, and the reason was his father," Kass thought. "He told me his father died of a heart attack, but I found out that was not true. I don't remember him ever telling me how he died, and I don't know how I found out, but I think it was a horrible stigma. There wasn't a whole lot of talk, it was fleeting, but what I remember was that it was with real kindness and real feeling.

"I imagine his father was a very kind, wonderful person. I bet Phil adored him. Phil had to get his brilliance and his sensitivity from somewhere, and it was not from Bertha."

The irony is that, even while chafing under Bertha's wing, Phil was actually very much like her. It is possible that Spector didn't even realize how much his own possessiveness mirrored hers. "He was very, very jealous," Kass recalled. "I remember I once went to a friend's cousin's house to go swimming and I didn't tell him, and somehow he tracked me down by calling all of my friends. He found out I was there and he called over and over, had me on the phone for hours, jealous of why I didn't call and who I was with and so on.

"It was such a crazy thing. He was doing what his mother did to him. I was like fifteen, sixteen years old. He had no reason to ever be jealous, because everyone who ever came into contact with him, got to know him, adored him. But he didn't believe it."

On Phil's fifteenth birthday, December 26, 1955, Bertha and Shirley had taken him to see Ella Fitzgerald perform at a nightclub in Hollywood. In the band backing her was an Oklahoma-born jazz guitarist named Barney Kessel, whose work on the instrument riveted Phil. Almost a year later, in October, Phil was reading *Down Beat,* the weekly jazz magazine, when he saw an article about rhythm guitarist Sal Salvador, who played in the Stan Kenton band. In the article, Salvador mentioned some rhythm guitarists he favored, including Howard Roberts but not Barney Kessel, who Phil came to learn had also played in the bands of Oscar Peterson, Charlie Parker, and Bob Crosby. So offended was he by the omission, Phil wrote in protest to the magazine's Chicago offices. His letter sounded so knowledgeable that *Down Beat* ran it on the Letters page of its November 14, 1956, issue. On a page that regularly carried correspondence from luminaries such as Frank Sinatra, Dizzy Gillespie, and Nat King Cole sat the name of fifteen-year-old Phil Spector. The letter read:

Just finished reading your article entitled "Garrulous Sal" in the Oct. 3 issue and am a little disappointed that when naming his favorite guitarists Salvador left out the name of Barney Kessel, who in my opinion holds the title of the greatest guitarist.

Salvador mentioned Howard Roberts, a very fine jazz guitarist from the West Coast, and also mentioned the state of California, where Kessel is most well known, yet he failed to say a word about the man whose style of guitar is copied so much but never equaled and is a favorite among jazz fans everywhere.

This I cannot understand. Maybe you could ask Salvador, who I think is also a fine guitarist, just why Kessel does not rate. Sure wish you would ease my pain and have a story about Barney in one of your future issues.

After the letter ran, Shirley Spector—who, like her mother, would have run through brick walls to aid Phil in his musical rev-

⊙

erie—called Kessel's record label and found out where he was recording. She went to the studio and told Kessel that her little brother, Phil, was crazy about jazz guitar and loved Kessel's records, and would he meet Phil. Kessel, who recognized the name Phil Spector from the *Down Beat* letter, was shocked to learn that he was just a kid, and he agreed.

Bertha took such a meeting very seriously. Phil had said he wanted to become a jazz guitarist, and she was going to have to finance this cockamamy avocation that she knew nothing about. Already she had given him every available dollar she had so he could buy the guitar, music sheets, and books he wanted. But now both she and her son had to know the details and realities of a career in music. Calling Kessel, she arranged to meet him at a coffee shop called Dupars on Vine Street in Hollywood. There, all three Spectors squeezed into a booth with Kessel. Phil was awestruck meeting his idol—"He was very, very soft-spoken," as Kessel remembered—and Bertha did most of the talking. She asked Kessel about the hard realities for a boy like Phil in jazz.

"I remember telling her that if he did have talent, I thought it was a wise move to direct it more into the pop field," Kessel said. "Because there were so many great jazz artists who were not making a living in jazz. Jazz had fallen very far from grace, and guys were not able to sustain themselves. You couldn't go out and play jazz on the road anymore; it was all rock and roll. I said that he should get into the pop field and write songs and get involved in publishing and maybe work as an apprentice in a record company; to find out how to mix sessions and get involved in the multidimensionality of the whole thing, but from that standpoint."

The kid took the the advice to heart, as did his sister. Shirley had finished high school in L.A., at Fairfax, and there she had met a classmate named Steve Douglas, who played the saxophone. Douglas now had a fledgling band. Shirley talked him into letting her manage the group for him.

After several years in Hollywood, making little headway in show business, Shirley Spector's adolescent beauty had taken on an embalmed veneer; she had a hard, brassy kind of look, her hair teased and sprayed into cotton candy and her fingertips sporting long, long fingernails. A cigarette was perpetually stuck on her bottom lip, Bogart-style. Shirley was Hollywood all the way, but with a New York crustiness, convinced she knew all the answers. Her voice was piercing as a blaring siren and she was pushy in a bulldozing way. She obviously felt well suited to the show biz world, but now her outlook was as a hype maker, and she threw herself into booking Steve Douglas's band into gigs at frat house dances and in bowling alley lounges.

His own musical ambition having grown by giant steps by 1957, Phil Spector came to believe that he should be on the same kid rock circuit with bands of his own. He was now spending long hours in Marshall Lieb's living room at 404 Gardner Street, sitting at Belle Lieb's Hobart piano trying to hash out original songs, his horizon expanding as he was drawn to other capable young musicians. Spector walked into the music room at Fairfax High with his guitar one day and heard a kid named Michael Spencer playing jazzy licks on a piano. Spector joined in on guitar, and the two became fast friends, marveling at each other's grasp of music. Spencer, whose father was a well-to-do accountant, lived in a large house at 201 S. Highland Avenue, between Third Street and Beverly Boulevard—in the kind of high-tone neighborhood Phil was rarely invited to enter—and it became his Taj Mahal. The two boys jammed around Michael's piano. Phil was intrigued by Spencer's classical music background—he told Michael his prime musical influence was Richard Wagner—and how it could be made to fit into mainstream pop. The Spencers had rows of jazz, classical, show, and R&B albums, and the most monstrous hi-fi system in West Hollywood: huge, six-foot-high Patrician Electro-Voice speakers stood like grain silos in the corners of the living room, and the amplifier had a time-lag feature that could reverberate any kind of music to make it sound as if it were being played live in a concert hall. Spector tried it with everything from Sibelius to Gershwin to Larry Williams, playing along on guitar. Beginning with disjointed little riffs, maybe two-note fragments, song ideas would become concepts. Spector was aglow with enthusiasm, his drive furious.

Spencer recalled Spector as "very quiet, very sensitive, a little mouselike creature without a lot of confidence—but when Phillip was playing music, he had a tremendous aggression."

Spencer thought he knew why: "It was perhaps a desire to be independent from his mother. Phil was overly dependent on Bertha when we met, very coddled by her, smothered really. The relation-

⊙

ship they had was extremely intense, because they were both very emotional people, and Phil's aggressive personality burst out of there, as a way of compensating for being dependent so much of the time."

Spector, Lieb, and Spencer began taking gigs around Los Angeles and ran into bands making the same scene. One was called the Sleepwalkers, a group from Union High School. The rivalry between Fairfax and Union was fierce, and it carried over to the two bands. Spector took to talking himself up, and it was a technique that came easy to him. Without batting an eyelash, Spector told the Sleepwalkers' drummer, Sammy Nelson, that he had produced several hit records that were on the charts. When Nelson told this to his skeptical bandmates, Bruce Johnston and Kim Fowley—the latter the son of actor Douglas Fowley ("Doc" on television's "Wyatt Earp") and the grandson of composer Rudolf Friml—they went to a record store to check the records, seeing if Spector's name was anywhere on them. It wasn't, but Spector had already thought of that: he knew he'd be safe because producer's credits were never given. Still, the Union High bunch was not fooled.

"I guess they lied a lot over at Fairfax," Fowley said.

Having sung with a black L.A. vocal group called the Jayhawks, Fowley was not overly impressed with Spector's unnamed band.

"The Sleepwalkers were much more creative than whatever Spector was doing," he insisted. "Both of us played biker parties, bar mitzvahs at the Brentwood Temple, then we'd run across the street and do the Catholics' lonelyhearts club crap at the CYO. But when those guys played, we'd be out stripping cars in the parking lot and giving beer to kids our age and younger. We got wallflowers to let us use their houses; we'd give 'em money, set 'em up in a hotel with hookers, and we'd have our own house parties. Or sometimes we'd roll queers in Hollywood for beer money."

Spector's group was arrow-straight, clean-nosed Fairfax boys. In time, it grew to include various configurations built around Phil and Marshall and the doo-wop and Everly Brothers songs the two would choose for their gigs. Spector was always looking for people who could sing with him. He joined a Fairfax High music club called the Barons, and out of its ranks he plucked what became a rotating carousel of strong-throated singers to take on gigs, which usually paid less money than what it cost in gas to get there in Marshall's old Dodge. Among the singing partners were Spector's next-door neighbor, Steve Gold, as well as kids named Steve Price, Donnie Kartoon, Bart Silverman, and Harvey Goldstein. None but Phil played an instrument well, and Spector would play guitar and sometimes piano if Mike Spencer wasn't around, at which time Marshall would do a turn on guitar. One gig, by far the most profound for these nice Jewish boys, was at El Monte Legion Stadium, where they managed to place themselves in one of the shows hosted there by Johnny Otis himself. This was in the middle of black and Mexican ethnic L.A., a hotbed of purebred R&B, and while they played to a lukewarm response, Phil and Marshall had a giddy exhilaration simply standing on the hallowed ground of Johnny Otis's stage.

In the spring of 1957, Spector could actually swagger up the steps of the Fairfax High auditorium stage and perform on his guitar "Rock Island Line," the British skiffle tune popularized by Lonnie Donegan, at a talent show. It surprised nobody that Spector won the contest. Not long after, Spector and Lieb went on a late-night television program on KTLA called "Rocket to Stardom." Sponsored by an Oldsmobile salesman named Bob Yeakel, and broadcast from Yeakel's showroom, the program was a showcase of young amateur talent in Los Angeles. Spector and Lieb performed "In the Still of the Night" and won the night's competition. There were many talented people in Spector's circle now, but he was fulcrum; his moves were the ones all the others were watching.

"We all were moving, with our own ambitions," Michael Spencer said. "But it was Phillip who moved fastest."

Phil Spector, Marshall Lieb, and their loose conglomeration of soulmates continued gigging after graduation day at Fairfax High in June of 1957, but the world was smaller now, less open to flights of fancy. In the fall, Phil and Marshall enrolled at Los Angeles City College, and Michael Spencer was at UCLA. Marshall chose political science as a major, but Phil was undecided. With Paris-born Bertha as an influence and tutor, he had taken French in high school, and studied it with such a frenzy that he was now fluent in the language—fomenting what Michael Spencer thought was "a tremendous desire to master something, anything, to prove to himself he could do it." A more functional outlet for that urge in college became court reporting, a natural dalliance for fingers as nimble as his. With his usual abandon, Spector rapidly progressed; practicing at home, he spent every afternoon in front of the television, watching

Dick Clark's "American Bandstand" and transcribing the dialogue onto his stenotype machine.

During the winter months, it grew more evident that the last link in Spector's music chain had to happen now or be lost forever. Phil Spector knew he'd have to cut a record.

2

Everything was organized in a way that on the first run-through we'd do this, on the second we'd do these parts, on the third these parts. All those things we did took on names years later, like stacking and overdubbing. We innovated all that.

—MARSHALL LIEB

In the late spring of 1957, kids all over Los Angeles were descending on recording studios in such numbers that this buffalo run had emerged as the hub of the West Coast rock scene. The western record labels were mostly shoestring operations; they signed kid acts by the truckload, on the cheap, hoping for one record that would click. The demos the kids were coming in with were frequently sent out as-is to radio programmers. Major rock-and-roll record sessions were atypical in L.A., and most of the records produced didn't have the tight, clean sound of the expensive union sessions in New York and Memphis. In the mid-fifties, L.A.-based labels began issuing hits that were the product of a few instruments rattling around in a drafty studio. The echoey, muddy sound, though an accident of deprivation, was effectively a musical duplication of the wide, smoggy expanse of California, and people began imitating and extending it using artificial echoes and tape overdubs—both of which became staples of the newborn "West Coast sound."

Phil Spector, as was his habit, was knee-deep in the industry trends and techniques. He had begun to show up at studios around town, introducing himself and saying whatever would enable him to be allowed to watch sessions. A favorite haunt was Gold Star Sound Studios on Vine Street in Hollywood. This was the hot studio in town. The Hi-Los recorded at Gold Star, and the Four Lads, and their lushly echoed harmonies were a primer on the white-and-light sound. Gold Star had not one but *two* echo chambers, built with great foresight by the studio's owners, Stan Ross and Dave Gold, in 1950. That, too, was an accident of fate. Renovating an old store into two small studios, Ross and Gold had to conform to the store's dimensions, including a very low ceiling, fourteen feet—most studios cleared twenty feet—and a good way to keep the music from flattening out was to goose it in a reverberating room. At Gold Star, with its studios a thimble-sized thirty-five by twenty-three feet, the best echoes were heard in the bathroom, which became the primary echo chamber. Furthermore, Stan Ross was an engineer as well, and a graduate of Fairfax High School, and Phil thought he might be generous with time and advice.

"He was always looking for an open block of time, but while I let him stick around, I wasn't gonna give him time," Ross recalled. "That would've started a stampede. You would've had fifty thousand Phil Spectors coming in."

Ross grinned at Spector's big talk and liked the kid, but he had no inkling of what he could do with a record. Studio time, he kept telling Spector, was only $15 an hour, plus $6 per roll of 1/4-inch recording tape. "Okay, I'll be back with it," Spector told him, but when he came back it was with empty pockets. But Spector wasn't idling. He simply wasn't ready for the studio because he knew he would have to make the product good and he wasn't confident he had mastered the techniques he wanted to use. Working those techniques on a smaller scale, Spector and Lieb would record their voices on a small tape recorder and sing over it.

"What we wanted to do was double ourselves—not just by making a track, hearing it played back in the headphones, singing over that, and mixing the tracks. Everybody was doing that," Lieb explained. "We wanted the sound of the first track played back over the speakers in the studio and to sing to that—everything into the mike at once. That would make the sound bigger, fuller. There was a lot of overdubbing going on, but no one had stacked voices like that. But we knew what we could do. Believe me, we knew what the studio would be capable of."

The song Spector decided he wanted to take into the studio was entitled "Don't You Worry My Little Pet." It was built around a Chuck Berry–style guitar lick, a "wah-do-wah" background vocal. As with all the songs he sang on gigs, Spector wrote the lyric as strict harmony—no lead vocal. What he really wanted was to get it sung in the studio, so that he could work on overdubbing, bouncing the lead and background parts off each other.

When Phil went about trying to get the money to pay for a session at Gold Star, he knew an hour wouldn't do it, that he'd likely need twice that. Bertha, though, couldn't spare $40. She did promise him $10, and Marshall could get $10. Canvassing his singing friends, only Harvey Goldstein—who had gone on with Phil and Marshall to Los Angeles City College—was moved to contribute to the cause.

One more candidate came onto the scene as well. It was a shy, cherubic brunette named Annette Kleinbard, who was Donna Kass's girlfriend. Annette, who was tiny as a buttercup, lived in another school district, on Stearns Avenue south of Pico Boulevard, but she attended Fairfax High School so she could be close to Donna. By association, she came to know Phil, and Phil was more than interested in Annette's singing voice. This was *her* release, and, in her soprano voice, she belted out songs at Fairfax High talent shows that belied her small size. Phil had had little use for girl singers—in the rules of rock, girls sang with girls, like the McGuire Sisters or the Chordettes—and Annette was just a kid, like Donna. But Annette was constantly on the periphery of his music; when he'd rehearse songs in Donna's garage, Annette would be standing right there, learning the song and the harmony parts. Soliciting contributors for his first session, Phil half-idly asked Annette—but didn't tell her about the session, saying only that it would be a loan.

Her first reaction was to laugh. "Ten dollars! I don't have ten cents." "Well, can you get it?" he persisted. "Why do you want it?" With reluctance, he replied, "We're gonna go in and cut a record." Assured that she would be included, Annette secured the money from her mother. Spector took the $40 to Gold Star and reserved two hours for the afternoon of May 20.

Stan Ross engineered the session at which "Don't You Worry My Little Pet" was cut, and it was not an easy assignment. Phil was like a water bug in the studio, frantically racing from the control booth to the studio and back again. Unmistakably the point man for this group, he sang, he played guitar and piano, and when he ran into the booth to hear the playback, it was he who judged it acceptable or not.

When Phil wanted to do tricky things with tape—overdubbing a second clangy guitar part and a supplemental background vocal—Ross's own skills were tested. Much of what Spector wanted to do was unworkable on Gold Star's equipment or simply impossible, the product of a naïve youthful spirit. Still, some of his ideas broke practical ground. Ross had not engineered a session before in which the playback coming out of a speaker was rerecorded live with the overdub. But he knew it could be done, and tried it.

"We were experimenting, too, in those days," Ross said. "Every time engineers went into the studio, we were feeling our way, trying to find out what rock and roll was."

The process Spector and Lieb envisioned, however, was tougher than they thought it would be. Wearing big, bulky headphones as they overdubbed, "We couldn't hear what we were singing live," Lieb recalled. "It wasn't being printed on tape and coming back fast enough, because they didn't have the technology for that then. We had to feel around it until we got it."

In spite of the long, painstaking two hours, though, Phil gained energy. "He loved it; he'd never spent that much time in command of something," Lieb said. "Phil was at the top of his game when he was in the studio."

When it was over, Stan Ross cleaned up the tape, made a master, and cut a lacquer—an acetate, the first copy—for Phil. After leaving Gold Star, Phil and Marshall took the demo into the first record store they saw on Vine Street. "We just made this record," Phil told the clerk, hoping he might play it. "So what?" the clerk said.

The fact was, as much as they knew about cutting a record,

getting it played was something Phil and Marshall didn't have a clue about. But the acetate they had was a valuable piece of goods, as it might open a few doors. Mulling over his options, Phil thought he might have an in—Donnie Kartoon, one of the people who occasionally sang at gigs with him, lived next door on Alfred Street to the co-owner of Era Records, Lew Bedell. In business less than three years, Era had hit pay dirt with Gogi Grant's massive No. 1 hit in 1956, "The Wayward Wind," a song written by Bedell's cousin and co-owner, Herb Newman, and the label was looking to make a move into rock and roll. Almost immediately after making his record, Phil asked Donnie if he could get Bedell to hear it. Donnie called him, and Bedell said to bring the record to his office on Vine Street.

"I took Phil down there and, as soon as we got to the reception window he tried to ace me out," Kartoon remembered with a giggle. "He said, 'Wait here,' and tried to get into the office by himself, like 'I don't need Kartoon.' He tells the receptionist, 'Phil Spector's here'—not 'Don Kartoon is here,' and I'm the guy Lew Bedell knew— and she tells him he can't go in. It was like 'Who the hell are you? I don't know you.' So I told her who I was and I was there to see Lew, and it was 'Oh, come right in.' "

Lew Bedell was a garrulous man who masked a hardheaded business sense with endearing and sometimes annoying bluster. He had been the host of a television show in New York in the early fifties when Newman—working with another cousin, Si Waronker, the head of Liberty Records—had a falling out with Waronker and left Liberty to start Era. Bedell kicked in $7,500, lured Gogi Grant away from RCA Victor, and took her into the studio to record "The Wayward Wind." Bedell's charm and pushiness had gained Era strong distribution, and he had vital contacts in radio and television. Though not a music man, he could also pick a good record.

After spinning "Don't You Worry" on his office Victrola, Bedell called in Newman. The two men then listened to the acetate over and over—making Spector gnash his teeth as the needle ground into the record, putting crackles and pops into the delicate grooves he'd labored to create. Furthermore, Phil could tell that the Victrola wasn't providing an accurate rendition.

"Your machine is running slow," he remarked, barely containing himself. "It's not the way we recorded it."

Bedell and Newman were amused by Spector's cheekiness; when

⊙

not discussing his music, he was solicitous and deferential, a good kid. "I liked him," Bedell said. "I like all Jewish kids." And, minutely slow or not, both men agreed that the record was worth signing the group to a "lease of master"—a device used to buy a demo in lieu of an actual contract. Era Records gave them an option for four sides, and the four members—Spector, Lieb, Annette Kleinbard, and Harvey Goldstein—of the as-yet unnamed group would divide a 1½-cent royalty for each copy sold, the record industry equivalent of minimum wage. "Actually, they may have wanted to give us *less*," Marshall Lieb said. "My dad, who was a businessman, thought a lawyer should examine everything. That's when they came up with a penny and a half."

Bedell and Newman, in fact, had to face more hurdles with this bunch of kids than they may have thought was worth it. Because they all were legally minors, Era had to get a court order approving the signing under California's Jackie Coogan Law, which protected underage performers. "I had all these people in my office before we went to the court, all their parents and everybody," Bedell recalled. "I said, 'Look, if I'm gonna have any *tsouris* down there, I don't even wanna do this thing.' And they said, 'Don't worry.' And we got down there and there was nothing but *tsouris*, everybody talking all at the same time. I said to the judge, 'Do me a favor. Just ask 'em if they want to sign. If they do, fine. If not . . .' He did and they said, 'Yes.' And that was it."

When the papers were signed, Phil didn't forget what Donnie Kartoon had done for him. He told him, "Kartoon, you'll be well taken care of." Donnie laughed. "I mean, it was such a farfetched thought, that this thing would go anywhere," said Kartoon. "Lew had said to me, 'Donnie, why don't you manage them?' But I said no. Phil was into that 'big-time' thing; it was like a joke to me."

The signing done, the next piece of business was to cut a song to slap on the back side of "Don't You Worry." Phil talked to Bedell about several of his songs, and Bedell chose one titled "Wonderful Lovable You," a slow-tempo ballad. The group then took care of more business by taking on an official name. That was Harvey Goldstein's doing. "They'd been searching for a name left and right and couldn't come up with one," Goldstein said. "Elvis's 'Teddy Bear' was a big hit at the time, so I casually mentioned at one of our little bull sessions that we ought to name ourselves the Teddy Bears."

Goldstein, the bass voice of the group, had chosen to do summer Army Reserve duty instead of taking a chance of being drafted, and was slated to begin a two-week boot camp at Ft. Ord before the next session. Just before he left, he learned that Phil was intent on slipping in another song at the next session. "We had a meeting and they presented the new song to me, sang it for me. Since I was leaving, they said they were going to cut it without me."

When Phil did a quick run-through of the tune on the guitar, Harvey was knocked out. "It was dynamite. I knew as soon as I heard it that it was an instant hit."

It was the song that Phil Spector had been nurturing, trying to fit into a proper context ever since being jolted out of his sleep by Ben Spector's graven image. With a slight change of tense, the resulting song he had composed was called "To Know Him Is to Love Him."

On the surface, the only bond that this song had with Phil Spector's father is the tombstone engraving. The immediate influence was really Annette Kleinbard. When the Teddy Bears rehearsed "Wonderful Lovable You," her part—unlike in the solid four-part vocal harmony of "Don't You Worry My Little Pet"—was separated from the male vocals; the verses they did were repeated by her alone, and her candied soprano also rang out in the background, almost like an instrument. After the session, Phil told her "I love your voice" and that he was going to write a song to showcase it.

"He made it quite plain it wasn't me he loved, because of Donna, but the sound and the innocence of my voice," she recalled.

When he heard her in the studio, enhanced and layered by his overdubbing, he thought the new song would be the perfect vehicle for Annette to take a lead vocal. The gravestone phrase easily lent itself to a teenage girl's yearning. Phil refined a simple lyrical hook built around the title. The melody, which would revolve around three-beat repetitions on the words "know" and "love," was abruptly broken midway through by a minor chord—a ninth chord, which was common in jazz but radical for the straightforward arrangements of early rock and roll. This was Phil Spector's knockout punch, delivered in a spirited rush in the middle of the night.

But Phil could not find time to cut "To Know Him Is to Love Him" at the session for "Wonderful Lovable You." Lew Bedell and Herb Newman came to Gold Star on that Friday morning expecting

⊙

32

to be in and out in an hour. Instead, after two hours, "Wonderful Lovable You" was still unfinished. Though they expected to produce the side themselves, they were virtually elbowed out of the way as Spector and Lieb did their intricate overdubbing. "Phil and I knew more than those guys did," Lieb said. "Together, Phil and I were overly knowledgeable."

Not to Bedell. Three decades later he would still refuse to call what Spector did in the studio that morning producing. "He did *not* produce. I was the whole thing. He was sitting out there playing his *fershtunkenah* guitar all day and a few notes on the piano." Bedell and Newman had little patience with the notion that Spector was working on a "sound." Exasperated by apparently so little getting done in so long a time, Bedell threw his arms in the air and yelled, "Okay, that's it! We'll come back and finish this thing on Monday."

On that day, the Teddy Bears returned with a new addition, a drummer—Sammy Nelson, of Union High's Sleepwalkers, which had evolved into a band called Kip Tyler and the Flips, with a contract on Challenge Records. Up until now, Phil and Marshall had kept the backbeat by hitting a telephone book with a drum brush. Now they required a real drummer. Unfortunately, Sammy Nelson was the only one they knew.

"He was not a great drummer, he couldn't keep time real well," Lieb said, and adding a drum overdub on the session ate up a huge chunk of time. "We'd made the demo with tempo, our tempo, and it fluctuated. Sammy had to play at that exact tempo, and no one could have done that. So we wound up giving him the beat, pointing at him, like 'Now!' "

Bedell, who was paying Nelson $15 an hour as an outside musician, was spitting mad. "He stinks, Stan!" he yelled to Ross, who instructed Nelson to use only a brush stick scraped across a snare drum. Still, for over an hour Nelson played alone in the studio, and Bedell and Newman were so frustrated that they left. "They told me, 'Look, give 'em the two hours, then cut 'em off,' " Ross related. "They split because they didn't want to be around Phil. They couldn't stand him, they thought he was crazy. But he wasn't. He was ambitious, not crazy."

With minutes left, Phil asked Stan if he could squeeze in one more song. Now Ross was generous; he let them go for an extra half hour.

In that half hour, Phil Spector produced "To Know Him Is to Love Him."

With little time to get tricky, Phil was forced to keep things simple. But even after Annette had done her lead and Nelson overdubbed his drum, Phil and Marshall wrang every second they could out of Ross's generosity, adding more background vocals and a guitar and piano track. The record they took from Gold Star was reminiscent of the great L.A. demo hits such as Patience and Prudence's "Tonight You Belong to Me" in 1956 and Tab Hunter's cover of "Young Love" in 1957; even with overdubbing it sounded as if it could have been recorded in a garage between two parked cars. But there was an odd wonder in its grooves. Minus Goldstein's bass part, the feel was less studied and cliché-ish, not so much a West Coast kiddie version of doo-wop as sincere white R&B.

Annette's lead was remarkable, a little girl hurting with real pain. She was the glue of a record on which instruments can barely be heard—though, as Lieb told it, the whole thing was deceptively sparse. "It sounds real simple but it's very complicated. In the real Spector tradition, it was very planned. Even though we had a short time we knew exactly what we wanted to do, the nuances, everything."

"To Know Him Is to Love Him" was an epiphany of yearning in the placid Eisenhower years. For all its innocence, the song had an undercurrent of sadness and alienation. It swayed back and forth in a hammocklike lull, sounding like a mantra, then given a sudden urgency by a ninth chord that was dark and melancholy in itself. In its inscrutability, the title regained its original implication.

But while Lew Bedell thought it had "a magic sound" when he heard it, and decided to use it as the slow-tempo song on the first Teddy Bears record, he was unsure which side to plug. Although Bedell would later say he put the play on "To Know Him," Lieb and Annette Kleinbard recalled otherwise. "Herb and Lew didn't love it, they liked it . . . I don't remember them loving it until it became a hit," she said.

"First of all, to do a ballad at that time was absurd. 'To Know Him' was the first girl ballad of its time. There was no girl, innocent, white-type voice on songs like that."

Bedell, at least, thought he might have had a two-sided hit on his hands when the disc—on Era's brand-new rock-and-roll label, named after Bedell's son—was pressed and released as Doré #503, both tunes copyrighted to Bedell and Newman's publishing company, Warman Music. On August 1, Era sent out a cautious run of five hundred copies through a distributor named George Jay.

And then, for the next month, not a thing happened.

Harvey Goldstein, returning home from boot camp, rehearsed "To Know Him" with the group, but they rarely got to sing it anywhere. In September he and Lieb began their second semester at L.A. City College. Annette and Donna Kass began twelfth grade at Fairfax High School. And Phil Spector, unconvinced of musical stardom, primed his court reporting skills at a business school in Los Angeles. The Teddy Bears did sing their two songs on a local television show hosted by deejay Art Laboe, but there was only sporadic airplay in L.A. B. Mitchell Reid, on KFWB, spun it—but he played "To Know Him Is to Love Him," not the A side. "We heard that deejays were flipping the record over," Lieb remembered. "In L.A., we heard the song for a couple of days, then the station dropped it."

The Teddy Bears were almost an afterthought at thriving Era Records, but the trend to flip over its rock-and-roll entry did not go unnoticed by Lew Bedell. With "Don't You Worry My Little Pet" dead in the water, George Jay put the play on "To Know Him Is to Love Him." Invariably, the response from distributors was "It sounds too much like a demo."

Finally, early in September, a deejay in Fargo, North Dakota, Charlie Boone, was the first non-L.A. deejay to break the record, and he put it in regular rotation. Then Bedell got word from his Midwest distributor: Lou Riegert, the program director at Minneapolis station KDWB—a sister station of KFWB—had said he had fallen in love with Annette's voice and put it on the air. The response was fantastic.

Inside of a week, orders came in for "To Know Him," 150 at first, then 300, then 1,000. By mid-September, Bedell and Newman were looking at an order from Minneapolis for 18,000 records.

Spector found out about it when he came in to Bedell's office to ask how the record was moving. "Hey, we got a little order here," Bedell told him coyly.

The week of September 22, 1958, "To Know Him Is to Love Him" hit the *Billboard* chart at No. 88. But it still had little airplay outside the Midwest. Bedell then played his biggest card. He knew Dick Clark, and he called him in Philadelphia to ask a favor. He pushed hard, saying he had a peculiar problem—a No. 1 record in Minneapolis that he couldn't get played anywhere else. The first thing Clark wanted to know was if Universal Distributors—a giant distributing depot powerful enough to own its own record labels, and closely linked to "American Bandstand"—was handling the Doré record in Philadelphia. It was, and that bit of good fortune may have led Clark to listen to it.

"He heard it, thought it over, then put it on 'American Bandstand' and *boom*—we wound up selling 1.4 million copies," Bedell said.

The nationwide after-school audience of "American Bandstand" could give a song megaton force, and "To Know Him" ran up the charts with frightening speed. Four weeks on the chart, it hit the Top 40 the week of October 11. It was No. 16 a week later, No. 5 two weeks after that. In mid-November, Dick Clark called Lew Bedell to request the Teddy Bears come to Philadelphia to appear on his show. Bedell took the opportunity to send the group on a promotional tour through Philadelphia, Washington, D.C., and New York during a four-day whirl around Thanksgiving. Suddenly, almost without time to focus their eyes on what was happening, the clean-nosed Teddy Bears were the hottest item in rock and roll.

Phil Spector was not too breathless, however, to make a hard business move. The victim was Harvey Goldstein.

"When the Dick Clark thing happened, they told me they didn't want me to make the trip," Goldstein said. "They said Dick Clark was paying expenses and he didn't want to pay for somebody who didn't sing on the record. This was the excuse for acing me out of the group. I knew this, but it was confirmed years later when I ran into Dick Clark. I introduced myself and told him the whole story, and he said he never paid expenses for people to do that show.

"I have a feeling that the greed factor came into it. Phil thought they might only have to split the money between three, not four, since I wasn't on the record. It was probably easy for him to make the decision, because I wasn't really close to Phil in school; it was Marshall who approached me originally about coming in, not Phil.

"I wasn't Phil's idea of a music person. I couldn't read music and they had to teach me my parts, and that was a pain in the ass

⊙   36

because sometimes I caught on, sometimes I didn't. I didn't have the talent they did, so it probably wasn't hard to convince them I should go."*

When the Teddy Bears went off to Philadelphia, a hurt and fuming Goldstein consulted an attorney and later filed a lawsuit against the group, claiming he in effect owned 25 percent of the name "The Teddy Bears." "I'm sure they thought they were smart when they pulled what they did on me," he said, "but they weren't smart enough." Ultimately, the group settled with Goldstein: bonds were placed in trust for him, and he continued to draw royalty checks for a decade. In return, Goldstein agreed not to use the group's name in any music venture of his own—a promise that was very easy for him to keep. He went to Cal State to study accounting, never to sing another note, and with acrid memories. "We were eighteen-year-old kids fighting like animals over a few dollars. There's something extremely sad about that."

The change that came over Phil Spector's personality in the wake of this explosion was vivid. Donna Kass saw a "much more confident" Phil. Lew Bedell and Herb Newman saw a monster. "The kid became so haughty," Bedell said. "Before the song was a hit, Phil used to come in and say 'Anything doing today, Mr. Bedell?' He was so obsequious I figured he was half-Japanese, this guy. Then, after it was a hit, he walks in and it's 'Hey, Lew, baby, we're doin' good.' He starts calling Herb 'Hey, you.' You never saw such a complete change in a little fuckin' Jewish kid."

Bertha and Shirley Spector didn't have to change. Always sure of his singularity, they now shared his vanity; anyone who Phil felt was not a proper ally became their immediate enemy. When Harvey Goldstein was cashiered, he felt that the women may have been behind it. "Phil's mother and sister virtually tried to control everything he did, and he tried to control us. I'm sure they had a real impact on my being booted out of the group. Shirley and his mother were like wild people. They wouldn't have hesitated doing it."

---

*Lieb and Kleinbard, whose recollections of most matters concerning the Teddy Bears were vivid, recalled Goldstein's departure only in vague terms. Lieb said: "I think Harvey and Phillip had some kind of falling out . . . something along the lines of . . . I don't know," while Kleinbard (who later changed her professional name to Carol Connors) said: "Harvey was in for about four seconds. It just didn't work, he just wasn't a part of it."

Donna was next to feel their wrath. Not particularly excited by the show-biz glitter being sprinkled on her once-shy and sensitive boyfriend, she was distressed by the upcoming East Coast swing, because it presaged more of the same. Several times she asked him if he had to go—the kind of request any girlfriend might ask of her boyfriend. Bertha and Shirley were livid. "They felt I was trying to hold Phil back," Kass said. "But what kind of power did I have? I was fifteen, sixteen, I was nothing. I was a lowly little Jewish girl that went to high school and was crazy about him. I'm totally nonmusical, and I kind of . . . if I look back now, I was jealous of it, his career. I tried to get him to stay in school and not to travel because it took him away from me, and yet here he was with my best girlfriend out there somewhere and it was real hard for me."

Once, at a rare meeting with Phil at his place, Donna was stunned when Bertha and Shirley lit into her, openly accusing her of trying to short-circuit his mission in music. "They attacked me, not physically but yelling and tormenting me for hours.

Phil tried to defend her but, predictably, it became an argument. "It was just ranting and raving for a long time. They accused me of all kinds of things, that I was taking him away and not encouraging him about his music, and he was spending too much time with me and he couldn't write . . . just everything."

Donna, seemingly paralyzed by the ambush, finally freed herself when her mother called. "I was crying my eyes out to her, and she came and got me. She said, 'Why are you involved with them?' "

But for Phil, liberation took a back seat to family loyalty created by the stigma and guilt he felt about Ben's suicide. That he was, and would be, the male legatee under the Spector roof, kept him affixed, stuck in place even as his legs itched to run out the door so he could make his music in peace. Indeed peace could only come from music, and music could only come after paying a toll in anger and frustration. To Bertha, he was still her little boy. Somehow, Phil knew that no matter how far he'd be able to spread his wings, he'd never really clear that roof, at least not in his own mind.

Shirley Spector hurled herself into the whirlwind of the Teddy Bears' ride up the charts. Welding her ambition to family loyalty, she convinced Paul that she should manage the group. The thought of the

⊙ 38

Spectors' fratricidal bickering interfering in the affairs of the group so horrified Marshall and Annette that they agreed to let her in only on a quasi-official basis, more as a bone thrown to the Spector women for their support of Phil. The real decisions were already being made by seasoned people in the business; an agent named Ned Tanen had put together the appearances on the East Coast trip, and a public relations man in New York, Bud Dollinger, was hired to do promotion. In Philadelphia, Universal's promo man, Harry Finfer, would escort the group to "American Bandstand." When the Teddy Bears went on the trip, Shirley stayed home.

On the morning they took off, Phil was so terrified about getting on an airplane—an old phobia—that he took his pillow along for security during the flight. That week, the Thanksgiving issue of *Billboard* had "To Know Him Is to Love Him" at No. 3. *Cash Box,* on whose chart the song first appeared on October 11, placed it at No. 2, after an incredible leap from No. 22 to No. 7 four weeks earlier.

Upon landing in New York, his physical and emotional breeding ground, Phil had two pressing pursuits: the first was to see his uncle Sam. The second was to visit the grave of Ben Spector.

After talking Marshall and Annette into coming with him to see Sam Spektor, who with his two sons and daughter had moved to a house across the Hudson River in Clifton, New Jersey, the trio boarded a bus at the Port Authority terminal. They arrived at Sam's house like conquering heroes. Phil, who had sent Sam one of the first few pressed copies of his record, sat with him for hours reminiscing over old photo albums of a family of Spectors and Spektors who once all lived within minutes of each other in the Bronx but now was spread from coast to coast.

Later in the day, Phil went to see the gravestone that was a source of such incredible despair and inspiration. He went alone.

A day later, on November 28, the Teddy Bears went on "American Bandstand," following by one day Buddy Holly and the Crickets, and lip-synched their sizzling hit song. Phil and Marshall wore powder-blue, V-necked sweaters with their first names embroidered in small script on the chest. Annette wore a red gown. All of them were petrified.

The appearance hastened the inevitable. The following week,

"To Know Him Is to Love Him" had pushed "Hang Down Your Head Tom Dooley" out of the No. 1 slot on both pop charts.

Phil talked on the phone with Donna constantly during the trip, but when he and the Teddy Bears came home, the relationship hit the rocks. Tooling down Sunset Boulevard in his new metallic-blue Corvette, bought out of the first rush of royalties, seventeen-year-old Spector met more girls than he once would have thought possible. Behind Donna's back he began seeing a girl named Karen Oster. "I found out he was cheating on me, and it was very painful," Kass recalled. Suddenly Spector's once-captivating little lies weren't so endearing. When Ritchie Valens's song "Donna" became a big hit in early 1959, Phil told her he had actually written the tune, for her— but said he had sold the song, its rights and writing credit, to Valens, who also recorded at Gold Star. On February 3, while on tour in the Midwest, Valens was killed with Buddy Holly and the Big Bopper in a plane crash. Donna Kass saw the Donna of the song—Donna Ludwig—crying on the newsreels.

Spector's ongoing mendacity was absurd, but Donna could sense it was pathological. "It didn't matter to Phil that he was hot, or that everybody wanted him," Kass said. "He was very manipulative. He had no good role models. The only good role model he ever had killed himself."

Plainly, Phil thought he had outgrown not only Donna but everything in her world. Gradually, and mutually, they drifted away from each other—but not before Spector had shaped the direction of her life. So skilled was he in his court reporting that a fascinated Donna began to study it herself. Three decades later, she would still be a working court stenographer in Los Angeles.

Now that Donna was out of the way, Annette, as her best friend, wondered if she would be the next target. Shirley had eased her way more and more into the inner sanctum of the Teddy Bears, and she began reigning with a fist of iron—which Annette thought was aimed at her. "Shirley was really tough on me," she remembered. "I think she really wanted to be me, in a sense as a singer, someone who had talent and could make it in show business." Shirley tried to govern Annette's role

☉

as she saw fit, in clothes, makeup, telling her when to smile and what to tell interviewers. Her words of criticism came in torrents, her words of assurance in trickles. Just her presence could unnerve both Annette and Marshall.

"Shirley really was an extension of Phil, but a lot more unpleasant," Lieb said. "She was a very hyper, very nervous person. She was very loud, very New York. She smoked a lot, and when she would sit with you, it gave you that turn-off feeling."

Feeling in charge after the headiness of the group's "Bandstand" triumph, Shirley barged into Lew Bedell's Vine Street office late one Friday afternoon to pick up a royalty check for Phil. Bedell, talking business around a conference table with an associate named Danny Gould, was nearly knocked off his chair when she came through the door and announced, "I'm Shirley Spector and I've come for my brother's paycheck!"

"Here . . . I got it right here,' Bedell said, reaching into a pile of papers on his desk and handing over a check for $38,000 in artist's and writing royalties made out to Phil.

Shirley expected cash. Her response, according to Bedell, was a flood of blue language in between which she said she couldn't cash the check because it was too late in the day. "And Danny Gould, he's lookin' at me. He says, 'Lew, I didn't know you did that sort of thing.' I said, 'I don't, I don't . . .' So, anyway, I told her, 'Listen, the United California Bank is open till six o'clock on Fridays,' and she goes out in a huff and that's the last I saw of the *meshugenah*."

Bedell had a bigger problem with Phil, about what would be the follow-up to "To Know Him." Spector had come in with a song called "Oh Why," a bluesy piece replete with minor chords similar to the kind he used for the bridge in "To Know Him."

"I don't wanna do it, Phil," Bedell told him. "I don't like minor songs, very few of 'em make it."

Spector would not budge. "Then I'm leaving. I'm gonna go somewhere else," he said.

It was no idle threat either. Spector had by this time gotten feelers from Lou Chudd, the head of Imperial Records, one of the biggest of the L.A. independent labels. Chudd was dangling a real contract, at twice the royalty rate, before Phil's eyes. Bedell knew he was boxed in, that Spector had him at his mercy because Bedell hadn't torn up the original lease of master for four songs with a real, binding contract delineating responsibilities. In effect, Spector was working on speculation and Bedell had no control over the material. But Bedell held *his* ground as well.

"Hey, I wanted to keep 'em, but I wanted to pick the material, because I'd been pickin' the material," he said. "But I made a mistake. I should've given 'em a contract where I had complete control. So we had an altercation about this song and I said to my cousin Herb, 'You wanna handle this kid? I don't want to. I don't need this aggravation.' And Herb didn't want anything to do with Spector. He was a *meshugenah* too. And when you got five things in the Top 20, like we had, you don't need this *tsouris*. If I could've taken the aggravation, I'd still be with him today."

Late in 1958—with "To Know Him Is to Love Him" hanging strong at No. 3 in *Billboard*—the Teddy Bears had signed on with Imperial, the prestigious label of Fats Domino and Ricky Nelson. With royalties hiked to three cents per copy sold, Marshall thought it was time to ask Phil about possibly sharing a few writing credits with him. Lieb didn't fool himself; he knew he wasn't close to Phil as a composer, but he felt his lyrical contributions were helpful. "When Phil came up with 'To Know Him,' I liked it, but I told him, 'We need to do some things with it,' " Lieb said. "The background part that goes 'And I do and I' . . . that was mine.

"To us, when we started singing, it was always the both of us. We were open and flowing with each other, and all things could happen. And at that time, there was no money in it, and Phil allowed my ideas to be dumped in his lap. Phillip wrote most of the stuff, and I did the backgrounds, because I was the background freak.

"We talked about me getting some credits a couple of times, and he said, 'Don't worry, I'm gonna give you half my royalties anyway.'

"Phillip was more familiar with the business, and he was slowly— or quickly—becoming what he later became, in terms of deceiving people. My whole thing then was, we'd grown up together, we were close friends, and it was gonna be okay. While I called him on it, we'd fight, and I didn't want to fight with him so I just said, 'Phillip, if you make a promise then you better keep it.' And, of course, he didn't. He never paid me any royalty."

Donnie Kartoon didn't get anything either, on *his* promise from Phil. He never tried to collect on it. He knew better.

⊙

．．．

On January 3, 1959, the Teddy Bears went on national television, flying to New York again to appear on NBC's "Kraft Music Hall with Perry Como." The show was a tribute to composer Harold Arlen, who was a guest, along with actor Louis Jourdan, singer Peggy King, and vaudevillian Eddie Foy, Jr.

For Annette in particular, the trip was a nightmare. Shirley came with the group this time, and she was to room with Annette at the Plaza Hotel. By the time the Teddy Bears arrived, Annette remembered that "I was so frightened of Shirley that I ran into Phil and Marshall's room and sat there all night crying. They took care of me. . . . Shirley was, in my mind, evil."

The next afternoon, at rehearsal, Shirley strutted around the stage of Broadway's Ziegfeld Theater—from where the show would be broadcast live—puffing clouds of cigarette smoke and trying to co-opt the director. "She would argue that the lighting wasn't right or that we weren't standing in the right position," Lieb said. "She made a real spectacle of herself."

When the Teddy Bears did a run-through of "To Know Him Is to Love Him," accompanied by the Ray Charles Orchestra, a weary Annette couldn't hit the song's high note. Phil told her sternly, "Annette, if you don't hit that note, I'm never going to talk to you again!"

Annette was numb with fear as showtime approached. "I was so frightened that I wasn't going to hit that note on the show. Phil had driven me crazy. He said, 'You can't do this. You *must* get the note right. You can't embarrass me.' "

Further auguring disaster, as the jittery threesome waited to go on that night, Phil accidentally stepped on Peggy King's gown, ripping it slightly. The singer turned around and glared at him, and Phil wanted to crawl away. But on stage, everything went well. Phil and Marshall wore sharp-creased black tuxedos, their hair sheared into crew cuts. Annette, wearing a pink dress, managed to hit the high note of "To Know Him Is to Love Him," and they then did a pleasant rendition of Harold Arlen's "It's Only a Paper Moon."

Fresh off that coup, the Teddy Bears began cutting their first album. Lou Chudd gave Spector a lofty budget to work with, and in March—with "To Know Him" only *now* having fallen off the chart—the group went into the studio, though it was not Gold Star but Master Sound Recorders, an old, hovellike studio on Fairfax Avenue

43

a block away from Fairfax High School, which was used by a number of Imperial artists. Gold Star was out now, unofficially off limits because it had a close working arrangement with Lew Bedell and Herb Newman, and the fallout from the Teddy Bears' defection would have made a session with Phil sticky for Stan Ross. But Imperial had a tremendous lure. "It was *Fats*'s label," Lieb said. "God, do you know how exciting that was for us?"

The studio at Master Sound was an even smaller room than Gold Star's and had less equipment. Spector and Lieb were hardpressed to duplicate the tonal ambience they had carved with Gold Star's walls and low ceiling, although for the first time they got to work with union musicians: two of Lou Chudd's top session men, bassist George "Red" Callander and drummer Earl Palmer, who worked all of Fats Domino's sessions in New Orleans and many L.A. rock dates. Callander and Palmer were used to breezing through sessions in which they would rip out four songs in two hours. Now, even with simple arrangements, they sat for long periods, as the two teenagers fiddled with echoes and fooled with knobs on the control room board.

Lieb remembered it as much more: "We were working on the transparency of music; that was the Teddy Bears sound: you had a lot of air moving around, notes being played in the air but not directly into the mikes. Then, when we sent it all into the chamber, this air effect is what was heard—all the notes jumbled and fuzzy. This is what we recorded—not the notes. The chamber."

Phil and Marshall believed they had reached the point where "we could get a kind of pseudostereo," Lieb put it. "We could channel the high end on one side, lower end on the other. We'd be situated between the two speakers and have this big monaural ball in front of us, yet it was from two sides; if you took one of the sides out, the ball would move. We could actually get a guitar to shoot off one of the speakers, by mixing and using equalizers. What we were doing was splitting sound—before stereo."

Lou Chudd and Bunny Robyne, the owner of Master Sound and its studio engineer, considered it mostly wasted time. Trying to move things along, Chudd would say, "Why don't you try it this way, Phil?"

Spector would tell him, "I don't want to try it that way."

"We had ideas and we had rehearsed those ideas, and we were

gonna do them our way," Lieb said. "When we came in to do it, if it wasn't working, Phil and I would reorganize it. We would experiment with the mixing board beyond the engineer's capabilities. We didn't need anybody to help us—we didn't *want* anybody to help us."

However, after two weeks of sessions—most albums of the day were done inside of a week—a mere six songs were in the can. Spector refused to believe that Lou Chudd expected him to cheapen anything on the album—in the normal manner of album-making, two or three good songs were showcased, buttressed by filler—and he would hunker down between speakers playing back tracks endlessly at screechingly loud decibel levels. Other times he would shut off the lights, just like the atmosphere of his bedroom on those nights of revelation, so that he could concentrate on the sound and nothing else.

Chudd, a bottom-line type, lost all patience. This seemingly juvenile exercise in indulgence was costing him a small fortune. In late March, fed up, Chudd took the album out of Phil's hands and gave the job of finishing it to Jimmie Haskell, Imperial's top staff writer/producer/arranger. Haskell took three days to record six songs. In the name of haste, he forbade Phil from playing guitar on the sessions, rightly assuming that would make Spector want to alter the arrangements that Haskell wrote. Each song was completed in one or two takes. Relegated to the unaccustomed role of a bit player, Phil petulantly said nothing beyond a few civil words to Haskell— who himself would take few bows for the album.

"I did the songs that sound like they were hurried," he acknowledged, unlike the Spector-produced tunes, which Haskell thought were "very well blended. . . . As a general rule then, we did everything live. If we overdubbed, it was with a single voice, not a group the way they did it." Haskell was fascinated by how Spector and Lieb overdubbed their voices as the playback was piped in live. "They couldn't hear themselves so they'd wear a headphone on one ear and cup the other ear—which everyone picked up on in the business, and is still being done today."

But, rushed through production, the album—*The Teddy Bears Sing!*—was a limp and soggy effort, a telling argument. No matter how well Phil Spector could tailor the sound of a record, the subliminal angst of "To Know Him Is to Love Him" owed its life to the death of Ben Spector; the genesis of that song was the culmination of dark forces Spector tried to push out of his psyche but which rose up in Freudian vengeance in the dead of night. Now, with no emotional context, the Teddy Bears' songs, well crafted to be sure, were essentially heartless, derivative pinwheeling of a now-empty teen cliché. This doomed the Teddy Bears as an example of country fair cute instead of white R&B. Three Spector-penned songs were as banal as the filler songs picked by Lou Chudd—including standards like "Long Ago and Far Away," "Little Things Mean a Lot" and "Tammy," "True Love," the country ballad "My Foolish Heart," and "Unchained Melody," which had been covered previously by both Fats Domino and Ricky Nelson, per Chudd's orders. Two of the Spector tunes, "Oh Why"—the work rejected by Lew Bedell—and "I Don't Need You Any More" were sides A and B of the first Imperial release in the early spring.

As the Imperial record died, barely scraping the bottom of the charts, the schism between group members caused by Shirley Spector widened into a gulf that could not be bridged.

"Shirley never had the approval of Annette and me," Marshall Lieb recalled, "but then she wanted to sign papers with us making it legal, and we wouldn't do it."

"In my mind," Annette Kleinbard said, "it became a matter of integrity and honor. I said, 'I'm not selling myself to the devil for anything or anybody.'

"It was hard for Phil too. He knew there was a problem, but blood is thicker than water. I think sometimes he just said, 'I can't deal with this. I'm under siege!' "

Spector had for months tried to walk a shaky tightrope between family solidarity and peace within the band. Now it was painfully obvious that there was no solution to the problem.

The Teddy Bears limped into the spring, fulfilling contract obligations with two more records. And Phil cut a session without the other Teddy Bears, a perk allowed him in his contract. He indulged himself by hiring two guitarists he yearned to be in a studio with. One was Ernie Freeman, who made albums for Imperial. The other was Howard Roberts.

As thrilled as Spector was to have him, Roberts did not enjoy doing the bland, three-chord movements he and Freeman were required to play. Spector regarded the pair of instrumentals that came out of the session as blues-rock. To Roberts they were pap, not pop—the same as the rest of the rock gigs he was called to. "At that time, everything was produced with the intelligence of a fern," Roberts said. Titled "Dumbo" and "Willy Boy," the first song was later changed to "Bumbershoot" when Imperial released the two sides—under the name Phil Harvey—into a marketplace that ignored them.

Seeing that the breakup of the Teddy Bears was becoming inevitable, Phil Spector was a restless young man now, again without direction and bitter about his broken dream. While he didn't sever his friendship with Marshall—"We had too many years behind us," said Lieb—things were clearly not the same between them.

For Annette, whom he blamed the most for the rift, he had nothing but loathing.

Early in September, Annette was at the wheel of her white MG convertible, coming around a winding turn high up on Mulholland Drive, when she swerved and lost control. The car spun wildly, went off the road, and tumbled down a mountainside and into a ditch. Annette was pulled from the wreckage. Her face was ravaged, her nose almost completely sheared off. For weeks she lay in a bed at the UCLA Medical Center as doctors reconstructed her features. She required four operations. When she was well enough to receive guests, Phil was not among the bedside visitors. In fact, one of Annette's friends told her that when Phil had heard of her accident he responded with venom.

She recalled, "His comment, which broke my heart, was: 'Too bad she didn't die.' I was devastated by that."*

In the fall, Imperial released the two last Teddy Bears singles—"If Only You Knew (the Love I Have for You)"/"You Said Goodbye" and "Don't Go Away"/"Seven Lonely Days"—and Doré put out "Wonderful Lovable You." They all failed. The nation's romance with the Teddy Bears had turned out to be the staggering twenty-three-week run of "To Know Him Is to Love Him," nothing more.

Crippled months before by internal strife, the Teddy Bears finally dissolved.

Though Phil could not have mustered the grit to fire Shirley, he

---

*Phil Specter has denied ever making this statement.

47

now became aware of how deep the problem with her was. After the Teddy Bears signed on with Imperial, Era had disbursed a large sum in writing royalties to Phil, which he had allowed to be assigned to Shirley. When the group broke up, little of that money was left.

"It was $200,000," Lieb remembered. "Phillip told me he gave it to Shirley, and it didn't reach him. I think he told her, like you would trust a relative to put your money away for you: 'Here, put it in the bank for me.' When you're seventeen, eighteen years old, you don't know what to do with it. And if she pays some bills with it, or buys a new car, with the expectation of paying it back, you just accept it."

When Marshall and Annette wanted to close the book on the Teddy Bears by settling up on money matters, they were told that any money Shirley owed them had been used to pay expenses. They did not dispute that, nor did they choose to have the books audited. To them, the breakup was more tragic than infuriating. Exhausted and battered, the three ex-Teddy Bears moved on, scarred by the price of stardom.

3

The Teddy Bears are a good example of how today's teenagers have a chance to become famous in the record field. In no other field of creative or industrial endeavor can the youngster express himself for so many and reap the lucrative rewards.

—Liner notes, *The Teddy Bears Sing!*

When "To Know Him Is to Love Him" hit Los Angeles, Phil Spector became the center of gravity in a West Hollywood rock-and-roll scene that was bustling because of his example. Comforted by this, Phil stuck close to his home turf, aligning himself with the local talent. One of these was Steve Douglas, whose early band Shirley Spector once managed. Douglas had since gone on to play saxophone with Kip Tyler and the Flips. Backing them on a Johnny Otis show at El Monte Legion Stadium, Steve had caught the attention of a black vocal group called the Sharps, who did the screaming background vocals on Duane Eddy's twangy guitar records. Eddy was going on tour and needed a backup band. Douglas, recommended by the Sharps, joined the group and also recorded with Eddy in the studio. As he lived in the area and knew Shirley, Steve had once let Phil sit in with his early band. Now Steve wanted very much to sit in with Phil.

"He was the local star on the scene," Douglas remembered.

With the chance to jam with the hotshot, Douglas began to bring other members of the Duane Eddy touring band to Michael Spencer's house, and it became the word-of-mouth place to be. On Friday nights, jam sessions there blew sky-high, with a combination Teddy Bears/Duane Eddy's Rebel Rousers: Spector and Lieb, Douglas and guitarist Mike Bermani, buttressed by drummer Johnny Clauder, another neighborhood guy, who played in jazz pianist Don Randi's band. Large numbers of kids from the area considered themselves lucky just to catch the music from the street outside the house.

More fortunate were those who by some twist of fate could step inside Spector's circle. Marshall Lieb's girlfriend, Sue Titelman, had a younger brother, Russell, who was in junior high school when he got to hear the acetate of "To Know Him Is to Love Him." "We had a Magnavox 78-rpm phonograph," Titelman recalled, "and Phil would play those demos on it. Sometimes they rehearsed in the living room, and I was completely fascinated, transfixed by the way Phil played guitar. And then when he was cutting the album, he'd bring over the stuff and play it, and say, 'What do you think of this?' Can you imagine? Here I was, a fifteen-year-old kid exposed to all of this."

Lieb also was responsible for finding a younger guitar player named Don Peake. Phil, who now owned a truly princely guitar—a sunburst mahogany, hollow-body Gibson L-5 with a double F-hole and mother-of-pearl inlay—was amused by the guitar Peake had: a frayed, green, Japanese-made slab of knotholes. But Peake could play the daylights out of the thing. "Dig this guy," Phil would say to friends who hadn't heard Peake play, at which point Peake would blow everybody away.

There were others, too, whom Spector touched by proxy, by what "To Know Him Is to Love Him" meant to them as aspiring rockers. Elliott Ingber was one of those thousands of fifties' teenagers with a guitar when his family moved to West Hollywood in the summer of 1958. He decided to go to Fairfax High as the song was burrowing its way into a generation's subconscious. "I put up with Fairfax High very grudgingly," Ingber said, "because I didn't think

⊙ 50

it was hip at all. The main thing was, this guy had a hit record, his name was Phil Spector, and this girl who sang on the record went there."

Ingber wanted badly to meet Spector, and introduced himself to Annette. "I told her I played guitar, the whole thing. She was the connection between me meeting him. Either that or she warned me *not* to get involved with him."

Phil allowed Ingber into his scene, after the latter showed he was a comrade in arms, not a leech. "I knew what the blues scene was and so automatically we had a base level of communication, sort of unspoken . . . there weren't many people around then who knew what the fuck that scene was. I mean, I didn't know what Phil's motivation was with 'To Know Him Is to Love Him,' but I knew he expressed himself with the odd chord change, the basic blues thing."

When it became all too clear in the spring of 1959 that the Teddy Bears were goners, Phil had taken his frustrations out by playing jazz, doing the "Bumbershoot"/"Willy Boy" session. Now, straining to break out of a mold that had gone stale, he took a live gig as Phil Harvey. To form a band to go out with him, he turned to Elliott Ingber.

"He wanted to go out and do something on his own scene, and he figured I knew some people who could help him," Ingber said, "and I got a guy, Larry Taylor, a guitar player. At the time, Larry and I were just startin' out—Phil had to bring us up to a level where we could be on the same stage with him. Like, Phil showed me what a ninth chord was. That was a big deal, but it wasn't to Phil, because the guy was a monster on the guitar. He was on top of it. He was fire. He could play 'Guitar Boogie Shuffle' like the record. I tell you, man, he and Michael Spencer, they'd have sessions over at Spencer's house and they'd be playing things like 'It's Wonderful,' way up tempo. That takes some real doing for any guitar player to play that shit and bring it out the way Spector could. He wasn't fucking around. He was actually playing *jazz*."

Spector rehearsed the Phil Harvey band at Ingber's house on Stanley Street, teaching the ringing guitar harmonies of "Bumbershoot" and other jazz and blues material to Elliott, Larry Taylor, and Larry's brother Mel. The band was filled out with others of Ingber's buddies, a pianist named Howard Hirsch and a drummer, Rod Schaffer.

Elliott had a much younger brother, Ira, who was only nine at the time. But he could still see something disturbing and adrift in Phil Spector. "He was this lost soul. My mother was a real mom to everybody, and I think Phil liked to be around us, as a family feeling. But he was a lost soul; he got pretty out there and unapproachable during that time."

Esther Ingber thought so too. Though Phil seemed to want to be around her son and her home, she recalled that he was "a very, very cold person . . . one of those people that don't show any affection."

Shirley Spector may have felt the cold breath of her brother's alienation more than most. As the primary cause of the Teddy Bears' demise, Shirley worried endlessly that Phil would cut her out of his music, even his life. Shirley, and Bertha, still made a habit of checking Phil's whereabouts closely, and when Shirley found out how attached he had become to the Ingbers, she imposed herself on the household as well. "It was like Shirley and her mother wouldn't trust Phil," Esther Ingber said. "They loved him, but you can smother someone with kindness too."

Esther Ingber barely knew Phil's family, yet she would be the recipient of a hail of phone calls from Shirley in particular, each one more distraught than the last, and they would go on for hours. It was as if Shirley could find no one else to relieve herself of a terrible burden, and Esther would be supportive. "She would say she was proud of her brother and I would tell her she had every right to be. Phil was the closest thing to her, and Shirley was hurt that they weren't close. All she could do was cry about it."

When Phil saw how torn up Shirley was, his way of reassuring her was not verbally—open expressions of love would have had to be extracted from him, like rotting teeth—but to ask her to write a song with him. Out of the collaboration came a tune called "Be My Girl."

Phil's idea for the Phil Harvey band was to sell hot jazz to rock audiences with a flourish of hip show-biz kitsch. The gig was at the Rainbow Roller Rink out in the valley, a roller-skating palace that was converted into a concert hall at night. When the band came out on stage the whole bunch was clad like gangsters—wide-lapel, double-breasted suits with ankle-length overcoats and snap-brim hats pulled down over their faces.

⊙

Kim Fowley, who with Bruce Johnston had gone on from the Sleepwalkers to Kip Tyler and the Flips, happened to be in the audience that night. He recalled it as a kind of rock-and-roll predestiny, with Spector a visionary far ahead of his time:

"What a brilliant idea. He had the 'Untouchables' concept. What Brian DePalma did in a movie in 1987, Phil Spector did in 1959. These guys came out and did this amazing . . . it was like Duane Eddy with *Miami Vice*, or *Scarface*. It was brilliant, a little too heavy for the little girls . . . but the visuals, the sound, it was black shit, Duane Eddy shit, all the elements. It's too bad he never took that anyplace."

"The gig wasn't a howling success," Elliott Ingber agreed. "It was okay, but Phil couldn't go to point B with it."

As it was evident to Spector, he ended the Phil Harvey band and flitted on. "He was here and gone," Ingber said. "I only knew him a month to six weeks: a three-week rehearsal shot in getting a band together, and then two weeks after that. He was spaced out on the Phil trip, and then he was gone."

Though he would cost Lou Chudd many thousands of dollars with little return, Spector's value was high around the time of the initial Imperial release. Not long after, knowing the Teddy Bears were about to break up, Phil tried to make a deal for himself as a solo act.

He needed to go no further than his first stop—the Hollywood office of Lester Sill.

Perhaps the most ubiquitous and well-connected figure in the West Coast rock scene, Lester Sill had his hands in many pots; beginning in the late forties as a promotion man for L.A.'s Modern Records, he later managed the enormously successful Coasters, he co-owned his own labels, and with Lee Hazelwood he was now managing and producing Duane Eddy. Sill had an eye for talent on both sides of the control booth glass. In the early fifties, he discovered a pair of Fairfax High kids, Jerry Leiber and Mike Stoller, and guided them as a writing/producing team. In the late fifties, the duo's profusion of Latin-flavored R&B hits with the Coasters and then the Drifters, and the songs they composed for Elvis Presley movies, had made them an industry sensation and power. They were in New York now, highly sought independent producers whose names appeared on the labels of their records.

Still a publishing partner with Leiber and Stoller, and with immense goodwill on both coasts, Lester Sill had extraordinary latitude. He and Lee Hazelwood produced Duane Eddy's country-influenced guitar records for Jamie Records in Philadelphia—a label owned by Dick Clark and the top two men at Universal Distributing, Harold Lipsius and Harry Finfer—and they co-ran a small record company called Trey, which although it had no appreciable talent, was being distributed nationally by Atlantic Records, the New York R&B label for which Leiber and Stoller did most of their work.

Providentially, Phil Spector met Sill during the March sessions at Master Sound for *The Teddy Bears Sing!* Cutting a master of a Duane Eddy record in another room, Sill overheard what Spector was doing in Bunny Robyne's studio. "I heard these great harmonic sounds, and that's when I saw him," Sill said. "I didn't know who he was. He was with the two other kids, and Bunny briefly introduced us." Spector knew of Sill's industry pull, and when he needed to make a move before the Teddy Bears' corpse was cold, he followed up on the brief encounter. He called on Sill at his N. Argyle Street office, saying "Mr. Sill, can I speak to you?" Sill quickly gave Spector a commitment, and in a matter of days, on April 24, he purchased one of Spector's songs for Gregmark Music, the Sill/Hazelwood publishing company. It was "Be My Girl," the song written by Phil and Shirley Spector, though Shirley used the pseudonym Cory Sands.

The contract that Phil would sign with Lester Sill was colossal, surely unheard-of for an eighteen-year-old kid; a three-year pact with spiraling royalties totaling 6 cents per record; 1½ cents of that was for producing alone, a separation of power hardly ever acknowledged with a performing artist.

"Actually, I wasn't happy about the artist part—Phil is not a good singer—but he wanted it so we included it," Sill said. "But I saw him right away as a producer, and I think that's what he really wanted to do."

Spector immediately began going with Sill to Phoenix to observe Duane Eddy sessions. The studio there, Ramco Audio Recorders, was Lee Hazelwood's bailiwick, and by watching Hazelwood work there, one could ingest the process of making high art with crude implements. Towering and bony, Hazelwood had been a deejay in Phoenix when he found and began to produce Duane Eddy in the city's lone studio. Ramco was a hovel, accommodating no more than one track of recording tape, but Hazelwood worked wonders with echo and tape delay and reverb—using an echo chamber that was once a water pipe. As a result, Eddy's guitar was so smooth that it seemed to vibrate in apple butter.

Eager to learn these techniques, Phil breathed hard on Hazelwood's neck. A temperamental man, Hazelwood answered Phil's questions and put up with his suggestions, but privately he told Sill not to let Spector in any more. "Lee was the angry young man, and the two of them clashed," Sill said. But this potentially explosive situation was warded off because Lester gave Spector the go-ahead to make his own records.

Phil wanted to resurrect the sound he had invented. His head-clearing jazz respite over, and with the Teddy Bears idiom still viable and marketable, he was now ready to fly with it again.

"I always felt Phil thought he was folding the group only as a way of getting rid of the Shirley thing," Marshall Lieb said. "The breakup of the group was not because we thought we'd failed. To Phil and me, it was like we made an arrangement to come back and do it in another way. I'm pretty sure I was supposed to be part of the new thing, but I was either away or in the studio with somebody else."

Ironically, in fact, Marshall had started working with Elliott Ingber, cutting demos at Gold Star. Annette was still recovering from her accident—and a nonperson in Phil's mind, anyway. And Phil himself had made a break with the Teddy Bears' breeding ground. Drawn to Lester Sill's large family and his spacious home in Sherman Oaks, Phil had taken up quarters there, sharing a room with Lester's ten-year-old son, Joel.

Distanced by geography as well as inclination, his seamless hours in the studio the epicenter of his life, Spector's design for a Teddy Bear–style revival came to be centered almost completely around the studio mixing board. When he went into Master Sound in the fall of 1959 to cut songs—under the name of the Spector's Three—the songs were an entirely synthetic product; a female session singer named Ricki Page, wife of a songwriter crony of Lester Sill's named George Motola, provided the female line, a high, nonverbal soprano that Spector filtered across the songs' musical image, embellishing his already-overdubbed vocals. Cloying and drippy, but convincing enough as smoky white doo-wop, Spector reidentified his signature product with these songs the way he could not with the Teddy Bears.

With several Spector's Three tunes in the can, Phil now turned to selling the group as a human entity. For that, he brought Russ Titelman further into his circle. In the year that he had known him, Phil had provided Russ with a musical education. Spector sent him to Burdell Mathis, the same man who'd taught him the guitar, and had also taken Russ into the studio to do backing vocals on demos. Russ, who was a young boy when his father died, saw Phil through eyes tinted by idealization.

"He was the male figure in my life," Titelman said. "I remember Phil as always very unusual: a quirky, odd character. But what always superseded everything else about him, and what affected me, was that he was completely into his music. That was his whole life.

"It was amazing to me. I'd hung out with him and he'd always have the most incredible records. He'd play *The Genius of Ray Charles* or *Ray Charles at Newport*. He played Larry Williams, stuff you'd never hear. He'd have Hunter Hancock on the radio, Lowell Fulson, Jim Randolph . . . all this stuff most white kids didn't hear. He turned me on to all that."

Titelman sang at the Spector's Three sessions. But his real use was on the outside. Russ was a dark and handsome teenager like Marshall, and Phil wanted him to front the touring group—which Spector wanted no part in. For one thing, Phil was now ready to accept that his pinched, adenoidal voice was inferior beyond the studio walls. For another, without Marshall as a buffer between him and people he did not know, his old insecurities resurfaced. His growth halted at around five foot six, his beloved hair thinned into snarly strands swept over gaps of bare scalp, Phil frankly came to see himself as a geek. "There was a time when he just didn't want to be seen any more," said Lieb, who may have known him better than anyone. "I can remember him not being in love with Phil at that time. He wasn't happy with the way he looked.

"Phil always liked to appear on stage with us, because everywhere he went he had his best friend and a girl that everybody liked. And if he got in trouble with his mouth, which he often did on the road, I'd be there to say to his adversary, with an amp in my hand, 'This is a very heavy piece of equipment and it could really hurt you if I crushed you with it.' On his own, I don't think he looked forward to that kind of thing happening."

⊙

The ersatz Spector's Three were Russ, his girlfriend Annette Merar—a very pretty blonde, who was a grade ahead of him at Fairfax High—and another classmate, Warren Entner. Late in 1959, they went on a television show hosted by L.A. deejay Wink Martindale and lip-synched the first Spector's Three release on Trey Records, "I Really Do."

This was a song born in cynicism, and it paid the price. Spector had been beaten in the evolution of the Teddy Bears' sound by another West Coast coed vocal group, the Fleetwoods, who had a No. 1 hit the previous spring with a trembling song called "Come Softly to Me." In a roundabout irony, and an open theft in a bid for recognition, the lyric of "I Really Do" played with the same kind of "dum-dum, dooby-doo, dum-dum" riff of the Fleetwoods' song—which itself was derived from "To Know Him Is to Love Him." Spector's rip-off failed, as did two other more original Spector's Three records.

Even so, Lester Sill could separate Spector from his chart performance. He gave Phil an arranger's credit on the label of the Trey records, the way Jerry Leiber and Mike Stoller acknowledged their orchestra leaders, though Sill would not go as far as a production credit. Leiber and Stoller had earned the right to that high ground, and eighteen-year-old Phil Spector had no business standing on it. Sill believed in Spector, loved his drive and grasp of recording, tolerated his unorthodox ways. Although Spector continued to consume time and money in the studio, Sill did not get on him about it. "I'm tolerant when it comes to great talent," said Sill, who did not even pretend that he could keep up with the young man in the studio. "Phil had complete control on his dates. He told us he had something and I said, 'Let me hear it,' and that's when I knew about Spector's Three."

Sill's house was now Spector's creative brewery. Lost in his art, shut out from the world, he walked around in a fog of words and music. Once, after a session, he went into the kitchen to make a sandwich and, thinking he was putting the salami back, left his wallet in the refrigerator instead. He looked all over the house before he found it. Sharing a bedroom with ten-year-old Joel, Phil soon had him copying music charts for him. The night still his refuge, Phil confined his work to the late hours. By day he hung around with Sill's other son, Mark, and his stepson, Chuck Kaye, delighting in a brotherly kind of bonding his own home could not have even let him imagine. Lester Sill could reasonably think he was playing surrogate father; Phil rarely saw his mother and sister, and Lester could understand why Spector jerked away when his wife, Harriet, would reach out to touch him on the arm or shoulder. "She thought he didn't know *how* to be close to anybody," Sill said.

A year after Donna Kass left his life, Phil's contact with the opposite sex was minimal, at a wistful distance. Sometimes after late sessions—Spector preferred the late evening hours for his work—he and Russ Titelman would drive for hours around the valley, and inevitably Phil would park in front of a house on Ventura Boulevard where a girl named Lynn Castle lived. Just like in a bad movie, he would wait until the lights went out in the house, then honk the horn for Lynn to come to the window. She would then climb out and get into the car. "We'd just drive around and they'd be kissing. Sometimes they'd drop me off and Phil would pick me up later," Titelman recalled of the routine, which never seemed to get any more serious.

Spector had other, more meaningful obsessions in his life. Semiemployed as a court reporter, he was called to do stenotype when depositions were taken and legal papers filed in the Los Angeles courthouse during the interminable appeals case of Caryl Chessman, the convicted murderer who was sentenced in 1949 to die in the gas chamber. As Chessman's decade-long Death Row bid to stay alive became more heated, and a public *cause célèbre*, the compulsive Spector, devouring reams of details about the case, took to defending Chessman fanatically. In Sill's office, he'd try to talk everybody over to his side. "He was very liberal, which was unusual for a teenager in those days," Sill said. "A lot of the kids around the place thought he was communist."

Most pressing, however, was for Phil to park himself in the studio. Early in 1960, Sill signed a black singer, Kell Osborne, who sang in the high-pitched, sorrowful style of ex-Drifter Clyde McPhatter, whose voice Sill loved. Shunted to Phil to produce, Spector and Sill rehearsed Osborne for two months, then flew him to Phoenix to record him at Ramco. But when Osborne got off the plane, he was so nervous about making a record that he lost his voice. For five maddening days, Spector tried to coax him to sing. Finally two sides were cut, a remake of "The Bells of St. Mary's" and a Spector tune, "That's Alright Baby." Back in L.A., Phil overdubbed with regular Sill sidemen, saxophonist Plas Johnson and bassist Ray Pohlman. The songs, released on Trey, were starkly, bizarrely opposite: the A side was mawkish, the other tough-teen rattling, on which Osborne sounded more like Eddie Cochran than McPhatter, fitted with booming drums and gnawing guitars.

The songs' lack of airplay irritated Spector and prompted him to shift his sights. He was tired of the limited scope of the L.A. rock scene, which was still lowercase compared with New York and Memphis; where music gushed from a thousand geysers in those places, it seeped here. Indeed, Spector's own group had been L.A.'s most viable product, and now *that* was gone. There was no shape or form to the local scene, no reliability to its structure, no broad power.

Lester Sill was Phil's link to the bustle and glamour of the real power. Sill had taken him to New York a few times when he went there on business. Jerry Leiber and Mike Stoller would call Sill from their studio, and then meet with him when he got to New York. Then Sill would go over to Don Kirshner's office at Aldon Music, the biggest publisher of rock-and-roll music, to find songs for his acts. Along for the ride, Spector *felt* like an industry scion.

"He saw all the activity going on," Sill said, "because at the time the rock-and-roll business was really New York . . . the Brill Building, 1650 Broadway, Leiber and Stoller. Phil knew it, he saw it. He was so bright about how the business worked. And Spector by then had a certain amount of notoriety."

Eager to use that as a lever, Spector bugged Sill all the time to find something for him to do back east. "He wanted to go to New York. He knew of my relationship with Mike and Jerry and he asked if something could be arranged with them."

Knowing Phil was unhappy on the L.A. treadmill, Sill phoned Mike Stoller in the spring and obtained a position for Phil on the Leiber and Stoller payroll—Spector's contract with Sill/Hazelwood would still apply to his work in L.A.—as a songwriter and as an apprentice producer. As Sill explained it to Mike Stoller, Spector would not be one to blend into the wallpaper.

"He's strange, this kid," Sill warned. "But you won't believe how talented he is."

Mike Stoller sent airfare for Phil Spector.

Kim Fowley hadn't heard much about Spector since he saw the Phil Harvey band perform at the Rainbow Roller Rink. Fowley had now secured a job at Arwin Records, a small label owned by actress Doris

Day and her husband Marty Melcher, which had just had its first hit, Jan and Arnie's "Jennie Lee." Fowley—"I was an office boy, quasi-publishing assistant, and song-plugger"—was looking to sign acts, having brought to Arwin Bruce Johnston and other remnants of the old Sleepwalkers—minus Sammy Nelson, now known as Sandy, who had notched a hit of his own in 1959 with a drum instrumental called "Teen Beat" and was signed to Imperial—and Johnston had begun recording with Doris Day's son, Terry Melcher, as Bruce and Terry. Pondering people who could make Arwin big time, Fowley called soul singer Johnny "Guitar" Watson and then Phil Spector.

"Hey, man, I'm at Arwin now," he told Spector. "If you want some studio time, we'll back you. Or you can just come hang out here."

With typical overstatement, Spector said, "No . . . I just did a deal with Leiber and Stoller. I'm going to New York any minute now to deal with 'em."

In mid-May, just before he left, Phil dropped by Russ Titelman's place to say good-bye. He gave Russ a guitar, a snazzy Defender Telecaster model, in apparent gratitude.

"Hold this for me," he said to Russ, as if giving himself a reason to return.

Eight hours later, Phil Spector was on Broadway.

4

*Mike and Jerry had no idea that he was going to be such a manip-
ulator.*

—BEVERLY ROSS

When he landed in New York, Phil had no plan or itinerary beyond
getting to 40 W. 57th Street. This was the location of Jerry Leiber
and Mike Stoller's office, and for Phil, having made no arrangement
for lodging, it was the width and breadth of his world. After arriving
at the narrow office building between Fifth and Sixth avenues, he
ascended to the penthouse suite and appeared before his two new
mentors—who, to his dismay, did not remember him from the so-
journs he had made with Lester Sill. Indeed, Spector's edgy, inscrutable manner made Leiber and Stoller uneasy.

Mike Stoller said years later: "He seemed very bright, a very
sharp young man, witty and sarcastic. I sensed a rather angry young
man. He dressed like a businessman, he wore a suit and tie, and he
looked like a man on the make."

Implying that he couldn't afford to go elsewhere, Phil was allowed to crash that night on the couch at the rear of the office, and he would do the same in following days. The truth was, Spector had money in his pocket, but part of his New York music assimilation was to assume the guise of bohemian deprivation.

"He didn't *want* a place to live," Lester Sill explained. "He was happy where he was. I imagine he thought he was in Paris."

"Phil wasn't broke when he went to New York," Marshall Lieb agreed. "Phil was good at camping out, he did that a lot. He did that because he truly liked that bag-lady lifestyle. That to him was how good music was made. He didn't want to be too set, too comfortable. He wanted to be where if a song came to him at three in the morning, he could get up when everyone else was wasted and get started with it. And where better to do that than in the atmosphere of Leiber and Stoller's office?"

And yet Leiber and Stoller were too busy to think about figuring him out, or even to notice him much. Left to fend for himself, Spector looked around at a rock-and-roll bureaucracy he had studied from afar, and he was avid to dip his feet into the pond. Hanging around at the restaurants and other haunts where the music crowd congregated, he ran into many of the working and aspiring songwriters who covered the canyons of Broadway like locusts; but these were mainly scratching, clawing low-level types, in Spector's mind inferior to him.

The first person of substance he found was a young woman named Beverly Ross, a staff writer at Hill and Range Music, the highly important rock-and-roll publishing arm of Chappell Music, the largest music publisher in the world. Spector was lunching at a Howard Johnson's on Forty-ninth Street, across Broadway from the Brill Building, when another writer and Brill Building habitué made the introduction. Phil was in New York less than a week and was still carrying around the big, bulky valise he had arrived with. As Ross saw him, he looked every bit the waif.

"He told me he was sleeping on Leiber and Stoller's couch, and I could believe he was stone broke and didn't know where his next meal was coming from," she remembered.

Tall, swarthy, and Italian-looking though she was Jewish, Beverly Ross was one of only a sprinkling of female writers to make it in a vehemently male structure. Only a year older than Spector, her track record was also impressive; as a teenager she had written "Lollipop," a No. 1 hit for the Chordettes in 1956, as well as songs recorded by Bill Haley and the Comets and Elvis Presley, and she had also recorded briefly for Columbia Records. Writing songs at the E. B. Marks publishing house with a lanky, rail-thin partner named Jeff Barry, she was then recruited by Jean Aberbach, the top man at Hill and Range. In 1960, Beverly Ross and Carole King at Aldon Music were the two top women writers in rock, and Ross was making a top-shelf $250 a week plus advances on royalties.

Spector was at once drawn to Ross as a career propellant. Hill and Range was *the* power in New York. Beginning as a pop music division beside Chappell's catalogue of Gershwin, Cole Porter, and Jerome Kern, Hill and Range first published primarily bluegrass songs, and its biggest early seller was "Frosty the Snowman." Then, when Jean Aberbach published the Elvis Presley catalogue, any writer hoping to get Elvis's attention had to deal with Hill and Range. Leiber and Stoller's access was a valuable chit: they produced records for the Hill and Range–owned label, Big Top, and when they began a publishing company called Trio Music, Hill and Range bankrolled it and took a one-half interest in it. As a prominent Hill and Range staffer, Beverly Ross had status and privileges that made Spector's pulse quicken.

"I was kind of a queen bee up there," Ross said, "and I had an open budget for demos."

Beverly saw a lot in Phil too, though when they spoke at the Howard Johnson's she recalled that "He had a shifty way of looking down at the floor, like he was afraid to make eye contact. . . . But he was very personable and very funny. He had an incredible sense of humor. He was funny and charming to the point where he could win anybody over." Later, when she took him up to the Hill and Range office and Spector took out his guitar, she was hooked. "He was the best guitar player I'd ever heard." Loosely planning to write together, Beverly foresaw a traditional, long-standing connection. "I took him up and introduced him to everybody," she said, "because they didn't know him from a hole in the wall. He had that one hit but now he was just a kid writing with Beverly. He used to borrow five dollars from me because he was broke, and I opened my heart to him. I wanted to trust somebody and have a new partner as dynamic as Jeff."

When they began collaborating, in one of the little piano cubicles at Hill and Range or at Beverly's W. 45th Street apartment, Phil was cast in the unlikely role of junior partner. "I don't think I ever found his strength as a writer," Ross said. "I was strong in melody and I needed a lyric writer and he wasn't it. One day he came up and we were real chummy and friends and we were all excited about our ideas, and he played me some terrible song he'd written called 'Little Red Riding Hood.' I said, 'Uh, gee . . .'

"I don't know, there was something strange about it. When you write, it's with great passion, you give everything you have, and you expect the other person to do as much. Yet it struck me as peculiar that Phil seemed to hold back, as though there was always something subliminal that he wasn't sharing with me, or that he was thinking of something else. I used to ask myself: is it that he's not a good writer, or was he insecure working with me, or what?"

Even so, Phil had an innate wisdom about music; it was uncanny how his instinct could get a song on the right track. "He could find interesting chord changes in raw material, or an interesting hook. Like he'd start playing a couple of chords on the guitar and I'd throw a melody at him and he'd say, 'Let's not go that way, let's go this way.' He was great at directing a song a certain way or shortening phrases to make it better. What he was was a great editor."

The union came up with a number of songs, mostly in the bubblegum-blowing idiom, with titles like "Planet Love," "Don't Believe Everything You Hear," and "Bandit of Love." Beverly thought they were good enough to book a demo date, and she and Phil went into Associated Sound Studio on Seventh Avenue and Forty-seventh Street, a drafty hall known for turning out cheap, quickie demos. Phil played guitar, Beverly the piano, and they both sang. And Phil employed his California overdubbing style, bouncing tracks around the studio while recording over them. In the booth, Nat Schnapf, who owned Associated, looked quizzically at Beverly. "Neither Nat or I had ever seen that done before," Ross said. "Nat thought Phil was out of his mind. But I liked to overdub also. I liked that fat echo, that lively sound. I knew what Phil was after. He was ingenious with the things he did."

A few days later, Beverly took Phil to a recording session held by a lesser Hill and Range writer/producer at Bell Sound, on Fifty-eighth Street. This was the studio where Leiber and Stoller had done many of their Drifters sessions, yet as brilliant a guitarist as Spector was, they had not given Phil a gig or done much of anything with him. "Phil would say he was with Leiber and Stoller, but it was a misnomer," Ross said. "Leiber and Stoller were hot as hell, they were very busy. They had Ben E. King, the Drifters, the Coasters, this one, that one. With Phil, I just think they were trying to be nice to Lester, patronizing Lester by letting this who-is-this kid hang around. It wasn't until they saw he was working with me that they accepted him and gave him a chance."

At the Bell session, Phil sat next to Beverly in the booth—but only until he felt he was needed. "This producer was a middle-aged guy and of course Phil and I were arrogant kids. This guy was fumbling around with the artist, who was all upset, and Phil just got up, right out of the booth, and went in and took over. Everyone was shocked, and the producer walked away with his tail between his legs.

"The producer just didn't know how to handle this artist, who was black, and Phil's favorite artist in the whole world was Ray Charles; he was mesmerized by Ray Charles, he loved him, he'd put on a Ray Charles tape and play his guitar to it. So he related to the artist in there and he put this other producer down who didn't know what he was doing. I remember that Phil changed the lick on the piano, changed the guitar, had a whole new drum sound, made the singer do another thing . . . and just ran the session.

"There was a lot of gossip about it, which Phil probably loved. He had the nerve and confidence to do something like that, and it was where he first showed me his incredible lack of conscience and lack of concern for others."

Eventually, Jerry Leiber and Mike Stoller got around to using Phil on dates, at $41.40-an-hour union scale. For Phil it was a frustrating chore. Weaned on jazz peaks and flourishes, Leiber and Stoller's lock-jawed precision in the studio inhibited him. This was a completely alien way of recording for Phil. Atlantic's engineer, Tom Dowd, had been working with an eight-track recording machine since 1957, the second such machine in existence next to the one in Les Paul's basement studio in Bucks County, Pennsylvania. The sound that came through it was bell clear and could define the mob of instruments that Leiber and Stoller put to work, including multiples of guitars and pianos, tympani, strings, triangles, and Latin percussion. They also cut fast, four sides to a session. This demanded that musicians be good and economical, and inured to Leiber and Stoller's strict precepts. Spector, surrounded by career musicians, was lost.

"In those day, Jerry and Mike would sit down with me and the group by a piano for two or three days and drill the melody and the vocals and the backgrounds," Tom Dowd said. "They had lines, counterlines, dialogue, dialect, then they'd come in and fly it live. So if they said, 'Hey, Phil, play on this date,' he wouldn't have been in their faces during the rehearsals. And because he wasn't tuned in to what they wanted, he was just playing to defend himself. When he was sitting in with somebody like Eric Gale or George Barnes beside him, when he was given a part he just made sure he wasn't screwing up any other part. He'd stop playing and you'd say, 'Why didn't you play there, Phil?' And he'd say, 'I couldn't do what I wanted because it doesn't fit, the other things around me don't complement it.' And then he'd come slide in the booth like 'I don't belong here,' and kinda slink down like Don Knotts."

Worse, some of the musicians were not kind to him. Spector had no reputation among this hard-boiled crowd, and as an outsider his unsolicited ideas—and even his musicianship—were sneered at. Gary Chester, who did a huge amount of drumwork in New York, remembered Spector playing right next to him on a number of sessions. "I asked him to move, to get away from me because his time was so bad," said Chester. "So he moved over by Charles Macey, a great guitar player, and Charlie threw him the hell away from him completely."

Still, Spector was in the lane now, heading somewhere. All around town, on his own fuel, he was leaving his trail. Shuffling constantly between the two buildings where American pop music took form, he became soldered to 1619 Broadway—home to Don Kirshner's Aldon Music and Aaron Schroeder Music—and to the Brill Building.

The Brill, squatting over Jack Dempsey's restaurant, had its own mythic lore, its eleven floors of piano cubicles and sheet music a museum of Tin Pan Alley and Big Band history. But when Phil Spector strode under its brass-grill archway and through the mirrored art-deco lobby, he had business in mind. Beverly Ross had provided the entrée to glad-hand the Vienna-born Hill and Range hierarchy:

☉

owners Jean Aberbach and his brother Julian, and their cousins Freddie and John Bienstock. All except John Bienstock had been longtime song-pluggers at Chappell Music, and while none of the cousins knew anything about rock and roll, Jean's wisest move was bringing Paul Case with him from the Chappell stable to be General Professional Manager at Hill and Range. Tall and urbane, his full head of silver hair at once marking his presence among the industry elite, the Iowa-born but very Jewish Case presided over the commerce of song publishing: extracting the best material from the writers and getting them played through his network of promo men in every corner of the land. Cajoling and stroking his writers, Case kept the conveyor belt going with competition that was cannibalistic. "People were taking things from each other, and you had a hard time knowing who you could trust," Beverly Ross said. "You'd trust somebody one day and it turned out they would undercut and undermine you the next day. It was a lot of politics and unfairness in the end. For example, I thought Paul Case was a misogynist. Women would be put in their place by Paul, if not in front of you then behind your back as soon as you walked out of the room."

But Paul Case loved Phil Spector and thought that he could be a fountainhead of hits for the company. When Phil went on about music and talked his big talk, Case leaned back behind his desk, puffed on his cigar, and nodded in agreement. The big-gun writers at Hill and Range came to know Spector as Case's pet and realized Case would look kindly on anyone who could form a working partnership with Phil. Early on, Case fixed Spector up with his biggest gun, Jerome "Doc" Pomus. Pomus, with his partner Mort Shuman, boasted a vault-sized stock of hits, having written for Elvis ("Little Sister," "His Latest Flame," "Viva Las Vegas"), Dion and the Belmonts ("Teenager in Love"), co-wrote "Young Blood" with Leiber and Stoller for the Coasters, and in 1960 wrote "This Magic Moment" and "Save the Last Dance for Me" for the Drifters. Forced to walk with braces and crutches because of a degenerative bone condition, Pomus nonetheless was a bearlike, peripatetic figure on the New York jazz club scene, and the embodiment of carefree cool. When he met Spector, Pomus wasn't sure whether the bug-eyed, elfin teenager was incredibly hip or simply disordered.

"Paul Case told me he wanted me to meet this young fellow who Lester Sill sent to New York," Pomus said, "and Phil paced the floor up and down. He kept looking at himself in a mirror and combing his hair with a brush. This went on and on and it was like a comedy act. Up and down, up and down. He was a very nervous kid, but he started getting friendly and after a while you got the feeling by what he said about music that there was a raw talent there."

Pomus lived during the week at the Hotel Forrest, just across Forty-ninth Street, and they continued their music discussions there. "Phil and I would talk all afternoon about songs. We'd sit around and go over old songs, 'cause he wanted to know about really old standards, the evergreens. And then we gradually started writing some songs in the lobby of the hotel because the lobby was great. Late at night everybody would be there. It was like one of those Damon Runyon–type hotels. We had a group that hung out. In fact, Damon Runyon, Jr., lived up in the penthouse. He was an editor on the *New York Herald Tribune* and his father lived with him there. And we had Joe Morgan, who was Duke Ellington's press agent, and Johnny Mel, a professional gambler, and Artie Ripp would come in. He was George Goldner's assistant at Gone and End Records. So this was our group, and Phil used to hang out in the lobby with us all night long."

Comfortable in the company of wolves, Phil was soon joining in on the pranks carried on by and among this motley fraternity. Huzzahs swept through the hotel the night Spector and Pomus set up Artie Ripp to believe that Elvis's manager, Colonel Parker, was calling him from Memphis. "Artie Ripp was an obnoxious little shit," Pomus said with a laugh, "and Phil and I worked hard to get him. We made him think the Colonel wanted to use Ral Donner—an Elvis soundalike that George Goldner had under contract—in the studio for $100,000 because Elvis had lost his voice. Now, George Goldner was a very hip, New York type of tough guy, and you can imagine the hell Artie Ripp caught after he woke Goldner up at three in the morning to tell him this bullshit story." Phil knew he was accepted in the brotherhood when Artie Ripp began sending him bogus telegrams from his draft board. Phil, who lived in cold fear that he'd have to go into the army, would quake all day each time.

By the time Phil was moved to leave Jerry Leiber and Mike Stoller's couch and find himself a place to live—a sparsely furnished, $100-a-month studio apartment on the first floor of an E. 82nd Street brownstone—he was a distinctly different-looking creature from the boy who'd come to town a month before. Spector arrived in a suit. Now, embraced by the New York industry heavies, he dressed his individuality in pants with mismatched legs, long, black, Zorro-like capes, and galoshes. The crowd at the Hotel Forrest could get hysterical about how he looked, but they did not begrudge him his eccentricity—they *all* were nutty there, that they agreed—nor did they believe Spector was going for attention any more than he was finding a way to frame, and live with, his peculiarities. Pomus could not get over how some of Spector's nuttiest habits were so commonplace to the young man. "One thing he did was, he carried around this briefcase with him all the time. And in the briefcase was a loaf of bread, a hairbrush, and a pencil and paper. That was it. He'd break off a piece of bread and sit there eating and he was the happiest guy in the world. We used to put him on, 'cause he was so funny. But he was very smart and very politically oriented too. You couldn't figure him out, whether he was putting *you* on."

On weekends, Pomus took Spector to his house on Long Island, where his wife, Willie, cooked ethnic Jewish food that Phil inhaled. Because Pomus could not get around easily, he rented a red convertible. Phil would get behind the wheel and the two of them would go off on day-long jaunts through the city. For a time, Phil seemed joined at the hip with Pomus, and when he was with others he did a dead-on imitation of Doc's raucous, saliva-rich manner of speech. After only a few weeks with Pomus, they had written a dozen songs— mostly the older man's work—in the Drifters' quirky, elegant style of rhythm and blues. When they were presented to Leiber and Stoller and Atlantic Records, Spector had yet more footing on the New York turf.

Up at Leiber and Stoller's office one day in the summer of 1960, Jerry Leiber wanted Phil—now on a $150 weekly salary—to meet a writer named Terry Phillips, who had just been added to Trio Music. When Spector came in, he was wearing a vest, he had his galoshes on, and he was toting an umbrella—even though it was a bright sunny day. Seeing him, Phillips laughed loudly.

"What are you laughing at?" Spector asked.

"Nothing personal, man," said Phillips, "but you look like Jiminy Cricket."

Spector, acting deeply offended, told him: "You know, man, that's not funny."

Jerry Leiber laughed, too, and immediately thought there was a kind of chemistry in the dialogue. "You two guys are gonna work together," he said.

Terry Phillips, born and raised in Brooklyn as Phil Teitelbaum, was nearly a negative image of Phil Spector. He had blond, teen-idol looks and in fact had once sung a song he'd recorded on "American Bandstand." A tough kid who talked with his fists, he eventually passed his entrance exam to law school and was about to begin when Leiber, meeting him at a cocktail party, hired him as a writer. Phillips retained some of his nail-hard qualities, and when he started working with Spector, he perceived that Phil "saw in my eyes and my personality somebody who could not be intimidated, who if you bothered or annoyed me, I wouldn't verbalize, I'd just break your jaw. Phil is very perceptive; he read this in me like in a second.

"But on the other hand, he also sensed that I was open. I expressed what I felt and I was a guy who liked people. Phil wasn't like that. He was very suspicious of people, very mature in the sense of business but wary of people. So, in me, he knew what I was, he didn't have to be wary."

Leiber and Stoller were going to record Ruth Brown for Atlantic, and Spector and Phillips were asked to write material for her. "We sat down with his guitar, and that's when I knew I was overmatched," Phillips said. But Terry came up with an idea for a song smoldering with sexual references called "Change Your Ways" and in developing it, he learned what Phil could and could not do. "I was a lyric writer and Phil was like Jerry [Leiber], he could sit down at the piano or guitar and in two minutes, you threw out a line to him and something was happening. It was really amazing. Nobody could sit down and instantly have a direction like that . . . or if the direction was bad, throw it out and, three seconds later, have another approach.

"Phil needed a collaborator, though. He was not a lyricist, and I think that was because his emotional nature did not allow him to express himself openly."

In writing that song, and a couple of others for Brown, Phillips said he and Phil "crossed a valuable bridge. I saw . . . there was a side to Phil that was absolutely terrific, and very nice if he saw you weren't looking to use him or cut his balls off. He sensed in me a guy not trying to ride on his coattails, or engulf him. Because the jungle drums had started to beat for him by then. It was before he did anything, but his ability was well known. Hill and Range had flipped out for him. Aaron Schroeder wanted him. Ahmet Ertegun [at Atlantic] pursued him. The goings-on between Phil and all these people were mysterious to me. There was so much inner stuff I never knew about.

"Paul Case used to take Phil and me to dinner fourteen times a week, and I realized Paul would have me along only because Phil wanted it. I could live with that, because I understood I wasn't as talented as Phil. Plus, it didn't mean as much to me. It meant everything to Phil."

Beverly Ross firmly believed that she and Phil were still a team, because he made sure to keep that lifeline open by continuing to get together with her around the piano. But on Beverly's end, the relationship was much more intense. In her mind, "I was really his only friend, and we got very attached to each other." Beverly even thought their writing was uniting them in romance.

"I thought that, but I don't think Phil did . . . maybe not romance as much as . . . you just become attracted in a strong way when you're so connected because of the art and the passion that you need to write. At that time, when you're that young, you feel you're influencing the world, and you attribute a lot of emotional things to the people around you. He was just so special, so creative . . . I cared for him a lot."

There were times when the emotional commitment was mutual, and at those times, Phil revealed himself to her as he did to few others. The agony of Ben Spector's death, the conflicting feelings about Bertha and Shirley, all fanned out before her.

"He said his father killed himself, and I knew it was a terrible blow to this little boy, this intelligent, high-IQ, sensitive child. Kids feel they've been betrayed when their parents kill themselves; they feel guilty all their lives.

"Phil was very insecure. He was always trying to prove that he could win this or do that . . . maybe to his mother or maybe to his dad. It seemed like he still had a relationship with his dad. He sort of had a residual feeling of tremendous fondness and loss."

Phil also told her that Shirley had gone over the edge since he left L.A., possibly because he thought Beverly could understand the pain that brought him.

"I had a retarded brother and I was always so filled with feelings of guilt: what could I do for him? And I told Phil about it, and I remember he said, 'Yeah, my sister is crazy. She's been in institutions.' It was yet another albatross upon his head—that he could not help her. We just kind of commiserated as close friends would."

Phil kept that side of him to a minimum, though, and Beverly faced his wrath when he wanted to shut off the personal anguish—abruptly, he would snap out of introspection with a gush of sarcasm, or a flip remark about her brother that would hurt her. Deadening his inner pain often numbed his entire being. "It seemed to me that his nature was not to have any conscience," said Ross. "He didn't want to feel anything for anybody."

Working at Beverly's place on a midsummer night, they were fiddling around with a riff. It grew out of an old song of Beverly's called "The Widow's Walk," in which three quick notes kept repeating in a *da-da-da, da-da-da* pattern. After they began working on variations of it, Phil suddenly leaped to his feet.

"I have to go over to Jerry's; we have to talk over some business," he said as he rushed out the door.

Unbeknownst to Beverly, Jerry Leiber had given Phil the lyrics of a song he had written and earmarked for the Drifters, "Spanish Harlem." With Mike Stoller out of town, he asked Spector to see if he could come up with a melody. Now the riff had given Phil a brainstorm, the three-syllable repetition, and when he got to Leiber's West Side townhouse, he sat at the piano and played what he had. Mike Stoller had returned and happened to be in Leiber's kitchen making himself a hamburger. Hearing the "da-da-da, da-da-da" hook, he came in and worked it into the centerpiece of the song, to be played on vibraphone from first bar to last. But Stoller begged off a writing credit—Spector had worked up a full melody, and Stoller gave him his due.

Artie Ripp heard the song before most of the world did. Ripp was taking two young women up to his room at the Hotel Forrest one night when he saw Spector.

"Phil, come on up," he told him.

Upstairs, Artie announced, "Okay, girls, now we're gonna get crazy," and instructed everyone to get naked.

Slowly, unsteadily, Phil complied. But after peeling off his shirt and pants, he stopped.

"He yelled, 'Wait a minute!' and he picks up the guitar and he sits on top of the television, which was the only place to sit because the girls were on the bed and the chair," Ripp recalled. "So he sat on top of this Admiral console TV in his underwear and starts singing about Spanish Harlem.

"Now here I am, lusting to jump on these crazy nymphomaniacs, and I look at him and I say, 'Listen, Phil, we can sing later.' But when I turn around a minute later, Phil is gone, with his guitar and his clothes, and I'm left with the two girls. I got the job done on both of 'em, but Phil got the hit. I don't know at what point the song was at, but he may have gotten some idea for it in that room."

In early October, Paul Case finally put Phil Spector to work for Hill and Range. Ray Peterson, the country singer who had a big hit with Jeff Barry's "Tell Laura I Love Her" in 1960, had broken with RCA Records after five years and begun a label with his manager, Stan Shulman. The label was called Dunes, after the Las Vegas hotel where Peterson did a four-month run every year, and Shulman made a deal with Hill and Range to be distributed as a subsidiary of Big Top Records. Shulman then took an office in the Brill Building, four stories below the Hill and Range penthouse offices. As it turned out, Peterson, crippled as a result of polio, had met Spector in Los Angeles in 1959, and the two had hit it off.

When Leiber and Stoller—Shulman's first choice to produce Peterson on Dunes—were booked solid, Spector moved in.

"He'd gotten real friendly with all the guys at Hill and Range," Beverly Ross said. "Mind you, he had the run of the place because I had brought him in there, and he was really feeling his oats. He was spending a lot of time in Stan Shulman's office with Paul and the other guys, and there'd be a lot of loud talk and laughing all the time. These were very macho guys, and Phil charmed 'em all, and he convinced them to let him produce."

"He was bitching and bugging us about it," John Bienstock recalled. "He said we didn't need Mike and Jerry, that he could do it himself. He was a confident little kid."

Contracted by Shulman to do a session for $150, a royalty cut, and a label production credit, Spector had no idea that he was stepping into a tempest of discord between Peterson and Shulman. The manager, a constantly sweating, cigar-chomping ex-Marine, could become carried away with his domination of Peterson. "Stan used to do things like knock me down stairs and throw me on my head and beat me up," Peterson said. "I had braces on my legs and I weighed ninety-eight pounds, and he would insult me, tell me I looked like a queer on stage, the way I held the microphone. Once he put me in the hospital with internal bleeding, but I told people I slipped in the bathroom. Stan was sick, obsessed with the power he had over me—in fact, he told me about the Svengali story. Stan would lock me in my room. I'd have to practice for five, six hours a day in front of a mirror so I'd learn how to walk, so people wouldn't feel sorry for me."

Peterson became a boffo performer because of it, but his relationship with Shulman was on a slow, curdling boil. Spector did not like Shulman and, as with many music people, had not a whit of respect for his expertise. Recently Shulman had turned down "Hello Mary Lou," a song written for Peterson by Gene Pitney, a hugely talented writer/singer managed by Aaron Schroeder. Ricky Nelson then took the song to No. 1. "Stan always had two lead ears," Peterson said.

Still, Spector grabbed the chance to get in the studio with a major artist. He and Peterson decided to cover the old Joe Turner blues song, "Corinna, Corinna"—Phil had been turned on to Turner by Doc Pomus, and Peterson had been doing the song in his act. Phil then went back to Beverly Ross. "He said, 'Let's write a song for the B side,' " she recalled. They came up with a tune called "That's the Kind of Love," but Beverly had a foreboding feeling. "I already smelled that he was being dishonest with me, because he barred me from the session."

When Spector and Peterson went into Bell Sound, it was with four songs—"That's the Kind of Love" not among them. "I had thousands of songs I could've done," said Peterson, "but I didn't have to go through thousands with Phil. He was a tremendous judge of music."

Phil insisted on only one song, and it became the B side of "Corinna, Corinna." It was "Be My Girl"—thus guaranteeing that Phil and Shirley Spector would enjoy a royalty windfall.

The Spector/Peterson version of "Corinna, Corinna" was considerably softer than the grit of the Joe Turner record. Arranged by

⊙

Robert Mersey, who had worked on numerous sessions for Leiber and Stoller, Spector used violins for the first time—and, later, he confided to Beverly Ross that he had been "scared shitless" by the challenge of going from small rhythm sections to a full orchestra— and he sought a sweetness of sound that bordered on icky. "Phil had a new thought for the song," Peterson recalled. "It had always been done gutteral and funky. I did it as though I was singing to a little girl, not a lover." Spector and Bell engineer Eddie Smith balanced out and mixed the vocals and the instrumentation so that the background was broad and dreamy, but Peterson's vocal intimately close to the ear. And, amazingly, Spector cut it in record time for him. Vocals sung right over the orchestra, everything was done live, and in just two takes, inside of half an hour.

Not long after, Beverly Ross found out about the omission of "That's the Kind of Love" from the session. "I was heartbroken over it," she said. "I had a screaming, hysterical fight with him about it. But when you confronted Phil like that, he would just cringe and walk away, before he could feel anything."

But before long, he was back. "He still wanted to be my friend. He said, 'I could never match you, Bev. I've looked for people like you all over this business and I could never match you.' He didn't want to burn down any bridges, but I later felt this was the beginning of his terrible two-facedness. I was just too naïve and trusting, and I believed him."

On October 27, just weeks after the Peterson session, Jerry Leiber and Mike Stoller went into Atlantic's new studio on Sixtieth Street, built by Tom Dowd, to record songs with Ben E. King, who had quit as the Drifters' lead singer for a solo career. King recorded four Drifterish tunes, his own "Stand by Me," the Spector/Pomus "Young Boy Blues" and "First Taste of Love," and the Spector/Leiber "Spanish Harlem." Originally intended as a B side, "Spanish Harlem"—an extraordinary piece of beauty that used the Latin *baion* beat of "Save the Last Dance for Me" and the piercing, frontal strings that created crossover soul on "There Goes My Baby"—was the first side to be released from the session.

Before Christmas and his twentieth birthday, Spector took to the studio twice more. Leiber and Stoller turned over to him Houston-born reggae singer Johnny Nash, who recorded on the ABC-

Paramount label. At Bell Sound, and again with Robert Mersey as arranger, Spector cut two string-laden Drifters-style songs he'd written with Terry Phillips, "Some of Your Loving" and "A World of Tears," and a cover of "A Thousand Miles Away."

The second job was for Stan Shulman and Dunes, to record Curtis Lee, a vegetable picker Ray Peterson had discovered singing in a Yuma, Arizona, nightclub. Lee came to New York with four middling songs he had written with L.A. songwriter Tommy Boyce. Spector's ears heard them as white doo-wop, but not with Lee's squeaky voice as the focal point. Instead he brought in a black quartet, the Halos, who recorded for Seven Arts Records and worked background sessions all over town. For $250 per Halo, Stan Shulman received four strong sides; the best was "Pretty Little Angel Eyes," which bridged the tail end of doo-wop and the new era of dance records.

Spector wanted to use a different studio for the session. He had come upon Mira Sound Studios, which sat in the rear of a forlorn building on W. 47th St. called the Hotel American. Pimps ran in and out of the building and rats had to be rousted from the studio, but the walls were thicker there, and the fat echoes seemed to squish off the plaster like ripe tomatoes. Phil hadn't had as thick a live echo—or "blur," as he called it—since Gold Star, and the engineer at Mira Sound, Bill MacMeekin, was a visionary in his own right; among other measures, he was the first engineer to put a separate microphone on a bass drum rather than over the entire drum kit, isolating a pounding backbeat not heard before on vinyl. Hunting for a chamber he could send the music through, Spector put a microphone on an outside stairwell. Pleased with the result, he vacated Bell.

Spector, arranging himself and again cutting in haste, recognized that Lee could not carry a tune and turned loose the Halos to pump life into "Angel Eyes." "We came in and he gave us lyric sheets and told us to do what we felt," recalled Arthur Cryer, the Halos' bass man and leader. The Halos' churning and shifting riffs— "We stole all those bomps and ha-ha-has from the Spaniels and Cleftones," Cryer said—made the song infectious.

Early in 1961, Phil Spector had no less than four works on the charts: "Corinna, Corinna," which was about to peak at No. 9 in *Billboard* and No. 7 in *Cash Box*, "Some of Your Loving," "Pretty

Little Angel Eyes," and "Spanish Harlem." The last, backed with another Spector-Pomus song, "First Taste of Love," had been released on the last day of 1960 and was now scrambling up the ladder.

Beverly Ross had heard "Spanish Harlem" back in November when Phil played an acetate of the song in Freddie Bienstock's office. She heard the familiar riff that she had worked on with Phil the night he ran out, and her heart sank. She knew she'd been had. Now the grapevine was abuzz with talk about Spector's hard upward thrust and she knew that he was not concerned about taking her on his ride.

"He'd done that song and then he suddenly was writing with some guy named Terry Phillips, and I didn't know from where this Terry Phillips sprang," she said. "It wasn't like Phil said anything about breaking off, he just started avoiding me. He started gaining power—and he wanted people to be influenced by *him*." And yet, against all hope, she didn't want to believe Phil would never write with her again.

Phil, meanwhile, was informing people that he had produced "Spanish Harlem," which in its glory and power dwarfed the songs he had produced. He took no official credit, he implied, out of deference to Leiber and Stoller's preeminence. Hearing this kind of scuttlebutt, Tom Dowd would bellow, "Horsefeathers!" since, in fact, while Phil had attended the session at which it was cut, he had neither played on it nor had any real input.

"I seem to recall him leaning against a wall or something," Ben E. King said.

Doc Pomus heard the poop too and would chuckle about it. "Phil always told a lot of stories, but here's the reality: what actually happened, what Phil wished could have happened, and what he *says* happened."

As the calendar ran out on 1961, to Phil Spector, spread all over the canyons of New York music but in his mind owned by nobody, only one reality mattered: he was omnipotent.

5

He had to find himself, but I'll tell you one thing. He was complete when he walked in. He was like Minerva coming out of Jupiter's head. He had it all in him. I don't think he had to learn too much. All he had to do was implement.

—JERRY WEXLER

Phil went home to Los Angeles for Christmas but it was not merely a sentimental journey. Lester Sill had called and asked him to do a job, and Phil owed it to Lester to do whatever he would have wanted. In fact, Phil was not convinced anything would come out of the job—which was to produce a trio of blond teenage sisters who did a McGuire Sisters–style act. Priscilla, Albeth, and Sherrell Paris—the Paris Sisters, professionally and otherwise—had recorded for Imperial briefly, but they were in a three-year drought when Sill bought them from Jesse Rand, who also managed the Lettermen. Sill solicited producers for the group, but he got no takers; by no stretch of the imagination were the McGuire Sisters a sixties boom.

⊙

The Paris Sisters were an odd fork in the road for Sill, given that he and Lee Hazelwood were in dire need of a hit act in 1961. Not long before, on a plane ride from Phoenix to L.A., Hazelwood and Duane Eddy had a spat, and Eddy demanded a break with Sill/ Hazelwood Productions. Trying to play hardball, the two men insisted that Harold Lipsius and Harry Finfer, the Jamie Records strongmen in Philadelphia, return master tapes of Eddy sessions that Sill and Hazelwood had paid for. But when Lipsius and Finfer refused, Universal's dominion was such that Sill and Hazelwood were forced to back down.

Now, with the Trey label dying and with no sure-fire talent, Sill was in crisis. Spector made plane reservations.

Longtime Gold Star clients, the Paris Sisters had cut a number of unsuccessful demos, engineered by Stan Ross, and Phil remembered that he'd heard the group in the studio and that—despite the Sisters being a group-harmony act—he thought that Priscilla Paris had a purring voice similar to Annette Kleinbard's. That made him think he could refashion yet another version of the Teddy Bears. He called Stan Ross to set the date.

"He wanted to make sure I could do the session, but he also was afraid to fly and he had a wonderful concept for getting over it," Ross recalled. "His theory was that if he spoke to the place he was going to end up—a music place, because that was his destiny—that he would get there okay."

It still didn't prevent Phil from squeezing the armrests of his seat every mile of the way, and a knowing Bertha Spector was at the airport to meet him with sandwiches. Checking into the Players Motel, a picaresquely dingy Hollywood music lodge, Phil went next to see Russ Titelman. He took back his Telecaster Defender guitar but gave Russ a gig as a guitarist at the Paris Sisters session. Having dealt, sometimes uneasily, with prickly New York musicians, Phil wanted a more conducive, familiar air in the studio. Michael Spencer, who had gone from UCLA to Harvard Law School but had dropped out after three months, was back in L.A., and Phil brought him onto the session as well, along with Johnny Clauder, the drummer for Don Randi who had jammed at Michael's house on those grandiose Friday nights. Moving Priscilla Paris out in front as lead vocalist—a move her two sisters resented—Spector cut two of his songs, the A side a cover of the tune that was currently making big money for him and Shirley as the flip of "Corinna, Corinna," though with the gender switch it was now called "Be My Boy."

Sill shopped the master to labels around town. Again, there were no bites. "I couldn't sell the record to anybody, couldn't lease it, nothing. Snuff Garrett at Liberty turned me down flat. Capitol hated it." With no recourse, Sill pressed and released it himself, creating a new label with Hazelwood, Gregmark, a combination of two of their sons' names and which was also the title of their publishing company. That's when Herb Newman at Era Records agreed to distribute the disc, and a promotion man named Clancy Grass was hired to plug it.

Spector didn't hang around for these machinations. Like a wisp of smoke, he left town quickly. There was too much on the burner in New York.

A few days after getting back, Phil had stunning news for Terry Phillips.

"We have a chance to do the songs in the new Elvis picture, *Blue Hawaii*," he said.

Terry had no idea how this incredible coup had come about, but then Phil had more news: they were also going to write songs for Bobby Darin and Connie Francis—both of whom were managed by Don Kirshner, now a close Spector confidant. Terry had barely digested all of this before he was caught in a tornado of dizzying activity. He moved in with Phil on E. 82nd St., they began working furiously on all three projects, and Phil took him on successive nights to the Copacabana nightclub, first to meet Connie Francis, then Bobby Darin.

"We played Connie a couple of songs," he remembered. "I'd written the lyrics, totally, to two or three songs, which she heard in her dressing room. And she flipped out over them. We then got with Bobby and played him a couple of songs, and he loved 'em. And then Hal Wallis, who was producing the Presley movie, heard the stuff we did and we got the affirmation that they loved all our songs for the movie."

Terry was ecstatic about this sudden turn of events in his still-brief career. But even though he had worked himself into exhaustion churning out lyrics, he could not quite understand the business logistics of it. He and Phil were both under contract to Leiber and

⊙

Stoller, but they were doing this new work under the auspices of Paul Case at Hill and Range. Often he tried to get an answer to how they could square this conflict of interest.

"It's cool," Phil would tell him. "It's been worked out."

Terry accepted it, trusting that Phil knew much more about this sort of accommodation than he did. Furthermore, Spector was in great demand, and in a power structure not unlike the five families of the Cosa Nostra, vicious competition could be mitigated by "gentlemen's agreements" benefiting any number of sides. Spector was constantly on the phone, dealing. "It never stopped ringing," Phillips said. "Everybody was stroking Phil, because of what they could get out of it. Phil was so many years beyond his age. I mean, I was a college graduate, I could've gone to law school, and Phil Spector absolutely made me feel like I was eleven years old in the business."

At times, Terry wondered what was being discussed during those phone calls, but Phil wouldn't open up. "He was like Ollie North. It would've been nice to hear the conversations, but if he saw me listening he'd hang up the phone. And if he would tell me things and he thought he was getting too close to something hush-hush, he would close up.

"I would say, 'Listen, Phil, if you don't tell me, I'm gonna beat your ass in.' He would say, 'Man, I'm tired of this business shit,' and he'd punch me in the shoulder—he absolutely was the weakest person I ever met in my life, God love him—and that would be his way out of it, like it all was getting to him."

And all the while they would be working, nonstop, because Paul Case told them there were tight deadlines. Terry would go as long as he could keep his eyes open, then fall out. Phil would never cave in. "He never went to sleep," Phillips said. "I'd go to sleep and Phil would sit on his bed and listen to the radio until 6 or 7 A.M. and he'd have his guitar in his hands, playing riffs. He could not go to sleep. He was afraid of the night, afraid to sleep . . . that if he didn't control himself, he might die before he woke up."

Inside of two weeks, songs for all three projects were done, a phenomenal output that had Terry euphoric. "I'd written the complete lyrics to everything we did, and now the Johnny Nash thing was like a bullshit little thing. This stuff was gonna put me on the map. I told my mother, 'I'm here only a few months—and I'm writing for *Elvis!*'" Phil then went into the studio and cut several songs with Bobby Darin.

At that point, life was good inside the first-floor apartment on E. 82nd St. The two young music men were bonded by cause and a unique personal chemistry, and Terry found that he was now possessive of the funny little man he knew had great depth and hurting inside him. Phil just naturally seemed like the little brother who needed protecting, and while Terry came to know some of the hairier details of Phil's personal heartaches and guilt, the hurt in Phil's eyes when he told of his home life made his pain so palpable that Terry would wince. He didn't need to hear one word to know that Phil Spector was a lost soul.

That also seemed to be Phil's attitude about women. He had a terrible time trying to find a love interest in New York. Terry, on the other hand, while not savvy like Spector in the business sense, left him in the dust during carousing hours. Running in a pack of happy wanderers that included songwriters Burt Bacharach, Bert Berns, and Bobby Scott, Phillips frequented downtown clubs like the Harwin. He and the others would attract a horde of women. Spector would sit alone on his bar stool, sipping 7-UP all night. "It was ridiculous," Phillips said. "He was the king and I was the serf, but I always wound up with the best-looking chicks in New York, I mean women ten years older than us. They'd spend time talking to him but then they'd go to bed with me. I'd get home the next day and Phil would be so pissed at me.

"It hurt him because he always wanted to be sexually attractive based on the fact that he was a human being. It was not that Phil was weird; he wasn't. Phil was a sweetheart. He was sensitive and hurt and brilliant and charming. He couldn't connect with women because he wanted one lady who was pretty and sexual and bright enough to be his lady. Someone who was classy and kind and honest.

"Phil wanted a love, he wanted to love and be loved. But every woman he ever met used him. The women he was screwing were doing it because of what he might do for them. And he was very well aware that these women would hurt and use him."

Eager to prove that he too could be a rogue, Phil came home one night with a very overweight female songwriter—and woke up Terry to invite him to join in as he and the woman undressed.

Casting a tired eye at them, and especially at the woman, Terry said he'd rather not. But Phil was insistent. "You gotta do it, Terry. You gotta do it for me," he pleaded.

Relenting, Terry crawled into Phil's bed to join them. But as hands were reaching and bodies touching, Terry began to quake with laughter. "It was just so funny, because this woman was so fat. I couldn't believe I was doing what I was doing," he recalled.

Phil was furious. "Terry, fucking Terry!" he kept snorting. They tried to begin over, but this time it was Phil who couldn't keep from breaking up.

"Then I went crazy again. And in the middle of this torrent of laughter, the lady got up, put on her clothes, and left, and Phil and I were still lying there in bed, laughing our asses off."

The elation at Eighty-second Street was shattered when Phil picked up the phone one night in February. Terry assumed it was just another routinely hushed call, until Phil began hollering angrily into the mouthpiece.

"There's a problem," Phil said, his face flushed, when he hung up. "Jerry and Mike have gotten wind of the whole thing and called up Freddie Bienstock."

All three deals, he said, were dead.

"Mike and Jerry found out and they put their foot down," Phillips explained. "They wanted half the publishing on the songs we wrote and Hill and Range said no."

Mad enough to kill, Terry glared at Phil. "You know something? You're all full of shit," Terry told him. "I love you as a person, man, but why didn't you tell me we didn't have the right to do it?"

Phil answered meekly, but unconvincingly, "I thought I understood that we could do it."

It was now possible to put the pieces together. Leiber and Stoller apparently had never been in on the dealing, and they had every justification to step in with an axe to protect their interests. Whether it was Phil, Paul Case, or Don Kirshner, in any combination, or whoever else had tried to pull this end run, it failed. "They gambled and lost," Phillips said. "You're talking about a man named Phil Spector. They wanted him and were willing to bend a few rules to get him." Hill and Range may have attempted, or planned all along, to settle with Leiber and Stoller after the fact; but Trio had a powerful attorney, Lee Eastman, and when he threatened to sue over the matter, Hill and Range junked everything. And yet, even though

Phil was bitter about the crumbled house of cards, he seemed not to be genuinely shocked.

"I think my reaction was much more emotional and angry than his," Phillips remembered. "I think he knew all the time what was going on. Maybe he misunderstood, but even if Phil knew, even if he overstepped a bound, the point was, everybody was going to make a lot of money, goddamn it. It seemed to us that the thing to do was for people not to be hard-assed and say, okay, 50 percent of a lot of money was better than 100 percent of nothing. That's why we were both pissed at everybody. I know Phil was very pissed off at Mike and Jerry."

Phillips, fearing Leiber and Stoller suspected him of treason, told Jerry Leiber: "Listen, I knew nothing about this. I was told it was okay." Spector, however, did not care about covering his back-side. He had an attorney inform Trio Music that he construed his contract null and void, on grounds that he had signed it as a minor without court approval, unlike his previous contracts with Doré, Imperial, and Sill/Hazelwood. As with most Spector moves, this was not done rashly. His association with Leiber and Stoller had tremendous leverage; however, in positioning himself for independent power, exclusivity was something he no longer wanted. Leiber and Stoller were also ambivalent about the rupture. To Lester Sill, they decried Spector's ingratitude. "They were angry," Sill recalled, "because they groomed him, helped him, honed his craft. They took Phil in, they took care of him, and they were gonna make deals with him and the minute he got hot, he walked."

But, clearly, there was nothing they could do, and when Phil asked for a release from Trio Music, they let him out. Yet Spector never really left. Mindful not only of their feelings but of the political danger of crossing Leiber and Stoller, Phil—who could play this game well—continued meeting with them as if nothing had ever come between them. What's more, he could do this because Leiber and Stoller wanted his modern brand of brilliance around them and their stable and were willing to eat their grudge against him. "More than anyone else, Mike and Jerry understand Phil Spector," Terry Phillips said. "Psychologically, they knew exactly where Phil was coming from, because they'd been there first. All three were such brilliant creatives, they were of the same mind. Mike and Jerry absolutely loved Phil. They did not want to lose him."

⊙

Spector thus proceeded with the uncertified imprimatur of Lei-ber and Stoller, and when he made his next move, finally acceding to the endless solicitations of Ahmet Ertegun to come to Atlantic Records as an A&R (artists and repertoire) man, as a kind of security pillow he went to work on his first day accompanied by the two men he had just jilted.

Spector went to Atlantic* with a wreath of chart hits: "Spanish Har-lem" would top out at No. 10 in mid-March, and its flip side, the Spector-Pomus "First Taste of Love," broke out for a run to No. 53. Curtis Lee's "Pretty Little Angel Eyes" hit the chart running in early February, at about the time that "Some of Your Loving" made a one-week appearance at the bottom tip of the chart. Spector's atti-tude upon entering Atlantic's ranks was that he would revitalize the company. The proud and preening Atlantic of the fifties was wob-bling now, stunned by the double-barreled defection in 1959 of both Ray Charles and Bobby Darin, and was struggling to isolate a new font of mainstream R&B besides the Drifters and Coasters. Phil often sat in Jerry Wexler's office, guitar in his hands, as he, Wexler, and Leiber and Stoller sifted through material. If Wexler ventured a criticism or even a suggestion, Phil verbally strafed him. "He came in as an instant sore winner," Wexler remembered. "To him, he was on equal ground, a peer. He'd say to me, 'Hey, baby, what the fuck are you talkin' about?' Whatever it was, I might've said 'Change the bridge,' or 'Get a new line here.' He said, 'No way! This is the way it goes down!'

"That quality was a great thing about him. I respected it. 'Cause he knew what he had and he didn't need to defer to anybody. Right or wrong, he pursued his own way, and it turned out to be right in the long run, didn't it?"

At the time, though, Wexler was not as philosophical or chari-table about Spector's impudence. A ruddy-faced onetime newspa-perman with a flashing temper—in the studio when "There Goes My Baby" was recorded, Wexler thought the song sounded so bad

*When he was interviewed for this book, Ahmet Ertegun claimed that he had originally brought Spector to New York, after signing him to Atlantic in Los Angeles as his "assistant." That version of history was rebuffed by everyone else in a position to know. "That's total bullshit, and I can't believe Ahmet said anything like that," Lester Sill said. "Ahmet met Phil after I sent him back to Leiber and Stoller. Jerry and Mike took him up to Atlantic. Ahmet had nothing to do with Phil coming to New York. He's full of shit and I'll tell him that."

that he hurled a sandwich against the wall—he complained loudly about Spector to Ertegun. "Jerry wanted to fire Phil the first day," Ertegun said.

The Turkish-born Ertegun, by contrast, was an industry diplomat whose urbane slickness Spector idolized. More than any other industry prototype, Phil was turned on by Ertegun's savvy and integrity in standing hard by soul music as a writer, producer, and executive. Spector may have played fast and loose trying to land *Blue Hawaii*, but Terry Phillips never believed that Phil wanted to be an industry nutcracker; the music was his motive in everything. "That hard-ass shit . . . you're talking about the George Goldners, the Freddie Bienstocks, guys that dealt a whole different kind of ball game, man," Phillips said. "You know what Phil Spector identified with in the business? He was totally influenced by Ahmet. Ahmet started a jazz and R&B field when there was no such thing. Phil was a great jazz lover, and Ahmet made an industry out of it. That was so great to him." People around town for months had noticed that Phil's hipster mannerisms and jargon were really Ertegun's. "The prefabricated stutter that Phil did, that's an Ahmet lick," Wexler said. "It's part satire, part emulation, and then it gets ingrained."

Erratic as Spector was, Ertegun wanted him to have at the depleted Atlantic roster. Gone now were Joe Turner and Clyde McPhatter; and Ivory Joe Hunter, Ruth Brown, and LaVern Baker were in decline. Besides the Drifters, the Coasters, and Solomon Burke's pulpit-style blues, numerous acts were in need of a shakeout. Spector went in with brash confidence, but he was wary of life as a staff producer bouncing from act to act and making art by the time clock. He came aboard as a loose kind of employee, without a signed contract and with latitude on the outside. His salary was small—"a pittance," as Wexler recalled—but what he wanted, and got, was carte blanche in the studio.

The problem was, high as a balloon on the "Phil trip," Spector used his time capriciously; if he didn't feel right on any given day, he'd forget about coming in. "Apparently, he was given authority to start auditioning people," said Tom Dowd, who as chief Atlantic engineer ran the studio. "I guess they'd given him some leads on people he should listen to. Either they had good songs or a good singer or a good harmony or something, and they wanted to see if Phil could marry off with any of these people. He'd tell them to meet

⊙

him in the studio. And I used to . . . I was in the middle of trying to get the product out, and somebody would put their nose in the door and say, 'I'm here for Phil Spector.' And I'd say, 'Wait in the studio for him.' At the end of the day I might have twenty or thirty groups sitting there sending out for sandwiches still waiting for Phil Spector.

"This went on for a couple of days, and I finally said, 'Wait a minute, this is getting impossible.' I had more people there that I didn't know who they are or what they're doing. I was hiring musicians and I couldn't tell whether a guy in the studio was on my payroll or not. Everybody was in everybody else's way."

Spector did cut sides on a good number of people, including Ruth Brown, LaVern Baker, and Billy Storm, the last a find of Lester Sill's who had previously recorded for Columbia Records. But many of these were in collaboration with other producers, some with Ertegun and Wexler, and Phil felt stifled. He was suffering more for his art now, punishing himself and all those around him to effect his concept of rock, and the self-induced pressure made Tom Dowd wonder if Spector was coming unwrapped.

"A musician might play or somebody might sing at the wrong time or pitch, and it would just unnerve him. And then he would break off all communication and input from anyone else," Dowd related. "You could see him get tense, and then all of a sudden he'd be out the door into the studio and screaming at somebody. He'd wrest the guitar out of a guy's hands and say, 'This is what I told you to play!' and it didn't matter who the guitar player was."

At those tortured moments, Dowd said, "I could get in about two or three sentences and then he'd be in another space. The more you fed into him, the farther away he got, the more intent he was on getting his one little microcosm going, until he got it right. If you rushed him, or tried to placate him, it wouldn't do a damn bit of good, and the frustration would make you feel like it was you he was against; but it wasn't, because he'd be sitting there carrying on a conversation, and then if something went by wrong, he was like three worlds away.

"Jerry Leiber was a lot like that, but he had Mike Stoller as a buffer against taking it out on somebody. Mike was always very solid, very steady, always positive. Jerry was positive until the first little obstacle and then he'd go off and you'd have to settle him down like a pigeon fluttering. But with Phil, there was no way I knew of how to settle him down. He just wouldn't recover."

Spector's predicament was time; unlike Leiber and Stoller, he needed too much of it to make the job work at Atlantic. And teaming him with another producer was to nobody's gain. Co-producing with Wexler a group called the Topnotes, a unit built around soul singer Derek Martin, the two had a blowup over who had final say. The songs suffered for it. "Together, we created negative synergy," Wexler said. "There was absolutely no consonance in the studio. I liked him, but we could not collaborate. I don't think Phil's a collaborator; it's his way or none."

The nadir was their co-production of a Bert Berns song, "Twist and Shout." Berns hated what they did to it but could only sit in the studio in pained silence. "We stashed him in the mezzanine, with the spectators, and we went out there and proceeded to murder his song," Wexler said. "There's a thousand ways to make a bad song and only one way to make it a good one. We never caught the right groove, the right spirit. When Bert went in and cut it himself [with the Isley Brothers in 1962], he did."

Atlantic was more than a clash of egos and will. For Spector, it was a clash of geography and technology. Having cut his teeth on the West Coast's archaic recorders, and continuing on similar equipment in New York, the culture clash of Dowd's eight-track machine made him swallow harder. "Phil was in his element with a two- or three-track, at most a four," Dowd said, "where he could allocate one track to all the rhythm, one to the backgrounds, one to the group. And then he'd play checkerboard with the tracks, bouncing one to the other. That was very California. He had better ways available to him, but if it impaired or impeded or made him insecure, technology means nothing. Let him do what he does best and capture the genius of the work. You don't make a Phil Spector a victim of technology."

Ertegun and Wexler never put Spector under the gun. "We didn't play that 'get your ass in gear' thing," Wexler said. "We knew how difficult it was." But in the early spring, Phil was writing Atlantic out of his world; abashed by his record of failure at the company, he was no longer mentioning Atlantic in conversation. He was dealing again on the outside, and Atlantic was merely a mental apparition by the time Phil told Ertegun and Wexler that he was walking

⊙

away from them. But if Spector's job performance had been mediocre, his timing was perfect. Only days after Phil left, Lester Sill got an agitated call from Jerry Wexler. "That son of a bitch Spector owes me $10,000!" Wexler bellowed. Atlantic had given Spector a number of cash advances, and Wexler believed—accurately—that Phil was not going to return the money. Wexler also believed Spector had ripped off the company for hundreds of dollars in long-distance phone calls after office hours. Working late one night, Wexler discovered a note under a blotter on the front desk. "It was a letter from the switchboard girl to Phil, telling him how to use the phones, which were shut off at night," Sill said. "Evidently Phil developed a relationship with the girl and was making all these calls. It got me into a very embarrassing situation with the Atlantic people."

Wexler, however, did not press the case. He chalked it up to the experience of living with Phil Spector.

The courting of Spector did not abate during his Atlantic detour, nor did Phil's desire to get on the good side of as many industry heavies as he could. One of these was Aaron Schroeder, the hard-selling, cunning, and likable song publisher and manager of Gene Pitney. Schroeder tried feverishly to charm Phil into coming onto his staff and finally reeled him in with an offer to produce a record for Pitney—who had recently had a self-produced hit, "(I Wanna) Love My Life Away" on a custom label begun for him by Schroeder and Art Talmadge called Musicor. Pitney was going in to record again and, with typical overkill, Schroeder had already lined up Leiber and Stoller to produce one of their songs at the same session.

Schroeder, who had written over twenty songs for Elvis Presley, was fanatical about getting his own company's catalogue material recorded, but he allowed Phil to pick the A side for Pitney. Spector, who wanted to link up with Don Kirshner's coterie of unorthodox young writers, tabbed Carole King and her husband and writing partner, Gerry Goffin, and they penned a melodramatic song called "Every Breath I Take." Schroeder also offered Phil another sop: Gene Pitney recorded a demo of a song written by Spector and Terry Phillips, "Dream for Sale," which would later end up as a cut on one of his albums.

Pitney had met Spector once before, during an early visit Phil made to Schroeder's office at 1650 Broadway. At the time Pitney had done very little in the business, and Spector had yet to get a New York gig. But Phil left a definite imprint when the two young men dined at a Chinese restaurant. "He understood the big picture of the whole thing, and what he wanted to do in the business," Pitney recalled. "He talked fast, like a machine gun, and he dropped a line on me that floored me. He said, 'My sister's in an asylum—and she's the sane one in my family.' "

Schroeder booked Bell Sound for the session, and the control room quickly was transformed into a zoo. Along with Leiber and Stoller and Spector, it was filled with writers of songs to be cut—Goffin and King, Burt Bacharach, and another married couple under the Kirshner domain, Barry Mann and Cynthia Weil—as well as Schroeder, his top hand Wally Gold, and Kirshner. Listening for direction from the booth, Pitney found he had not one producer per song but anywhere up to a dozen. "It was a real problem," he said. "Because every time somebody would be satisfied with something, somebody else would say, 'Yeah, it's all right, but you should've done this.' And I'd have to do it again. There were so many egos in there. Nobody wanted to step on anyone else, but that's all they did."

Scheduled to run from 7 to 10 P.M., the session stretched long into the morning hours, at double-scale overtime for an army of musicians. "Every Breath I Take" was the final song cut, and Pitney, suffering from a head cold and his vocal cords wrung raw, concluded his vocal by jumping into an unexpected falsetto. "Everybody said, 'Yeah, great idea, Gino.' What they didn't know was that was the only way I could get it out." It cost a startling $13,000—the average date ran around $500—but Spector, Pitney, Schroeder, and Kirshner got a song that they all swore would blister the pop chart. Phil used the Halos once again as a background choir, and a string section rose like great heaving breaths in a wild interplay with Gary Chester's choppy, booming drums.

Gerry Goffin recalled Spector on that night as a mercurial blur. "It was really something to see him work,'" Goffin said. "He was all over the studio, telling everybody what to do. He was hardly in the booth. He was always out there on the floor. I remember he was telling Gary Chester what fills he wanted. There was a great drum fill after the instrumental, and Phil practically directed that himself."

The result of these meticulous, back-breaking hours was Spector's boldest and most ambitious work, a spectacle of sound and fury that he had been building toward for over a year. Aaron Schroeder was pleased. After the session he reached into his pocket, pulled out a $50 bill, and tried to stuff it in Phil's palm. Spector, who received absolutely no compensation for the gig, declined.

"That was Phil's way of saying 'You can't buy me. I did my thing, I did you a favor, but that's it,' " Gene Pitney believed. "Aaron wanted to grab Phil, put him under contract, but Phil was too smart for that. You could see what was comin' with him. Phil purely had designs on creating his own little empire."

6

He would have all kinds of things going on. He was just wheeling and dealing. And he couldn't believe what he was doing, how easy it was. He would come home and say, "Mike, you won't believe this one . . ." and go on to describe the deal he cut that day.

—MICHAEL SPENCER

To everyone's surprise, the Paris Sisters' "Be My Boy" made a respectable display on the chart, reaching No. 56 in late May of 1961. In search of a follow-up record, Lester Sill came to New York to make the rounds on Broadway. At Don Kirshner's office, Artie Ripp, who was now working at Aldon, sat at a piano and played Sill and Spector a ballad by Barry Mann and Larry Kolber called "I Love How You Love Me." Ripp could hardly hit the right keys and had a voice like a hinge, but Phil loved it; the long pauses in the lyrics made it compatible with strings, and it intrigued him that the old Teddy Bears sound could be buffed with violins.

Spector flew back to L.A. with plans to cut the song as part of

⊙

an album of similar lachrymose love songs. Needing an arranger, Sill matched him with Hank Levine, an independent Hollywood producer and orchestrator. But neither Levine nor the musicians Phil booked—including Earl Palmer, Ray Pohlman, and Howard Roberts—for May and early June sessions envisioned what an ordeal recording the Paris Sisters' drippy ballads would be.

Roberts, the old jazzman, was still far removed from the ferment of rock and roll, and he had not the slightest notion of what Phil had done or where he had been since "Bumbershoot." But he had every reason to think that Spector's lead sheets two years later would be something more intricate than the three-chord cycles of 1959. He was wrong. "He'd walk in and it would say 'C-F-G' and that was it," Roberts recalled. "And the next tune would say 'C-F-G' and the next after that was 'C-F-G.' " Given this, Roberts could not understand why Phil pushed him and Pohlman on the same stuff again and again, with little or no variation. "With other producers, there would be some little fine adjustments here and there, and you'd do four sides in three hours and leave. With Nelson Riddle, it sounds great. But with Spector, we'd sit there for hours on end on one tune, strumming these three chords."

"He always seemed to have an idea of what he was after," Pohlman said, "but I don't know if he could always *express* it. He would let it happen with the band and let it evolve."

To the musicians, Spector's recording process seemed chaotic and unplanned, something on the order of knitting an afghan in the dark. And yet, as difficult as it was for them to comprehend, Phil— three years more skilled in the "broad mono" with which he and Marshall Lieb made aural images dance across the music image of a song—was working on a higher plane: it wasn't melody but the blend and the balance of that image that consumed him. Thus, even though the rhythm section would be barely discernible in "I Love How You Love Me," buried by eight violins and the sugar-plum voices of the Paris Sisters, it would be that way precisely *because* drum, bass, and guitar merged into a "feel" rather than separating into select instrumental noises. The balance of a Spector song was diaphanously sensitive; it could happen at any moment, like a sudden hiccup. Accordingly, Phil no longer cut strings along with the rhythm track. Hank Levine's violinists had to overdub the same way Sammy Nelson had tried to keep the drum beat on "To Know Him Is to Love

Him": listening to a disembodied track. It was a hellacious task for Levine, and Stan Ross had to mix and match sound levels to make the finished product sound natural. And because Phil thought that the acoustics at Gold Star would stunt a major string arrangement, he cut the violins at another studio. Ross was amazed at how well Phil and Hank Levine did under these trying circumstances. "It was a perfect meeting ground of strings against rhythm," Ross said of the song. "The string overlays were done in good taste, very subtle, crisp and sharp but not distracting."

However, before Phil would put the song in the can, he took the raw tapes back to Lester's house, where he was camping during sessions, and listened to them in a monklike trance. "He spent hours with that song," Sill recalled. "We came home at 3 A.M. and he must've played that thing fifty times that night, in our little den. There's a certain point where the strings come in and out. He wanted to make sure that the level of the strings was just right. He turned the sound way down, because he wanted to make sure the strings cut through, that they wouldn't fade out, even for a split second. Even after he thought it was right, he would listen and listen and listen."

As the Paris Sisters' sessions ran on, Lester became rooted in the studio. Although he had drifted away from the studio over the years, he now was by Phil's side during the interminable hours at Gold Star. "I saw what he was doing, the sounds he was getting. Like the way he muted the strings as he blended them. Seeing what Phil was doing, it just made me want to get back in there," Sill said. It would get to be a problem, because Lee Hazelwood thought Lester was putting in more time with Phil than was necessary—an opinion no doubt reinforced by Hazelwood's festering dislike of Spector. Two years before, the acrimony between the two had become so intense that when Stan Ross heard that Phil was sent to New York, he swore it had to be because Sill wanted to keep the peace with Hazelwood. Now, with Phil's star screaming skyward, Hazelwood was forced to take a backseat to the kid he abhorred. It ate him like battery acid. In the studio to offer Sill his help during the early sessions, Hazelwood cringed and his pride burned when Phil, wallowing unabashedly in his new power, showed him little respect. "Phil was running around crazy and giving people a hard time, and he was picking fights with Lee," Stan Ross said. "Phil wasn't really

⊙   94

being disrespectful—he was being Phil Spector, not the easiest guy for anybody to love. Lee said, 'I'm not gonna go in the same room with that little fart.' "

Still seeking an act he could get behind now that Duane Eddy was gone, Hazelwood would want to meet with Sill, only to be told constantly that Lester was at Gold Star with Spector. Finally, the irritable producer snapped. In a huff, he went to Gold Star and, in an ugly scene, confronted Sill.

"I'll never forget it," Sill said. "I was there with Phil cutting the Paris Sisters and Lee walked in all pissed. He said, 'Look, I can't handle it. I'm doin' work, too, but you're spending all your time with Phil.' He said, 'Look, you keep Phil, I'm gonna go back with Duane.' Lee and I hadn't been getting along, and I said, 'Fine,' and that was it. It was the end of our relationship, though we kept the publishing company for years.

"Lee thought I was neglecting our thing, which wasn't true. It was really that Lee saw Phil as a threat, creatively. That's how much Phil had grown."

Witnessing the disintegration of Sill/Hazelwood productions before his eyes, Spector was not too preoccupied to sense how it could affect his life. The cadaver of Hazelwood's abandoned partnership was still not cold, but Phil pounced. Only days after the blowup, he approached Lester with a proposition.

"Now that Lee's gone," Phil told him, "I'm ready to step in."

For Lester, it was a logical proposition. He had little to lose by bumping Phil up to a co-ownership and co-publishing position; Spector's contract with Sill/Hazelwood was about to run out, and a writer/producer future, at any cost, would not have made Phil want to get on an airplane and keep coming to L.A. Sill was in crisis losing a partner on the order of Lee Hazelwood, and Phil Spector was the hottest item in rock. Where the New York heavies were unable to reel him in, Sill could now have him in perpetuity in shared royalties by granting Phil his overriding wish. Right there, with not a beat of delay, he told Phil, "Let's get it going."

The deal necessitated a new label and publishing company. In keeping with the Gregmark acronym custom, the label was christened as an amalgam of Phil and Les—Philles Records.

The publishing company was named Mother Bertha Inc. "Mother Bertha was a double-edged thing, a big joke."

The immediate problem for Philles Records was money. Sill had dealt small, and Phil Spector meant big—Sill could only imagine the production costs on records Phil would make for his own label—and even hit records could not guarantee profits for a small, independent label. Distributors routinely took advantage of such companies, holding back on disbursing funds to see if the labels would fold before they could collect; often the windfall of a hit record outran a label's ability to collect all the cash it was owed. It was much too risky for Sill to go neck deep into Philles with his own money. Instead, he called in another chit, turning to a convenient if not beloved ally. Sill had sagely refused to go toe-to-toe with Harold Lipsius and Harry Finfer over the Duane Eddy master tapes. Now, with the line between them still open, Sill opted for the clout of Universal Distributing.

Universal had recently suffered a setback itself. Harry Finfer, who was its general manager and promotion head of Jamie Records, had been implicated in the rock-and-roll payola scandals that bloodied rock's nose. Testifying before a congressional committee in 1960, Finfer admitted that he had slipped under-the-table cash and favors to deejays. Finfer, like Dick Clark, came away relatively unscathed—technically, it was ruled, no laws were broken by payola—but Jamie Records eventually divested of its management interest in Duane Eddy, who went to record for RCA Victor, again produced by Lee Hazelwood. Knowing well about Phil Spector's fire storm in New York, Harold Lipsius readily agreed to finance, press, and distribute Philles Records in exchange for a one-third financial stake in the profits; in turn, Sill and Lipsius gave Finfer an override on all Philles releases, and because the Philles stock would be owned by Jamie Records, both Lipsius and Finfer were instant shareholders.

It was unclear when the first Philles product would come about. Phil would go back to New York, free to sign acts and book sessions. Projecting costs, Phil had no doubt that these sessions would burn more dollars than Lipsius and Finfer could ante. A disposable financial angel was what he needed, and he believed he had one. Months before, Phil had met Helen Noga, the manager of Johnny Mathis, at Hill and Range. Noga was a windy, matronly woman, enormously wealthy and desirous of show-biz power. While still in L.A., he dropped in at her Beverly Hills house and inflated her head with dreams of mutual conquests. When she went to meet with Lester Sill, Lester could see why Phil honed in on her. "She was an obnoxious human being," he recalled. "She said to me, 'Lester, when I come to New York, I just reach out and pull the money in.' " For a piece of the first Philles record, Noga agreed to kick in on the initial sessions. She assumed there would be bigger and better agreements to be made later.

During the Paris Sisters' recordings, Michael Spencer gave a party at his house attended by many of the old gang, including Russ Titelman and Annette Merar, the girl Russ had brought into the Spector's Three touring group. When Phil dropped by, he was immediately mesmerized by Annette, whose shaggy blond hair and soft green eyes left him short of breath. Trying to keep from toppling off his platform-heeled boots, Phil stood as tall as he could and lied about wanting to use her as a model on an album cover. As an ice-breaker it worked, but it wasn't until he came down from the Phil trip, played his guitar, and revealed himself as vulnerable that she turned on to him.

"I knew Phil before that, of course, but it was at that party when I realized I was very attracted to him," she recalled. "The way he played his guitar and just his persona were extremely interesting to me."

When it got late, Phil dropped hints. "I've got to go out to the valley, and I don't want to make that long ride alone," he said to her.

Annette, seeing how hard he was trying, laughed and told him, "Okay, I'll go with you."

It was around midnight and Annette, who was in the eleventh grade now, was usually in bed by this time. But she was enthralled by Phil. They drove to Lester's house and talked until the sun came up. When Phil drove her back to L.A., "We just sat in the car and there was a lot of silence," she said. "And I remember saying 'I've never felt so comfortable with anybody not saying anything.' "

Phil, who had also been having a fling with Priscilla Paris, began seeing Annette almost daily. Moving from Lester's to a Hollywood motel, the Plaza Lodge, he brought Annette back to his room one night. A little while later, they were startled when someone started to pound on the door.

"Open up, Phil!" came a scream from outside. "It's me, Russ. Open up!"

Recognizing the voice of an angry Russ Titelman, Phil—who had not bothered to inquire if Annette was still Russ's girlfriend—whispered, "Be quiet." The two of them sat silently in the dark until they heard Russ's footsteps trail away.

"I don't know why we did that," Annette recalled. "Phil and I weren't doing anything, we must have been watching television. And I was no longer going with Russ at that time. I didn't cheat on Russ to go with Phil. But for some reason Russ was very . . . maybe he wasn't over me. Russ must have found out I was with Phil in his room, and he freaked out."

Russ, feeling betrayed and sick about Phil romancing Annette, jumped in his car and started driving aimlessly. Finally he rolled to a stop in Lester Sill's driveway. "The poor kid, he was broken-hearted," Sill said. "Russ was going with Annette and then he found them there. He had to stay with me for a couple of days before he was ready to go back. He was all shook up."

In reality, very little was actually going on between Phil and Annette. "We were not sexually fast or anything," she said. "Phil was very slow in that area. I thought he was gay at the beginning. I asked him too, and he got real insulted and wouldn't talk to me for a while. But then we started dating, and he took me to Palm Springs and we'd have dinner, we'd be in the studio and I got to watch his creative efforts from the germ to the fruition. He'd be playing his guitar and he'd come up with a little riff that he liked and he said, 'I'm gonna do that in the studio,' and he'd work on it and expand it and make it happen.

"I was very creative myself, I wrote poetry. I loved what he was doing. And then I remember he took me to lunch one day and he finally kissed me."

But by then, his work done with the Paris Sisters, he was ready to go back to New York. They would continue a long-distance love affair—"We had a romance by phone that you would not believe, hours and hours every night, talking about everything from math to sex," she said—and Annette would send him love poems that would leave him gasping. But in the summer of 1961, other things took priority over romance for Phil Spector. His career, and his whole world, was about to break wide open.

Phil returned to New York early in June, and for the Philles sessions he brought with him an arranger named Jack Nitzsche, who was working for Lee Hazelwood in the new office Hazelwood had taken one floor below Lester Sill's. After arranging several of the songs for the Paris Sister's album, Nitzsche went to Hazelwood with the New York offer. Hazelwood, who could have been balky out of spite, gave his permission. In New York, Spector kept Philles under his hat, and it was useful that the first Philles sessions would be held under the official banner of Jamie Records. Phil had too many favors to do yet, too much industry goodwill and perks to earn. And building up working capital was still a consideration. For Phil, the Hill and Range connection was vital; not only were acts drawn to the Brill Building like flocks of geese but Paul Case and his minions could judge the marketability of an act and a song like no other industry meter. Besides, Case and the Bienstocks were, as ever, willing to pay him beneficial stipend money to hang around the eleventh floor and feel disposed to produce for Big Top. So many acts streamed through the place that Spector could bird-dog for Philles and do an occasional Big Top turn without changing his step.

Still ensconced on E. 82nd St., Terry Phillips watched ambivalently as Phil played his shell games. To be sure, there was some poetic justice in Phil's duplicity, given that the *Blue Hawaii* fiasco had hardened Terry's overview of the recording business. "Big Top was a bunch of fucking whores," Phillips said. "Freddie Bienstock and Jean and Julian Aberbach had millions of dollars, they were people who looked at writers as scum. Phil saw that. Phil saw everything, man. He knew they were trying to take advantage of him. But they didn't, because he was too smart. Phil took advantage of them and they didn't even know it."

Phillips, however, had no stomach for finagling or wanderlust, yet the current of intrigue and deception at E. 82nd St. had only gotten hotter since *Blue Hawaii*. "These people were so different than me. I thought it was all greed and stupidity. Everybody was fuckin' everybody, and that was bullshit to me. It started to get awfully complicated and I said, man, I don't wanna deal with this. Because it wasn't interesting to me, being around it wasn't fun anymore. But I understood Phil's problem. Phil was a young man who had matured enough to be concerned with his future career. I was a young man who was only interested in the next beautiful blonde I could have."

Terry knew it was over when he suspected that Phil, out of sheer self-interest, was holding him back. "Phil knew more about the business but I also felt he was concerned about my personality—that while he really cared about me, he kept me two steps behind him because I was an open guy and people liked me. Phil knew I was talented, if he had a meeting with Aaron Schroeder or Art Talmadge [the head of Gene Pitney's Musicor label], I wasn't allowed there." And so in early June, Terry moved out. He began collaborating with a writer named Jerry Vance, whose brother sang in a Brooklyn quintet called Jay and the Americans. Phillips took them to Leiber and Stoller, who by now had broken with Atlantic and gone to United Artists, and they produced the group for the label. Every once in a while, Terry would bump into Phil along Broadway, saying little more than hello and good-bye. "My feeling was, if Phil didn't want to call me, I knew I could do things on my own. He was with a whole other crowd, and I didn't want to be perceived as trying to take advantage of what he was achieving. That was important to me because I wasn't gonna suck up to him, because I didn't need to."

Phillips's place at E. 82nd St. was taken by Michael Spencer, who came to New York to attend the Mannes College of Music. This arrangement pleased Phil: the quiet, taciturn Spencer had none of Phillips's wildman habits, and he had an understanding of music that could keep them busy for days on production ideas. Spencer also was put to work on sessions, as a pianist and leader, a double-scale perk that helped him pay his tuition. Uninterested in the business end, Spencer observed Phil's commandeering of Broadway as a lab experiment in environmental sociology. Michael was incredulous at the change in Phil; the mama's boy of West Hollywood could play the part of the New York honcho in high style. "He was much more flamboyant, his air, his attitude," Spencer said. "Making it in New York fed his ego and his personality." Because Phil had missed any period of struggle and adjustment as a young adult, Michael could see that his old friend was a strange hybrid: his insecurities had never been assuaged, and yet he was caught in an avalanche of success. Concerned that Phil was too shut off from reality for his own good, Michael tried to get Phil's mind off the business. He would drag Phil out of the apartment, out of the Brill Building, even down to the Times Square grind houses. Other times they'd get a car and roam the city, with one clear exception—Phil would not step on his old Bronx turf.

But these were mere interludes, marking time between business paces. Phil was racing recklessly to his requital, and he could not be stalled. At Hill and Range, Phil found, and later cut sessions with, three groups as potential Philles fodder. They were named the Ducanes, the Creations, and the Crystals. The first two sang ethnic white doo-wop, a dying idiom that Phil—who never really got the hang of eastern streetcorner harmony—put on tape only because he liked something in their voices. He soon backed off both groups, though, and he sold to Jamie the Creations masters for a one-shot issue on that label. With the Ducanes he notched a favor with George Goldner, the old tough guy. Goldner was a still-influential figure on Broadway even though huge gambling debts forced him to unload his big fifties' labels, the inverted End and Gone—for which he had produced and then plugged classic R&B hits by the likes of Frankie Lymon, Little Anthony and the Imperials, and the Chantels—to Roulette Records. Goldner was left with silk suits, Havana cigars, and a small label called Goldisc Records, and Goldisc was a logical home for the Ducanes' cover of the old Louis Lymon hit "I'm So Happy (Tra-la-la)."

The Crystals masters, however, would not leave Phil's hands. From the very beginning, he had the group earmarked for Philles. Five soft-throated black teenage girls from Brooklyn, they came in to Hill and Range with an uptempo song written by a friend named Leroy Bates, "There's No Other (Like My Baby)." As they sang it for him in an audition room, Phil had a different concept. "He was sitting there nibbling on pretzels, little tiny bites like a bunny rabbit, and he just told us to slow it down," recalled Mary Thomas, one of the Crystals. "Then he turned the lights out in the room and we sat around in the dark, because he thought it would make it sound romantic." For two weeks, Phil rehearsed the Crystals just that way, in the dark, so much that lead singer Barbara Alston, whose voice had little timber, would leave hoarse.

Spector was not the only one at Hill and Range interested in the Crystals; the group auditioned regularly for two other writer/producers, Bill Giant and Bernie Baum. But when Hill and Range lagged in signing the Crystals to Big Top, Phil signed them himself and hustled them into the studio. On June 28, graduation day at their high school in Brooklyn, the girls were paged. "We didn't even know we were gonna record," Mary Thomas said. "All of a sudden we got a message, 'You gotta come to Manhattan.' We went flyin' there that night."

Spector, without Jack Nitzsche, who had gone back to L.A., went into Mira Sound with his own arrangement for three songs. Joining Mike Spencer on the date were Gary Chester, guitarists Bob Bushnell and Wallace Richardson, and bassist Richard Ziegler, and when the Crystals did the vocals, Spector came back the next day and conducted a light string arrangement. Yet even with Helen Noga's and Jamie's foot money, Phil did not have the unlimited resources of his Atlantic and Gene Pitney sessions, and "There's No Other," the A side, was not prime Spector stock; the few instruments splattering against the thick Mira Sound walls sounded small, muddy, and impossible to mix clearly. Still, the languid and sensual beat and the title hook worked well, and recalled the drafty auditorium sound of the Chantels and the Shirelles' cute, imperfect harmonies.

Lester Sill heard the masters and sent word to Jamie to issue "There's No Other (Like My Baby)" and a Spector song called "Oh Yeah Maybe Baby" on the yellow and red label of Philles Records—with Spector listed as a co-writer with Leroy Bates.

Over the summer, while the Hill and Range staff were still unaware of the heist of the Crystals, Spector proceeded to do Big Top's bidding. He produced a Sammy Turner record as a follow-up to Turner's "Lavender Blue," and another for a singer named Karen Lake. During his hours in the studio, he was difficult, often vexing, and always excessive.

"The thing that used to bug me was that he ran overtime so much," John Bienstock said. "It was hard to have a budget come in that made sense. But he didn't give a shit. His artistic endeavor was more important to him." To Bienstock too. Spector was where he wanted him: in the studio for him. And so he was allowed his surfeit.

⊙

"I happen to have liked him a lot," Bienstock insisted. "We used to fight a good deal because we had differences of opinion. But we loved each other. We were real friends." As a favored son, Phil was thick with the entire Hill and Range clan. When he took a liking to Bienstock's pretty daughter, Jackie, Bienstock did not object to him taking her out one night. Phil went to the Bienstocks' home in Teaneck, New Jersey, well dressed and groomed—"not in his goddamn doo-dads and jeans, but perhaps he did have a cape"—to pick Jackie up. It was the last she wanted to see of him. "She thought he was a kook," Bienstock said.

Phil's place in the Hill and Range bosom lasted only until summer's end—until they found out through the grapevine about the Crystals and Philles Records.

"We were very angry because we felt they were Big Top artists," Bienstock said. "He was merely supposed to produce them for us. There was no question about the fact that he was just rehearsing them for Big Top—hell, he rehearsed them for weeks in our offices. And then he just stole them right out of here. That precipitated a breach of contract with us.

"We were just incensed because that was a terrific group, and for him to do that shows the type of character he was. We felt he was less than ethical, and, obviously, he was then shown the door."

Phil did not believe his crime was heinous—to him the Crystals had been fair game. Nevertheless, when told to clear out, he did not feel he had to defend himself, and his reaction was much the same as with the *Blue Hawaii* abortion. He did not flinch.

"He showed no remorse whatsoever," Bienstock related, "just like the typical piece of shit he was. He was talented, but he was a piece of shit."

The sacking—along with the failure of his Big Top records— was part of a double-barreled blow for Spector. "Every Breath I Take," on which Aaron Schroeder had banked so much money and hope, went to No. 42 in mid-September and then died, a killer of a letdown for Spector, Gene Pitney, and Schroeder.

Nervously, Phil turned to sweating out the record he had been waiting to put out all his life.

7

I felt like I was in the center of the universe when I was with him.

—ANNETTE MERAR

"There's No Other (Like My Baby)" was released with the catalogue number Philles 100 in late October. But it wasn't Philles business that occupied Phil when it came out. More important was the staggering blast up the chart of the Paris Sisters' "I Love How You Love Me." After landing on the *Billboard* chart in early September, the record zoomed into the Top 40 four weeks later, en route to a No. 5 peak and a fifteen-week run—a mandate for Phil to cut a third single with the sisters. In early November, with "I Love How You Love Me" one of the hottest discs in the land, he flew out to Hollywood once again, carrying a song written for the sisters by Gerry Goffin and Carole King, "He Knows I Love Him Too Much."

Phil had won over Goffin and King's allegiance very early in his New York career. While up in Don Kirshner's office just before "Spanish Harlem" was released, Spector sang them the tune to his

⊙   104

own guitar accompaniment. "The way he sang, with his vocal intonations, he sounded like Bob Dylan," Goffin recalled. Phil, with his tangled mop of thin hair and torn blue jeans, struck Goffin as an *artiste* and a "character," a wraith of uniqueness that he and his wife had not yet encountered along Broadway. Trying to break out in a Kirshner barn pervaded by the vapid, homogeneous teen pap churned out by the Neil Sedaka-Howard Greenfield team, Goffin and King—both Brooklyn-born, and married in 1958—were not merely beguiled by Spector; Phil's pluck and nerve and his keen musical palate made him seem almost like an oracle to them. "He would play us records that he loved," Goffin said. "He was very much in tune with what was happening."

A year later, Goffin-King and Phil Spector had both taken massive strides in carving rock's sixties' identity. Goffin and King were really what was happening in rock prose. They were writing progressively daring, two-minute psychodramas in which the protagonists—based on the couple themselves—were troubled, self-destructive lovers for whom love was a battle zone. Redefining the boundaries of rock realism, they had a massive hit with the Shirelles' "Will You Still Love Me Tomorrow" in 1961; in 1962, they would provide an anthem for the sadomasochistic minefield of love with the Cookies' "Chains"—a theme very similar to that of "He Knows I Love Him Too Much." Cooed from Priscilla Paris's quivering lips and moistened by Hank Levine's weeping strings, the pathos was bitingly real.

Happy as he was with the record—which would make it to No. 34 in March—Phil could not be pleased with this trip back to the California sun. Weeks earlier, Lester Sill had found out that an assistant had accidentally discarded the master tapes of the intended Paris Sisters' album. "It was my fault, really," Sill said. "The guy was cleaning out the dubs and never came to ask me about it. I had them stacked with all the other demos and filed wrong, and he just threw 'em away." The heart-crushing accident became the focal point of a bitter contention among Phil, the sisters, and Sill. The huge success of "I Love How You Love Me" had led Phil and the sisters to believe that big money was due them. But when they queried Lester about it, he told them that the expenses in making the album had eaten up almost all of the royalties. "There actually was a *debit*, but I gave 'em both some money," Sill said. "The cost of the album was horrendous. I showed 'em the figures. It may have been $10,000. That was the way Phil recorded. He was a perfectionist." With the album now lost, none of that money could ever be recouped.

Trying to live with this terribly cruel turn of events, Phil cursed an unkind fate. But he also wondered if Lester was being completely honest or fair with him. Biting his lip hard, he refrained from arguing about it, and he soon split for New York, still simmering.

The Paris Sisters were more demonstrative. They were so angry they staged a series of nasty scenes in the office, demanding their money. If they were frantic, they had reason. When Phil left, his haste had made it clear that he was through with them for good. "Phil is like that," Sill said. "When it doesn't happen the way he wants, he doesn't give a shit what it does to other people involved. He will destroy those people—although in this case, the Paris Sisters destroyed themselves, because they got very salty with me and forced me to drop 'em. Besides, when Phil went back to New York, no one else wanted to record 'em. I loved the Paris Sisters but I don't think anyone could've made hits with 'em but Phil." Sill did release two more Paris Sisters' records that he had in the can, but he in effect "washed my hands of them" the day Spector walked out on them. They signed with MGM in 1963, but never relived the heady days Spector had given them.

Still unsure about the future of the Crystals' "There's No Other," Phil sought to close some wounds with Hill and Range. Operating on the periphery of the eleventh floor, he did two more sessions for Stan Shulman and Dunes, one with Ray Peterson, one with Curtis Lee. Each would yield a minor hit: Lee's "Under the Moon of Love" and Peterson's "I Could Have Loved You So Well." And when the Bienstocks and Paul Case got into a sticky political fray with George Goldner, Spector agreed to be the peacemaker. The problem came about when Big Top signed Arlene Smith, the strong-lunged former Chantels lead singer, as a solo act. Goldner was irate about Smith leaving Roulette Records, and he and the Roulette people began making intimidating noises about it to Hill and Range.

"They thought of me as 'George's artist,' and they were giving Big Top a hard time," Smith recalled. "I was caught in the middle of it."

Burt Bacharach was slated to produce Smith at Big Top, but

when Goldner put the heat on, Big Top shuddered. Rumors about Goldner and the mob were a longtime undercurrent on Broadway, and no one wanted to find out whether there was any truth behind them. "Big Top was afraid of George and Roulette," Smith thought. And so Bacharach was taken off the gig, to be replaced by the kid who had done Goldner right with the Ducanes, as part of an arrangement leading to Smith eventually being sold back to Roulette.

Phil was thrilled to get Smith's powerful voice in the studio, and he took the extraordinary step of having her do a cover of "He Knows I Love Him Too Much." Released at about the same time as the Paris Sisters' record, Big Top didn't push it hard, and it was heard almost nowhere. Nor was Smith happy with the product, though she liked working with Phil and later wrote a song with him called "Pretty Face." Smith would fondly recall his energy and his bizarre wardrobe—he wore pointy-toed desert boots and a little cap, reminding her of Robin Hood—but the song struck her as "a stock arrangement, and the attention wasn't focused on me. I was lost at the bottom of a big orchestra mix, and it didn't work. If I'd been out front, it might've been very special."

Phil figured in the second stage of the Smith exit plan as well, which was to reunite her with her old Chantels producer and Goldner protégé, Richard Barrett. When Barrett cut his record, it was released not on Big Top but on a one-shot label sticker under the name "Spectorius." That was George Goldner's payback to Spector for his generosity with the Ducanes.

Helen Noga, acting on Phil's hints of a shared march to glory, greeted the release of "There's No Other" with a decided effort to wiggle further into the Philles picture. On October 17, after consulting with Phil, she had her lawyers draw up a contract of terms and conditions financing more sessions by the Creations, Ducanes, and Crystals, in exchange for a 50 percent cut of the profits. How Phil hoped to reconcile this with Harold Lipsius and Harry Finfer only he knew, and it was possible he had no intention of ever going that far with Noga. But, pending the showing of "There's No Other," he signed the contract—including a make-good gesture to the Bienstocks: a clause stating "Paul Case of Hill and Range Songs Inc. is to be given first consideration for material to be recorded."

The truth was, Spector had come upon a better means of life

support for Philles. For months he had been quietly dealing with Liberty Records, the L.A. label founded by Lew Bedell and Herb Newman's cousin Si Waronker in 1955 and which had consolidated the range of West and Northwest rock—it was Liberty that distributed the Fleetwoods' "Come Softly To Me" and the hugely influential guitar-rock records of the Ventures, each recorded on a small label in Seattle. The Spector-Liberty romance began with overtures by Tommy "Snuff" Garrett, a skinny producer who was also Liberty's head A&R man on the West Coast. Garrett was, in Phil's mind, the only L.A. producer who really mattered in sixties rock. An ex-deejay from Texas and a close friend of Buddy Holly's, Garrett came to L.A. in 1959 and produced gigantic hits for Liberty with Bobby Vee, a Holly soundalike from Minnesota, and Johnny Burnette by adding opulent string arrangements to rockabilly.

Garrett was Spector's idea of Dixie hip. He wore cowboy boots, spun homilies about horses and pigs, and was fond of saying—and proving—that he could not produce a flop record. Only three years older than Phil, Garrett's long, gravelly face was excavated by the force of a thousand Texas saloons, and if Spector tried to faze Snuff with the Phil trip, he got nowhere. In New York once to bird-dog songs for Liberty, Garrett invited Spector up to his hotel room for breakfast. Phil asked if anyone else was there, and Snuff told him he was with a certain female writer. Phil, who knew the woman, said, "I don't like her." Snuff told him, "Well, then don't look at her." Moments later, Spector came to the door—with his eyes jammed shut. "He had a plastic bag and in it was a half-eaten dinner roll, a razor, and a broken comb," Garrett recalled, "and all the while we talked he sat lookin' at me. He would not look at or talk to the lady." Garrett never blinked. After breakfast, Phil "closed his eyes again and I helped him to the door and he left."

When Phil buried himself in the postproduction of "I Love How You Love Me," he took the record to Garrett for an opinion, knowing he'd get a square count. "He came runnin' over and, God, we went over and over that record," Garrett said. Months later, Liberty producer Clyde Otis—head of East Coast A&R—quit the label, leaving unfinished records he had been working on. Garrett offered the A&R job to Spector, and the two of them kept increasing salary figures until, almost in jest, Phil said he'd accept $25,000. "It was ridiculous, unheard of for then, but I gave it to him because I believed

Spec to be a great fuckin' talent," Garrett said. "I thought the two of us would really put Liberty on the map." Garrett had to talk Liberty president Al Bennett into approving—"Al bitched and moaned. I was enough of a problem to handle. They didn't want two children in A&R."

But Garrett talked well. Not only did Al Bennett okay the contract, he also capitulated to a clause drawn up by Spector and Sill that gave Phil the leeway to go on producing his three personally owned acts—the Crystals, Creations, and Ducanes—on his own time, as well as liberal travel privileges. For Bennett, this was a very risky clause; at worst, Phil might hoard the best songs he could find for his own label, and at best his attention and purpose might be divided. As Bennett needed signs that Spector would perform well for Liberty, Garrett assigned Phil the unfinished mix of a song Clyde Otis had cut with Timi Yuro, "What's the Matter Baby." "He went into Mira Sound and redubbed it down," Garrett said, "and he did a helluva job on it." Outwardly, at least, Spector seemed gung ho about the job, and this convinced Bennett as to his ability and intentions. And so Bennett gave in to one more of Phil's requests, for a cash advance on expenses. Sitting in his office a continent away, on top of a roster of rockabilly acts, Bennett had ecstatic visions of beating the New York labels on the important new rock acts. Spector was clued in, he was hot, he was good. Suddenly, placating him didn't seem such a gamble. Bennett drew out an entire year's salary, up front, for Spector, with another $5,000 thrown in.

This incredible war chest socked away, Phil no longer needed Helen Noga. But neither did he need to alienate her. Guaranteeing her a piece of the first three Philles records, he made a cash settlement, buying out her dream before it began.

Next came a change of address, to a bigger apartment, a one-bedroom on W. 58th Street. Liberty was one block away, at 171 W. 57th Street. Phil inspected his office there and decided that he did not want the desk provided to him. "They had a conference table in a big room, and Spec wanted that as his desk," Snuff Garrett remembered. "So of course I had to get it done for him. Liberty wanted to hang me." The first few weeks in the new job, Phil sat in his office, dwarfed by the titanic table, and did almost nothing besides play with an air hockey game, either by himself or with a still-paternal Paul Case.

As New Year's 1962 arrived, Spector had signed one act to Liberty, a black singer named Bobby Sheen, who was sent to him by Lester Sill. Sheen was, like Kell Osborne and Billy Storm, another in the Clyde McPhatter mold. Tall and thin, with a towering, pomade-juiced pompadour on top of his forehead, he was discovered by Johnny Otis, who guided his career before Sill used him in an offshoot edition of the Robins. Sheen had gone to high school in West Hollywood, and he vaguely knew Phil when they were teenagers, recalling him as "kind of doofish." No longer. Watching Phil at work in New York, Sheen was dazzled by Phil's darting, swarming energy and command of all before him. "He was push, push, push, let me do it, I can do it," said Sheen. "He could do anything. He was invincible."

However, Phil's work at Liberty was knocking nobody out. Nor did it seem to matter overly to Phil. Apart from two sides he cut with Sheen, and another with a singer named Troy Shondell—none of which dented the chart—Phil stirred mainly for non-Liberty concerns. The chart performance of "There's No Other (Like My Baby)" had much to do with this. By Christmas it had vaulted to No. 26, with plenty of steam left in it. As if on cue, Phil arose from his big desk in mid-January and journeyed to L.A. to cut Philles material with Jack Nitzsche at Gold Star—the site where he wanted to eventually make all of the Philles records. Before he left, though, he made a mental note about a girl group he had seen perform at a dance club. Called the Ronettes, they were a trio of caramel-skinned black girls from New York—two sisters and their cousin—who were signed with Don Kirshner's Dimension Records. Rare among the day's girl groups, the Ronettes advertised themselves with knee-length wigs and skirts slit to the hip as a mascara-caked vision of sexual paradise, and from what Phil heard, he thought they might be able to sing gritty blues, especially in the quivering, heaving voice of their sultry lead singer, Veronica Bennett. Phil promised himself that he would steal them from Dimension, where they were being regurgitated in a rut of larded white pop that misused their talents.

Eighteen-year-old Annette Merar, who had begun her freshman year at Cal State–Berkeley, transferred after one semester to UCLA just as Phil came to town. For two weeks, he took her out and about L.A., his obsession with her unnerving the Merar family. "My mom and dad didn't like Phil at all, because he would drive everybody crazy when we were dating," Annette recalled. "He'd scream and yell and bring me home at all hours of the night, call at ridiculous hours." Such disruptions led Annette to move in with her sister Renee in Hollywood. By then, Phil was ready to return to New York. He did not want to go without her. Believing in her heart that the two of them shared a deep and special love, Annette agreed to go with him. Hurriedly she threw clothes into suitcases and together they caught the flight back. For once, Phil had no trouble flying. "We made out the whole way," Annette said.

After moving into his apartment, Annette was inseparable from Phil. She went to the studio with him, copied and printed his lead sheets, and continued the idyllic conversations they'd had on the phone. About the only thing she didn't do was to sleep with him—literally—because even after they made love long into the night, Phil would not be able to sleep. "I'd usually be in bed way before him. He'd go to sleep at about 5 A.M. and get up at 10. I was up at his Liberty office real late one night and I went to sleep on the couch. I remember falling asleep watching him screaming his head off at somebody. I thought: Why does he always have to scream like that?"

This was no longer the Phil Spector of the capes, chukka boots, galoshes, and tousled, tangled hair. He was a figure of New York power now. As much as it pained him that his hair was receding rapidly, he now wore it neat and short, arranged by high-priced coiffeurs. On his bony body and in his closets at home, he boasted Italian seersucker suits, silk ties, and shiny leather boots. Once, with nothing to shield him from the New York cold, Phil had asked to borrow an overcoat from Beverly Ross, and wore it even though the buttons on the left marked it as women's wear. Now his own overcoats were made of fine cashmere. "I never saw him dress weird," Annette said. "He was dapper. I liked that, that cut-velvet vest and the silk socks. He was always very elegant."

The spoils of his success, however, were irrelevant to Annette. "I didn't go with Phil for his money. The part of him I loved most was his genius, seeing an idea develop and come to fruition. Phil Spector was the rock-and-roll Mozart, and he shared his plans and his dreams with me. Oh, yes, late at night he talked a *lot* about his dreams."

111

In early February of 1962, as "There's No Other" peaked at a very edifying No. 20, nearing the end of an eleven-week spurt, all of Phil's dreams circled around Philles Records. Seeking an edge on his competition, he conferred with Don Kirshner about a pooling of efforts between Philles and Aldon. There was much about Kirshner that Spector liked. In fact, they were intrinsically alike. Bearlike but with the plump cheeks of an infant, Kirshner was pathologically ambitious; a failure as a songwriter in the fifties, he drew vicarious satisfaction from owning outright the best young writers in pop music in the sixties. More than anyone else Kirshner had made rock and roll a profession rather than just a vehicle of rebellion, and his power was sultanlike: he could deign which labels and producers should have his catalogue—his writers' copyrighted material—and exact a price in return. His label, Dimension, allowed his writers— primarily Goffin and King—to produce some of their own songs. Like Spector, Kirshner could act like an overage child, and his pouting temper tantrums were notorious. But where Spector believed his own puerile side was a subterfuge, a hiding place for manipulation, he thought Kirshner to be somewhat naïve and malleable, and the idea of swaying and controlling Kirshner, with all his power, was arousing. And so Spector and Kirshner waltzed with each other, and in mutual recognition of their corpulent egos they half-facetiously called each other "The Kingpin." In late January Spector took one of Aldon's best new songs—Barry Mann and Cynthia Weil's "Uptown"—for his second Crystals record, but only after he agreed to put a lesser Aldon work, the Larry Kolber–Jack Keller "What a Nice Way to Turn Seventeen" on the flip side. Through Kirshner's largesse, Spector got to redeem at least part of the deal that Leiber and Stoller squashed a year before. He co-wrote (with free-lance writer Hank Hunter) and produced a Connie Francis record for MGM, "Second Hand Love," which went Top 10 in June.

Annette was privy to the Spector-Kirshner shadow dance and never thought the two would give enough to work in tandem. "Phil was gonna have an empire with Donnie Kirshner, but he was also very competitive with Donnie—Phil is competitive with everybody," she said. "His thing was, who's going to have the biggest empire, him or Donnie. That's how he talked—and, you know, if Phil weren't so talented he would sound like he was totally full of shit. But it was really true, he could think that way."

⊙

"Kirshner never spoke his true feelings about whether he liked or disliked Phil," Gerry Goffin said, "but he had a lot of respect for Phil because he liked his records and he was a great vehicle for us. And Phil knew Kirshner could motivate Carole and me and Barry and Cynthia to write. Kirshner would call and say, 'Phil needs a song' and we'd be hot to do it. So those two really got a lot out of each other."

Kirshner confided much about his dealings with Spector to Lester Sill. "Donnie never trusted him," according to Sill.

It was a feeling that Lester himself would come to know during the early months of 1962. "I began to smell things falling out a little bit with Phil," he said.

This happened once it was clear that "There's No Other" was a hit and Phil followed it up with a personal *tour de force*—his production of "Uptown." The record that he took out of Mira Sound was like an oil painting of Spanish Harlem, now hued in frustration and not just the innocent charm of the Jerry Leiber-Spector work. Phil's tableau of brooding violins, cellos, mandolins, and castanets was an echo of the Leiber-Stoller black/Latin Drifters idiom. But it was much more urgent and restless, and it gave an aching anxiety to a lyric that Barry Mann and Cynthia Weil intended to be high-mindedly liberal but unwittingly branded *barrio* men as docile and addicted to servility—the protagonist dutifully shuffled downtown each morning to be a little man in a world "where everyone's his boss." Spector saved it with the intense, sensual beauty of every note.

Watching the session from inside the booth, Gerry Goffin was knocked out by the song. He asked Phil who wrote it, and Phil said, "I did." Not until later did Goffin learn otherwise. "The weird thing was, it was the kind of lie Phil knew he'd be caught on," Goffin said. "I never understood why he told lies like that. Maybe he thought he could *make* it his if he said it was." Released in March, "Uptown" would rise as high as No. 13 in *Billboard*, No. 10 in *Cash Box*, by early June.

As it climbed, Phil produced only one record for Liberty, with a singer named Obrey Wilson. As Al Bennett feared, his commitment to the label was only transitory. Snuff Garrett, in fact, heard from Spector just once after the new year—when Phil complained that the plants in his office weren't being watered by the Liberty staff. He did try to cut a Liberty record with the Ducanes, but with ill results. "Liberty tried to tie Phil's hands, they didn't give him the creative freedom he needed," said Eddie Brian, one of the Ducanes. "Phil couldn't stand Liberty. They wanted us to do a country-western song called 'Tennessee.' You don't give a song like that to New Jersey teenagers who sing doo-wop. A Liberty executive came in during a rehearsal as we were making fun of it with cow and pig noises. After that, we were out on our asses. They gave the song to Jan and Dean, and they had to flop with it."

As Annette read Phil, however, his discontent had more to do with personal than creative freedom.

"Phil just didn't like working for anybody but himself," she said.

Again working in his own interest, Phil cut a third Crystals record in May. As with "Uptown," Don Kirshner held the option on both sides. The A side was a Goffin-King work with the lurid and provocative title of "He Hit Me (and It Felt Like a Kiss)," and it was the most literally bruising love/pain theme of all by the tortured couple. Goffin explained that the song grew from a sob story they heard from their live-in babysitter, Eva Boyd—the teenage girl who, as Little Eva, sang the Goffin-King "The Loco-Motion," a No. 1 hit that Goffin produced for Dimension in mid-1962. "She had this boyfriend and she was off for the weekend and when she came home she was all black and blue. She said, 'He hit me and that must mean he really loves me.' " The Goffin-King lyric echoed that sentiment. Years later, Goffin would allow that the tune was "a little radical for those times."

So too was Spector's arrangement, which seemed to justify violence against women as a way to true love. The song began with an ominous drum-and-bell thudding that sounded as if it could be a fist hitting bone, then lifted in a crescendo of stringed *schmaltz* as the girl realized how lucky she was to have her brute. The ending was a prayerlike font of soprano voices echoing into silence, the girl's blessing.

Hearing this bizarre vinyl soap opera, Lester Sill was horrified. "I hated that record," he said. "I got into a big fight with him over it. I thought it was a terrible fucking song."

Gerry Goffin, immersed in his and his wife's personal obsession with battered and bruised romance—"It was the mood we were in, a phase we were going through," he said—clearly found Spector to be an indirect inspiration and direct market for the darker themes. "Phil was sort of a masochist himself," he said. Asked by Spector to write material for the Crystals after "Uptown," Goffin and King not only gave him "He Hit Me" but two other harrowing songs: "No One Ever Tells You" and "Please Hurt Me." Spector took all three, using "No One Ever Tells You" as the flip side of "He Hit Me" and saving "Please Hurt Me" for an upcoming Crystals album.

And yet the caricature of Phil Spector as a physical beast was not one that Annette could recognize. "That was just a good song," she said. "Phil thought it was a great hook, and he never had any other musical rationale than what was a good song. Yes, Phil is definitely a sadist—but of the mind, not the body. He was a gentle lover, a very fine lover. He was not a ferocious tiger who was some kind of a crazy sadist in the bedroom."

In June, Phil called Al Bennett and said he was quitting Liberty Records. He told Bennett he was "burned out" and was going on a sabbatical to Spain, to get his head together. Phil, who padded his alibi for weeks by registering for a Spanish study course at Berlitz and ostentatiously leaving the language school's pamphlets all around his office, left Liberty with no apparent inclination to pay back any portion of his $30,000 advance. Like Jerry Wexler, Al Bennett and Snuff Garrett knew they had been had.

For Garrett, it was a kick in the pants. "It was my deal, I brought him in, and I felt bad about it not workin' out," he said. "That's the only thing in my life that never worked out well. But my reaction was: who cares? That it didn't work out didn't mean anything to me. All I knew was that I knew Spec was a talent and I really liked Spec a lot and we had fun, man."

Spector and Garrett would never hook up again, but they had a chance reckoning with fate just weeks later.

8

The group has a winning sound on this new ballad. They handle it with much feeling over a martial-styled big ork background that builds. Watch this one.

—*Billboard* review of "He's a Rebel"

Phil did not walk out on Liberty until he had two must-do items checked off on his list of priorities. One was the courting of the Ronettes. Phil preferred not to deal with Don Kirshner on this one, and indeed never let on that he was interested in them. Instead, so convinced was he that he and the group were right for each other, he wanted to have no ties and no conditions in connection with their services. When Phil found out that the Ronettes were doing session work as background singers, he passed the word that he wanted them to contact him—but that they should not be told his identity. Although Phil loved these kind of secret games, it is likely that Kirshner would not have objected to letting the Ronettes go, since their records for Dimension under the name of Ronnie and the Relatives and the Heartbreakers were failures. In fact, Kirshner had asked Gerry Goffin to produce the group. Unimpressed with them, Goffin said no.

"I remember going through rehearsals with them and trying to get them to sing harmonies and they seemed pretty terrible," Goffin said. "I turned 'em down because I couldn't stand Ronnie's voice."

Born on Manhattan's Upper West Side, Veronica and Estelle Bennett and their younger cousin, Nedra Talley, began singing as the Darling Sisters, playing local hops in flare dresses and ponytails. The hardening of their image came when they started dancing for pay in New York's Peppermint Lounge during the twist craze. Their name was changed to the Ronettes—a fusing of their first names— as they danced on the holiday rock shows hosted by the influential New York deejay Murray "The K" Kaufman at Brooklyn's Fox and Paramount theaters. Their recording career was less fruitful. Signed to Columbia Records' Colpix label, then to Dimension, they were handled for Kirshner by a capable producer named Stu Phillips, and also appeared in the movie *Rock Around the Clock*. But their records, candy-coated gruel with titles like "I Want a Boy" and "What's So Sweet About Sweet Sixteen," kept them obscure. Eventually, Phillips quit Dimension after a spat with Kirshner, and the girls had little to do but work outside sessions.

On one such gig, they got a message with a number to call for more work. They called and were put through to Phil. "When he came on, it was not who we expected," Nedra Talley recalled, "and he told us to meet him at Mira Sound. We went, and not much later we were recording as an act for him." Their ears ringing by his promises of stardom, recording much better material with a super-star producer, they didn't bother to terminate their Dimension contract. At Spector's behest, they told the Dimension people they were quitting the business—an alibi delivered at about the same time Phil gave a similar story to Al Bennett. "We weren't pulling any hits where we were," Talley reasoned, "and if you have another situation, you go with what reeks of success."

On May 26, mere days after he quit Liberty, the Ronettes were with Phil in L.A. and cutting demos at Gold Star, a process that would determine what kind of material he would want to put out when the time came. For now, though, that time was not yet close. To lend credence to the lie about them quitting the business, and pending what he knew would be long months of drilling them to be his big act, he put the Ronettes on the back burner. Knowing he had them under contract was good enough.

The second factor that hastened his departure from Liberty was the sure-fire song he had been waiting for. Finally, in June, it came—from the recipient of one of his favors: Aaron Schroeder. Schroeder played him a demo Gene Pitney had made of a new song he had written, "He's a Rebel." Though Spector did not know it, there was irony in him coming upon the song. "Uptown" had led Pitney to write it. " 'Uptown' was the first song where I ever heard anyone use funky strings like that and especially low strings, violas and cellos down that low," he said. "I fell in love with it and it hit me. I said, 'I'm gonna write their next single, another song they could do just like that."

An idea came out of a mind reflex, a sudden memory of a tune Pitney had heard years before, "something with the word 'rebel' in it. It was goin' around in my head for some reason and I thought, wow, what a great word, a great color word to use in a song. Twice I tried and twice I trashed it. Then I hit the groove and I knew I had a winner." Pitney's demo, with its recycled James Dean movie theme ("He is always good to me / Always treats me tenderly / 'Cause he's not a rebel, no-no-no / He's not a rebel no-no-no, to me"), was so catchy that the Crystals' tie-in was forgotten. "That had kinda faded out of my mind," Pitney said. "The first time Phil heard it was when he came by looking for material. But Phil did always get the A material. For most A&R guys, or guys like a Stan Shulman, Aaron would pull out the C material, fair stuff you'd say was great, or if a guy didn't know what he was after he might take. Phil always knew what he wanted. He'd come in and say, 'Don't play me the crap.' He'd listen to maybe eight songs and he'd know right away if something was there.

"The minute he heard 'Rebel,' his eyes lit up. He was still with Liberty and that's when the fun began. He may have been there on a fishing trip for Liberty, but he knew he was gonna cut it himself. And Aaron used to give people exclusives on songs. He'd say, 'Exclusive, you got it, I won't show this to anybody'—but then when the guy was out the door he'd give exclusives to everybody."

Knowing Schroeder's method full well, Spector took no chances. As soon as he got "He's a Rebel," he was gone from Liberty and on his way to Gold Star to make the record of his life. "That was so Phil Spector, going through all that to do one session," Gene Pitney mused. "But he knew what he had in his hand, and I think he would've gone through anything to get that onto a disc."

"All I knew was that he had to go to Gold Star right away," Annette Merar remembered. "He didn't say why, he just knew he had to make that record there."

One specific reason for the shift of scenery were the problems Phil had been having with the musicians' union in New York, the American Federation of Musicians Local 82, concerning his known use of overdubbing; although the technique was becoming common-place, union leadership was resisting it on grounds that no session should be without a working quorum of musicians, and full accep-tance was still years away. Similar resistance existed in L.A., but there monitoring was less likely due to the city's size. In New York, studios rubbed elbows along Broadway, and the chance that a union snoop could walk in while he was cutting just strings or vocals put Phil under minor but growing duress. "He would have to be surrep-titious about it," recalled Michael Spencer, who was married now and still booking and playing on Phil's New York sessions. "We would do vocal tracks but wouldn't use them. He'd come back at 2 A.M. with the girls to put the real vocals on. It was a hassle. He would tell me that the union was driving him out of town."

If so, he did not need to be pushed far. Already making demos at Gold Star, Spector was constantly aware that his two biggest hits had been made there, in Studio A, a room he still adored for its acoustics and echo chambers. He never considered moving out of New York—there was no change in the centralization of the music industry, and the sway he had now in the big city was an ongoing high—but "He's a Rebel" had to be cut in Studio A.

"He called me and said to get a band together in a matter of days," recalled Steve Douglas, who had booked several Spector dates in L.A. Douglas, the saxophone player Phil had once begged to jam with in West Hollywood, was more and more becoming a product of Spector's domain. After Douglas booked some Paris Sisters ses-sions, Lester Sill signed him to a production deal. Cutting his own records on the Philles label in early 1962, Sill produced two instru-mentals under the name of Steve Douglas and His Merry Men, the A side a version of the *Bridge on the River Kwai* movie theme song.

Phil went out on such short notice that he not only didn't wait for Stan Ross to return from a Hawaiian vacation, he didn't wait for the Crystals, whose record this was to be. At first, when the Crystals refused to make the trip because they didn't want to fly, Phil looked frantically to alternatives. "I'm comin' out there and those son of a bitches won't come out. I gotta get some girls," he told Lester over the phone. Sill was nonplussed. There was a wealth of black soul singers around L.A. One group, a trio called the Blossoms, were very hot background singers; they were the chorale on Ed Townsend's "For Your Love" and Sam Cooke's "Everybody Likes to Cha-Cha-Cha," and Sill had used them as the "Rebelettes" on Duane Eddy's "Dance with the Guitar Man." They weren't teenagers but they were versatile enough to pass.

"Phil, I'm tellin' you," Lester assured him, "with the song that we got, these girls are better than the Crystals. They're adults; you can bend them and do what you want with 'em."

Legally, Spector and Sill could use proxies, since Philles owned the Crystals name. If a moral issue was involved, Spector in particular was undisturbed. "Phil thought of everybody he worked with as his puppet," Annette believed. "He was immoral or amoral about things like that. He did connect with me on a human level, but except for me he didn't like people at all. He treated people like shit."

Phil also had to be reassured about a new engineer. When he booked the studio time, Stan Ross said he might not be in town then. Agitated, Phil asked him, "Who's been working for you?"

"I got Larry," Stan said.

"Who the hell is Larry?" Phil raged.

"You know Larry. Larry Levine. He's my cousin. He works here."

A year older than Ross, Larry Levine had worked at Gold Star since the mid-fifties, and he engineered Eddie Cochran's "Summertime Blues" and Toni Fischer's "The Big Hurt." On the latter, Levine—by accident, as was generally the case with engineering trickery—helped establish a milestone in overdubbing; layering a copy of the tape over the original at a slightly different speed, it caused an in-and-out "phasing" effect that Levine wanted to redo but later came to characterize the record. Levine had also done vocal overdubbing similar to Spector's, with the Pied Pipers. Yet as much as Spector was at Gold Star, he and Levine had not met, and for Levine that was intentional. "From what I saw of Phil, I didn't like him," he said. "He just seemed like a spoiled brat, and this was when he was coming in with the Teddy Bears. His personality was so grating. It's apropos, 'To Know Him Is to Love Him,' because without knowing him, there's no way to love him. As a mild acquaintance, he's totally abrasive."

To calm Phil, Stan lied that he'd see if he could get back for the date, but at the July 13 session for "He's a Rebel," the engineer was Larry Levine.

Except for Howard Roberts and Ray Pohlman, most of the musicians that Steve Douglas came in with on short notice that day had not worked a Spector session before. Phil, more and more stuck on the concept of bigness as his rock-and-roll mother lode, wanted to double up on the basic rhythm, thus Roberts was paired with guitarist Tommy Tedesco, Pohlman with bassist Jimmy Bond—and the request for a second bass bewildered Douglas. "Two bass players was ridiculous," he thought. "*Nobody* used two bass players." Two other new pieces were pianist Al DeLory and drummer Hal Blaine, and Blaine had to rush in off a road tour he had been on with singer Peggy Lee. Phil did not want to be caught that cold with the vocalists; in addition to Blossoms Darlene Wright, Fanita James, and Gloria Jones, he had brought with him a girlish-sounding voice that he knew: Bobby Sheen.

The arrangement that Phil dictated to Jack Nitzsche was, as ever, threadbare, and Larry Levine, like others before him, had to get used to Spector's grueling balancing and feeling-out procedure—which, with more instruments, was even more tedious and brutal for the guitar players. "You just didn't know what was gonna happen until he had his guitars playing," Levine said. "They'd play the first four bars over and over and he'd have 'em play fifth notes and then change it to sixteenths. He'd start the guitars, add instruments, then take 'em away and start the guitars all over again. Everyone else was waiting for his turn, but the guitars never got a break. Howard Roberts played for hours on end that day, and I remember him saying that his wrist was killing him."

"Howard's fingers were bleeding," Hal Blaine recalled. "He said, 'I can't take it anymore.'"

While Gene Pitney intended "He's a Rebel" to include strings, his stringless demo was so good as it was that Spector cut the song as pure, jazzy-licked blues-rock. The orchestration shook Studio A. Turned loose to improvise much of their parts after hours of antsy waiting around, Al DeLory played an itchy be-bop piano figure from end to end, Hal Blaine played a cascade of stylish drum fills and Douglas a blazing sax solo when the recorder was finally turned on for the actual take. In the booth, Phil listened to the playback at his usual ear-numbing levels—"We just looked at each other, like, how can he hear anything?" said Douglas. "It just sounded like a roar"—knowing he not only had made a great record, he found something indefinable in the synergy of a big band, Gold Star's acoustics and his own perfectionism: a large sound that hung together in one piece, with no drops or drifts or wasted echoes. A sound that would pour out of a transistor radio like cake batter.

"We all knew we were listening to something different," Douglas said. "I remember how excited Phil was, he was glowing. We all were, but Phil was so happy with the band, and especially with Hal Blaine. He just fell in love with Hal."

A dissenter in the midst of the love-fest was Howard Roberts. He had decided that he'd had enough of Phil Spector.

"You have to understand that the guitars were primitive and rough to play then," Roberts said. "A twelve-string guitar had a huge neck and you had five hundred pounds of pressure on the strings. And the kind of thing Phil was into was to let all the chords ring as long as possible. You'd never take your hand off the fingerboard, just keep it down under maximum pressure. When we'd play a thing through, my hand would be about to fall off."

As bad as the physical pain, Roberts still found little challenge for a top jazzman in Spector's method. Unable to peer into Phil's mind of musical subtlety, and as much as Phil believed jazz players would give simple white chords a jazz varnish, it was still just rock and roll to Roberts. "If there is ever a decline in Western civilization, that period of music will be high on the list of causes. After coming out of a period of Jerome Kern and like that, it was like being thrown back to the dark ages to play stuff I played when I was eight years old.

"I would come to a Phil Spector date after having been at Twentieth Century-Fox with Alfred Newman or Hugo Friedhofer, playing with some of the world's great orchestras. There, you'd walk

⊙

in and see music that was virtually impossible to play at first glance—and you played it perfectly the first time. Those people knew not to overwork the orchestra, because stress produces mistakes. Once you've mastered something, the worst thing is repetition. But Phil was using repetition, it seemed to me, to get his piece figured out."

Then there was Spector himself. The polite fifteen-year-old who sat in Roberts's living room was now "aloof, very distant, there was no more closeness. Phil slipped into that Never-Never Land of Hollywood success and really strange weirdness, and I never saw him again after that. Even when I was seeing him, I couldn't see him."

When Phil first heard Darlene Wright sing, he forgot about Barbara Alston and the real Crystals. Toothsome and with hair dyed bright orange, Wright at twenty-four years of age sang the "Rebel" lead as a convincing teenager, smug and sarcastic, but her gospel-oriented vivacity humanized and broadened the pubescent aspect of the lyric. Wright's was a loud, powerful voice, and if she lacked heartfelt romantic emotion and wasn't suited to love ballads, she could do anything else. The daughter of a Pentecostal minister, she was singing in a church wedding when Fanita James heard her and began using her as the lead singer of the Blossoms, who had been found and originally managed by Johnny Otis. The group recorded for Capitol from 1958 to 1961, then on Challenge and Okeh before making their mark as a background unit. Given $3,000 to do the "Rebel" lead that she thought of as nothing more than bubble-gum music, Darlene split the money with Fanita, continuing a practice she had started with the Blossoms. Fanita, with Gloria Jones and Bobby Sheen, had received a standard session fee. The session done, Wright doubted if she would ever see the little sprite producer again.

Only weeks later, she and Sheen signed personal services contracts with Philles Records.

With the tapes of "He's a Rebel," Spector and Sill rushed out of Gold Star to the well-equipped United–Western Sound Studios to make the master of the song. As they worked in United's Studio A, musicians on a break from a session in Studio B drifted out into the hall. "One by one they came in and heard our record. They said, 'Hey, man, we were just playing the same goddamn song!' " Lester Sill remembered.

Sill and Spector stiffened in surprise when they heard this. Aaron Schroeder had indeed given a second "exclusive" on "He's a Rebel"—and it went to none other than Snuff Garrett and Liberty Records. Garrett, in Studio B, was cutting the tune with soft-pop singer Vikki Carr.

"By the time Snuff finished recording, our master was in the bath and done," Sill said. "I heard his record and I said to Snuff, 'You don't have a chance.' "

Garrett was purple-faced, incensed not at Phil as much as he was at Schroeder. "Aaron screwed us on the song, and I stopped doing business with him for a while after that," Garrett related. "I wouldn't have done that to Spec for anything, and I don't think he would've done it to me *intentionally*. That's not the way it played between us. I didn't know he had the song and I don't think he knew I had it—or else he knew I had it because Schroeder tipped him and he went and cut it. I wouldn't blame him for runnin' with it."

Learning about Garrett's record, Phil issued a terse order to Lester's stepson, Chuck Kaye, who had been recently put to work doing promotion for Philles.

"Bury it," he told Chuck.

Pitching the Crystals' version of "He's a Rebel"—hardly a difficult chore to begin with given that a Phil Spector record was now like a gold doubloon—Chuck found himself pitted against longtime Liberty promotion man Tommy LiPuma. "Tommy had a gimpy leg," Kaye recalled, "and we were both outside the building where KFWB was with our records. I got ours played first solely because I could beat him up the stairs." Chuck was young and green, but he had been taught the tricks of record hustling by the best, his father, one of the first rock-and-roll song-pluggers. Snuff Garrett found out how sly Chuck Kaye was.

"The thing that made me maddest out of the whole thing," Garrett said, "was not Spec or anybody else but Lester Sill's son out on the road and tellin' everybody that I went in and 'covered' that song. Because that was a fuckin' lie. I never knew anybody else had the song, but he was out there hawkin' the deejays and sayin' how the big giant Liberty was covering the little bitty Philles."

With the Crystals' record on the market first, Liberty tried to retrench by taking out huge ads in the trade papers heralding the Vikki Carr record as "The Original! The Hit!" However, when both records were on playlists, Snuff Garrett's plight was pitiable, framed

⊙

by the serious mismatch he faced in Spector's finest work to date. "Ours crashed and burned on takeoff," Garrett remembered mournfully.

Phil could fully anticipate a hit with "Rebel," and it was released even though "He Hit Me," out only a couple of weeks, was just beginning to make a move. However, "He Hit Me" quickly became Philles' first misstep. Although it was played freely by stations all over the country at the beginning, some major station chains and national networks—with outlets in most big cities—were getting mail protesting the all-too-stark imagery of male violence against women. Spector and Sill knew this kind of publicity could not help Philles, and with "He Hit Me" just outside the Top 100, they yanked it off the market and recalled thousands of copies from store shelves before a large storm could ferment. Now "He's a Rebel" became doubly important, and because it would no longer have to compete with another Crystals record, Phil and a grateful Lester barely blinked at the loss of "He Hit Me." "Rebel" would be *big*.

However, just as exciting to Phil as individual records now was that incredible sound he'd unearthed at Gold Star. He returned to Studio A a month later, after picking a song he could get crazy with in that studio, something that could *really* take off with that monster block of alloyed rhythm. Phil by passed all the usual song sources for it—Kirshner, Schroeder, even Mother Bertha. Instead, he went to Walt Disney for "Zip-A-Dee-Doo-Dah" from the 1946 Disney movie *Song of the South*. "The memory of that song is so strong to me," Annette said. "It was at the time of the Bay of Pigs invasion, and I can still see Phil working on it, expanding it. He was fooling around on the guitar and the song popped into his head. He played the riff and said, 'I'm gonna make this a hit,' and before I knew it, it was a record. He did that all the time, and whenever he did it was like every man's dream come true, to have an idea and then create something with it."

The session was on August 24, a Saturday, and Stan Ross was again away. Larry Levine was astonished when Spector came in with a cavalry of musicians and began going through his repetitive paces. Phil had two guitarists—Billy Strange on electric and John Anderson on acoustic—and *three* different-sounding basses: Jimmy Bond played a big upright, Wallick Dean a higher-pitched Fender, and Carole

Kaye—the first female musician on a Spector date—a crisp-toned Danelectro. Al DeLory was back on piano, but he shared the bench with another player; DeLory played half of the keyboard, Nino Tempo the other half. Steve Douglas, on tenor sax, was paired with another horn player, Jay Migliori, who played baritone sax. Only Hal Blaine and percussionist Frank Capp played by themselves.

"It was a mob," Levine recalled, "and Phil started in and he has me raising this up and that up and adding this and that and making it louder—'Bring up the bass, bring up the guitar.' We're like three hours into the session now and we're still just rehearsing, and all my meters are pinning, they're just stuck over on the end and I know I can't go on with that but I don't know what to do. Phil is Phil, he's gotta do it his way, but I can't record that way because it's too loud and it'll all be distorted. So, finally, I turned everything down, turned all the mikes off."

The suddenly-mute control booth hit Phil like a slap in the face. "What the hell are you doing!" he screeched at Levine. "I just about had the sound! I just about had it and you ruined it! Three hours and you ruined it!"

Levine, a big but mild-mannered man, tried to explain why he couldn't record. Phil turned away from him and slumped deep in his chair, saying nothing. As Spector pouted, Levine swallowed hard and began bringing in the instruments again, aping Spector's odd routine as best he could. "I started at a level around zero on the meter and I brought each of the parts in, fitting it all together like Phil would." Just before Levine got to the final element, Billy Strange's electric guitar solo, Phil came to life.

"That's the sound!" he cried. "Let's record!"

"But I don't have Billy's make in yet," Larry told him.

"Don't turn it on!" Phil said, meaning Strange's microphone. "That's the sound, just like you have it. Let's record!"

Levine wanted to label the tape. He asked Phil what the name of the song was. "He said it's 'Zip-A-Dee-Doo-Dah' and I thought he was joking. The whole room is shaking with this *boom-boom-boom* and he's telling me it's a kid's song. When I realized he was serious, I fell off my chair. So I rolled the tape, saying 'Zip-A-Dee-Doo-Dah,' take one—and that's all it took, one take."

When Strange did his solo on the bridge, his amp leaked into all the live microphones and it came out a fuzzy, tinny coil of disembodied noise. "Phil didn't care," Levine said. "He didn't care what

⊙   126

the break was gonna sound like. We played a full chorus before we got to the break, and you don't sell a song with a solo on a break. Phil heard it, that was enough." It was also opportune. The guitar solo was so funky that it would be the lure for many who heard the song.

In actuality, it was only when Bobby Sheen, with Darlene Wright and Fanita James doing the backing, laid in a fabulously emotive lead was the song discernible as the Disney classic. The melody simply offered Phil the chance to erect the most deafening instrumental effect he could, and the clanking *chink-a-chink* beat was more Bo Diddley than Mickey Mouse. As a rock-and-roll form, it was a dip into the still-to-be-tested waters of metal-rock. "That was one record I knew absolutely was a smash," said Levine, whose baptism by fire earned him a loyalty from Phil that few humans knew. Though Phil never told Larry how much he valued him, the message of "Zip-A-Dee-Doo-Dah" was implicit: Larry Levine was now Phil Spector's engineer.

Phil had to know for himself if the record was sellable. He took it back to New York and, saying he wanted to sell the master, played it all around Broadway. To a man, everyone he played it for thought it couldn't miss. After hearing only eight bars, Stan Shulman lifted the needle off the record and offered to buy the master for $10,000. Spector smiled and Shulman thought they had a deal.

"I don't think there was anything vicious about Phil when he led people on like that," Gene Pitney said, "but Phil was not a straight-ahead type of a guy. That's part of his creative mentality. I can just picture him going in and saying 'Yeah, man, we'll do it, great,' and the people he said that to didn't forget it like he did."

"Phil told me, jokingly, that he had to put the record out because everybody, on both coasts, had already heard it," Levine said. "That's because when he was in New York, I was playing it for everybody who came into Gold Star. It would knock your ass off, the way it sounded. You could hear the total joy of it."

It was now mid-September. "He's a Rebel"—released with a very crowded label, including the names of Spector, Jack Nitzsche, and Larry Levine—had hit the chart on the dead run, with not a bullet so much as a rocket. "Zip-A-Dee-Doo-Dah" was in the wings. Riding an emotional crest, Phil made a critical decision, one that would strain the limits of his impudence.

Lester Sill had to be purged from Philles Records.

9

Jerry Wexler and Jerry Leiber told me this long before I was aware of it. They said, "He's a snake, he'll stab his own mother in the back to get ahead."

—LESTER SILL

By the time "He's a Rebel" came out, Phil's peevish independence had eaten away the partnership with Lester Sill. Lester heard from Phil infrequently and never could reach him on business matters. Phil started to sign papers and make some moves regarding Philles without informing Lester, moves that could reach all the way down to minor changes in distributors. While the Philles office was in L.A., Phil was making it clear that he considered the office to be wherever he happened to be. When Sill could get through, Phil would be tense, curt, and would ring off quickly. If Phil was in L.A., he would call and arrange a meeting, then fail to show. Lester knew what was going down.

"The problem was, when it got to the point where it was a

⊙

successful venture, he didn't want anybody around him," Sill said. "He felt no one else was carrying his weight—creatively, no one carried his weight with Phil."

Though he said nothing to Lester, in his private moments Phil was foaming about ridding himself of his onetime mentor and godfather figure. If it was Sill's benevolence and stability that began Philles Records, he reasoned, it was his own genius that got it off the ground. Spitting venom in Sill's direction, it was as if he thought he could further convince himself. "It was a vicious thing," Annette would remember. "He was saying, 'I want Lester out. It's my juices he's riding on. He's a parasite, I want to be on my own,' and all like that. He wanted it all to himself. Phil wants total power, total control. He had no guilt about it. He just put Lester down and that was it."

When he caught on that Phil felt this way, Lester did not go away meekly. Insulted by Spector's arrogance, he made adversarial gestures of his own. Sill had been cutting his own stuff for Philles, recording unknown singers and instrumentals like Steve Douglas's. Phil hated these records and was offended that they broke the Philles string of Crystals hits. Knowing of Phil's discontent over the records, Lester went on making them. "I knew they were shitty records, and I did it for a reason. I intended it to be a personal affront, only because I couldn't stand his fucking attitude and I wanted to aggravate his ass. I knew it was breaking up. I knew it was over."

In September 1962, Sill and Harry Finfer were in New York on business when they both got word from Harold Lipsius that Phil was going to force the issue. They were told Phil would call Lester's hotel room and that they both should be there. As Sill and Finfer waited for the call, recriminations flew. "Harry got mad at me because he thought I was in on a plot with Phil and Harold to get rid of him," Sill recalled. Lester, meanwhile, suspected Lipsius carried a dagger for both of them. "Harold helped Phil get me out. When the call came, it was from Harold, and Phil was with him. Harold was already unhappy with Harry, and this was an excuse for him to get rid of Harry at the same time Phil did me in."

It certainly abetted Phil's purge that Lipsius and Finfer had fallen out and were connected now only by Philles Records. Recently Finfer had stunned Lipsius by quitting Universal Distributing and selling out of Jamie Records—though his Philles override remained. Like Helen Noga, Finfer felt aggrandized wearing the Philles wreath; not only did he want to do things with Spector, he now wanted to run his own independent labels as well. He even sent memos to the trade press claiming that he was "running" Philles, which riled Spector, Sill, and'Lipsius. But when Lipsius agreed to Phil's buy-out offer, it meant that Finfer was automatically out and left Phil with two-thirds of the stock. An inducement for Lipsius was that Phil retained Universal as national distributor for Philles.

When Lipsius told Sill and Finfer that he was stepping aside and that Sill should work out a buy-out deal with Phil, Lester did not capitulate easily. "Harry had a handshake deal with Lipsius, and Lipsius paid him off, but I wasn't gonna take anything from Phil right then, because to me, no matter what it was it wouldn't have been enough." Eventually, though, Sill gave in and agreed to talk about a buy-out.

"What do you want?" Spector asked him.

"Look, Phil," Sill said, "I'm not gonna just walk away from this thing, because I started it."

Impatiently Phil repeated, "What do you want?"

Goaded into exasperation, Lester grunted. "Look, you figure it out," he said, and told him to base it on a year's royalties. But in the end, he got nothing close to that.

"I sold out for a pittance," he recalled. "It was shit, ridiculous, around $60,000. I didn't want to but I had to. Let me tell you, I couldn't live with Phillip. I could've been a millionaire with this guy—don't forget, I owned half of Mother Bertha. I owned all those masters, and if I'd held on to them, he would've had to start a new company. But I just wanted the fuck out of there. If I wouldn't have, I would've killed him. It wasn't worth the aggravation. No matter how important it was, it wasn't that important. I didn't even want a lawyer. I said, 'Send me the check.' "

Sill's haste proved costly. "I made the mistake of signing the paper before I got my check, because I trusted him." Months later, still with no check, Sill met with Spector in Phil's apartment. When he walked in, he again had to go up against both Phil and Harold Lipsius. Lipsius, a lawyer, was now advising Phil on legal matters. Phil was prepared for Lester's demand for payment, and his rationale for holding back on it stretched far back in time—to Lester's refusal to cough up royalties on the discarded Paris Sisters' album.

Only now did it become clear how much of a grudge Phil had nursed against Lester.

"Phil wants to see some figures," Lipsius told Sill, who went over them again and again but could not elicit a promise from Spector to pay up. Reaching an impasse, Sill hired a lawyer and sued Phil Spector.

A short while later, in late January of 1963, Phil went into Mira Sound with the Crystals, Michael Spencer, and two other musicians and cut a song titled "Let's Dance the Screw Part 1 and 2." The record was not intended for release, and the only person who received a copy was Lester Sill.

"He wanted to get me," Sill said. "That was him saying 'Fuck you, buddy.'"

Incredibly, Chuck Kaye stayed on as Philles promotion man, working out of Lester's new office in a converted bowling alley on Hollywood's El Centro Avenue. "Phil wanted me to continue," Kaye said. "We'd been pals since we were teenagers and he tried to separate the business end from the fact that he knifed my father in the back. And my dad was great. He thought it was a great opportunity for me. Philles was the hottest label in the country."

At the El Centro office, there was a strange combination of bad blood and mixed blood. While Sill feuded with Spector, his son and two of his salaried assistants—Steve Douglas and now Jack Nitzsche—went on working Spector's sessions. Nitzsche had a philosopher's name and a Huck Finn face, he wore thick black-framed eyeglasses and his dark hair swooped forward over his eyes like a sheepdog's. Spector asked a lot from his arrangers—his long hours and capricious chart alterations during sessions had driven away a number of past conductors in a jumble of frayed nerves—but Nitzsche had an intuitive sense of where Phil was going, and he had endurance. Like an athlete, Nitzsche would dart from musician to musician, translating Phil's whim to notes on paper. Out of the studio, Phil would awaken him at ungodly hours and call him to ungodly motels because Spector wanted to develop an arrangement.

Nitzsche's sweat and stamina surely was not bought with money— Spector paid him just $50 per chart. For Nitzsche, Spector was an icon, a solitary man making a rock-and-roll testament and changing the industry's rules purely because of his love of music. Nitzsche was not without self-interest, of course—"The label credits he gave me got me jobs in this business for years," he said—but Phil Spector was the fountainhead. Spector was there, he was king, he knew the business, but never did he give an inch in creating what he had to.

"In those days, A&R men would hire me for a three-hour session and we had to get it done in that time," Nitzsche said. "But if Phil needed two sessions to do his rhythm section, that's the way it happened. Maybe other producers liked their records; Phil *loved* his records.

"Phil really was the artist, and it wasn't just out of ego. Phil understood the teenage market, he related to their feelings and impulses. It was like he was a kid himself—he'd call me at 4 A.M. and want ice cream—and he could commit those impulses artistically like nobody else."

Seven weeks after its release, "He's a Rebel," backed with a Spector song called "I Love You Eddie," sat at No. 3. The next week, in early November, it was No. 1. It would stay there, looking down at every other piece of grooved vinyl in the United States, for three weeks, and it would not fall out of the Top 10 for another three weeks—nor out of the Top 40 until Christmas.

Just before "Zip-A-Dee-Doo-Dah"—under the name of Bob B. Soxx and the Blue Jeans—was released in early November, Ray Peterson split with Stan Shulman. Dunes Records had done $11 million in business in 1961, thanks in large part to Spector, but Peterson was paid very little of it. "That was my record company, I was vice president," he said. "It was supposed to be 50–50, but Stan became extremely greedy. He was cheatin' me. I found out that he was keepin' two sets of books. I told him, 'You pushed me around but you're never gonna do it again!' I was so angry I threw him against the wall, this marine.

"I told Phil about it. We sat in my car for three hours and I said, 'Phil, I'm leavin' Stan and I don't want to see the same thing happen to you. Stay away from him.' "

Phil was so angry that he told Shulman he was going to sell him the "Zip-A-Dee-Doo-Dah" master. Shulman ran around the Brill Building boasting that he had a smash Dunes record. Only days later Shulman heard it on the radio, soon to be a smash Philles record.

One facet of the record would become a Spector trademark for two years, and it was indelibly Spector-like: the B side, "Flip and Nitty," was not a real song but rather a few impromptu licks played by the band at the very end of a session. By attaching these shams, Phil knew he would not run the risk of a deejay flipping over a record and would instead focus all attention on his uncompromised work. Not incidentally, Phil could also collect up to a quadruple royalty by taking a writer's credit on the bogus side and publishing it through Mother Bertha. Or he could use the trick to reward a favored musician by listing him as writer. Several times Phil would list Shirley as writer—helping to pay the bills for her periodic stays in the psychiatric ward of a Palo Alto hospital, which he considered his responsibility—or Annette.

"Zip-A-Dee-Doo-Dah" got as high as No. 8, in early January. By then Spector and his "little bitty label" were so hot that, from September of 1962 to November of 1963, not one month passed without a Philles record on the charts.

The first record after "Zip-A-Dee-Doo-Dah" was a true Spector anomaly—the result of a rare deal he made with another producer. This was Lou Adler, a fifties' protégé of Lester Sill's. Teamed with writer-producer Herb Alpert while working for Sill, the two men wrote and produced Jan and Dean for several years. Now both men were making entrepreneurial moves on the West Coast. While Alpert began an independent label called A&M Records, and cutting his own mariachi-flavored trumpet instrumentals under the name of Herb Alpert and the Tijuana Brass, Adler handled Don Kirshner's West Coast office and then became an A&R man with Columbia Pictures–Screen Gems. As Phil was looking to record a male group, Adler rushed in to link Screen Gems with the name of Phil Spector. Adler had Billy Storm—whom Spector had cut on Atlantic and who now was Bobby Sheen's brother-in-law—under contract with a five-man L.A. soul group, the Alley Cats, and their records did well on the West Coast. Sheen touted Spector on the Alley Cats, and Phil agreed to a one-shot record to benefit him and Adler. A 50–50 deal from top to bottom, Adler would produce the B side.

Phil's side was called "Puddin' 'n' Tain (Ask Me Again and I'll Tell You the Same)," an old nursery rhyme expanded into an up-tempo bubble-gum teen love song by Alley Cat Gary Pipkin. It became a Top 40 hit in late February of 1963 and was Phil's most convincing doo-wop record, ladled with the big band bite. However, in making the record he clashed with Adler. Ambitious and chummy in an unctuous, talent-agent way, Adler seemed to fancy himself as a West Coast Phil Spector. "He was kinda out there too," said Bobby Sheen, who sang backup on the session. "They all wanted to be different then." Making his presence felt, poking into Spector's studio time, he seemed to be trying to compete with Spector on his own turf. Phil had known Adler for years, and through him he met and became friendly with Brian Wilson of the Beach Boys, who revered Phil and whose creative outflow Phil liked to be around. But now Adler made his skin crawl, and by the end of the session Phil had turned Gold Star into a battlefront.

"Phil could never accept anybody being on a level with him," Larry Levine said. "I could feel the animosity between them, and I found that Phil's dislike for Adler spilled over to me years later when I worked with Lou too. I didn't like him, just because of Phil. At first Lou would come in when Phil was doing things and they'd be acting friendly. Then Phil was funny. He'd turn up the speakers as soon as Lou came into the control room. That was like stepping into a scalding shower.

"Phil would love to blast the sound because it was a great feeling of all this coming at you, but he'd start off at a moderately low level and grow used to it. But when a visitor would walk in, he'd crank it up, like, hey, let's impress him. And they wouldn't make head or tail of it."

Crowding Lou Adler out of the studio was Spector's way of ignoring a potential rival. "He had no respect for anyone he thought was a threat to him in any way," Lester Sill believed, and by 1963 that applied to Don Kirshner as well. After recording Mann and Weil's brightly upbeat but again too-fatalistic song, "He's Sure the Boy I Love," the next Darlene Wright–fronted Crystals hit, Phil did not go to Aldon for two years. "He thought he was making Kirshner too big," Annette said.

His alternative became a a young woman from Long Island, Ellie Greenwich. Mostly unknown around Broadway, Greenwich had recorded briefly for RCA in the late fifties, taught school for a while, and now was writing under the Leiber and Stoller banner at Trio Music—in another irony of mixed industry blood, it was Terry Phillips who recommended her for a job while he was dating her best friend. Greenwich was a melody writer of immense ability, and her songs were inventive teen tripe, with beguiling chord changes and cute hooks. Armed with songs, the blond and spunky Greenwich tried to play some for Phil one day in the Brill Building. Spector looked in a mirror, combed his hair, and ignored her. Greenwich scolded him, yelling "Are you going to listen?" and he huffed out, apparently turned off to her. But when Phil heard her demo of a song she'd written with a Trio collaborator named Tony Powers, "(Today I Met) The Boy I'm Gonna Marry," he thought they could do business and invited them to his apartment. Phil came home very late, and Greenwich accosted him in the lobby, again berating him for being rude. This time Phil smiled at her, as if she had passed a test. He took her and Powers up to the apartment, sat them at a piano, and heard much that he thought he could use.

The first Greenwich-Powers-Spector tune, correctly listed in that order, was "Why Do Lovers Break Each Others' Hearts?", a chugging, glockenspiel-punctuated piece sung in unison by Bobby Sheen and Darlene Wright and released as a Bob B. Soxx and the Blue Jeans record. The second, "(Today I Met) The Boy I'm Gonna Marry"—credited as Spector-Greenwich-Powers—made Darlene Wright into an unlikely torch singer. Wright sang the ballad the only way she could, as if she were in a pulpit, and it was a loud wail that Phil did not want to use as a Crystals record. When released, it was with the name of a new Philles act: Darlene Love.

Phil was in the studio all the time now, hopping from coast to coast, cutting mostly in L.A. but also doing album fillers with the real Crystals at Mira Sound. He stepped away, briefly, on a February day in 1963. On that day, he married Annette Merar.

As much as she loved Phil, and though things were good between them, Annette was not happy as a live-in love interest for a man almost never at home. She was young, still friendless in New York, and she had seen a darkness in Phil that was disconcerting. As had Donna Kass, Annette felt the hot breath of Phil's jealousy. When Phil was in L.A. cutting "He's a Rebel," she told him over the phone that she was about to go sunbathing. "He got freaked out and so pissed that I was wearing a two-piece bathing suit that I couldn't sunbathe in it," she said. "He made me promise not to wear it." All too often, Annette stood in the firing line of his temper. "The worst of it was his verbal abuse and arguing. Phil loves to argue, and he would destroy me, and I'm no dummy. But he'd have to win." Trying to cope with his bottomless pit of insecurities, Phil had begun seeing a Park Avenue psychiatrist named Dr. Harold Kaplan, on Mondays for group therapy plus two or three private sessions during the week.

Annette believed that their love was the only emotional cement of their lives. Phil said as much when he proposed marriage. In January, he gave her a glimmering 2½-carat diamond ring. They also moved to an apartment Annette had secured from a realtor, a magnificent terraced penthouse at Sixty-second Street and York Avenue with a breathtaking view of the East River and neighbors that included Steve Lawrence and Eydie Gorme. They took the apartment completely furnished, the living-room walls painted in shades of olive, expensive French frying pans dangling on hooks in the kitchen. The only new piece was a television sent as a gift from Don Kirshner. On February 18, they were wed in a rabbi's study of a synagogue on Central Park West. The ceremony was attended only by three of Phil's friends: Arnie Goland, an arranger who charted many of Phil's New York sessions, was best man, and the other witnesses were a Liberty Records producer named Ed Silver and Peter Bitlisian, a show-biz photography who sometimes took Phil to Las Vegas to meet celebrities. The reception was held at Helen Noga's sprawling Central Park South apartment.

Joyous as the wedding day was, it ended in tears. "We had a fight that very night," Annette said. "I don't remember why, but we were arguing again. I'm telling you, he loved to argue. And I remember sitting there on the floor of the dining room crying my eyes out." Only days later, Phil left for another session at Gold Star. "I was devastated. He just walked out and left me there. I couldn't believe he could be that cold."

Annette, reaching out on her own, began school, studying English literature at Hunter College. And in the coming months, life as Mrs. Phil Spector seemed good to her. "We had a high life," she said. "I had beautiful clothes, a maid three times a week, and a limousine to and from school. We went out to the Copa, sat at the best tables, went dancing and discothequing, the whole thing." At home, Phil could seem like an endearing little boy. "You know how he lives? He lives like a middle-class Jewish boy, with his salami and bagels in the refrigerator. He liked to sit with a cup of coffee and watch a little TV we had in the kitchen." Now growing into domesticity, Bertha Spector instructed Annette about how to please her little boy. "The only thing his mother ever said to me was to tell me how to freeze bacon, to wrap it in four-strip packages and put it in the freezer. That's all I remember of Bertha. I ran into a lot of Phil's craziness, and I was the love of his life."

In time, the partying and domestic tranquility ended, and the biggest problem for Annette became her alienation from Phil's life. He still took her to the studio with him, but that now bored her. "I felt very out of place in the studio. I was very mubh in the background. I'd take one of my French literature books out and read so I could do something. Sometimes it was great. I went to rehearsals with Jeff and Ellie that were phenomenal, and with Darlene Love, who would sing and make you want to cry. But those sessions, God, those were hard work—just sitting there was hard. I liked him much better at home just with his guitar.

"I just never felt part of his circle, the rock-and-roll people, like Kirshner and Leiber and Stoller. I was friends with Doc Pomus and Michael Spencer and his wife Ruth, but I never would allow myself to ride on his coattails, because it was not *my* success. I never gave up my identity to him and he didn't like that, because he wants everybody to be a moth around his flame."

Eventually Annette was cut out from his life almost completely. For long periods Phil never wanted to go out of the apartment. Annette, a nature lover, felt caged. "We'd just stay in and argue. One perfect example was when I told him there was a difference between a dictator and a demagogue. He said there was no difference, and we got into a big fight about that. If I said red, he'd say it's green, just to be contentious." After that, he would leave and be gone, for hours or days.

Marrying Phil, it seemed, had reduced his capacity to love her. It was as if, having become a part of him, he could not accept her being that close.

"Phil seemed to thrive on destroying his opponent, even if it was his wife," Annette said. "He changed after we married. He never let me sit next to him and he gave me little affection. Sex was okay, it was, but as far as affection, he was like a hummingbird. He was an emotional tease. He would appear to be the sensitive, lovely genius, but the minute you expected it to bloom, it would fly off."

To Annette, the arguing and the little symbols of neglect arose from a cavity in his soul.

"I think the man doesn't really know how to love. I think he loves his music and that's it. So I was slowly being destroyed, by waiting for his calls, and he would never come home and then he would walk in at five in the morning.

"Phil is so charming and sophisticated and talented. But he has a shadow side, as everybody does. And his shadow side is violent, and it came out; he has no control over the beast inside of him. That's the trouble. He's a victim of his own mind. He doesn't control it, and I'll tell you something. To be subject to that on an intimate level was devastating, and it has affected my whole life."

Together now, and separately, they began to see Dr. Kaplan. "But there was no change at all," Annette believed. "Kaplan was like another fan for Phil, an ego trip for both of them."

Disheartened as she was, even darker storm clouds were on the horizon.

10

His music gave him so much altitude and respect as a person. That was his power source, and it was such a tremendous source that it just drove him higher and higher.

—SONNY BONO

Phil Spector had a peculiar kind of hit factory by mid-1963. As he stepped into Gold Star and rolled more and more records down the echo-chambered assembly line, he knew that few cared who the artist on the label would be. The startling fact that a producer mattered more than the artist suggested that Beethoven had not rolled over for rock and roll after all. Spector was, as he always had dreamed, an apparition of Richard Wagner right in the middle of pimple-cream music.

Befitting a latter-day classic master, Spector fiercely protected his musicians' interests. Hal Blaine earned thick steaks after sessions and the forbearance to poke fun at Phil's recording methods. Sitting at his drums for a typically long haul awaiting his cue, Blaine one time pulled out an alarm clock and let the bell sound, rupturing what the band was playing. Phil laughed with everyone else. A brilliant new pianist, Leon Russell, once played a solo that moved Phil so much that he came onto the studio floor and wrote him out a $50 check. "Phil always took care of us. There was never a problem with bread, never," Steve Douglas said. "In fact, one time I remember him being pissed because we hadn't been paid for something by Warner Brothers. He yelled, 'Goddamn it, stop this session. Fuck those people! I'm gonna get you guys paid!' We had to convince him it was cool, that they really weren't that late with the money."

One time, after arranging and contracting a session, Arnold Goland submitted a bill that Phil wouldn't accept. "He wanted to pay me *more*," Goland said. "He said, 'You're not charging me enough.' He wanted to pay me double what I asked for."

As a joke, but a telling one, the musicians came in for one date wearing T-shirts bearing a picture of Phil's face—a take off of his habit of wearing shirts with Beethoven's face. "Phil was flabbergasted," said Ray Pohlman, who devised the joke. "He loved it."

Conversely, although Barbara Alston, Darlene Wright, and Bobby Sheen were crucial to his records, they were now little more than tools. Phil demanded that they be available to him, but no one ever knew what group name would be chosen for each song—and he seemed to delight in this arcane power to make kings and break hearts. "He'd talk about it," Annette recalled. "He would say, 'They're all mine. Without me, they're nothing. They will do what I want.' Again, it was full power, full control."

No one inside Phil's inner circle could ever fail to see that. No man, no musician—not Larry Levine, not Jack Nitzsche—was allowed to penetrate his wary omnipotence and to know him too well. "Phil had yes-men, but he didn't like to surround himself with people, that didn't make him feel good," Annette said, "because they'd want to know him and want to get close, and he doesn't want to— even though he feels very small if he is just himself. That's where his bravado and lying come in."

One confederate who came closer than most was a short, swarthy industry hustler, Sonny Bono. Squinty-eyed, and with a casaba-sized nose, Bono was a West Coast rock denizen for years, including a spell when he was partners with Jack Nitzsche. Bono sold his first songs while driving a meat truck in the mid-fifties, and he was hired as a writer/producer at Specialty Records in 1957 when he just happened to come in after the R&B label fired Sam Cooke and his producer Bumps Blackwell. At Specialty, Bono placed two of his songs on the flip sides of Larry Williams's hits "Short Fat Fanny" and "Bony Maronie." Meeting Nitzsche, Bono hired him to do lead sheets at $3 apiece. Bono and Nitzsche went on to write songs for the Robins, and then Jackie DeShannon's "Needles and Pins," but neither man prospered. When Nitzsche went to work for Lee Hazelwood and Lester Sill, Bono went into promotion at a Hollywood distributing firm. But Bono longed to get back to making records, and when Nitzsche fell in with Spector, Sonny considered it *the* job in music. Because his distributing house handled the Philles line, Bono, a huge fan of Spector's records, offered himself up as a quasi-promotion man, sideman, and all-around stooge.

"I was Phil's flunky," Bono clarified affably. "Sometimes Phil would get hungry at four in the morning, or if he wanted company, that's what I was around for."

Bono was a faithful and obedient basset hound—"Sonny had his nose up Phil's ass a mile," said Lester Sill, who gave Bono office space at the El Centro office as well—but in return, Phil included Bono on every session after he came on at a $175-a-week salary in early 1963. Bono sometimes contracted the musicians, played percussion, and sang with the background singers, but Bobby Sheen, who recorded for Bono as a teenager at Specialty, remembers him now as "a coffee guy." The dialogue between Phil and Sonny would go like this:

"Doesn't that sound good, Sonny?"

"Yeah, Phil, great!"

"Should we get it up higher?"

"Yeah, that sounds good, Phil!"

"Go get me some coffee."

"Okay!"

All the while, though, the amiable and shrewd Bono was watching and learning how to make quality records.

"I was blown away when I saw what he did in the studio," Bono said. "Even back then, the thing to do was isolate your sound as much as you could. But Phil was like Muhammad Ali with the rope-a-dope. He did everything the opposite of what you were programmed to do. Everybody wanted a clean sound, and then he comes up with this slop over and over, bigger and bigger each time, and makes a sound everybody flipped over."

Bono was not, however, permitted a hard, honest appraisal of the music, or to make a contribution. After coming aboard, he started bringing around his seventeen-year-old girlfriend, Cherilyn Sarkasian LaPier, who was called Cher. Tall, lean, and very pretty, Cher, a runaway who had moved in with Sonny, had dark hair down to her waist, a crooked nose, and little to her name except a white pant-suit that she wore almost every day. Bringing her to the studio, Sonny was able to insert her into the coterie of Spector's background singers. "Phil loved it that Cher could sing because he could get a background singer for $15 instead of a standard fee," Bono said. But Sonny had more in mind for her.

"I always wanted Phil to record Cher. But they didn't get along. Cher was a young girl and she was overwhelmed by Phil. The communication was really weird between them; it wasn't easy because Phil was sometimes open, sometimes introverted, and you didn't know whether you said something wrong or not. Conversation didn't flow with him, and it was never a piece of cake to hang out with him."

Those around Phil learned quickly that conversation would be scarce, a nicety he considered a distraction. "The studio was his life," Bono said. "He ate, slept, and breathed music. Sometimes he'd go to the Beach Boys' sessions and listen to what they were doing and talk to Brian. He was all-consumed by record studios and songs. There was no other life that I could see."

If Bono was Spector's pet, Nino Tempo was his pet musician. Tempo became the same kind of one-way sounding board as Bono. He was put to work on keyboards, saxophone, percussion, almost everything, and while he played nothing extraordinarily well, no session would run without him. Dark and stocky, Tempo spoke gruffly and out of the side of his mouth, gangster-style. Phil had run across him early on in New York. Trying to sell songs to Leiber and Stoller, Tempo shared an elevator one day with a nervous Spector. "He shied away from me, pressing himself as tightly as he could against the back wall," Tempo recalled. "Later on he said he thought I was going to rob him." Jerry Leiber had wanted Phil and Nino to write together, and when Leiber vacationed during the summer of 1960, the two of them and Tempo's sister, April Stevens, lived in Leiber's town house for a few weeks. Tempo then went to L.A., and when Phil happened to stop at a red light on Wilshire Boulevard two years later, Tempo was in the car next to him and Phil invited him onto the "Zip-A-Dee-Doo-Dah" session.

As a profusion of Spector hits ensued, this human good-luck charm developed a distinctive strut inside the studio. Years later the other musicians would hear about how Tempo claimed real influence on the hits. "Nino was another one who wanted to be a producer, a big *macher*," said Hal Blaine. "He was kinda considered not a whole lot by the gang. He was like Billy Strange. Billy, with his big bulk, was a little bit intimidating, and when he'd say, 'Wait a minute, let's do this,' everybody would do it. Nino wanted to always take over sessions and tell everybody what to do."

With a breathing apparatus attached to Phil Spector's incredible power source, Tempo could inflate rapidly. And though Phil could be difficult, the relationship was a joyous lark. "He's got a much better sense of humor than most people think," Tempo stressed. "Yes, there is another side of him. He can be a very hostile guy. But my memories are of fun and laughs and kicks and screwing around like two crazy young guys."

Bono and Tempo could be useful flunkies, but Larry Levine was the only absolute essential. No other engineer was allowed his wide berth; Levine could turn down the sound level of one instrument to compensate for the cranking up of another, he could move microphone placements, he could tell Phil when the distortion was *too* much. He could even edit tape, something Phil at one time would not have tolerated with his "live" sound. Levine earned the right to do that after accidentally garbling some tape while mixing. When it happened, a self-pitying Spector walked from behind the console board and crawled under a table, drawing his knees up in front of his face. But, luckily, Larry was able to make a copy of a similar passage and splice it in. "It worked perfectly, and from that point on, Phil let me edit tape," Levine said.

However, one thing Phil would not let Levine do was record in stereo after Gold Star acquired a three-track recorder in 1963. "I said to him, 'Why don't we separate the horns, or the guitars maybe, so we have a little more control?' He said, 'Absolutely not. What I hear today is what I wanna hear tomorrow, when I come back to the mix. And you can never bring all those elements back precisely the same in stereo.' And he was right. Even today, stereo is an *approximation* of what's heard in the studio. For Phil, the only sound he wanted was the sound he recorded after three hours getting everything to fit. He cared that much about it."

Cut in mono, parts of Spector's big orchestrations were obscured or lost completely. Phil willingly parted with them. His sound was an overview, a primordial feel of joyful noise, although many technical people in the business could not comprehend it. In New York, removed from Larry Levine and his unspoken command, engineers would jump on Phil about his decibel level and the resulting distortion of sound, to little avail. "He'd say, 'I don't care if the dials jump off the meters, I *want* it to sound distorted,'" Arnold Goland said, "so what would happen is, on the master the needle would literally jump out of the grooves, that's how loud it was cut. Sometimes there'd be recalls on his records and he'd have to do them all over again. But he didn't care. He was going after what he wanted."

Tom Dowd, still manning Atlantic's clear-channeled, eight-track board, heard Spector's massive hits and shook his head. "Thinking of what the man was doing, it could have been done easier and less expensively," Dowd said. "Tracks got bounced around so many times they were inarticulate. Phil never measured, was it worth it? If it didn't sound like he wanted, it's not ready yet, keep on going, hunt and peck. It's like shopping for a doctor. It's a state of confusion.

"I wish I could've made a couple of those records, or had some contribution. There were a lot of brilliant parts in his records that were wiped out. But high fidelity is not what's sold. Novelty and timeliness is the strength of a record, and he always had that."

For the Crystals, the association with Phil was maddeningly contradictory. By the spring of 1963, they had four hits, and while none were actually theirs since "Uptown," they could go on lucrative tours with no one aware of it. But the strange conflict was personally humiliating. When "He's a Rebel" broke on the radio, the Crystals were on the road in Ohio. "We were in the car late at night when all of a sudden we hear: 'Here's the new Crystals song'—and our mouths fell open," remembered Mary Thomas. "I mean, goodness gracious, but what could we do? There was nothing we could do."

They also now had to perform the song live—luckily, Gene Pitney was a performer at their next show, at the Howard Theater in Washington, D.C., and he taught them the words—and this created an instant problem because Darlene Wright's emphatic voice was so unlike the wan softness of Barbara Alston's. The only one who could take the lead was Dolores "La La" Brooks, who at age thirteen had been brought into the group after "There's No Other (Like My Baby)," to replace a pregnant Crystal. Much younger and not part of the original core of schoolmates, Brooks felt the sting of frustration that the girls could not direct at Phil.

"It was a lot of tension," she said. "When I started doin' 'He's a Rebel' on stage, Barbara just said, 'The hell with it, let her do "Uptown" too, and everything else.' She didn't care anymore."

The truth was that, even as the Crystals continued to tour as one of the hottest vocal groups in rock, they had been stripped of their identity by their own producer. One hard sign of Phil's neglect was the dearth of royalties they received. At the very beginning, Lester Sill, acting as a temporary manager and helping book their appearances, had met them on tour in Washington, D.C., to give them a $1,000 check. "I was worried that we didn't have the proper pay setup," Sill explained, "and I just wanted to make sure the kids got paid." Now, with Lester pushed out, all they had gotten from Phil was one check for $5,000, and that came when they marched *en masse* to his apartment building. "We had such a hard time getting that out of him that we went right to his bank and cashed the check," La La Brooks said.

The Crystals faced constant reminders of their identity crisis. Booked on the Murray the K shows in their hometown Brooklyn, they also had a hard time getting the deejay to pay them. Murray the K, who wore fedora hats over a bald head and loud, tablecloth-print sport jackets, was one of the most aggrandized, and disliked, deejays in the business. Mouthy, pushy, and overbearing, he valued acts according to how much they doted on him, and he apparently had it in for the Crystals. "We worked our buns off for Murray the K," La La said, "but when he had to pay us, he'd say he didn't have it, he was in debt, or he'd act like he was ill, pretend he was having a heart attack. We'd be standing over him and he was laying on the couch and all his people were saying 'Oh, he's sick,' and he was holding his heart. Meanwhile, he was putting our money in his pocket."

145

On the other hand, when Bob B. Soxx and the Blue Jeans—really no more than a studio concoction—went on tour, Murray treated Darlene Wright, Bobby Sheen, and Fanita James courteously. In fact, the deejay, with whom Phil maintained a patronizing kind of friendship in deference to his impact on airplay, utilized Bob B. Soxx to degrade the Crystals. Inviting Bob B. Soxx, but not the Crystals, to appear on one holiday show, he told his audience that the Crystals did not record "He's a Rebel," and Bob B. Soxx were the "real" Crystals. Mary Thomas, who happened to be sitting in the audience at the Brooklyn Fox that night, was mortified. So was La La Brooks, who listened to the show on the radio at home.

"He was getting back at us because we didn't take anything from him, we stood up to him and demanded our money, even if we had to sit there all night," Brooks said. "We weren't the type of girls that you could sleep with instead of having to pay."

The Crystals had made up their minds that such was not the case with Murray the K's "dancing girls," Ronnie Bennett, her sister, and their cousin. However, in 1963, for the Crystals and Bob B. Soxx and the Blue Jeans there were other much more ominous signs involving the Ronettes. Rehearsing in Phil's new office, on the lobby floor of his apartment building, the Crystals were startled one day when the Ronettes came to the door and then strode in and made themselves comfortable.

"Ronnie was paying a lot of attention to Phil, and he was married to a very nice girl," La La recalled. "We were really upset because we couldn't rehearse any more. All of a sudden he wanted to rehearse them."

Never having met Ronnie Bennett before, La La sized her up. "She was more advanced than we were. She was a hard rocker, even then, you know what I mean? She had hard language, was a hard person. She had a hard inside."

Actually, Ronnie Bennett, Estelle Bennett, and Nedra Talley seemed more like vipers and harpies than they were. All lived at home, none smoked or drank, and rather than being on the prowl, Ronnie's mother Beatrice chaperoned them almost wherever they went. All the same, eighteen-year-old Ronnie, a tiny china doll with large eyes, full lips, and a nasty wiggle, had a trashy, kittenish kind of sexuality that could make men's knees buckle. It was evident now that Phil had a major hunger for her. When Ronnie was with him,

⊙

he seemed to see only her. In no time, they were neck deep in a secret love affair.

When La La Brooks left the building the day she met Ronnie, she ran into a dour and depressed Annette Spector on the street walking her dog.

"She was very, very unhappy," Brooks said. "She said she couldn't deal with Phil. She said he was crazy."

The Crystals' "He's Sure the Boy I Love" went to No. 11 in late February of 1963. Neither "Why Do Lovers Break Each Others' Hearts?" nor "(Today I Met) The Boy I'm Gonna Marry" did more than nudge the Top 40, but Phil was cutting a lava flow of vinyl. He released only about a quarter of what he recorded, at the rate of one a month, and all were quality records. He paid no attention to how a previous record was doing in deciding to put out another one. A one-man label, he did not have the luxury to release a slew of scatter-shot records and hope one would hit. As Phil Spector, he had to come through without pause.

In March Phil went into Gold Star to cut a song that had grown from a piano riff Arnold Goland had improvised one night in his living room. Presenting it to Ellie Greenwich and, now, Jeff Barry—Beverly Ross's onetime writing partner had married Greenwich in late 1962 and begun to write with her—Phil told them to do something with it. What they worked out was a seriously silly song with a title the writers originally inserted as a gibberish filler phrase until they found a workable line. Finding nothing that worked, Greenwich and Barry concluded that their gibberish line worked on its own as rock-and-roll patois. It also became the title of the song: "Da Doo Ron Ron." Phil took the tune and touched off a sweaty fervor around it that made it sound like it was recorded in a bar. The rhythm, three guitars, three horns, and now three pianos grinded in a reverberation that created its own echoes and undulated in a great fused mass of reeds, tinkling keys, and hand claps.

Though Darlene Wright—so cemented in her Darlene Love persona that she had now adopted the name as her own—did a lead vocal on "Da Doo Ron Ron," Phil turned away from her loud, studied impeccability. He had heard La La Brooks sing in New York, and thought he was blessed. Still only fifteen, Brooks spoke in a whisper, like a breathy sparrow, but when she sang she could knock down a building. She had a Brooklyn accent and a slight vibrato that rippled like a sneering lip through a song. Phil flew her to Gold Star, tried her on "Da Doo Ron Ron," and axed Darlene's lead. La La made the simple love cupidity of the song a visceral thump of a young girl's heart. Darlene had no idea the lead wasn't hers until the record came out, and Fanita James, recalling Darlene's studio take, which she thought was brilliant, assumed two decades later that it *was* Darlene on the record.

Stepping on the faltering tail of "(Today I Met) The Boy I'm Gonna Marry," "Da Doo Ron Ron," released as the sixth Crystals record—Arnold Goland went uncredited but was listed as nominal writer of the bunco B side—ran all the way to No. 3 in June. It was still on the chart in mid-July, when the next Philles single, "Not Too Young to Get Married," by Bob B. Soxx and the Blue Jeans, was here and gone after peaking at No. 63, and Darlene Love's "Wait 'til My Bobby Gets Home" reached the chart on its way to No. 26 in early September.

La La Brooks, whose prickly, little boyish voice sharpened Phil's music scalpel, claimed her second lead on the follow-up to "Da Doo Ron Ron." This was a similar Greenwich-Barry wall-banger, "Then He Kissed Me," and the song gave Phil the chance to get back to strings. Mixed with savage-sounding horns and overheated casta-nets, it was "Uptown" stirred into a frenzy and ablaze with spirit. With "Then He Kissed Me," Spector's musical vernacular at last was truly symphonic, the tight, slightly distanced nature of the wad of rhythm forming a suggestion of awesome power while still preserv-ing the intimacy of the vocal through a radio speaker, and remaining recognizable as rock and roll.

An integral part of the mix was a billowing echo, one that dwarfed any other so far on a Spector record. As it happened, it was an accident, though one forced by Phil's endless demands for greater and greater exhilarating voltage. "Phil needed volume in the control room on the playback," Larry Levine said. "No matter how much level we had he wanted more. So I doubled the track, put it on the left and right channels, knowing I would erase one channel because Phil cut in mono. But when I erased one, I was still getting echo from both left and right on the one channel. The echo crossed, it didn't stay on its own channel. I was left with a double echo with half the musical presence. But it worked fine, Phil liked it, and from then on I knew how to get as much echo as Phil wanted, although I don't think we ever used more echo than on that record."

In August of 1963, Phil finally released his first Ronettes record. Over a year since taking them on, he found the right song for them, the Barry-Greenwich-Spector "Be My Baby." He cut it, a month before, with an obsessive furor incredible even for him. Four hours into the session, Larry Levine's recorder was still not turned on. The musicians, their sweat-drenched shirts sticking to their bodies, believed that they could get their parts down no better, only to see Phil tear up the lead sheet and start again. Michael Spencer, back home in L.A. for the summer and invited to play on the date, sat on his piano stool almost comatose. "It took forty-two run-throughs to get it the way he wanted it," Spencer remembered. "I know that because I destroyed the forty-first. On the break, there's a pause where the drum goes *bom, bom-bom*. I played right through that, that's how punchy I was."

"The things Phil was doing were crazy and exhausting, but that's not the sign of a nut, that's genius," Levine said. "I mean, if something was remotely possible, he was gonna do it, and we just went ahead without a second thought. There were no rock-and-roll rules for Phil, because he was making them up as he went along."

Softly couched by acoustic guitars chewing an unbroken line of repetitive notes, the steady three-beat drum accent and a dramatic entry of horns, Ronnie Bennett's gushy, seductive voice, with a vibrato that fluttered like bird wings, burst onto the rock-and-roll landscape. The Ronettes were not polished singers—"They sang flat," Bobby Sheen noted—and Estelle Bennett and Nedra Talley's backing vocal tracks had to be overdubbed several times and buffered with other voices. But Ronnie sang the way she looked—it was possible to fall in love with just her voice, and the 'whoa, ho-ho-ho-ho" riff she sang was a come-on that needed no words.

Phil was to become fixated with her, more so than with the group as a whole. Ellie Greenwich and Jeff Barry were charged with writing a whole series of plaintive, first-person love declarations that Phil would regard as the longings of his own heart.

"Be My Baby" was on the chart by the end of summer. By then Phil knew he had Ronnie Bennett right where he wanted her.

11

The records are built like a Wagnerian opera. They start simply and they end with dynamic force, meaning and purpose. . . . It's in the mind. I dreamed it up. It's like art movies. I aimed to get the record industry forward a little bit, make a sound that was universal.

—PHIL SPECTOR, *London Evening Standard,*
January 24, 1964

Phil began work on one other project during that fateful summer of 1963. It was an album of traditional Christmas music done in the untraditional idiom of rock and roll. Spector and Jack Nitzsche laid out arrangements for twelve carols and one original song—a teary, bittersweet Greenwich-Barry-Spector ballad, "Christmas (Baby Please Come Home)"—in the same manner as rock songs, with hip R&B styling, copious strings, and a big band kick to the age-old hooks of pieces like "Frosty the Snowman," "Sleigh Ride," and "I Saw Mommy Kissing Santa Claus."

"He thought it was good music, he respected it," Annette said

⊙   150

of Phil's motivation. "It was like 'Zip-A-Dee-Doo-Dah.' God knows why these things came into his head, but if a song was good, Phil had creative input with it."

"He probably saw the novelty and absurdity of the idea," Larry Levine said, "but I don't think there's any way for anyone to know where he got it any more than any other idea. I can't overstate that Phil was just different. When I was with Phil, things happened to me that wouldn't happen to me with anybody else. Phil was a magnet for unexplained behavior, his kinetic energy was so . . . I mean, people would get into arguments, fights, and not necessarily with him. When you're part of Phil's entourage, strange things happen because his mind doesn't work the way other people's minds do. You don't know why they happen, but you know they will."

And once Phil began on this anomaly, his commitment grew to a level bordering on insane. Day after day for six weeks, sessions ran almost without seams. The artists—Darlene Love, La La Brooks, the Ronettes, and a shoal of background singers—and the musicians did not know what day it was, whether it was light or dark outside, and cots were set up in the studio.

If the album had been done without genuine care and sincerity, there would have been no audience for it. Instead, when it was finally completed, it was a feast of cool and mawkish, a hipster's way of appreciating the seasonal standards that had become stale and depressing for a burgeoning generation of young adults.

But when Larry Levine heard Spector's *coup de grace,* an effulgent soliloquy spoken by Phil himself over the final cut, "Silent Night," he thought he had figured out the motive for the project. This was not only to be Phil's message of good tidings to his record-buying public, but, as he went on and on in unrelieved vanity about his privilege to make such an album, Larry cringed. If Phil could not sing on his records, now he would at last be the presence that verified his endowment.

"He started on this thing, and it was 'I want to say how fortunate I am at twenty-three to do this . . .' and what he was doing was extolling his virtue, how great he was, while trying to sound humble with 'Silent Night' in the background," Levine said. "I'm only sorry I didn't save it for posterity, but I did make him cut it down because it was unbelievable. It got past funny, after five minutes it wasn't funny at all."

The version that remained barely skirted bad taste. "Of course, the biggest thanks goes to you," Spector told his public, many of whom still did not know who he was, "for giving me the opportunity to relate my feelings of Christmas through the music I love." The album, titled with similar presumption—*A Christmas Gift to You from Phil Spector*—was released in November with a jacket designed by Phil; the front cover showed his four acts popping out of gift packages, and on the back were pictures of him and a longer, signed message from "Phil Spector, Producer."

For Levine, making the album was six weeks spent in hell. "I told him after we did the album that I didn't want to work with him anymore. Because it was too hard for me. When you engineer for Phil you have to work every second, you're always mixing and re-mixing and it's physically excruciating. I told Phil, 'Look, you're great, you don't need me' and I walked away. He went back to New York for a long time and I thought that was it for us."

Starting with "Zip-A-Dee-Doo-Dah," the inner groove of each Philles record had been etched with the words "Phil & Annette." But by fall of 1963, it was an empty love symbol. Phil's adultery with Ronnie was now an open secret, and it was causing trouble between Ronnie and her cousin. Nedra Talley had been aware of the illicit romance for months, ever since Phil began calling her house in a snit demanding to know where Ronnie was. Nedra, who was firmly against Ronnie seeing a married man, tried to dissuade her.

"It's wrong," she told Ronnie. "Weren't we brought up to know it's wrong?"

As much as the marriage issue, Nedra worried about Phil himself. She warned Ronnie that he was weird, a man with problems. Ronnie thought Phil's jealous calls were "cute," but Nedra insisted that it was a harbinger of insanity, that later on he would be horrible to her. "If a man cheats on his wife," Nedra said, "he'll cheat on you."

But whatever Nedra said, Ronnie would not listen. "She would just say, 'Oh, I'm not really getting involved, he's just cute'—but let's be real. Phil is not cute. Ronnie fell in love with power," Nedra believed. "Phil talked funny, he looked funny, and he was married. But he was successful and he turned her head with who he was. Ronnie was young and he could give her the world."

All through the winter and spring of 1963, the union got hotter. Ronnie, left fatherless as a young girl when her parents divorced, clung to the security and social ladder Phil offered. Her mother, Beatrice, mindful of her daughter's interests, did not seem to object. "I think my aunt was going along with what Ronnie was doing," Nedra said, "and saying 'Well, you know, she's got a catch.' "

Phil and Ronnie took their affair coast to coast. They lived together while recording in L.A., and in New York, Phil gave nerve new meaning by coupling with her in his office, eighteen floors below where his wife sat in their apartment. Phil thought he was safe there; he could carry on with Ronnie under the cover of rehearsing and other record business. And, for a long time, he was right. Annette Spector knew nothing of the romance. Then Annette visited a girlfriend of hers named Lindy Michaels, who ran in music circles.

"Have you heard about your husband and the Ronettes?" Lindy asked.

"What are you talking about?" Annette said.

"He's working with this group, the Ronettes, and there's a rumor he's having an affair with one of them."

Annette wanted to believe it was a lie, but something told her it was not. Before she'd left the apartment, Phil had told her he would be in the studio recording that night. When Annette got back, she had to know the truth. Calling Mira Sound, she asked for Phil and was told he wasn't there, nor scheduled to be. Next she got on the intercom that connected the apartment and the office. When Phil answered, her heart sank. Saying nothing to him, she raced into the elevator and went to the office, to bang on the door. Knowing he had been caught, Phil wouldn't open it, but when Annette got back upstairs the intercom was buzzing.

Answering it, Annette screamed, "Who are you with down there? Get your whore out of my building!"

At this point, Annette suspected that he was cheating with Nedra. "She's the one who bothered me most, Nedra was the prettiest," Annette recalled. "I said to him, 'Which one is it, Nedra?' and he said, 'I'm rehearsing, and I'm not with Nedra'—he thought that was his out. He made me come down so he could show me it wasn't Nedra."

When Annette went down and the elevator doors opened, she saw Phil and Ronnie, in dark silhouette, standing in the rear of the lobby face to face, their noses almost touching. Annette let the doors close and rode back up. "I just about died," she said. "I was too young to accept that kind of thing." When Phil got in later that night, he flew into a rage.

"What the hell are you doing to me, what is this bullshit?" he screamed at her. "What are you doing spying on me? Who the hell do you think you are?"

"Goddammit, Phil," she said through tears. "If you're having an affair, I wanna know!"

Phil's response was to storm out the door. "You know something? He never admitted it—and he never to this day has admitted it," Annette related. When he was gone, Annette slumped on the living-room sofa. On a table next to her was a picture of Phil. "I looked at it and it seemed as if he was shaking his head back and forth. I kind of hallucinated and it freaked me out. I called a girlfriend who came and took care of me." Much later that night, Phil came home, and for a week they went through the motions of living together. Then, nothing resolved, Annette told him to move out, and he found an apartment two blocks away at York Avenue and E. 64th Street.

"I just couldn't take it anymore," she said. "I was in the middle of finals when that happened and I could not sleep or eat or work. I think I had a walking nervous breakdown. Even today, I still can't take it at age forty-four. I'm very much a moral person. I never cheated on him."

Some weeks later, Phil asked her if they could reconcile. "I'll drop the Ronettes from their contract, I'll just forget about 'em," he insisted—a promise Annette did not believe.

"I can't, Phil," she told him. "It's too devastating to me. You tore me in half."

For the next several months they remained apart, with Phil speaking civilly with Annette and never writing off the marriage. "I believe—no, I know—that I was the only real love of his life," Annette said years later. "Phil dug Ronnie physically, and he dug controlling her and creating an image of a Svengali with her singing. When Phil talked about Ronnie, it was as a slut, a whore, and he thought she was illiterate and ignorant. With me, he had something he could not find with anyone else."

•   •   •

☉

And yet, by late 1963, Phil was deliriously hung up on Ronnie. "Be My Baby" had gone to No. 2, and Dick Clark invited the Ronettes to appear on a barnstorming tour of the East and Midwest called the Dick Clark Cavalcade of Stars. Worried about Ronnie seeing other men once she was away from him, Phil forbade her to go.

"Phil wants me to stay in New York with him," Ronnie told Nedra.

"He's playing one of his stunts," Nedra said. "He's playing emotional games with you, and you know who's gonna win in the end."

The Ronettes went on the tour with another cousin, Elaine, as the third member and with Nedra taking over Ronnie's lead vocals. Then, with the tour almost over, Phil relented and allowed Ronnie to go on.

But now the Ronettes were hot. In early 1964, the follow-up record, "Baby, I Love You," hit No. 24, and another invitation came in—this time from England, where the Ronettes' records were selling heavily. Promoters wanted the group to co-headline a tour with the Rolling Stones, who were in the vanguard of the exploding British rock scene but thus far known mainly as an unwashed, uncouth answer to the skyrocketing Beatles. Phil reluctantly gave Ronnie the go-ahead, but only because he would be there with her. The fact was, Phil had wanted to go to England in any case. His records sold well there, all the way back to "To Know Him Is to Love Him," and in recent months he had negotiated a historic deal with England's Decca label, which had been distributing the Philles line on its London Records sublabel. Though Spector was given the largest known advance from a foreign record company, he recouped the entire advance for London with his first new record, "Be My Baby." Even as the Beatles and the British band scene was sparking tremendous worldwide attention, establishing England's first real rock identity and crowding American pop music off the charts there like never before, Spector's girl-group sound was highly popular. Thus, with the Rolling Stones—who recorded for Decca—geared up for their second national tour, importing the Ronettes was wise planning. In addition, Andrew Loog Oldham, the twenty-year-old Carnaby Street industry bumblebee who was co-managing and producing the Rolling Stones' hard-bitten records, was doing publicity work, gratis, for Phil out of his promotion company. Oldham idolized Spector at a transatlantic distance, and linking up with the Ronettes had been his suggestion.

For Phil, the trip gave him the chance to present himself amid the clangy guitars and high nasal harmonies of the Merseybeat sound as the biggest force in pop music since Elvis, immune to a change of the rock guard but born out of the same rebellious spirit as the English rockers.

On January 24, 1964, a limousine came to his apartment to take him to the airport. As the car pulled out of the driveway, Annette Spector happened to be on the terrace of her apartment. "I watched his limousine roll down York Avenue and suddenly I thought, 'I'm nineteen years old and my husband's going to England,' and I freaked out. I realized I was all alone."

Phil—clad in a scarlet-lined suit and vest, pin-tucked mustard shirt and matching handkerchief, gold watch fob dangling from his vest pocket, a pearl stickpin and pointy brown shoes with spats—landed in London to find that Andrew Oldham, and his business partner Tony Calder, had stirred the interest of the English press about his arrival. Newspaper reporters clamored for interviews with the American Mozart. "It was pure manipulation," Calder said. "We told them, 'Phil Spector's coming but you can't talk to him.' And of course then everybody wanted to talk to him." The first interview, by Maureen Cleave of the *London Evening Standard,* took place in the back of the limousine that carried Spector from Heathrow Airport to his hotel. Phil, who had not encountered this kind of media notoriety at home, reveled in it. "I've been told I'm a genius," he said to Cleave. "What do you think?" Cleave wrote of him as a mercurial homunculus—"He walks like Chaplin, for every three steps forward he takes one back or to the side"—and a loner. "I'm the least quoted man in the industry," Spector said. "I stick to my little bourgeois haunts and I don't bother with the masses."

The Ronettes had preceded Phil to England by two weeks. They appeared on the television variety show "Sunday Night at the Palladium," and their month-long tour with the Rolling Stones was proceeding excellently. The Stones were received wildly by big, enthusiastic crowds, yet the band itself seemed to be more interested in the Ronettes. As both groups spent days together, and went to local clubs and parties, the real prize of the tour for the Stones seemed to be if any of them could get a Ronette into bed—although Ronnie was deemed off-limits. "She was always a no-go area," Tony Calder remembered, "but I've got to tell you, I think everybody in the band was in love with Ronnie. She didn't play around, and everybody presumed it was because of Phil. But we were all madly in love with all of them, because they were the Ronettes. I mean, the Stones were in awe of them. To them *they* were the stars, not Phil, because not everybody knew who Phil was yet. The Ronettes had a special magic right from the start, and everybody was after them."

Yet so good were the vibes that by the tour's end it was of minor importance that none of the Stones could bag a Ronette. Mick Jagger and Keith Richards tried with Estelle, Brian Jones with Nedra, but the girls thought the Stones were grimy and foul-smelling, their hair *too* long. Nondrinkers, they reeled from the band's hard drinking and pill-popping, and they did not care for the Stones' music. Still, they loved being in the spotlight so far from home, and for them the tour was lit with a neon glow.

Phil was lit up too in London. After a few days with Andrew Oldham, he was orbiting the earth, kept in the ionosphere by a nonstop ingestion of marijuana and pills from Oldham's pockets. "Andrew used to have a pill box with every different color under the sun," Calder said. "I'm quite sure he gave Phil something to take him up a little bit and something to calm you down a little bit, and something not to make you overanxious, and after a half dozen of those there's another pill to make sure you don't black out."

Phil had not used drugs before he came to England, fearing they would strip him of his self-control and leave him at the mercy of his neuroses. But the English scene, with its self-aware notion of being different and happening, made easy demands, and Oldham made a convincing Brahman of the new order. Hollow-cheeked and urchinlike, with long strands of blond hair and a mouthful of hip jargon, he was actually a latter-day, if less uptight, analogue of the early Spector. At the time they met, the Rolling Stones had released only two songs, and they were only on the outer edge of stardom. Oldham's publicity work for the Beatles and Freddie and the Dreamers was mostly volunteered, a willingly uncompensated hustle for attention and favor. As Oldham began to wrest control of the Stones from the band's other manager, Eric Easton, he and Tony Calder rented a two-apartment office in a row house at Ivor Court in London's Gloucester Place section, eating up every cent they had. Oldham had to bum tea and biscuits from friends, but he was known far and wide on the British rock scene.

There were not many people Phil could have taken cues from, but he did from Oldham. "Andrew and Phil considered each other to be oddballs," Tony Calder suggested. "I think Phil admired in Andrew the fact that he really did break the rules, and knew how to deal with people. And for Andrew it was near to the point of worship in respect to Phil's ability to produce a good record."

Taking an almost paternal interest in Andrew and the Stones, Phil decided he wanted to distribute the band's records in America on the Philles label. He and Andrew worked out a deal that would have Decca license the Stones' catalogue to Philles, and then went to see Sir Edward Lewis, the aging head of Decca Records. They presented the plan to him, and for forty-five minutes Lewis, who spoke in a pinched old-world British tongue, prattled on by way of saying no. Phil did not understand a word Lewis said, but it was clear the Stones were forbidden to go through any other channel but London Records and its usual outlets. Phil and Andrew left, mad.

That night the Stones had a session at their studio, a small and musty place called Regent Sound on London's Denmark Street. Andrew brought Phil and also Gene Pitney, who was in England during a foreign tour of his own. Since "He's a Rebel," Pitney had fallen out with Aaron Schroeder and gone on to have a number of hits. Cultivating the British market, he turned to Oldham to do promotion, and Oldham later produced Pitney singing a Mick Jagger-Keith Richards song, "That Girl Belongs to Yesterday," which became a hit in England. Two other rockers filtered into Regent Sound that night, Graham Nash and Alan Clarke, who were the core of the Hollies. But at first it was difficult to get anything done.

"It was one of those days where the Stones all hated each other," Pitney recalled. "Later on I realized why Andrew was the best thing they ever had goin' for them. He had a nice ability with them in the studio to get them to put things out. Left on their own egos, they always had a problem with each other.

"So that night, I had just come in from Paris with five fifths of duty-free cognac, and I had a fifth with me at the studio. It was my birthday that day and I told everybody they had to drink to me.

⊙

And it did the trick. Everybody got a little mellow and started jammin' around a little bit."

Half wasted, all of them sang a musical piss-off to Sir Edward Lewis in which everybody shouted "Fuck you, Sir Edward" and other obscenities. Oldham recorded it, gave it the title "Andrew's Blues," and pressed copies to give to his friends as an inside joke. The real work that night, though, was cutting the Jagger-Richards song "Not Fade Away," which Oldham produced in what must have seemed a dreamscape, working with America's top producer.

"Phil really produced that one," Tony Calder said. "It was just one of those magical nights when all kinds of forces came together. Phil actually sat there in the booth and said, 'Hey, Andrew, let's do it like this' and 'Hey, Mick, let's put the maracas in here,' and he went outside and he was playin' the maracas with Mick and showin' him how to play 'em. It was one of those scenes you never forget. And on the record you can actually hear Phil tapping a coin on the cognac bottle and Brian Jones sayin', 'Drink some more cognac to change the note on the bottle.' It was that ridiculous, and that wonderful."

Released as the Stones' next single, "Not Fade Away" would become their first big hit in America, going Top 5. Phil would be credited with co-writing the British B side, "Little by Little," although this was just a few riffs jammed on the spot, and that song would draw royalties for him by its inclusion on the Stones' first album. Also on that album was an instrumental version of Marvin Gaye's "Can I Get a Witness"—which Oldham retitled "Now I've Got a Witness (Like Uncle Phil and Uncle Gene)."

Phil was buoyant throughout his stay in London. Assuming the role of the hip hobgoblin that the media had created for him, he brushed his hair straight out like pinecones and began to wear dark glasses wherever he went. He appeared on the television shows "Ready, Steady, Go" and "Juke Box Jury," alternating thoughtful insight with playacting. Riding around London one night with Decca promotion man Tony Hall in a long black Rolls-Royce hired by Hall, Phil asked the driver to stop and go out to a grocery store for a container of milk. "We were somewhere in Mayfair and the driver got out and Phil jumped in the driver's seat, did a quick U-turn, and drove off," said Hall, "this funny little man wearing the chauffeur's hat behind the huge wheel of this Rolls-Royce and driving on the sidewalk. I was in the backseat and I was freaking."

Tony Hall's house on Greene Street in Mayfair, the site of many parties attended by members of the top rock groups in London, was right across the road from the flats of John Lennon, George Harrison, and Ringo Starr. Hearing that the Ronettes were in town, the three Beatles asked Tony Hall if they could meet the girls. Again, Ronnie was the Beatles' focal point, the known commodity, and when Hall gave a party for the meeting, they had no reason to think Phil would be there. But Phil did come, with Andrew, and it was a disastrous entrance.

"Phil was very weird that night," Hall said, "and the atmosphere was strained to begin with because the girls weren't exactly overflowing of personality. And Phil was never easy to get along with. Whenever you'd meet him he would be extremely moody."

"I remember Phil came in that night and he was talking high, like a girl," Nedra Talley said. "He would stop and it got embarrassing."

"I think Andrew encouraged him, just as Phil encouraged Andrew," Tony Calder said. "It was just a game to be . . . you see, we would call it weird now, but at the time it was not weird. They were camping it up, they were taking unlawful substances, and they were just talking nonsense and sending people up. They were havin' a giggle."

Still, Andrew knew he had to get Phil out of there and get his head together. "Andrew dragged him off someplace and they returned a couple of hours later and everything was fine," Hall said. "I think Phil was a bit stoned when he came back, he'd had some smoke. He started telling the Beatles about his records, who played on them and things that happened on the sessions, and it was a great atmosphere, everybody was getting on fine."

Before the evening ended, George Harrison and Estelle Bennett retired to an upstairs room. And while Phil did not have the instant affinity with the Beatles that he did with the Rolling Stones, they parted as friends. A week later, on February 7, the Beatles were about to depart on their first trip to America, to appear on the "Ed Sullivan Show" two consecutive Sundays. Before they left, apprehensive about stepping onto a strange land, they called Phil over to tell them about what they should expect in New York and how to

⊙

handle it. To continue the indoctrination, they asked him to fly to New York with them.

And so Phil Spector flew back across the Atlantic with the Beatles, on a flight crackling with anticipation, fear, and excitement about what Beatlemania would do to America. Five years later Spector would describe the flight as "a lot of fun. It was probably the only time I flew that I wasn't afraid, because I knew that they weren't goin' to get killed in a plane.

"That plane was really an awful trip. I mean there were twenty-eight or thirty minutes where that plane dropped thousands of feet over the ocean. It scared the shit out of me, but there were 149 people on board who were all press and Beatles right-hand men and left-hand men, and we just sat together and talked about the Apollo [Theater] and all that jive. Lennon was with his first wife, and he was very quiet. Paul asked a lot of questions. George was wonderful. It was a nice trip."

At John F. Kennedy Airport, the very nervous Beatles asked Phil a favor. "It's really funny but they were terribly frightened to get off the plane. They were really frightened of America. They said, 'You go first.' 'Cause the whole thing about Kennedy scared them very, very much. They really thought it would be possible for somebody to be there and want to kill them."*

As thousands of shrieking teenage girls watched the Beatles climb down from the plane and stand in front of a battery of microphones and cameras, Phil Spector, a sylph in a cap and dark glasses, lurked unnoticed and unknown just behind them, a firsthand witness to the thundering genesis of rock's new age. He was convinced that he belonged.

*From the Rolling Stone interview, Jann Wenner (November 1, 1969):25.

12

He had a funny sense of drama, and he was always shocked that people took him seriously. His whole thing was: let me see if I can create a drama about myself, throw a few bombs, and look around and see if I can get a response out of all these people. Maybe because he was a lonely little boy and didn't look like Erik the Norwegian.

—BEVERLY ROSS

He was insecure and it was a weakness across the board.

—NEDRA TALLEY

Phil's single use of La La Brooks in the studio, recording songs the Crystals knew nothing about, finally caused the original Crystals to rebel. After the Christmas album—which displayed the entire group on the jacket but only La La's voice—Barbara Alston and Mary Thomas were sick of the charade and quit, leaving only Dee Dee Kennibrew from the unit that recorded "There's No Other (Like My

Baby)." "See, we were young, wide-eyed, we didn't know that things that come out of people's mouths were going to be lies," Mary said. "You believe everything they say, that you're gonna do this and that. All Phil Spector did was record us and then left us on our own out in the cold."

Phil, picking his teeth clean of the Crystals' remains, seemed sorry that Kennibrew did not grind under the heel of his boot. "The one girl that Phil did not like was Dee Dee, out of all of them," La La Brooks said, "because she was a die-hard, she was a pusher. She didn't have any talent but she had the guts to keep on and keep on."

Thus proving that he could scatter a group to the wind even as he was making hits with their name, Phil next played similar games with Darlene Love. Having snubbed Darlene on "Da Doo Ron Ron," he put her through the same charade almost every time she sang. Darlene, who did not like being used as a front for the Crystals, was happy to be doing songs under her own name. But only a fraction of the records she cut made it past the acetate stage. "Or he would use Darlene but he wouldn't let her know if he was gonna really use her or go to La La," Bobby Sheen said. "I don't know why he did that. It was his strategy. You'd have to study generals to be able to figure out that type of mind, like maybe Napoleon."

Phil apparently did have some hard reasons of his own to undercut Darlene. For one, Phil never lost sight of the locus of his own fame vis-à-vis his artists. "He didn't want to build up Darlene too much, he didn't want her to be too big," Lester Sill believed all along. For another, Phil was not happy with Darlene's independent streak. As soon as he began using her, Phil disregarded the Blossoms as an entity of their own; they, and especially Darlene, were his property, as he saw it. The Blossoms, however, had a rich pipeline of session work, from Doris Day to Buck Owens, and Darlene never considered leaving it. In 1964 she, Fanita James, and Blossom Jean King took a regular gig on the weekly rock-and-roll television show "Shindig," which further irritated Phil. He gave her several ultimatums, but Darlene—who never let Phil bully her—called his bluff and would not budge.

"Darlene was the only one who stood up to Phil," Sonny Bono said. "Phil would just back everybody down, but Darlene didn't give a shit. She was tough. She would say, 'No way, Phil.'"

Jerking Darlene around on the records, Bobby Sheen thought, could have been the result of Phil's vindictive attitude.

Darlene was also unbending about money, of which she was seeing little. Since Darlene was a Philles employee, Phil did not have to pay her anything close to what he had on "He's a Rebel," merely a standard session fee, and her royalties were scotched by session costs that were contractually paid by the artists—precisely the technique that Lester Sill utilized to explain the loss of Phil's revenue on the Paris Sisters' album. On August 15, 1963, Darlene and Fanita James received the same royalty statement covering "Not Too Young to Get Married" and "Wait 'Til My Bobby Gets Home." The total was $2,948.47, but the balance due was only $1,015.27. It was then that a disgusted Fanita ended the 50–50 pay arrangement with Darlene, giving her almost everything. "I was trying to be fair to her," Fanita said, "but also I didn't want to be part of the Darlene Love thing any more. It was all very unpleasant."

For Darlene, the ensuing rewards were little better; thimble-sized, she reckoned, by comparison to what she was really owed. And yet she was reluctant to move away from Phil's cruel kingdom. "For a long, long time," Fanita recalled, "Darlene didn't think any-one else in the world could record her but Phil Spector. He had led her to believe that. Ahmet Ertegun came after us and Darlene wouldn't go. Oh, what a mistake. I think that stopped us from really being superstars, that little move right there. I wanted to go, but Darlene was afraid of leaving Phil."

Bobby Sheen hung around too, as a favored background singer now that Phil had decided to dispose of Bob B. Soxx and the Blue Jeans. And for Sheen, it could be profitable. "Phil was good with me about money—but in his own way. He'd rather take it out of his own pocket than put it in a statement. If I told him I needed $5,000 right away, he gave it to me. I would've liked it on a statement, but he wasn't really the greatest businessman in the world." Sheen laughed. "Either that or he *was* the greatest. But most of his inter-est was creative, and if I'd come in for a date he would give me triple scale. That was his way of payin' without his accountants get-ting in the way."

When Arnold Goland went to United Artists as an A&R man in 1964, Phil took on as his New York arranger a young man out of the

Leiber and Stoller fold, Artie Butler, who had produced, arranged, and played every instrument but guitar on the Jaynetts' hit "Sally Go Round the Roses."

"I remember Phil saying one day that he discovered a formula for making hit records and he couldn't miss," Butler said. "He said it in front of a bunch of people in the control room. And he wasn't wrong. Phil Spector had the ability to capture innocence, even when he had forty guys pounding and scratchin' and blowin' their brains out."

The New York sessions were important to Phil because he sometimes took tracks cut on a whim at Mira Sound out to Gold Star to be embellished. Yet it was becoming harder for Phil to work out of New York. Artie Butler often hired musicians for the sessions through Artie Kaplan, a top saxophone player and part-time writer for Don Kirshner, and Kaplan was also awed by Spector. "He was the leader of the pack, the guy who started it all, the image of being young and brash and strange," he said. "He took the idiom another step." However, the men Kaplan booked were icily indifferent to Phil. Unlike the Gold Star brigade of musicians, the New York sidemen had little reason to identify with him or to consider living in his studio bunker a point of honor and virtue. At that time, many of these men did not believe rock and roll was a legitimate musical form, and to sit through Spector's long and bristly dates filled the air with tension.

"He was not alone, but he was one of those guys who came around then who seemed to have great authority and we didn't know why," recalled Dick Hyman, the popular jazz pianist.

"I never could understand what he was doing," agreed pianist Mo Wexler. "All I did was play triplets for him, ba-ba-ba, ba-ba-ba. I never played a melodic line."

"We had a big session at Mira one time and he started badgering everybody, pickin' our brains," drummer Buddy Salzman said. "It was four hours and he still couldn't get what he wanted, so he'd badger us, like 'Do something, play something.' We said, 'Hey, Mr. Genius, you're the genius. We're only musicians.' Then he got all upset and Jeff Barry came in and said, 'Fellas, the session is canceled. Phil doesn't feel well.' He was very unsure of himself, very insecure."

The worst incident involved Charlie Macey, a veteran guitarist who had played with the Jimmy Dorsey and Glenn Miller bands and who had insulted Phil's guitar work during a Leiber and Stoller session a few years before. From the booth, Phil said, "Let me hear the guitar." Macey began playing, but was interrupted by Phil yelling "Wait!" Macey asked what was wrong. "You can't play wrong chords for me," Phil said. "What chords? You said to just play," Macey told him angrily. When Phil repeated his critique, Macey put his guitar down and bounded into the booth. "If you open your mouth one more time I'll put your head through that window!" he screamed into Spector's face. "Don't you ever tell me how to play!" Badly shaken, and physically afraid of Macey, Phil could not go on with the session. Then, weeks later, at another session, he saw that Macey was again in the band and asked, "Who hired that guy?" "I did," Artie Butler said. "Charlie is the best around." "No, he's not gonna play for me," Phil decreed. Again, the date was aborted.

"He was scared to death," Macey recalled. "He was scared if he opened his mouth, I would bury him in front of all those people who he wanted to respect him. See, that's what he was doing with me. He was trying to show his authority, but he didn't. Nobody liked him. He was a kook."

"Phil was not a guy who could take charge effectively," Artie Butler said, "because he was all emotional and his ego was hurt easily. Phil's really a little boy."

After constant arguments, by early 1964 Bill MacMeekin, the engineer who worked most of Phil's sessions since "Pretty Little Angel Eyes," had had enough. He gave the assignment to a bright, antsy twenty-year-old named Brooks Arthur, who was nicely suited to the difficult job. Arthur didn't hesitate to ride the meters into the red zone and was a whiz rigging tape-speed tricks to add echo. He made mistakes other engineers would not, but soon Phil would not work a New York session without him. "Brooks was a creative," Artie Butler said. "He let his ear control his heart instead of his brain—just like Phil."

What Arthur would remember most about the job was how much he had to sweat. "Phil was so intense that it carried over to me," he said. "I'd be just wringing wet." After one long and damp session, Phil and Brooks came out of Mira Sound bedraggled and wrung out and were refused admission to a restaurant. "They thought we were bums off the street," Arthur recalled. "Phil went into his 'I can buy this place!' routine. And the funny thing was, at that point he could have."

Phil's odyssey of success and power was a bitter pill for Beverly Ross to swallow. Beverly had a big year herself in 1963, writing two massive hits, Lesley Gore's "Judy's Turn to Cry" and (with Tony Powers) the Earls' "Remember Then." But as her career had progressed, she could push aside the hurtful memories of Phil pulling away from her trust and affection and then breaking the bank without once including her. Traversing the same Broadway acres, they continued to bump into each other, and at those times Phil would almost hurt himself trying to be gracious.

"I think he really did like me very much, and I think he felt a little guilty about what he had done to me," she believed. One time Phil asked her to write a song for Darlene Love. Spector cut the song, "Mr. Love," at Mira Sound, but he never used it. "I guess recording it was some sort of mercy," Ross said. Another time, Phil invited her to his penthouse and cooked her an omelette. "That was how he dealt with guilt. He had no conscience so he could only show remorse by making me an omelette. Besides, I think he just wanted to tout his superiority. His apartment was very plush in a kind of show-off way, just like he was." When "Remember Then" went to No. 1, Phil called her. "He said, 'Hey, you got a smash,' and my attitude was, Why are you telling me that? Are you amazed that I survived? I said, 'Don't pat me on the back, Phil, after you tried to demolish me.' "

Despite her hits, Beverly found it hard to write. "I remember going into a suicidal depression for about a year." She did not renew her contract at Hill and Range, and she turned down Mike Stoller when he offered her a staff job at Trio Music. "I would have been in the machinery of all the production. But they were so involved with Phil and I didn't want to be anywhere near him because I didn't want to walk into a snake's den. I felt my trust had been completely dismissed and violated."

Phil, on the other hand, seemed to have a built-in barrier against feeling guilt. "His morality was that if you violated what *he* decided were the rules, he would penalize you, because you deserved to be penalized," Beverly said.

"Phil once came up with a line in one of our songs that went:

'If you hear them talkin' just walk away.' And that was indicative of how he felt about things. If anybody in the slightest offended or hurt him, he wouldn't give him a second chance. He would just walk away. That was his defense mechanism; he didn't want to be hurt by anyone so if he got to know you really well he'd wind up hating you."

For many months it was Sonny Bono's job to ease Phil's fear of flying and deliver him to the airplane. During these sallies, Phil would sometimes rant and rave at the mosaic tile on the airport wall, yelling that the money should have gone into the plane's radar equipment. Often the only way he could make it onto a plane was by stuffing enough sleeping pills down his throat to knock him out on his feet. One night, as Sonny was escorting him down the long corridor to the American Airlines gate, Phil collapsed. "He was holding a big suit bag chin-high, and he's shorter than me so it's like you couldn't even see him," Bono said. "All of a sudden I'm walkin' along and wham, Phil is down, he just flopped forward because of the bag and the pills. And you can't laugh at Phil, so I pick him up and somehow get him on the plane and I go home and got in bed with Cher. And it's like, oh man, finally he's gone, I can rest for a while."

Then the phone rang. Cher picked it up. "Sonny," she said, "it's Phillip." "Phillip!" he repeated. "He's supposed to be in the air an hour already."

Sonny took the phone and heard Phil mumble, "I didn't take the plane, man."

"What happened?"

"I made 'em turn the plane around on the runway and come back."

Bono recalled: "As the plane had taxied to get in position for takeoff, Phil freaked out. He was screaming, 'I'm not flyin' on this plane! These people are losers and the plane's not gonna make it!' Phil always thought the people he thought were losers were cursed. So they came back to the gate, which is against all regulations, threw him off, and banned him from flyin' American Airlines ever again. They took his credit cards and took down all his identification, everything. They hated him, and I think they fired the pilot for bringin' the plane back."

Unable to pull himself out of bed, Sonny sent Cher to the airport to get Phil onto another flight on a different airline. She found him out cold, on a lounge seat at the same gate. Calling Sonny, she said, "He's asleep and a crowd of people are lookin' at him." Rousing him, Cher found the only way she could get Phil on another plane was to give him the St. Christopher medal she wore on a chain around her neck. "Phil, put it on," she told him. "It's blessed." Phil, the medal dangling down on his thighs during the flight, prayed to a Christian God all the way to New York.

Having been around Phil for many months, Sonny believed he had outgrown his toady's role. By early 1964 he felt he could confide a criticism about the music Phil was making. Over the past year Phil had invariably asked Sonny the same question at almost every session. "Sonny, is it dumb enough?" he would ask—hoping that he had preserved the teen innocence in his ever-growing sound but not really caring about what Sonny had to say. Now Sonny felt that the question was irrelevant. Dumb or otherwise, he feared that the music was stuck on a treadmill and losing its edge.

"It was dynamite for a while," Bono said, "then it kept coming, and as promotion man I couldn't get the records played as much any more, because the jockeys got tired of that sound. What used to be automatic airplay got tough, and records started bombing. So I called him when he sent me a new release one day and I said, 'Phillip, maybe we should change our sound.' And there was a long pause and he didn't say anything; Phil never reacted to anything, you never knew where you stood with him. But I sensed some kind of break in communication from then on. Things were different between us."

In mid-1964 Sonny wrote a song called "Baby Don't Go" and produced a master of it with him and Cher singing. Looking to sell it, he played it for Spector. Phil listened to the record and said he couldn't use it. But he did offer to pay Sonny for half of the publishing rights. "Phil's not always an encouraging guy, but the way I tested him was to see if he'd give you money for something. If he would, you knew he liked it. So when he gave me $500, at that time that was a big chunk of money to get all at once, it was a big validation of my work, as far as I was concerned."

With that impetus, and cash, Sonny—who had married Cher—went on to produce records for the Vault and then Reprise labels. Although he had no immediate success, Phil became decidedly cool to him. "Phil was very weird," Bono said. "You'd know that if you did something on your own, he would be weird to you. He didn't want to be that way, but he was. He was the same with Nino too."

Not coincidentally, Tempo and April Stevens had cut a song called "Deep Purple," which went to No. 1 in December of 1963. As Nino's attention to Phil became divided as he worked on more of his songs, he was invited to fewer Spector sessions. Amazingly, both flunkies had succeeded in becoming creative rivals to Phil Spector. In Phil's system of rewards and punishment, Sonny was at greater fault. By late 1964 his minutes were numbered.

In 1964 a good number of record producers did not share Bono's feeling that Spector's overstuffed sound was becoming stale. Quite to the contrary, like dogs nipping at the tires of a speeding car, they vied to duplicate it as closely as they could. Brian Wilson, a frequent visitor at Spector's sessions, swelled the Beach Boys' surf music with tidal waves of lush, tiered backgrounds, yet as brilliant as Brian was—and he and Phil surely were the twin leviathans of American rock and roll in the early and mid-sixties—he brooded endlessly about Phil always being one step ahead of him. Others, with not the tiniest understanding of the idiom, were miles behind.

Larry Levine, who thought he had broken permanently with Phil, found he could not get too far away from Spector or his sphere of influence. When Phil returned from England and came back out to Gold Star to record, Larry—at Phil's personal behest—was again next to him at the Studio A mixing board. And in the interim, and for a time thereafter, producers were coming to Gold Star and asking for Levine, in order that he might apply Phil's magical formula to them.

"One very big-name producer came to me and I said, you know, you gotta call all of Phil's guys, which he did. And then I'm starting to build the way Phil does, the three guitars playing and the three pianos melding in. So we're doing this for maybe forty-five minutes and this producer says, 'What's that guitar playing there?' He wanted to hear it so I brought it up. And he'd keep saying, 'I wanna hear this and that, bring 'em up.' I said, 'Well, that's not the sound, if you're hearing each instrument.' And he said, 'Well, I'm payin' and I wanna hear what they're playin'.' He missed the whole point of it, and it was a total disaster. But when you get down to it, it wasn't

⊙   170

what I or anybody else could do to make that sound. My contribution to it was minor. You really did have to hear what Phil heard, and nobody could."

Even so, Phil's was a much more temperamental, brittle genius now. The previous fall the Christmas album and the single of Darlene Love's "Christmas (Baby Please Come Home)" had been released into the shroud of gloom following the assassination of John F. Kennedy, and they sold poorly. Phil didn't feel rejected as much as hurt that the public did not hear the grandeur of his work. He then put Darlene Love's "A Fine, Fine Boy" in September of 1963 and the Crystals' "Little Boy" in January of 1964. Neither record did well, but he would not blame himself, or his music, as Sonny Bono had suggested. Instead, he ignored Darlene and La La almost completely afterward.

Peevish and very tightly wound, Phil lashed out at many things that made him feel insecure. For years, Bertha Spector, who with Shirley was being supported by Phil, had been coming by the studio to watch her son at work. But now there would be escalating arguments with her. Phil, unable to control his temper about the slightest of things, would lose focus. That, of course, was the last thing he needed in the studio, and his frustrations made him a figure of pity among those over whom he most needed to exert his authority, his artists and his musicians.

Once a commanding presence in the studio, his almost childlike tantrums, especially under the gaze of his mother, turned into grist for gossip around the L.A. studio scene. Phil, who loved his reputation as a taskmaster, even a heartless martinet—or even crazy—curdled at the thought that some in the business regarded him as a grown man still caught in his mother's apron strings.

People close to Phil were getting worried about him; never a ballast of stability, Phil's highs and lows seemed to be at polar ends. Flamboyant and garrulous when up—he had long, dawdling discussions with Larry Levine prior to recording that grew into raging, wind-blown debates about anything from politics to pastrami, and Larry indulged him because it seemed to charge Phil's batteries—he buried himself in Hamlet-like brooding when down. "Phil had a hard time with reality, especially with present-time reality," Sonny Bono said. "He was coming in and getting very depressed and we'd all have to wait until he'd go in another room to talk to his psychiatrist in New York for about an hour or two. That would bring him up and he'd be okay for a while." When Phil titled one of his B sides "Dr. Kaplan's Office," it was an in-joke that Sonny understood. "As he went on," he said, "the studio was like a roadshow Dr. Kaplan's office."

Phil was also growing more paranoid about his frailty, how physically vulnerable he felt in a world that hated people like him. He began to employ a bodyguard/chauffeur, a beefy Irishman known as "Big Red," to stand by him in L.A., and he took karate lessons from a black-belt, former Hungarian freedom fighter named Emil Farkas. Phil was zealous about the martial arts, but his real aim was to have a goon with him so that he could provoke people without fear of retaliation. Several times Phil picked fights with strangers, only to have Big Red and other bouncer types finish it off while he sat in the comfort of his limousine. To Phil, that was justice.

Phille's output had begun to dwindle. Only one record—the Crystals' "Little Boy"—was released through the first three months of 1964. It was not that Phil was cutting less; rather, having sold over ten million records to date, he was hesitant to release any song for fear that it would not quake the chart. "The pressure kept building on Phil," Larry Levine said. "He'd put out hit after hit, and when the pressure becomes so enormous you lose perspective about what makes a hit a hit any more.

"Phil would always bounce the songs off me, ask me what I thought of the records, and I always said I loved them, because I always did, they were so great. I remember the one time I didn't say it, he didn't put the record out. After that, I would make sure to say 'Hey, that's great, Phil,' because I thought that if I didn't say that, I really didn't know if he'd kill all these great records. He was that insecure about it. Each new record had to be *the* Phil Spector record."

One Ronettes song that Phil would not issue was the Barry-Greenwich-Spector "Chapel of Love." When Jeff and Ellie, with Jerry Lieber, Mike Stoller, and George Goldner, opened their own independent label, Red Bird Records, in early 1964, they were not content to let "Chapel of Love" go to waste. Jeff called Phil out of courtesy and asked if he planned to put the song out as a single, hoping Phil would say "no."

"He said, 'I don't know . . . I don't think so . . . no, no, it's never

☉   172

coming out," Greenwich said years later. "He always wanted to have total control over everything he had anything to do with. I don't know how happy he was that Jeff and I were going to do something on our own without him."°

Barry produced the song with a girl group called the Dixie Cups. When Red Bird's first release exploded on a ride to the top of the charts, Phil was outraged. Thinking he had been betrayed, he broke with Greenwich and Barry—who, in effect had already left him by virtue of their own work at Red Bird—and refused even to speak with them. He then sought another writing team with whom he could impose a similar three-way operating order. He consulted Paul Case, a man he had never strayed from, and Case was ecstatic that he might get Hill and Range on Phil's money wagon. Case pushed two new writers, a duo from Providence, Rhode Island, Vinnie Poncia and Peter Andreoli. They had been staff writers originally at Peer-Southern Music, and Poncia also sang in a lounge act at the Copacabana. Both lived at the Hotel Forrest—blowing all their money on room rent just to be in on the lobby scene there, where they had met Doc Pomus, who brought them to Case.

"Paul told us, 'Phil Spector is looking to replace Jeff and Ellie,' " Poncia recalled. "I've got to believe it was a personal thing between Phil and them and then Phil made it professional. So we went over to Phil's place, which for us was the opportunity of a lifetime."

Running through some song ideas, Phil stopped Poncia when he mentioned a title he had, "(The Best Part of) Breakin' Up Is Makin' Up." "With Phil, it could be just a snippet, a word, and he'd know if it was good for his acts," Poncia said. "He didn't care what the whole song was, because he knew he'd be changing it, break it down and make it a hit." If Phil had little input with the tightly knit Barry-Greenwich songs, he seemed to take a stronger hand now in attacking the more freely structured, insurgent concepts of Poncia and Andreoli. He collaborated in developing "(The Best Part of) Breakin' Up" for the Ronettes, and the structure was radical for a Spector song: a semispoken lead vocal, a choppy and uneven melody, and a false ending before the fade-out. Phil hoped Ronni's breathless "come on, baby, ooh-wee baby" cooing would smooth and carry the record, but the song went only to No. 39 in early Arpil, just as "Chapel of Love" hit No. 1.

°Alan Betrock, *The Girl Groups* (New York: Delilah Books, 1982), 90.

Still, he was comfortable with Poncia and Andreoli. Both were big, animated Italians; Poncia was doughy-cheeked and snidely sarcastic, while Andreoli's rock-jawed features and squinty eyes could scare dogs and small children. They could drink people under the table and they could use their fists—real men, from where Spector sat. Phil, in his new mind-set of vicarious masculinity, liked the idea of working with two men he could bounce around town with and do some manly damage. He even gave them staff jobs at Philles—buying half of their contracts from Paul Case and sharing them with Hill and Range, which would have a half cut of their songs. Poncia and Andreoli had written songs for Don and Juan and other acts, but now did almost all their work for Phil. Holed up in the office at Sixty-second Street, Phil would work with them on the two elements he thought made a song—the opening and the first verse—and then leave and let them do the second verse. "It was a very fair distribution of work," Poncia said. "Who gives a fuck about the second verse? He didn't want to deal with that."

But, again, Phil seemed to need them as much for companionship—and protection. "Peter and I doubled as his bodyguards, 'cause he was always getting into arguments with people. In a restaurant he'd say to someone at the next table, 'Who the fuck are you lookin' at, shithead?' He was studying karate and he'd always think he was a tough guy but he couldn't break an egg. I'd just politely escort him out of there.

"I was different than the bodyguards he had in L.A., who'd beat up people for him. I cared about Phil. Those guys didn't give a fuck about him. He was payin' them as bodyguards, they couldn't care less about Phil. They would beat up someone and figure maybe they'd get a raise. Also, he couldn't get away with that shit in New York. The places you went were music business places. It wasn't like you were goin' down to Pink's for hot dogs. He wouldn't dare pull that shit with a Paul Case or Jerry Leiber sitting two tables away."

The second Spector-Poncia-Andreoli song was the Ronettes' "Do I Love You?" Like "Breakin' Up," it bucked and jerked in separate but connected blocks of funky, brassy rhythm linked by a double-bass line. Ronnie, singing in a lower, more mature key, had no "whoa-ho-hos" or "ooh-wee babys." Rather than filling every spare moment with instrumentation, Jack Nitzsche's arrangement left

⊙

holes when no one played and Larry Levine's echo chamber filled the gaps with the previous strain of notes and voices, striking a mood of hushed contemplation.

"Phil was trying to move out, not stay confined," Vinnie Poncia said. "With 'Do I Love You?' we also started going with the Motown horns. The man was growing up."

All over rock, pimple music and girl groups were still dominant. Ellie Greenwich and Jeff Barry would turn Red Bird into a spurting geyser of juvenile hits with the Dixie Cups, Jelly Beans, and Butterflys—and they collaborated on the Shangri-Las' "Leader of the Pack," which made the girl group sound a grease monkey's paradise.

Meanwhile, twenty-three-year old Phil Spector was going adult.

Spector had received many offers to sell Philles, or have it distributed by a large label. Invariably he refused. Phil was into the one-man trip all the way now. Early in 1964 he no longer wanted to pay Universal Distributing to oversee his national distribution web, and he pulled a no-lose squeeze play on his onetime ally Harold Lipsius. "He wanted to limit the amount of money we could earn," Lipsius recalled. "He didn't want us working on a percentage but on a fixed fee, which would have been much less for us. We didn't feel it made economic sense, and so he took it over himself." That was really what Phil wanted all along: to sell directly to distributors and bill and collect from them himself. Local distributors craved his product, and Phil, who knew his sales figures inside out, used that leverage to demand every cent he had owed. Distributors got no guarantees, because Phil knew they could rip him off by buying cheaply from other distributors and then returning much of his shipments. They had to work only on his terms, and hard. "I remember a conversation he had with one of his distributors," Annette Merar said. "He said, 'Look, if you don't pay me on this stuff you won't get my next record.' He was so confident at that time. He could threaten everybody just by the mention of his next record."

Unfortunately, Phil did not bother with paperwork, leaving it to Chuck Kaye. Phil had named Chuck general manager and moved him to New York, and he ran the office with a secretary named Joan Berg. But when Chuck would try to check on details with Phil, he could only chase a shadow. Worse still, just being in Phil's employ during the winter of 1964 was a burlesque of misery.

"I'm living in the office because he wanted me to," Kaye said, looking back, "and there are no shades, an army cot, and a rented black-and-white TV. And he's in his apartment taking private French lessons and eating pâté. I mean, the guy was the worst. I'm starving to death, man. The winter hawk is blowin' off the East River and I went outside to go to the store for something to eat and I couldn't get half a block. And I'm dyin'. I'm on a $20,000 salary and it was like I was livin' like an animal. So I went to his place and pounded on the door and I'm yelling, 'You gotta feed me, Phil.' And he wouldn't open the door, he was bolted inside. I wouldn't go away and finally he had to open up and feed me.

"When you're young, you can find a Phil Spector charming. We were pals as kids and I'm glad I could learn from him. He was the most brilliant producer to ever live. He stylized record production and he created something that's legendary. But, as a human being, I came to see it as a moral choice: How could I keep working for a guy who did what he did to my father? My dad was suing him and here I was working for him and this guy's a lunatic, he's untouchable and unreachable, and it was demeaning to put up with him."

Before the end of that bitter winter, Chuck sent a memo to Phil. "Basically it said: 'Hey Phillip, I'm gone. Stuff it.' " Without waiting for Spector's response, Kaye went back to L.A. and began working for Lou Adler at Screen Gems.

With Chuck gone, the business was administered by an overburdened Joan Berg. "I used to call over there on business and she would be in tears," Gean Pitney remembered. "She was just beside herself because she could never find Phil. Things would have to be done and she would never know where he was because he would never tell her." Joan was vital to Phil. She had to keep the books, do promotion, book studio time, and make sure the records were pressed on time with the proper information on the labels. Phil knew of her thankless task and was good to her—he allowed Joan to contract musicians for some sessions, paying her per session so she could earn a few extra dollars—but when it was obvious that she had to have help, Phil wisely reached for someone who would be more than an office mule. For all his haughtiness, Phil's antennae were picking up the hurt feelings he could cause in the industry. Accordingly, he brought in a real industry guy, Danny Davis, a promotion man who knew all the angles and all the right people.

Phil had long known Davis. A round little man with friendly blue eyes and a cackling laugh that could rumble a room, Davis had once worked the Borscht Belt as a stand-up comedian while doing promotion for Eddie Fisher, and he carried that chattery arm-around-the-shoulder manner to rock and roll when John Bienstock hired him as national promotion manager at Big Top Records. Davis, who promoted Spector's records for Dunes, found Phil an endearing wacko then. "I loved being involved with him," Davis said, "because you knew he was brilliant and ahead of his time. He adopted the outragious garb and the Ben Franklin glasses before it was fashionable. They thought he was an absolute cuckoo at Big Top, and he was sleepin' on people's desks because no one would give him space, but they knew he was a genius."

Davis was a spectator as Phil fell out with Big Top over the Crystals, but even after the advent of Philles he had remained in Phil's good graces. "He helped me out because we had a good relationship. I'd bring program directors over to meet him. I was using Phil to get my own records played, by trading on his friendship. Phil knew that you do whatever it takes to get a record played. He knew I was the best in the business. But I don't know if Phil needed me or if he just liked me and wanted me to be around him."

Danny was in no position to quibble. He had left Big Top in 1963 to go to Don Kirshner's Dimension Records as vice president. Then, only a short time later, Kirshner folded Dimension when he sold Aldon to Columbia-Screen Gems and, his eye trained on television and movie music, began using many of his nonpareil rock writers to score witless theme songs for Screen Gems sitcoms like "I Dream of Jeannie" and "Bewitched." Kirshner, who was named president of the Screen Gems music division as part of the sale deal, retained Davis at rock-oriented Colpix Records. But then, given a limousine ride by Kirshner to Penn Station one day in 1964, Davis was stunned by what Kirshner told him. "He said he was gonna divert himself into motion pictures and close up the record division," said Davis. "He didn't tell me I was fired, but he literally held me like it was all gonna be through. I of course was gasping for a job because I loved my association with Columbia Pictures with him, but he didn't give me one and I felt completely betrayed. I had given him a tremendous posture in the industry, won all the awards goin', but Don Kirshner was an absolute megalomaniac and I was out in the cold."

Phil had offered Davis a job before. Now Danny called him and quickly accepted.

Vinnie Poncia knew for a fact that Philles needed a man like Davis badly. The hits had slowed, Phil was biting into different music styles, and his industry goodwill was in danger of atrophying. "He had to hire Danny to smooth things out," Poncia said, "because when the hits didn't happen Phil started blaming the distributors and their promotion people. The hits and the adulation, this was supposed to go on forever in his mind. Phil would never take stock of himself, look at what was happening, and see what he had to do." Indeed, when in the summer of 1964 Davis arrived at Sixty-second Street as Philles' new vice president, on an $800-a-week salary, he saw that the Philles empire was really one tiny room in disarray. "I was shocked," Davis said. "He had nobody that was fielding phone calls, nobody taking care of business at the radio level. Joan was great, but she could only do so much."

Davis set out right away on a cross-country mission seeing the Philles distributors, but his first assignment was something Phil considered just as pressing.

Danny had to fire Sonny Bono.

"Get rid of him," Phil ordered.

"Jeez, Phil, I didn't hire him," Danny protested.

"Well, you fire him."

"Phil said we just didn't need Sonny," Davis recalled. "Phil was a little disenchanted at what Sonny was doing. He didn't think Sonny was worth the money, or that he was doing much of anything. But Phil didn't want to face him. I'd never fired anyone before and I had a terrible aversion to being fired myself. I didn't want to do it and I asked Phil two or three times to do it. He told me, 'Don't be a wimp.' "

His throat tight and his mouth dry, Danny placed the call to L.A. Getting Bono on the line, he said, "Sonny, we're gonna let you go." Despite feeling Phil's cold shoulder for months, Sonny did not take it well. "He started to get very testy," Davis said. "He said he did an awful lot for Phil and this isn't fair. He didn't calm down the whole call, and it was highly embarrassing for me. In the end I just left it like I was the bad guy, the guy who fired Sonny Bono."[*]

Sonny would get back on his feet soon enough. Signing with Atlantic in 1965, he and Cher had a No. 1 hit, "I Got You Babe." The follow-up was "Baby Don't Go," and it went to No. 8. Both songs had a familiar ring. Using many of Phil's session men, the sound was "inspired and influenced by Phil," Sonny said. "I definitely ripped off his style of recording." Sonny and Cher would notch five more Top 20 hits through 1967 and perform as a major nightclub act.

"Phil and I were really amazed when he had those hits," said Davis. "Sonny was not a good songwriter, not a good musician or singer, and the act was certainly all Cher. But he had fed off Phil Spector. That made it all possible."

Before Sonny and Cher were gone, Phil used Cher, under the apple-pie pseudonym of Bonnie Jo Mason, singing a novelty song he wrote with Poncia and Andreoli as a play on Beatlemania called "I Love You Ringo." Because it was not material he could have issued on the Philles label, he released it on an off-label he named Annette Records—a bow to his wife's pain that was intended to "anesthetize the situation between them," according to Poncia. Although record sales were minuscule, Phil had use for the idea of offshoot Philles labels. He issued two more inane discs on Annette Records in 1964, one of which, "Oh Baby," he sang with Doc Pomus and released under the name of Harvey and Doc with the Dwellers. He also put out a cover of the Lennon-McCartney "Hold Me Tight," sung by Vinnie and Peter—as the Treasures—on a label called Shirley Records. More important were two solo records by Ronnie singing under the name of Veronica, "I'm So Young" and "Why Don't They Let Us Fall in Love?" He released these on a specialty label called Phil Spector Records, an emblem he trusted would have instant sales appeal.

While some of these records were made at full-blown Spector sessions, he saw none as fit for Philles—a label he viewed now with uneasy

---

[*]Bono's explanation of his parting with Spector skirted any mention of being fired as well as any other specifics. "When 'I Got You Babe' came along, that was the end of my and Cher's connection with Phil," he said.

ambivalence, his personal dominion but also the germ of searing pressure and discontent. "He really wanted to disassociate himself totally with the Lester Sill thing and all that stuff with the Philles label—but he knew he couldn't," Poncia believed. "So what he did with these records was . . . he just wanted a whole expanded set up which he could offer to other distributors and start fresh."

Stepping back from Philles, Phil used the other labels both as a haven and a cudgel, trying to find a new path without pressure while at the same time smiting the industry and even his trail of hits. "At this time, Phil had grown tired a little bit of his sound," Poncia said. "He was getting turned off with the teenybopper stuff. The Jeff and Ellie thing, that wasn't his music. Phil would never have written a song like 'Da Doo Ron Ron.' With something like that, he would tap the source for whatever it was and when it ran out it was 'next.' We were starting to get into some different kinds of songs, we'd come in with different angles, and he was happy with that.

"Phil knew what the power of Philles was, but he always had the idea . . . See, this is when he felt rejected by a business that he thought he gave so much to. So he did this other thing for a while and said, 'Fuck everybody.' And then too, in order to bring in Danny Davis and make it a viable working situation, he wanted to offer Danny a situation too." This would come about months later, when Phil opened yet another off-label, Phi-Dan Records; co-owned by Spector and Davis, it was a minor vehicle designed to feed off the reputations of both men, though Phil would have little to do with any product on the label.

However, Phil gave up the safe harbor of releasing inadequate material on cheesecloth labels when all of the records he made failed and a priority was to deliver a record with the appeal of "Be My Baby." Clearly, the timing of the Philles retreat could not have been worse. As Spector receded, the Beatles captured the imagination of the restless baby-boom generation, flooding the charts with as many as six Top 10 hits at once. The Merseybeat was in full bloom across the United States, on a rising tide with the rhythmic, pounding hooks of Motown. Spector had little voice in this important period of change. As the hot summer of 1964 was called to arms by Martha and the Vandellas' "Dancing in the Street," the Ronettes, "Do I Love You" rose to only No. 34. The one new Philles release was the Crystals' "All Grown Up"—and this record may have appeared more out of spite than art. Phil had cut the Spector-Barry-Greenwich tune a full year before. Then, when Jeff and Ellie recorded it with the Exciters, Phil—still smarting over "Chapel of Love"—put out his record, leading Jeff and Ellie to kill theirs. And while he won the round, the ploy was harmful to him. The Crystals' song, a mediocre Spector artifact, was gone in an eye blink, a whisper at No. 98.

The cool breeze of autumn rejuvenated Phil. He returned to the reliable lodestone of meretricious emotion, Barry Mann and Cynthia Weil. For this, his timing was perfect. Fairly drifting in Don Kirshner's television jingle world, their biggest recent hit was Eydie Gorme's "Blame It on the Bossa Nova." Kirshner wanted to keep his writers content and in the rock-and-roll elite, and that "Philly" was coming back to him made Kirshner believe in the prodigal son. Spector was so serious about his revival that he earned his one-third interest. For days, three titanic composing talents sat with each other around a piano, soldering viscous, romantic chords into a Ronettes ballad called "Walking in the Rain."

Phil cut the song in a minimal style, smothered in soft, salacious echoes and only horns and a triangle bell sticking out of the quietly massed arrangement. Given the literal imagery of the lyric, Larry Levine suggested using sound bites of thunder and rainfall, which he had in the special effects drawer in the Gold Star office. Normally, Phil would have gone for such effects only if he could create them musically, but Larry blended the taped clangor as he would have an instrument, not obliterating any other sound. Thunder booming and drops falling around her, Ronnie's gauzy, quavering plea for someone with whom to share the rain was every bit an operetta.

"With 'Walking in the Rain,' " Vinnie Poncia said, "he went back to goin' for the jugular again."

Phil had been going to release a Darlene Love song written by Poncia and Andreoli, "Stumble and Fall," and had already assigned it the catalogue number Philles 123. But he was so eager to unveil "Walking in the Rain" that he gave it that number. Released within days in early October, it climbed rapidly and blanketed the airwaves but, oddly, it stopped at No. 23, surely the lowest chart ranking for a song everyone assumed was a monster hit.

Phil was certain that the song would serve him well, and he did not wait for the chart's verdict. He was moving again now, pushing with the old confident swagger, and he was working on a record he wanted to hit people across the eyebrows. Satisfied that he had taken the Ronettes to a higher level, but fearful that the girl-group thing was dying, he had already cast his fate in a whole new direction.

13

I get a little angry when people say it's bad music. This music has a spontaneity that doesn't exist in any other kind of music, and it's what is here now. It's unfair to classify it as rock and roll and condemn it. It has limited chord changes, and people are always saying the words are banal and why doesn't anybody write lyrics like Cole Porter anymore, but we don't have any presidents like Lincoln anymore, either. You know? Actually, it's more like the blues. It's pop blues. I feel it's very American. It's very today. It's what people respond to today. It's not just the kids. I hear cab drivers, everybody, listening to it.

—PHIL SPECTOR, from "The First Tycoon of Teen,"
Tom Wolfe, *New York Herald Tribune*, January 3, 1965,
New York magazine section.

The concept of true "pop blues" was a promise that rock and roll had forsaken in the great rush to move the most vinyl. Phil himself believed he had gone back on his implicit blues genesis; in the seven years since "To Know Him Is to Love Him" made the *Billboard* R&B chart, he returned there with only one record—"Be My Baby"— and not since "He's a Rebel" had he turned loose the jazzmen in Studio A without care for any formulizing. Spector's vocalists sang blacker than Berry Gordy tolerated from his Motown artists, but in truth neither idiom was R&B in its brokenhearted and wailing sense.

Contemplating pop music after the initial wave of Beatlemania, Phil thought that as marketable as Motown and the Merseybeat were, they were still teenage idioms and that there really was nowhere for rock and roll to go but back to the heart of R&B, because that would close the circle of its evolution. The pity for Phil was that rock had virtually bludgeoned and whitewashed great black soul singers out of the business; in a mid-sixties that was riffling by like pages from a Greek tragedy, Sam Cooke was shot dead, and Ben E. King, the Drifters, and the Coasters had to work in supper clubs.

When Phil found a soul act with which he thought he could right the world, it was ironically a white act, but one that no set of ears would ever hear as anything but black. Indeed, when Bill Medley and Bobby Hatfield began vocalizing together, they took their performing name from the reaction of a mostly all-black audience who greeted their music with cries of "righteous"—black slang for that which is truthful and honest. Signed to the small L.A. label Moonglow Records in 1962, the Righteous Brothers were a local word-of-mouth sensation. They had a middling hit, "Little Latin Lupe Lu," in 1963 and cut songs written by, among others, Sonny Bono and Jack Nitzsche. But their hard gospel blues were their calling card. It kept them on the L.A. club circuit and landed them a regular gig on "Shindig."

Phil wanted Medley and Hatfield so much that he was willing to deal with Moonglow to lease their services, a sharing of the riches that usually was anathema to him. In early October of 1964, he signed papers with Moonglow's R.J. Van Hoogten that granted him an exclusive four-year license to record and release the Righteous Brothers on the Philles label in the U.S., Britain, and Canada. Van Hoogten, who was eager to make this step into the rock elite, retained the right to sell the records anywhere outside those three countries. Spector's cut of publishing royalties would be divided between Mother Bertha and the publishing company of Moonglow's owner, Ray Maxwell Music. Medley and Hatfield, eager for a national hit, met with

Spector and forwarded their approval in a signed letter on October 1, 1964.

Slim, dark-haired, and narrow-faced, Bill Medley, born in Santa Ana, California, was the Righteous Brothers' soul fulcrum. His voice was a bold and edgy basso that sounded like a Bing Crosby croon powered by a diesel engine. The turnip-nosed and blond Bobby Hatfield, from Beaver Dam, Wisconsin, was Medley's physical and vocal counterpoint, with a honeyed soprano that trilled with heated Jackie Wilson–style shrieks. Together, their tight harmonies soared in every direction, each note wildly exuberant and at times almost angrily emotional.

As such they were tailored to the Mann-Weil meat grinder of passion. They and Phil collaborated in a harvest of love's shameless irrationality called "You've Lost That Lovin' Feelin'." The lyric of this song indicted, derided, and then ultimately pleaded for reunion, and it would be Bill Medley, solo and almost *a capella* for a Spector song, who would carry the record into its raging currents by crooning the damning intro of eyes unclosed during kissing and fingertips bereft of tenderness.

Phil took the purgatory nature of the song literally. This record was to be a rebirth; far more so than "Walking in the Rain," this was a holy conversion of his music. To go with his new act, Gold Star's Studio A was fertilized with the seeds of new life. There were a number of new musicians in the room. Jack Nitzsche, busy elsewhere, was replaced with an arranger named Gene Page. Hal Blaine, who had mildly irritated Phil by refusing to cancel other gigs and stay on hold for him, was out and Earl Palmer back in. And, most significantly for Phil, an invitation was sent out to Barney Kessel, the great jazz guitarist who helped steer Phil to pump the fortunes of rock.

Kessel had never before played on a rock-and-roll session. Like Howard Roberts before him, he knew almost nothing of Spector's career or music, and was just as puzzled about Phil's conceptualizing of a record. But Barney could see that Phil was on to something. "It was all loose and laid back, but all the time he was working on a strategy, like he was going to invade Moscow," Kessel said. "He had a sketch, and there were very few things happening, but there was a lot of weight on each part. The three pianos were different, one electric, one not, one harpsichord, and they would all play the same thing and it would all be swimming around like it was all down a well.

"Musically, it was terribly simple, but the way he recorded and miked it, they'd diffuse it so that you couldn't pick any one instrument out. Techniques like distortion and echo were not new, but Phil came along and took these to make sounds that had not been used in the past. I thought it was ingenious." Spector had Kessel play a high-octave, six-string bass guitar on the bass-heavy "Lovin' Feelin'," in tandem with Carole Kaye's Fender and Ray Pohlman on stand-up. "Really, more than anything else, what he wanted from me was the jazz kind of energy," Kessel said.

Studio A was like a nuclear generator that night, but Medley and Hatfield, unaccustomed to anything like this grand-scale session, sat through the hours of mounting orchestration bewildered and bored. Waiting to lay down their vocals, they watched Phil ring-lead a circus of flash and noise and could not believe that they were the stars of the record. Larry Levine, who knew from the first guitar chord that something special was happening here, was incredulous that Medley and Hatfield didn't seem to care. "How can you sit there?" he admonished them. "You should be ecstatic about this!" Bill and Bobby remained impassive, but Larry would play the song for record people as soon as they entered the Gold Star doorway. "They'd come back after three hours and want to hear it again," he said. "All day long people would be comin' over to listen to that thing."

"You've Lost That Lovin' Feelin' " was not unlike "Walking in the Rain" in its dreamlike flow, but the emotion was rubbed raw. The slashing vocals and the massive chorus tore the top off the song, while the throbbing basses and tom-toms made the quiet passages a slightly surreal intimation of a molten heart. It was still white pop, but it was white pop cleaved by the forgotten pain and grieving of the blues. Over the radio, one could hear the embers burning.

"Lovin' Feelin' " ran three minutes and fifty seconds, a good half-minute longer than the average record of the day. Phil, who would not cut one second of it, released it with the label reading 3:05, just in case program directors would be skittish. He need not have worried. The record messed up some tight radio schedules at first, before the ruse was discovered, but it demanded to be played. Five weeks after hitting the chart in mid-December it went Top 10, and many black stations were playing it in rotation, a major break-through for a white act in the mid-sixties. Reflecting a revolution in rock tastes, teenagers bought the record in greater numbers than any of the earlier teen anthems. In England, Andrew Oldham gen-uflected to the record. When a British pop singer named Cilla Black put out a cover of "Lovin' Feelin' " before the Righteous Brothers record was imported, Oldham took it as sacrilege. He and Tony Calder took out giant ads in the London music papers screaming attention to the Spector disc. In an ad placed in *Melody Maker*, Oldham wrote:

> *This advert. is nor for commercial gain, it is taken as something that must be said about the great new* PHIL SPECTOR *Record,* THE RIGHTEOUS BROTHERS *singing* "YOU'VE LOST THAT LOVIN' FEELING". *Already in the American Top Ten, this is Spector's greatest production, the last word in Tomorrow's sound Today, exposing the overall mediocrity of the Music Industry.*

In solidarity with Spector, in the ad Oldham used the term that had become the quasi-monogram of Philles Records and imprinted on some Philles album jackets, "Tomorrow's Sound Today." In other ads, Andrew described the magnitude of the song by coining a new term, "Phil Spector's Wall of Sound," and that catchphrase would come to have a life of its own, cribbed by music critics worldwide as the definitive description of Spector's work. Realizing the power of those words, Phil would eventually register them as a legal trademark.

The Righteous Brothers, with Phil to pitch them, went to England in January to do a tour. By mid-February, "You've Lost That Lovin' Feelin' " moved ahead of Petula Clark's "Downtown" and became the No. 1 record on both sides of the water. On the American R&B chart, it was No. 3, behind only the Temptations' "My Girl" and Sam Cooke's "Shake."

Although Phil had stopped etching the "Phil & Annette" legend on his records with "Baby I Love You," he and Annette came together in several shaky reconciliations in 1965. During these interludes, Ronnie's name was never mentioned, and Annette dreamed that Phil had finally learned what was important to his soul. However, their arguments never ceased. Vinnie Poncia would be called up to the eighteenth floor and would step into guerrilla warfare.

"Things would be strewn all over the place and they'd be screamin' at each other," Poncia said. "She'd say, 'You better get him out of here, because I'm gonna kill him if you don't!' And he'd be threatening to kill her and it would get brutal. I'd go in there as a peacemaker and break it up but then they'd start again. Because Phil was just impossible to live with. He was way too involved with himself to give anything to anybody else. At one point Annette was a very normal human being. He made her a wreck. That's why both of them were in therapy all the time."

"There were tremendous fights," Danny Davis recalled. "Annette was no mouse. She was very tough and demanding of his time. She was very sweet and nice, but she changed too. I watched her change. But I tell you what, her change was fostered by Phil's actions."

Phil told Annette he still loved and needed her, but the romance with Ronnie did not cool. Neither did he allow Annette to get any closer to him or his success. In June of 1964, two months after the release of their first album, the Rolling Stones flew over to begin their first American tour. Phil entertained them in New York and provided Andrew Oldham the use of his office; some nights Andrew slept there. Their first night in, Phil took Vinnie to have dinner with the Stones at the Astor Hotel, where they were staying—"He said, 'Vinnie, you're not gonna believe what they look like' "—but he would not let Annette near them. Early in 1965, when the Beatles were filming their second movie, *Help!*, in the Bahamas, Annette, at that time again separated from Phil, was invited by her friend Henry Grossman, a *Life* magazine photographer, to visit the set. When Grossman introduced her to the Beatles, they sang "Happy Mrs. Spector to You." It was a thrilling moment for her, and she had to fight for it.

"Phil was so pissed that I went, he almost screwed up my whole trip," Annette said. "He told Murray the K, who was also there, to spy on me and try to keep me off the set but he couldn't.

"Phil didn't want me to do anything, or find any happiness, or be a part of anything. He had detectives on me when we were separated. I know because I read the detective reports. A private investigator was tailing my ass to see what I'm doing when *he's* the one who's screwing around."

Phil recorded "You've Lost That Lovin' Feelin' " while he was

⊙

separated from Annette. "He wrote 'Lovin' Feelin' ' for me, he told me that to my face," she related. "He said, 'This song is for you.' " That cut Annette like a knife. Gorgeous as the record was, the lyric was a harsh censure of blame for a failed love; not one word of it accepted blame.

"He has no right to tell me I lost the loving feeling," she said, "because he's the one who never had it."

Knowing there was no hope for them, Annette moved into an apartment removed from him and the memories, on Broadway and Sixty-eighth Street. Phil returned to the penthouse. Even so, there was still talk about reconciliation. "He never said yes and he never said no, he just left me dangling." She gave it one last chance when she went to L.A. with Phil one time, hoping the change of scenery would evoke old feelings. It didn't. "We fought our asses off," she said, "and I walked out one morning at 6 A.M. and got on a train— because he got *me* afraid to fly—and went back to New York alone."

Finally Annette spoke the word they had avoided. She asked for a divorce.

"First he said if I wanted a divorce, I had to go get it. But after some more time, he said he would arrange it. I had a lawyer and we made a settlement and Phil was very generous, but I felt I deserved it. He had his best year with me; he never before or after had a year like he had in 1963."

Late in 1965, Phil went to Tijuana on an overnight charter to obtain a Mexican divorce. The settlement gave Annette $100,000 in alimony spread out in weekly payments over five years.

"I never asked for royalties or anything. I only wanted his love— and that was the last thing in the world he was capable of giving."

In the months following his unpleasant departure from Philles Records, Lester Sill hit bottom. His production companies and talent scouting underfinanced and withering in a new world of rock, his royalty vein to Duane Eddy and then to Spector broken, Lester closed up shop. The man who tilled the rock soil with Leiber and Stoller, Phil Spector, Herb Alpert, and a dozen more was repaid by none of them. There was no work and no money. Being locked in legal battles with a stubborn Spector over the $60,000 severance pay was a major strain.

"I remember my lawyers deposing him, chasing him all over

the place, and I was in real bad trouble," Sill said. "I was busted, I was really broke and on my ass."

Aware of this, Phil wanted to turn the screw. "You know what he did? Shows you where his mind was. I owed money to Gold Star for my own projects. I owed 'em about $1,500 and I couldn't pay them. So Phil wanted to pay that and take over the bill, so he could sock it to me because I was suing him. It would be my debt to *him*. Stan Ross and Dave Gold told him they wouldn't do it."

Eventually Lester did get the money held hostage by Phil, but by the time the lawyers were paid it was only a moral victory. Still hurting, Lester was finally offered a job, by Don Kirshner at Screen Gems, where Chuck Kaye had landed. Called in to quell the writers' discontent and resign them to Kirshner, "I had to pay my own way to New York, that SOB," Sill said. Not sure if he wanted to take a long-term position, he signed two one-year contracts with Screen Gems. He wound up staying with the company for twenty-one years.

Only now was Spector getting exposure in his own country as a prime representative of the rock generation, though at times it could be as the butt of the straight world's smug derision. He appeared on David Susskind's television show, *Open End*, and was set on by Susskind and an elevator-music deejay, William B. Williams, both of whom held rock in contempt. Making a point, Susskind dryly intoned the simple-minded lyrics of "A Fine, Fine Boy," which mainly repeated the title over and over. As Susskind read aloud, Phil began tapping his hand on a coffee table. "What you're missing," he pointed out calmly, "is the beat." When Williams boasted that he played only "good music," Phil asked him how often he played Verdi. In conclusion, after enduring the ambush, Phil informed his attackers that he didn't have to come on television and put up with insults. "I could be home making money," he said.

Phil also appeared on Johnny Carson's "Tonight" show, a guest along with Ella Fitzgerald. At one point she asked him what his top act was and he said it was the Righteous Brothers. Ella confessed that she had never heard of them. A testy Phil replied, "They never heard of you."

In late January of 1965, with "Lovin' Feelin' " scaling the chart, Phil released the follow-up to the Ronettes "Walking in the Rain." A Spector-Mann-Weil song called "Born to Be Together," it was an unexpected flop, reaching only No. 52. Unhappily, this abrupt reversal came on the heels of a profile of Spector by "new wave" journalist Tom Wolfe in the Sunday magazine of the *New York Herald Tribune*. The piece, titled "The First Tycoon of Teen," was a broad-brush, not-entirely-factual caricature that made Phil out to be a kind of music Man of La Mancha reeling against the windmills of the rock establishment in a suede shirt, Italian pants, and Cuban heels. It helped establish Phil Spector as a major nutcase, but one who was singularly qualified as avatar of the recalcitrant new rock millennium. "Every baroque period has a flowering genius who rises up as the most glorious expression of its style of life," Wolfe wrote. "And in teen America Phil Spector is the bona-fide Genius of Teen."

Phil's life—minus any mention of Ben Spector's heavily cloaked suicide—was laid before America, how he sprang from the rock generation's desire to possess grown-up money and power without bowing to the grown-up world. "He is something new," Wolfe concluded, "the first teen-age millionaire, the first boy to become a millionaire within America's teen-age netherworld. It was never a simple question of him taking a look at the rock and roll universe from the outside and exploiting it. He stayed within himself. He *liked* the music." Now, having dragon-slain the rock establishment, Spector had no conciliatory words for his chosen enemies.

He branded industry people and rip-off record distributors as "animals" and "cigar-smoking sharpies," but neither was he comfortable with practically anyone in his world. Said Spector: "I find this country very condemning. I don't have this kind of trouble in Europe. The people of America are just not born with culture." And: "I even have trouble with people who should never say *any*thing. I go over to Gristede's to get a quart of milk or something and the woman at the cash register has to start in. So I tell her, 'There's a war in Viet Nam, they've fired Khrushchev, the Republican party is falling to pieces, the Ku Klux Klan is running around loose, and you're worrying about my hair.'" And: "You know what I'd like to do? I'd like to do a recording session in the office of *Life* or *Esquire* or *Time*, and then they could see it. That's the only chance I've got. Because I'm dealing in rock and roll, I'm, like I'm not a bona-fide human being."

Barry Mann and Cynthia Weil had been responsible for Phil's return to prominence, and shared with him one of rock's seismic moments when "Lovin' Feelin' " shook pop to its foundations. However, they also felt Spector went back on his word to give them the follow-up to "Lovin' Feelin' " when he instead renewed old ties with Gerry Goffin and Carole King and gave it to them. Promises aside, Phil believed that Goffin and King's bouncier style of introspection was a perfect Righteous Brothers recipe.

"Phil invited us to his apartment and told us we had the song," said Goffin. However, Gerry and Carole were lost in the wilderness of Don Kirshner's boob-tube preoccupation. "Working for Phil again was in our best interest at the time," Goffin said.

The first Spector-Goffin-King song was "Just Once in My Life," composed with almost no aid from Phil. It was crafted and produced in the same densely sumptuous style as "Lovin' Feelin'," with a near-identical Bill Medley intro and blended harmonic hooks, and it went to No. 9 in early May.

The Righteous Brothers' saucy vocal cords were a secure and prosperous headrest for Phil. With a catchy hook and the big-band dramatics, their blue-eyed soul flowered into a concerto. When their next single, the Spector-Goffin-King "Hung on You," did not explode up the charts, deejays flipped the record—the public's thirst for the Righteous Brothers' fervent vocals had ruled out any more sham B sides—and began playing their cover of "Unchained Melody," which was a solo by Bobby Hatfield. Hatfield's wild, hungry emotion and wide octave range tingled a million spines and rammed the song to No. 4 in mid-September. The Righteous Brothers were so hot that even as the Philles records came out, R. J. Van Hoogten released four Bill Medley–produced songs for Moonglow: "Bring Your Love to Me," "You Can Have Her," "Justine," and "Georgia on My Mind." Phil hated that these clinkers were on the market at the same time his Righteous Brothers records were, but the distributing run was small. Even so, riding the comet's tail, all four charted, way down the list.

At various times in 1965, Phil gazed around at other acts, but never in earnest, figuring that the Righteous Brothers were a perpetual meal ticket. Early that year, Danny Davis got a call from concert promoter Sid Bernstein, who was instrumental in arranging the Beatles' U.S. tours. Bernstein touted Danny on a four-man blues rock band, the Rascals, who were a regular act in a Westhampton, Long Island, club called The Barge. "Sid wanted Phil to hear 'em, so I dragged him out there," Davis recalled. Vinnie Poncia knew the Rascals and The Barge. He had been a running buddy of the group's lead singer, Felix Cavaliere, in the New York scene when Cavaliere sang in a latter-day version of Joey Dee and the Starlighters, of "Peppermint Twist" fame. Three members of the Starlighters then formed the Rascals, who performed in Edwardian knickers and cloth caps after the old "Little Rascals" movie shorts. Fronted by the bearded, soulful Cavaliere, they combined R&B with the self-contained rock band format then coming into vogue. As such, Vinnie, whose wife Joanna was working in a backup band at The Barge, agreed that the Rascals could be Phil's entree to the stripped-down trend of rock.

"At that time, the music had started to move away from the giant sound and more toward the personal kind of records," Poncia said. "And I thought that would be perfect for Phil. He grew up on that stuff, R&B, jazz bands. When we went in and made the Cher record, it was just two guitars, bass and drums, and he had a lot of fun. Phil liked to dabble with that kind of music because of the Beatles. He would always extol the virtues to me about how simple those records were. He'd say, 'That's what we gotta do. We gotta get back to just guitars'—and yet he'd be contradicting that all the time with his own sound going through the roof.

"Because that was the only identity he had left. He was the star, as far as he was concerned. He was the music, and he was afraid to go any other way. It was easy, he had it down, it was very comfortable: same engineer, same studio, you don't have to worry about some kid drummer, because that's another challenge. All he wanted was what he had."

But Phil did go to see the Rascals at The Barge, and the band was so elated that he was there that they performed some of Spector's hit songs in homage. Phil listened impassively, then turned to Danny and said, "Let's get the fuck out of here. They don't do anything original." Persuaded to stay, he heard the group's entire set and then went backstage to be introduced to them by Vinnie. "They wanted Phil to produce them," Poncia said, "but Phil said he wanted me to produce them, for Phi-Dan Records, which immediately turned them off. They liked me but I was new to producing. They didn't want me, they wanted Phil Spector." And so the Rascals declined, with the bitter taste of being brushed off by the godlike Spector. A short time later they signed with Atlantic Records, changed their name to the Young Rascals, and by the end of the year had their first hit, "I Ain't Gonna Eat Out My Heart

Anymore." Early in 1966, they had a No. 1 record, "Good Lovin'," followed by nine more Top 20 hits.

Phil received similar feelers to produce new acts, and Danny believed Phil wanted to widen his purview, not just to change with the times but for his own survival. By mid-1965 the Crystals and Darlene Love were forgotten and on the verge of leaving Philles, and the Ronettes were only a step behind in alienation. Danny certainly knew the risks of the label becoming too dependent on the Righteous Brothers. "We all knew it, the distributors, everybody. A lot of guys said, 'Jeez, Danny, you gotta break another act.' And Phil knew it. That's why people kept bringing 'em to him."

One such moment occurred at a party in L.A. given by Lance Reventlow, the race-car driver son of heiress Barbara Hutton. A band was performing at the party whose lead vocalist was a little fellow with round glasses, John Sebastian, who played a lute tucked under his chin. Phil heard the band, the Lovin' Spoonful, and said, "I don't like their name. They'll never happen." But Phil was mildly intrigued with their folk-rock sound, which was played jug-band style. The Lovin' Spoonful stemmed from the Greenwich Village folk scene, whose influence in rock was growing with the emergence of Bob Dylan; in 1965 the Byrds, an L.A. band, recorded Dylan's "Mr. Tambourine Man" using a loud electric guitar line and soft harmonies, creating a profound new rock form that seemed made for the plaintive, airy L.A. state of mind. The Lovin' Spoonful were as eager as the Rascals to be produced by Spector, and they sent Phil a demo of a record called "Do You Believe in Magic?" Phil liked it, and played it for Vinnie Poncia one day while strumming a guitar to the melody. But he never did connect with the group, and the Spoonful signed with Kama Sutra–Buddha Records, a label begun by twenty-five-year-old Artie Ripp and on which they had five Top 10 hits over the next three years.

"Phil was considering them but passed on it," Poncia said. "He would dabble with new groups, get involved to be associated with something, and then pull out, never commit to it. Which was a big mistake. Phil needed groups like that. Had he taken the Rascals or Lovin' Spoonful, he would have fulfilled his dreams of expanding. Had he gone through with all those people he was associated with, he would've been like Berry Gordy at Motown."

The biggest problem for Phil was facing the reality that working with a band that had songs and a sound would mean a reduction in his authority—which, unlike Berry Gordy, was tied directly to his own work. "Every artist wants to have a voice in something," Poncia said. "The Rascals and Spoonful would have come in with songs so left field and not of his character—or with any of his input in their development—that he would have to be strictly a producer, just to get the shit down on tape. He couldn't have the same stamp on it, and he didn't want to do that. It would have required a total revamping and a totally different outlook in the studio, making an entirely different kind of record.

"Not that Phil was incapable of doing it, because it was so much easier to make a Rascals record. But his ego was involved, it would've been too much sharing of the spotlight—which wouldn't have been the case, it was only in his head. Phil wouldn't have been any less effective on a Rascals song than a Darlene Love song. Once he got in the studio and made the record, it didn't matter who wrote the song. He could've done 'I Ain't Gonna Eat Out My Heart Anymore' and made a better record, because nobody makes a record like Phil Spector.

"But he was just so involved with himself at the time. Again, he never knew it was gonna end, he never knew that something like that was gonna make a difference. He never wanted to change, to adjust. He wanted complete autonomy and control, like he had over Ronnie."

As soon as Phil obtained his Mexican divorce, he began openly living with and squiring Ronnie around. Weeks later Ronnie, hoping to ease the family tension, told Nedra and Estelle that she and Phil had run off and gotten married. By then, though, Phil's obsession with Ronnie was the cause of serious dissension among the Ronettes. The solo Veronica ventures had not sat well with Nedra in particular, and she bridled when Phil released a Ronettes album—which was mostly a compilation of their hit singles—and titled it *Presenting the Fabulous Ronettes Featuring Veronica.*

"The way he used Ronnie, it was divide and conquer," Nedra said. "Because at that point, he was separating her off, which was understandable. They were involved with each other and she saw it as her way to fame. Anyone would feel that way with someone patting them on the back and promising to make them more special. But I did not feel Ronnie could be objective to what was best for the Ronettes. Sex, love, and business don't work well together."

195

Most crushing to Nedra was that Phil had succeeded in prying open the ties that had held the Ronettes: family unity and loyalty. When Ronnie said she deserved to get more than the one-third share each Ronette received, Nedra wanted to cry but what came out was anger. "When that happens," she told Ronnie, "count me out."

"My cousin Estelle was more under pressure, because it was her sister," Nedra recalled. "But my argument was: as long as we were the Ronettes, I started out in a trio and that's the way I stay. If Phil was getting what he wanted from Ronnie, I can understand him building her up. But he wasn't going to build her up at my expense. And he couldn't replace one of us, bring in another girl like with the Crystals, because we were family. So we stayed with thirds."

Phil may have been incurably in love, but Ronnie learned how strange and demeaning Phil Spector's love could be.

Danny, for one, was never really sure how deeply Phil cared for Ronnie. "He definitely threw himself at Ronnie. He romanced her pretty good," Davis said. "I remember him telling me at the outset he was crazy nuts about her because she was great sexually. He was very enamored at that, and I know for a fact that they were doin' ménag-à-trois scenes." As with Annette, Phil could at times treat Ronnie like his queen, lavishing her with clothes and, now, a three-carat diamond ring. And yet, at other times, he could be extraordinarily spendthrifty with her. "One time Ronnie went out to California with Phil on her own, without Estelle and me," Nedra recalled. "He brought her out as his girlfriend, or wife, but he put her in the studio just long enough to justify that we had to pay for the session. So her trip was paid for—by us, not him. He had his cake and he ate it too, and we paid for it."

But even these sessions were infrequent as Phil became more absorbed with the Righteous Brothers and veered hard away from any kind of Ronettes product. After "Born to Be Together," there was only one Ronettes record in 1965, the Spector-Goffin-King "Is This What I Get for Loving You?" which died at No. 75 in June. Nedra thought the neglect had as much to do with Phil's twisted insecurities as it did his musical interests.

"Ronnie getting involved with Phil caused the destruction of the Ronettes," she said. "Phil made a lot of promises to Ronnie, but the other side was that he couldn't do those things because if he did, he believed he would lose her. It was like: if you're special to me, I'm going to make you special and push you forward—but with one hand he's got strings and he's pulling her back. He's saying: 'I can't let her go *too* far off my leash because then I can't control her.'

"It was the extreme jealousy. Phil knew that Ronnie was not in love with him as a man. She was in love with who he was. I think he felt that if he made her a success in her own right and she became all that she could be, then maybe someone would come along who was good-looking and a producer and a genius—and then why would she need Phil Spector? So he would only do so much with her, he would give her an inch and take back two inches. And then he took back more than that."

14

The two of them weren't *exceptional talents, but they did have a musical contribution to make. I loved them. I thought they were a tremendous expression for myself. I think they resented being an expression.*

—PHIL SPECTOR on the Righteous Brothers

Phil had seen the creative weight of rock shifting westward as early as the autumn of 1964—the last important thing he did in New York was playing the funky guitar break for Leiber and Stoller on the Drifters' "On Broadway" in 1963. To prep himself for resettlement in the hip new L.A. rock community he fully intended to serve as headmaster, he leased an appropriately regal castle. It was one of those ego-assuring Lotus Land fantasies in wood and brick: a five-bedroom, twenty-one-room Italian-style house with a swimming pool, nestled off a hushed side road in Beverly Hills. The house and the leafy grounds at 1200 La Collina Drive, only minutes from the action on Sunset, had once been part of the enormous Woolworth

⊙

family estate, which was now subdivided into tracts. Other houses on the land had been made from the servants' quarters and the horse stables. Phil had the prime lot, the Woolworth master house, which was owned by the aging British actor Reginald Owen. Owen's wife, Barbara, leased it to Phil at the bargain rent of $1,000 a month.

The house, furnished down to the last napkin ring, greeted a visitor with a Louis XV credenza in carved gilt wood and a green marbletop table in the entrance hall. Louis XV doré-framed armchairs with Aubusson upholstery sat in a hallway lined with Piranesi prints, a Chinese Chippendale frame mirror with carved birds in a gilt finish, an antique French clock, and bronze candelabras. The living room, with its twenty-foot ceilings and gable archways, was a veritable Louvre, offering an ormolu Napoleon round table with miniature medallions, two beige satin sofas, portraits of King Louis XV and Queen Marie Thérèse in gilt frames, a large French clock on the mantel, rose velvet and red satin Louis Philippe armchairs, and a black ebony Steinway concert grand piano. Upstairs, Phil could loll on a blue velvet king-size bed next to a lavender silk chaise longue and a purple velvet antique settee and silver-leafed chests. The library had bookshelves of French and English classics, wing chairs, a Rembrandt print, ceramic Chinese horsemen, antique gravures of military men in uniform, and a red leather wastebasket.

All Phil needed to bring when moving into this palace was a toothbrush, yet for almost a year it sat unoccupied while he put off the move. He told Danny Davis to be ready to go to L.A. in April, and Danny, who lived in Philadelphia with his wife and commuted to New York, sold his house. When April came, Phil still wasn't ready, and Danny had to ask the real-estate agent for an extension. "We were down to one mattress, we'd sold everything else," he recalled. "So then April came and went and he never moved, and then June and nothing, July and nothing, August, September . . . he put us through some shit that was unbelievable. My wife was crying every night, she can't stand livin' this way." Realizing what he was doing to Danny, Phil bought him a Mustang automobile. Finally, in October, he made the move.

In L.A., Phil quickly ingratiated himself among the new breed of rock-and-roll crowd. This was not difficult, for it was Spector who showed the way to these young Turks. Phil was a legend, the prototype of weird antisocial behavior that now was the basis of cultural expression. But because he placed so much emphasis on the material end of his fame, people paid attention to him mainly as a conveyor of cheap thrills and for a free ride. His art now had less to do with his persona than his designer-pricey ruffled shirts and Edwardian suits, his big house (everyone assumed, and Phil made no effort to say otherwise, that he owned it) with Humphrey Bogart's former maid and butler—and his $100,000 white Rolls-Royce. And so, there he was, bounding from the Rolls with a retinue of bodyguards and bodacious bimbos, digging the Sunset scene with Roger McGuinn of the Byrds at the Whiskey-a-Go-Go, the Factory, the Daisy, and the other cabarets of mod rock. In a Hollywood of outlandish slimeballs, leeches, and phony backslappers, Phil was at home because the affected worship felt good and carried no compunction for him to like anyone in return, or to even have to care. "He wanted to be the most outrageous, the most noticed," Davis said. "He wanted to walk into celebrity parties and be the focal point. The broads that accrued to him were fuckin' knockouts. When he was riding the crest, everybody wanted to be with him. It was celebrity, it was money, and he played all of it very well.

"But at the same time, he would always back off people. He would never come up to people himself and he would like crush you, he would want to crush you with some kind of statement designed to negate any further conversation. He'd give you the *shpritz* and then you'd know to walk away."

The days and nights of Phil Spector's Hollywood were "a fantasy world," according to Davis. "Phil has a penchant for embracing certain things at certain times in which he absolutely throws himself whole-body because it's the thing to do. When he became a billiards aficionado, Minnesota Fats and Willie Mosconi and Cowboy Johnny Moore shot with him at the house, betting like $10,000 a game, and Phil couldn't make a shot at the table although he did become a fair player. With Phil, if that's what's current, or has a scent of perverseness, hipness, he will . . . believe me, Phil is the kind of guy who will tell you that Ollie North spent time at the house before he testified in Congress."

The figure, and cause, that Phil cared most about that fall of 1965 was Lenny Bruce. At the time, the tortured dirty-mouth comedian had been abandoned by his longtime claque of New York liberal intellectuals who now found him too depressing and self-destructive to get behind as he went from one court case to another on obscenity and narcotics charges. Bruce lived in a house in the Hollywood Hills and spent most of his time there alone, nearly broke and addicted to heroin and Methedrine. In the few stand-up gigs he was allowed to perform, he eschewed comedy for boring readings from his legal papers. Lenny no longer saw himself as a guerrilla for freedom of art but a martyr of social persecution. The problem was, in a time of exploding individual expression within the youth culture, he seemed a prehistoric apparition, a pitiful has-been bent on killing himself.

When Phil began running into him on the Strip, he took to the outlaw blues that spilled off Lenny. Both of them had huge New York Jewish egos, and Phil believed they both were symbols of resistance against the same establishment pincers. The fact that Lenny had few friends only made him more of a *mensch;* neither did Phil have friends. Lenny was a *real,* big-league rebel, with real smack in his veins and an arm's-length arrest record. Phil thought that was hip beyond belief, and if he wanted to outrage the right people, how better to do it than be seen with Lenny Bruce?

Lenny did not identify with Phil or with rock and roll. Forty years old, bred on the Borscht Belt and then in smoke-filled jazz clubs, the rock culture was alien, even a little intimidating to him; these wiggling and jiggling kids with long hair and disappearing skirts were somehow *too* free, definitely too freaky. Lenny would listen to Phil go on about his rock music and pretend to be interested. Lenny knew immediately what he wanted from Phil. He had Phil marked, and every time Lenny said he needed some bread, Phil confirmed it by faithfully going into his pocket. This Ferris wheel went around for many months, with Phil spending thousands of dollars paying Lenny's bills and tending to his needs. Whether it was for a pack of cigarettes or for unspecified "legal expenses," Danny Davis—who knew Lenny on the Borscht Belt and once had his wife type some of the comic's early legal briefs, a chore she now resumed—would draw it out for him.

This was the price Phil had to pay for riding on and trying to somehow save Lenny's half-dead body, and he complied with the usual Spector zeal. Not only was Lenny taken care of, but so was his nine-year-old daughter, Kitty. With Phil's house a garrison of electrified gates and guard dogs, Lenny got the idea to install iron and steel barriers in and around his house. Phil, the big idea man, also concocted with Lenny a gig not in a dungeonlike nightclub but at a legitimate theater; that way, Lenny could raise the conscience of the L.A. show-biz colony. The show, a ten-day run bankrolled by Phil and billed as "Phil Spector Presents Lenny Bruce," premiered at the Music Box Theater in Hollywood—and was a calamity. Despite the fact that Danny Davis pitched the show all over town, only a handful of people showed up, their eyes glazed in boredom as Lenny recited from his legal papers and ranted almost incoherently, his dilated eyeballs bulging. Phil was crushed by this curio of a burnt-out loser and wanted to close the show after one night rather than be tarnished by its bad and costly vibes. But Lenny would not have it. He demanded that the gig run its full course, and it did, each night more lamentable. Phil took a bath on the fiasco, but Lenny had no sympathy. The fault was Phil's, Lenny insisted, because he had "failed to advertise the show."

Nothing would hold back Lenny's rush to judgment day. One night, trying to surround him with caring people, Phil took Michael Spencer and his wife, who had also moved back to L.A., and Russ Titelman and his sister to Lenny's house. A strung-out Lenny barely noticed the guests. "He was very depressed, very down," Spencer recalled. "He tried to play tapes and couldn't get them on the machine. We had to put them on." Phil, almost always the aberrant in any group, was for once put off himself. "He said Lenny was acting weird," Spencer said.

Worried sick about Lenny and too committed to turn away from him, Phil could only keep plying him with handouts. Meanwhile, he posed in Lenny's scruffy perverse image. The house at La Collina became a hangout for the grungy poet Allen Ginsberg and others of Lenny's Greenwich Village loyalists, and Phil spoke of doing an album of Ginsberg's poetry. At times, Phil's sympathy pains seemed frighteningly real. In the studio, he would cower in a corner and call out, "I need my heroin." It would scare all but those who really knew him.

"People said he was a junkie, but I never believed it," Vinnie Poncia said. "You have to know Phil. He would've fainted at the sight of a needle. I never saw him get high, never even saw him with a joint. He was crazy enough as it is. Phil had that chameleon thing. If he was with smokers he'd say, 'Gimme a cigarette' and never inhale it. If he was hangin' out with Lenny Bruce he was sufferin' with him. He'd adopt a heroin habit without stickin' a needle in his arm."

"Phil wore Lenny on his wrist," Danny Davis said. "He loved Lenny, but it was one of those 'periods.' Karate, pool . . . Lenny Bruce was one of those."

Phil had his own explanation of Lenny's purpose. "He was at the time my closest friend," he told *Rolling Stone* a few years later. "He was like a teacher or a philosopher. He was like a living Socrates."

Phil transferred the business—now operating under the umbrella name of Phil Spector Productions—from New York to a penthouse suite in a tinted-gray glass office building at 9130 Sunset, mere minutes from his house and punctuating the "happening" juncture of Doheny and the Strip. Joan Berg, who elected not to move west, was replaced in the setup by a sales manager, Bob Kirstein. Danny Davis, as always, was the keeper of the cash drawer, which was now being opened less for music matters and more on rehabilitation cases. There was Lenny Bruce, of course, but no more so than the demands of the Spector family.

Regarding Bertha and Shirley, Davis said, "Phil has the classic love/hate thing with them; they, of course, think he's the end of the world."

Working on the love side of the equation, Phil put Bertha up in an apartment that he paid for and he bought her a car. If he hoped that relieved him of the frustrations he had about his family ties, friends doubted it worked for very long, because his mood never seemed to brighten when the subject was family relationships. There was, for one thing, the continuing distress about his sister. Shirley was still seeing doctors up in Palo Alto and Phil had an iron-clad pact with himself to pay for every cent of her care. "I'd have to send money to people at the hospital, the doctors, to keep her in," Davis recalled. "Once Phil wanted me to go up and get her out when she was bein' discharged. I got out of *that* job fast. No way I wanted to do that."

At the core of his unease about Shirley, Phil may have worried that he might somehow go over the edge as well. In his concern for Shirley's health, he pondered long and hard trying to come to grips with her descent and learning about her particular demons, as if that could distance his own. While he could be genuinely sensitive, empathetic, and even optimistic about Shirley's therapy, it still struck others that Phil had left himself unprotected, and in fact had put himself in line for a breakdown by his inability to assimilate into the world around him.

Vinnie Poncia noticed the telling contradiction that Phil could feel other people's pain, while being helpless to ease his own.

Vinnie Poncia said, "My wife killed herself in the seventies and Phil sent me a heartfelt letter that made me understand why it happened. He knew about alienation. Phil couldn't ever make peace with people around him. He always feared he was out there on the fringe looking in."

By this time, 1965, the West Hollywood boys touched by Phil's art and personal blessing were making *their* move on rock—some abetted, ironically, by Marshall Lieb. Marshall himself had edged upward after the Teddy Bears, as had tiny Annette Kleinbard, who under the name Carol Connors had written the 1964 Rip Chords hit "Hey Little Cobra." In 1960 Marshall sang in the road version of the Hollywood Argyles—whose big novelty hit "Alley Oop" was produced by old friend Kim Fowley—and then, working with Lee Hazelwood, played guitar on Duane Eddy sessions. He went on to produce songs for Timi Yuro and then the Everly Brothers. "When I got away from Phillip," Lieb said, "I was able to make some money." By 1965 Marshall's presence was formidable. When the Rolling Stones came to record in L.A. that year, Marshall gave a party for the band at his house. Phil, who did not miss the chance to play host to the Stones in L.A.—and played bass on the session at which "Play with Fire" was cut—nonetheless stayed away, his coolness to Marshall having turned bitter cold now that he was a creative threat.

Marshall, on the other hand, wished they could renew their friendship. In a way, he felt joined to Phil even now—by the Wall of Sound. Even in its evolved form, Marshall believed it was a style of music the two of them had worked out. "The loss of quality in the vocals, background, bass, the big wash of the mix, Phil and I had worked a lot on that: the transparency of music," Lieb said. "The Wall of Sound was a very transparent wall. People who tried to duplicate it did it wrong. They were always *adding* to make more sound. But it wasn't a lot of sound, not a lot of people playing a lot of notes. It was more air than sound.

"Phil always knew what he wanted, and the two of us were able to achieve it quickest. He could achieve it with Nitzsche, but it took him forever because he didn't have anyone that he could talk to. Nitzsche was close, but not where we were. The Teddy Bears was its own sound and Phil Spector was its own sound. But 'To Know Him Is to Love Him' is a classic and it outsold every Philles record."

When Phil went to New York, Marshall was the man who could make it happen for the next generation of rockers of West Hollywood, who were now out of school. One was Don Peake, the kid who made that green Japanese guitar wail on the Friday night jam sessions at Michael Spencer's house. Through Marshall's recommendation, the eighteen-year-old became lead guitarist for the Everly Brothers. Peake was the hottest L.A. sideman when Phil began inviting him to play on Righteous Brothers dates. There was also Ira Ingber, the younger brother of Elliott, who had played the "Bumbershoot" gig with Phil. Marshall produced a demo on a band that Ira was in. Others in the old neighborhood crowd were forging their own success. After two years in the army, Elliott Ingber was deep into the new scene in West Hollywood, which centered around Canter's Deli. Soon he had a reputation as a guitar fool—although years later he confessed that he still could not play "that be-bop shit Phil did"—and joined Frank Zappa's pop-and-protest band the Mothers, a cult fave on the freak underground circuit. Elliott's guitar partner on the "Bumbershoot" gig, Larry Taylor, was the bass player in Canned Heat, a rising electric boogie band. Kim Fowley's old partner in the Sleepwalkers, Bruce Johnston, was with the Beach Boys. And then there was Russ Titelman, who, playing a Spector-like game, made demos of his own songs that led to an apprentice writing job in New York with Don Kirshner. Back in L.A. now, he was an office rat at Liberty Records. "It was a vital, happening time," he said.

In the midst of this crackling vibrancy, Phil finally found a band he could produce in the hues of his vision. The Modern Folk Quartet, an ensemble that combined acoustic folk with modern vocal harmonies, had made two folk albums for Warner Brothers Records, and one of their single records was John Stewart's "Road to Freedom." As regulars at the Village Gate, they had opened shows for Woody Allen and John Coltrane. When folk and rock merged, the group electrified its guitars and jumped into the L.A. thicket, performing at The Troubadour, Whiskey-a-Go-Go, and The Trip. Phil saw the MFQ, as they were called, as a unit he could make into his version of the Byrds. Negotiating a deal with the band's manager, Herb Cohen, he went into it headlong with the Phil trip.

"We spent three or four months hanging out with Phil," recalled Henry Diltz, who was a member of the MFQ. "We'd go to his house and he'd keep us waiting, it would take him two hours to come downstairs and make his entrance. But then he'd be fine, and it was very inspiring to stand around the piano as he'd bang out chords and take us through these great old rock and R&B songs and try to get us to sing and harmonize a certain way. It was a nice feeling to have somebody famous like that interested in us."

Wearing the MFQ like a bib, Phil made the club rounds with them, the prince of rock and his new mid-sixties vanguard. In the fall he took the band into Gold Star and cut a song he had bought from a Van Nuys singer/songwriter named Harry Nilsson. An up-tempo folk-rocker titled "This Could Be the Night," the song sounded more like a Wagnerian folk march with the Wall of Sound, but Phil thought it was a certificate of Sunset Strip viability. Preening in the hippie crowd, he was on an extraordinary high one night at The Trip. As the quartet was doing its set, Phil bounded from his seat and onto the stage with a twelve-string guitar. In one of the least-known major events of the rock epoch, Phil Spector—who renounced public performing because he could not bear a roomful of hard eyes staring at his rodent features—unfurled his guitar, picked up the microphone, and began warbling fifties songs backed by the Modern Folk Quartet. "It was weird—this was Phil Spector up there! But it was completely unannounced and some people in the place probably didn't know who it was," Diltz said.

One of those fortunate to see and know was Kim Fowley, who happened to be at the club that night. Fowley, with his hulking size and black-vested, mortuarial foreboding, was a resident scenemaker, closely identified with Frank Zappa's freak circle. But few things blew Fowley away more than watching Spector front a rock band on a public stage. "Amazing, man, and the pity was that there was a lot of kids in there who didn't know what the fuck was happening," Fowley remembered. "I think about it now and it's like, how's *that* for a memory? And he was good too. I'd never heard his voice. He

⊙

had good mike technique, good delivery. He sounded like he would've been a good lead singer."

It was around this time that Phil became the central figure in a concert movie called *The Big TNT Show*. Shot intimately on video-tape and then transferred to film, *TNT* was modeled after the 1964 concert film *The TAMI Show*, which provided major exposure to the Rolling Stones and the Supremes and years later gained fame as a prime documentary of sixties' rock. Phil was signed by producer Henry Saperstein to serve as musical director and associate producer for a fee of $20,000 against 20 percent of the film's profits. Two concerts were taped, on November 29 and 30, at Hollywood's Moulin Rouge Theater. The talent Spector chose made up a strange rock, folk, and soul mélange of past and present—Joan Baez, the Byrds, the Ronettes, Ray Charles, the Lovin' Spoonful, Donovan, Petula Clark, Bo Diddley, and a veteran soul act, the Ike and Tina Turner Revue. Eager to promote the Modern Folk Quartet, Phil used "This Could Be the Night" as the movie's theme and ran the song over the credits.

Awed by the amazing sixteen-week run of "Lovin' Feelin'"—No. 1 for two weeks, the record spent seven weeks in the Top 3 before falling off the chart in late March—Larry Levine could not understand why Phil had no plans for a Righteous Brothers album. "Phil was so dumb. He was so brilliant but he was so dumb," Levine said. "Here you got this record and it was selling millions *before* it ever got to the Top 10 and then it kept going and going. I said, 'Phil, why don't you put an album out? Call it *Lovin' Feelin'*. He said, 'No, I don't do albums that way. I put out a bunch of singles. When I got enough singles, I put out an album.' I argued and argued and finally I said, 'Listen, Phil, let Bill and Bobby and me go in and we'll do it, just one album.' He said okay and we went in on a weekend and Bill produced it."

Phil would come to regret his decision. Medley produced ten tracks of his own choosing on the mid-1965 LP, *You've Lost That Lovin' Feelin'*, all but the title song. Two months later he produced all but two tracks of the second Righteous Brothers album, *Just Once in My Life*. As Medley's self-importance ballooned, Bobby Hatfield fretted. Bobby had not lived easily with Medley's solo vocal on the entire first verse of both "Lovin' Feelin'" and "Just Once in My Life," believing Medley was slowly eclipsing him. By the summer of 1965, Hatfield, flushed with the success of "Unchained Melody," refused to sing with him. Contending suddenly with fratricidal Righteous Brothers, and not able to stress business perspective with two men he thought were rather dim bulbs and had little common sense, Phil intended to use a third Righteous Brothers album—the first two had sold extremely well—as a vinyl demilitarized zone. Aside from "Hung on You," there would be three new songs by Medley and Hatfield; Spector would produce the Hatfield songs, Medley his own. In mid-September Phil cut Hatfield's covers of "Ebb Tide," "For Sentimental Reasons," and "White Cliffs of Dover." Medley completed the songs for "Loving You," "God Bless the Child," and "Hallelujah I Love Her So."

The album, though, was already under a cloud, not because the Righteous Brothers had a problem with each other but because they were at the end of their line with Phil and with R. J. Van Hoogten. Although Medley and Hatfield took a quantum leap with "Lovin' Feelin'," that first session was a hint of things to come. The Righteous Brothers—who had once quit as an opening act on an early Beatles tour because they couldn't stand the comparative anonymity—were now convinced that their popularity was as an echo of Spector's name. As promotion man, Danny Davis could commiserate. "It was particularly bad for the Righteous Brothers, more so than the Ronettes," he said. "I remember the jockeys getting on the air and saying, 'Here's the new Phil Spector record.' The Righteous Brothers railed at that. They hated Phil for it." Neither was Medley content with the doggie-bone reward of producing album filler.

For months Medley and Hatfield, believing they could make their own records and extend their own popularity without Phil, had wanted to break from Spector. Van Hoogten provided a way to go about it. In July Medley and Hatfield, who were receiving sporadic royalties from Moonglow Records, had hired an accountant and ran an audit of Moonglow's books. The audit showed that Van Hoogten allegedly shorted them by $28,600 on royalties. Van Hoogten, meanwhile, had his own beef with Spector, who had not turned over a number of Righteous Brothers masters to him for sale in the foreign countries in Van Hoogten's domain. Van Hoogten took this as a breach of contract. On September 15, a day after Phil cut "Ebb Tide," Van Hoogten sent Spector a letter terminating Moonglow's agreement with Philles. A week later Van Hoogten instructed the Righteous Brothers to refrain from doing any further recording for Spector. While Spector's lawyers threatened Moonglow with a lawsuit, Medley and Hatfield decided to meet with Phil to clear the air of their grievances, which also included not receiving royalties due them by Philles. In recent weeks their expensive Hollywood agent, Jerry Perenchio, had met with Phil on that subject. "Jerry couldn't get through to him," Danny Davis recalled. "Jerry knew faster than them he was dealing with a loony."

Now, because the album was sitting half finished, Medley and Hatfield believed Phil would have to listen. Phil told them to come to the house, and Danny Davis brought them over. But when they arrived, they were told he was out. Unfortunately, they could plainly see that he was in, and only feet away, hiding behind the door. "Phil had one of those two-way mirrors where he could see out but you couldn't see in," Davis said. "However, the house was always in a state of disrepair and, unbeknownst to Phil, the thing was broken and you could see him standing there. The Righteous Brothers saw that he wouldn't answer them and they were unbelievably pissed."

As they drove back through the gates, Medley and Hatfield decided they would break the four-year contract with Spector. On September 23, they filed a lawsuit against Van Hoogten and Spector, boldly—and speciously—claiming that because Van Hoogten breached their Moonglow contract, his deal with Phil no longer could be held in force.

While the three sides jousted in the courts of Los Angeles County, Phil was in a bind. He wanted the Righteous Brothers album to be out in time for the Christmas buying season, yet he could not get the pair into the studio. Van Hoogten, in a Machiavellian twist for mutual gain, agreed with Phil that Bill and Bobby finish the album pending the legal outcome. The appeal fell on deaf ears. For whatever reason—either because they believed they could, or they were advised by Jerry Perenchio that they could—Perenchio sought a contract for the Righteous Brothers with another record company. Even though any label would risk immense damages in signing the act now, an aggressive MGM Records was very hot for them. MGM was in the middle of a wave of a new big-name signings and rumors filled the air that they were close to notching the Righteous Brothers. With the potentially disastrous defection staring him in the face, Phil sent Medley a cheeky telegram on October 26. Designed to wheedle and shame the pair back into the fold, it read:

Dear Bill:

Well aware of current situation involving lawyers, managers and others. This is to let you know that during the present involvement, there is no possible chance for you to have an album out for the Christmas market, or to even have an album out in general, unless you record.

Bill, believe me, this can only hurt you. You may think not, at present, but no matter what the outcome and however long it takes to reach it, I can only lose money, you can lose a career. Please remember that it is Moonglow you're suing, not me, and you could by court order hold up all future monies payable to them by me. To protect yourselves, I don't think you can sustain without any product. I personally feel it's foolish for you to do so. 'Nuff said.

Phil Spector

Later, on December 1, Phil released the Righteous Brothers' album, titled *Back to Back*, and "Ebb Tide" as a single. To fill out the album, Phil had foraged through tapes of Medley-produced songs and slapped six of them onto the record. When Medley and Hatfield saw and heard it, they wanted to kill. Among the tracks that Spector chose was one song Medley had cut in September as a demo with only four musicians, "Without a Doubt." This, Medley said in court papers, was made for his "private use . . . as a first step in the production of recordings." In addition, Medley claimed that the tapes had been "pirated" after he left them stored in the studio. Of the remaining tracks, sung by Hatfield, one, "Hot Tamales," had been released in 1962. The other two, "Late Late Night" and "She's Mine All Mine," were incomplete.

In liner notes on *Back to Back*, Phil chose to subtly disassociate himself from the album as a whole beyond the separate producer's credits. While calling "Late Late Night" a "polished, skillful performance of a complete musical arrangement," he trenchantly added that "The Righteous Brothers thought you would like to hear it." If Phil thought this would also somehow placate the pair, he was wrong. Outraged that the release was kept from them, and believing Spector was trying to make fools of them, Medley said the album was "a disparagement of my talents as a producer." The Righteous Brothers demanded that the album be removed. They lost the motion, but the point was moot. Spector and Van Hoogten's battle now was to stop MGM from signing Medley and Hatfield. On December 5 Phil's attorney, Jay Cooper, wrote a stern letter to MGM's Jesse Kay, reading: "Please be advised that the sole and exclusive right to record the Righteous Brothers at this time is with Philles Records. Our client intends to, and will, use all available legal remedies for the protection of his rights." Four days later Van Hoogten's attorney, Jack Weinstein, called MGM lawyer Alfred Schlesinger and tried to strike a deal giving MGM permission to record the Righteous Brothers if it would agree to put sales money in escrow pending the court case. Schlesinger replied tersely: "No."

On January 3, 1966, Van Hoogten picked up *Billboard* and read that the Righteous Brothers had signed with MGM and would soon release a single and an album on its Verve sublabel, with a "super promotion." Both Spector and Van Hoogten bolted to their attorneys to try to void the deal. Phil could not mask his contempt for this treason. Bitterness dripping like battery acid, his court papers called the signing a "free ride" at his expense, as he had made the act what it was. The Righteous Brothers had done over $3 million in sales with him, he pointed out. As much as the pair disclaimed *Back to Back*, the LP had sold 200,000 copies in two weeks. The swirling, sonorous "Ebb Tide" was on its way to No. 5. By implication, they owed him.

But within Spector's papers was a hint of a self-recrimination too, the confession of a man who knew he fooled himself into a sense of eternal security. Danny Davis's warnings about investing too much in the Righteous Brothers was prophetic when Phil protested that "disc jockeys throughout the country associate Philles Records with the Righteous Brothers." Losing the duo, he said, "would mean losing the confidence of the disc jockeys at major stations . . . and destroying the goodwill and reputation of Philles Records with distributors. This will surely cause Philles to lose the business of many distributors, the loss of which cannot adequately be compensated in damages."

In late January, with the case still pending before the court, the Righteous Brothers went in to cut their first Verve single. For

Phil, this was a two-handed slap in the face—the record was going to be a Mann-Weil song, "(You're My) Soul and Inspiration." Although it had been bare months since Phil went back on his word to give Barry and Cynthia the "Lovin' Feelin'" follow-up, he now wanted them to rescind the song—in the name of loyalty to him. The hypersensitive couple was torn, but they went ahead with the song, resenting Phil for manipulating their emotions. "There were a lot of hard feelings over that song," Vinnie Poncia recalled. "Phil would've preferred that you just let them die, don't give 'em that song. If you're my friend, you'll let them die. But it was strictly a question of music with Barry. Hey, you don't want to do the song, I'm gonna go elsewhere with it. It was no mystery to Barry or Bill Medley: we'll make a Phil Spector record without Phil Spector. That really blew Phil's mind."

If he could not stop the signing, Phil hoped he could at least stop the recording.

"I came in that morning and he has me calling anyone in the country who could possibly stop that session, the musicians union, everybody," Danny Davis said. "The session was at noon and I'm tryin' at four o'clock to stop it. By then it's obvious we don't have a prayer, so now Phil is absolutely . . . I mean he's out of his mind, berserk."

Saying nothing, his eyeballs glassy, Phil locked up for the day. He walked around the office blankly, turning off every light. Then he pulled a chair to an open window high over Sunset Boulevard.

"I was freakin' out because Dr. Kaplan had already told me that Phil was suicidal and capable of taking his life," Davis went on. "There was no question in my mind he was gonna jump."

His fingers frantically dialing, Danny placed a long-distance call to Dr. Harold Kaplan.

"I explained to him what had happened, that we'd lost the Righteous Brothers, and I said, 'Can you talk with him?' He said, 'No, he's got that kind of thing that if I talk to him, he'll reject what I say. If he calls me on his own, I may be able to help him.' He told me to stay with Phil, not to let him be alone, and I took him home and stayed with him the whole weekend.

"Finally, like about Sunday, I said to him, 'You know, Philly, this is not right. You should really call Dr. Kaplan,' and he rejected it at the outset but we had some breakfast and then he went into another room and called Kaplan and I guess the crisis passed."

Eventually, when MGM realized that the impetuous signing of the Righteous Brothers was legally indefensible, Phil got a $600,000 settlement from the company. It was a comforting, but empty, victory. The whole nasty business knocked the wind out of him. Losing his appetite to risk failure with the Modern Folk Quartet, he turned his back on the group, never releasing a single record by them; forsaken, the quartet disbanded and it was ten years before they reunited.

Medley and Hatfield suffered as well, though. "(You're My) Soul and Inspiration"—a dead-on copy of the Wall of Sound that many thought was a Spector record—was a juggernaut itself, a No. 1 hit for three weeks in May of 1966 and a gold record. But it was the Righteous Brothers' denouement. Without Spector, they soon receded back into the background of the new rock and roll; they charted only once more for MGM, and by 1968 they were working as a casino act before they broke up. Medley had a modest solo career, and Hatfield recorded with a different partner under the Righteous Brothers name and performed in cocktail lounges.

Phil would take his vindication in their failure. To *Rolling Stone* he poured sanctity on the adage—advanced by him—that an act does not kiss off Phil Spector and stay anywhere near his level. "I mean it was really dumb," Spector said in 1969. "It doesn't matter leaving me; fuck that, that don't mean nothin'. The dumb thing was to leave and suck MGM into that stupid deal, and then die as an act!" Although Phil had made it easy for them to believe they *were* Philles Records, he insisted: "The Righteous Brothers were not Phil Spector [but] something happens to people's minds, and they start thinkin' maybe you are the cause of everybody's financial success. . . . I think the Righteous Brothers would admit it today . . . that they were wrong. The very fact that they settled meant that they did not want to go to court. I think Bill Medley, in an honest moment, which he *has* said since, would say, 'We really shouldn't have left Phil, and also we had no right to.' . . . I even ran into Bobby Hatfield one night about a year ago, and he had every reason to be apologetic, you know, he's really a strugglin' cat now.

"It's a shame, I really feel funny. I didn't get hurt, I really came out smellin' like a rose . . . but I was very upset that they blew their talent. I was selling more records in the colored market than I was in the white market, and yet *they* had a tremendous fan club of white teenie boppers. I mean they had it made. They could have been around for three or four more years *solid* with big records. [But] they only had three or four hits and then good-bye. They weren't around long enough to sustain with junk . . . because they themselves were not extraordinary talents. They were just *commercial* talents.

"They blew it because they tried, I think, to copy and emulate and use whatever it was that I did, and they did not know how—not that they should have known how, but they shouldn't have even tried."

In his gloating, Phil did not see the irony in his dig at the Righteous Brothers as "a strange group in that they really were non-intellectual and unable to comprehend success. They couldn't understand it and couldn't live with it, and accept it for what it really was—they thought it was something that could be obtained very easily, and once it was attained, be consistently obtained."*

For in early 1966, it was precisely that assumption that had brought him to the edge of giving up. Left with no bankable act, thrown off-rail and consumed by months of legal warfare, Phil lay in ennui for the first two months of 1966. Then he decided he had to draw at least one more big breath.

*From the *Rolling Stone* interview, Jann Wenner (November 1, 1969):26.

ברוך בר גדליהו
נפ׳ כא ניסן תשט״ט

Ben Spector

APRIL 20, 1949
FATHER HUSBAND

TO KNOW HIM
WAS TO LOVE HIM

Above: Ben Spector's grave site in Beth David Cemetery: laid to rest with the words that brought to life his son's genius—and torment (ANTHONY NESTE). *Above right:* From the Fairfax High School senior yearbook, 1957: the eyes stared far into the future (COURTESY OF FAIRFAX HIGH SCHOOL). *Right:* But first he had to break away from Mother Bertha's grip (JASPER DAILEY).

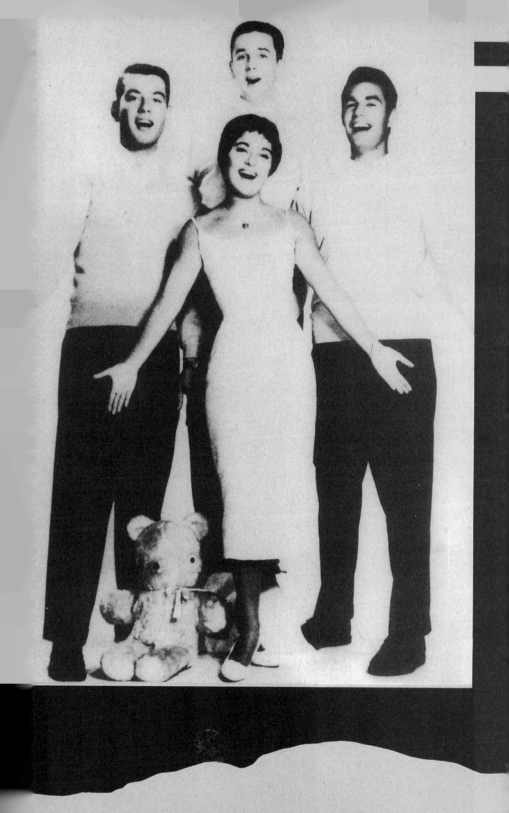

Opposite: In the beginning there were four Teddy Bears (COURTESY OF HARVEY GOLDSTEIN). *Above:* When they had a hit record, greed took Harvey Goldstein out of the picture. Spector, Annette Klein-bard, and Marshall Lieb got more—but smiled less. *Right:* Beverly Ross: she gave Phil her heart, but he only wanted her studio privileges (COURTESY OF BEVERLY ROSS).

EVERY BREATH I TAKE

GENE PITNEY

MUSICOR

Above: Gene Pitney: the first great Spector production—and a flop. But Pitney would help out later. *Opposite top:* The Paris Sisters: early proof that Spector could make something out of nothing (MICHAEL OCHS ARCHIVES). *Right:* The Ducanes: for them a momentary brush with genius; for Spector a favor paid off (COURTESY OF EDDIE BRIAN).

THE DUCANES

Above: Kingpins (from left): Spector with Don Kirshner and wife, Snuff Garrett, Gerry Goffin, and Carole King. Snuff wouldn't be smiling after "He's a Rebel" (COURTESY OF SNUFF GARRETT). *Opposite top:* Turning the studio into a conveyor belt of perfect rock-and-roll records: Spector (right) with Jack Nitzsche and Darlene Love (RAY AVERY/ MICHAEL OCHS ARCHIVES). *Right:* Larry Levine was master of the control board. Nino Tempo (right) was the good luck charm (RAY AVERY/MICHAEL OCHS ARCHIVES).

Right: Annette Merar: from bobby sox to the wife of the American Mozart. Then the tears began (COURTESY OF ANNETTE MERAR).
Below: The label said the Crystals, but the voices on "He's a Rebel" and many other hits belonged to Bobby Sheen, Darlene Love, and Fanita James—who sang as Bob B. Soxx and the Blue Jeans on "Zip-A-Dee-Doo-Dah" (MICHAEL OCHS ARCHIVES).

Above: Darlene Love and Sonny Bono take five. Later, Spector punished both of them for lack of loyalty (RAY AVERY/ MICHAEL OCHS ARCHIVES). *Left:* Cher, who once could only peek wistfully inside Spector's studio and wonder why he would not let her sing, helped Sonny get the last laugh (RAY AVERY/MICHAEL OCHS ARCHIVES).

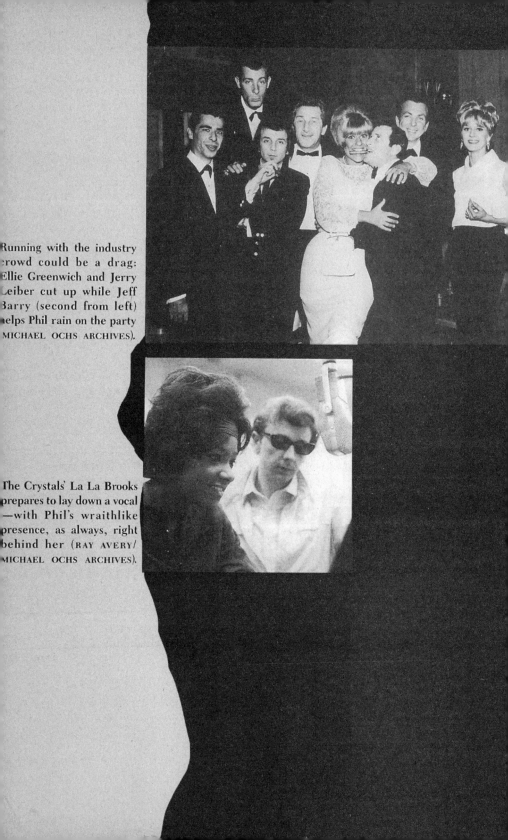

Running with the industry crowd could be a drag: Ellie Greenwich and Jerry Leiber cut up while Jeff Barry (second from left) helps Phil rain on the party (MICHAEL OCHS ARCHIVES).

The Crystals' La La Brooks prepares to lay down a vocal —with Phil's wraithlike presence, as always, right behind her (RAY AVERY/ MICHAEL OCHS ARCHIVES).

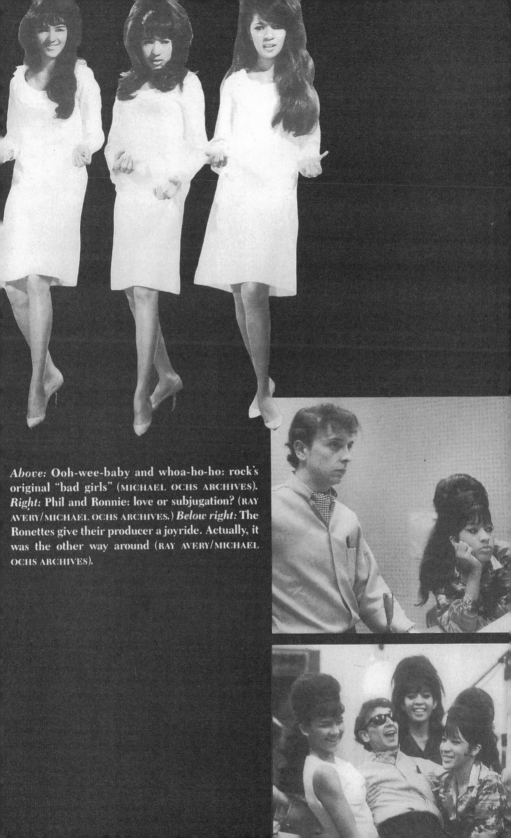

Above: Ooh-wee-baby and whoa-ho-ho: rock's original "bad girls" (MICHAEL OCHS ARCHIVES). *Right:* Phil and Ronnie: love or subjugation? (RAY AVERY/MICHAEL OCHS ARCHIVES.) *Below right:* The Ronettes give their producer a joyride. Actually, it was the other way around (RAY AVERY/MICHAEL OCHS ARCHIVES).

THE RIGHTEOUS BROTHERS
(I LOVE YOU) FOR SENTIMENTAL REASONS
EBB TIDE

Apple Records

THE BEATLES

Let it be

Opposite top left: **Estelle Bennett with Paul Mc-Cartney, January 1964: like everyone, the Beatles adored the Ronettes—but Ronnie was off limits** (COURTESY OF NEDRA TALLEY). *Opposite top right:* **The First Tycoon of Teen: a man who always put his money where his mouth was** (MICHAEL OCHS ARCHIVES). *Opposite center:* **With Beach Boys Brian Wilson (left), Mike Love (second from right), and Righteous Brother Bobby Hatfield (right). Brian knew his place —behind Phil** (RAY AVERY/MICHAEL OCHS ARCHIVES). *Opposite bottom left:* **The high point of Philles Records, a gold mine of blue-eyed soul: it was supposed to go on forever.** *Opposite bottom right:* **The Beatles' swan song, by way of Phil Spector.** *Above:* **Laying it all on the line with Tina and Ike Turner: a river too deep, a mountain too high** (RAY AVERY/ MICHAEL OCHS ARCHIVES). *Above right:* **A Phil Spector Christmas card, 1969. The picture was from Spector's cameo role in** *Easy Rider* (COURTESY OF JASPER DAILEY). *Right:* **John Lennon goes solo—in partnership with the world's greatest rock-and-roll producer.**

JOHN ONO
LENNON
INSTANT KARMA
(WE ALL SHINE ON)

PRODUCED BY
PHIL SPECTOR
APPLE RECORDS 1818

Spector made George Harrison's solo debut the most successful of the ex-Beatles' (COURTESY OF PETE BENNETT).

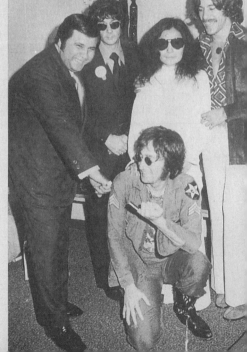

Lurking on the Lennon–Yoko Ono scene, New York, 1972 (with Apple promotion man Pete Bennett at left and television newsman Geraldo Rivera at right). A year later, there was booze, guns, and bloodletting (PHOTO BY PAUL SCHUMACH; COURTESY

Above: Solid citizen: a natty, dark-shaded Spector at a charity banquet with, from left, Pete Bennett, old mentor Ahmet Ertegun, and New York Senator Jacob Javits (PHOTO BY POPSIE; COURTESY OF PETE BENNETT). *Left:* Hanging out with Ringo (COURTESY OF PETE BENNETT).

The Ramones: eight months of hell, their best album, and a Spector farewell (GEORGE DUBOSE).

Living legend: Spector comes out of hiding to salute the music of the eighties, escorted by brothers Dan (left) and David Kessel (BRAD ELTERMAN).

Above: Spector's Pyrenes Castle at 1700 S. Grandview Drive in Alhambra. Thirty-three rooms of gloom and one gun incident too many. (AP IMAGES) *Left:* Lana Clarkson—tall, gorgeous, and dying for a break. The last part became all too literal when she found herself trapped in Spector's Castle with no way out on February 3, 2003. (AP IMAGES/RAY CAVALERI)

Above right: Indicted murder suspect Spector enters the courtroom for a September 27, 2004, hearing with personal assistant Michelle Blaine on his arm. Later, after Phil fired her, she would spill some of his tawdriest secrets. (AP IMAGES) *Right:* On May 23, 2005, Phil arrived in court looking like a mutant Mozart, his wig all aflutter. After more than two years since the shooting and more than two years of trial delays and courtroom high jinks, he wasn't conducting symphonies anymore. It was now "Waltz of the Cuckoos." (AP IMAGES)

15

It was like my farewell. I was just sayin' good-bye, and I just wanted to go crazy, you know, for a few minutes—four minutes on wax, that's all it was. I loved it, and I enjoyed making it, but I didn't really think there was anything for the public.

      —PHIL SPECTOR on "River Deep—Mountain High"

What he was doing was trying to top "Lovin' Feelin'." He had to create something greater than "Lovin' Feelin'," which I always felt was the acme. He shouldn't have had to do that. If he didn't he could have been making records for years longer. But he had to create the image of Phil Spector going higher and higher, and he ran himself out trying to do it.

      —LARRY LEVINE

No one who saw Phil around New Year's 1966 could have believed he had any appetite left to wage war for rock and roll's lost soul. Plainly, Spector was tapping out on music. He had just turned twenty-five, yet daggers of pain and fatigue tore across his forehead and cut down his spine. For five years he was plasma in the veins of popular music, making it jump and twitch. Now he was winded, the angry young man still but with an aging fighter's legs. With his label emptied—Bobby Sheen went to Capitol, the Blossoms to Screen Gems, the Crystals to United Artists—his music idled and his nights on Sunset were separated by longer retreats inside a cold, dark house that for him was a chrysalis of security.

"He was getting a lot more reclusive," Vinnie Poncia said. "I'd come in from New York and stay at the Sunset Marquis, and when I went to Phil's, he'd be playing his pinball machine and not want to do anything. In New York I could always get him out. In L.A. I was losing him."

Part of this was due to Vinnie's own growth. In early 1965 he and Pete Andreoli wrote and produced a moody surf-rock ballad, "New York's a Lonely Town." Vinnie took the song to Phil. "He said, 'I think it's a hit—but I don't want to put it out.' I was really disappointed. I said, 'Why?' and he didn't answer but I think Phil wouldn't put it out because if it was a hit, he'd have to come to grips with the fact, well, this guy can make hit records and maybe I'm losing touch. He was much more excited about the stuff I did on Phi-Dan, but none of those records did anything and I realized that the music and his tastes had nothing to do with the public's acceptance—with those records, he could say what's the big deal, I didn't care anyway. That was his cover against losing touch."

Vinnie sold the master to Leiber and Stoller at Red Bird Records and under the name of the Tradewinds it became a Top 30 hit. Poncia and Andreoli never wrote another song for Philles. By early 1966 Andreoli was beginning a singing career and Poncia had signed with Artie Ripp to produce records at Kama Sutra. By then Phil and rock were a Grand Canyon apart. Spector and the Righteous Brothers were dual riders into the dusk of rock's V-necked, spit-shined era. Though Phil took R&B up a mainstream notch with the Righteous Brothers, the rock of social conscience and the adult introspection of the Beatles' *Rubber Soul* album was passing by him and others of the era. For this, Phil blamed radio. Openly, he scorned a new generation of deejays and program directors who demanded that he make personal appearances to plug his records—*him! Phil Spector!* They wanted *him* to go to *them?* Were they kidding or *what!* No, he would not go. And if deejays thought it was cool to speak in the forked tongue of progressive and underground rock, he wanted them to know that he thought they were stupid and knew nothing about music. In the learned opinion of Phil Spector, radio could go fuck itself.

"He started turning off everybody in the radio end," Poncia remembered. "And they picked up on that and turned off to him. They felt the attitude of people like Phil Spector was: I'm gonna tell you what to play. And their response was: You're not the magic man anymore. We have this new thing, guys with long hair and stuff like that, and you can't take us for granted."

"He was a recluse before that, but Phil was that kind of an ego who wanted to be presented to everybody," Danny Davis said. "I didn't have a lot of trouble getting him to do things with jocks. But then he really got pissed off at them. He didn't think they held him in high regard anymore."

"The thing was, they thought he was, maybe he was losing it, starting to slide," Poncia said. "And yet, even so, even with all his arrogance, I don't think they could publicly dislike him until he failed."

For now, Spector merely bobbed in these unfriendly waters, almost as if he were waiting for the tide to wash him out. To some of those who knew him, he already had.

"Even before sixty-six, Phil felt that it was starting to come to a close," Jack Nitzsche related. "I remember we were in the studio with the Ronettes cutting 'Born to Be Together,' and during the playback Phil stood next to me and said, 'It's all over. It's over. It's just not there anymore.' The enthusiasm was gone. We had done it so many times. And now the musicians were changing, they didn't want to work overtime for him. It just wasn't the same spirit, the spirit of cooperation started to change."

"It really was over for Phil by sixty-five, really," Sonny Bono insisted. "Music left him in sixty-five. He was out of it then."

There were times when the once-impregnable Spector ego sounded like parody. Annette, who after the divorce would hear from Phil at times when he needed comfort, received phone calls all the time now in which Phil's self-doubt brought them both down. Routinely Phil would ask her, "Am I as big as Dylan?" "Yes, Phil. You sure are," she would assure him. "Am I as big as the Beatles?"

"You sure are! There's always been the Beatles and Dylan and Phil Spector!"

"It would be like a pep talk," Annette recalled. "But after a while, I don't think he believed it."

But if this was a broken man, sometime during those first weeks of 1966 he clambered from the sludge. He decided to record again, and with no halfway impact. He would either go all the way up or all the way down, but he would go with his own way, against the prevailing winds of rock. For many months Phil had thought about recording Ike and Tina Turner—actually just Tina, whose powerful, stinging voice cut through him like a drill. But while he put the act on *The Big TNT Show,* he could not find a rock context for her hardcore R&B sound. The Ike and Tina Revue was essentially an innercity nightclub act. Much like James Brown's revue, its idiom was gritty, gospel-style funk, jumping and shouting in spasms of rhythm. Ike Turner, however, understood rock and roll. Born in Mississippi, Turner produced "Rocket 88," an important No. 1 R&B hit in 1951 for Sam Phillips's Sun label. Through the fifties he was a top studio guitarist and produced sessions with Johnny Ace, B. B. King, Howlin' Wolf, and other soul giants, selling his records to Chess and Modern/RPM Records. In 1956 Ike's band, the Kings of Rhythm, was playing at a club in St. Louis when an eighteen-year-old girl jumped from the audience, grabbed a microphone, and began vamping with the Kings. Named Annie Mae Bullock, she had an electric glow. Ike soon hired her to front the band—high honor indeed for a woman then—and in 1958 he married her. In the early sixties he changed her name to Tina and put together a revue around her with nine musicians and three background singers called the Ikettes. Clad in hip-hugging short skirts, long wigs, and high heels, Tina and the Ikettes sang and did intricate dance routines, never pausing for a breath. At the *TNT Show,* they made the mainly white crowd hysterical with their volcanic renditions of the soul classics "Think It's Gonna Work Out Fine" and James Brown's "Please, Please, Please."

That performance told Phil Tina might have strong cross-over appeal, but it would be a risk. The Turners' sixties' records had dotted the R&B chart but Ike had only scattered pop hits. At first this scared Phil, as did Ike's baleful image. Long and lean as a two-by-four, with glaring eyes and a drawn face that fought every smile, Ike was a mercurial man who fired Ikettes on a whim and took out his inner rage on Tina with his fists; because he drank, used cocaine, and carried a gun, he was genuinely threatening to be around. But in summoning up a last big push, Phil became convinced that Tina's voice was the only soul venue left with which he could make his ultimate music statement. This would not be with drippy folk rock or a four-man band of long-haired, whining adenoidals. It would be with the music he loved—R&B, with the shameless excess of Wall of Sound, damn it. No pair of ears would fail to know that, and in the end he hoped it would blow away all the new proponents of rock. And if it didn't, well, he was going to go out his way. No compromise, no equivocation.

For this, he would need Tina Turner, but only if Ike stayed away from the studio. Phil was prepared to buy this condition with a promise of Ike producing songs on some future Ike and Tina album on Philles, but it turned out that he need not have worried. The chance of getting into rock mainstream excited Ike. After Phil obtained permission from Ike's current label, Loma Records, an R&B branch of Warner Brothers, to lease them for $20,000, Phil and Danny Davis went to Ike and Tina's Baldwin Hills house to close the deal. "I didn't know what to expect, Ike had a mean reputation," Davis said, "but he was thrilled at the time that no less than Phil Spector was interested in them." Although Ike had no objection to keeping out of the studio with Phil, "he did think he would be involved somehow in what came out and so forth. I remember there was a lot of talk about it because Phil wanted to keep him happy. He was scared to death of Ike."

Sizing up his Waterloo, Phil thought he had to invoke the magical symbiosis of the past; specifically, 1963, when nothing ever went wrong. To do so, he wanted to enlist the handcrafters of his great run of 1963 and 1964—Ellie Greenwich and Jeff Barry. That was no simple wish. Divorced in 1965, Jeff and Ellie continued collaborating but their paths had taken them far afield from Spector; Red Bird Records had folded, and they were working as staff writers at Bang Records—a branch company of Atlantic Records co-owned by Ahmet Ertegun, his brother Nesuhi, Jerry Wexler, and Bert Berns—where they were producing a young singer named Neil Diamond. There was also the ugly business about "Chapel of Love." Phil, always the charmer, came at them as if nothing had ever gone sour. "That's the way this business is," Vinnie Poncia remarked. "Phil may have hated you personally, but as long as he had respect for you as a writer or a musician he'd work with you again." Besides, Spector was still power and money, and it did not take long for Jeff and Ellie to capitulate. "There might have even been some kind of deal made at the time of 'Chapel of Love,'" Poncia said. "Leiber and Stoller may have smoothed some feathers, given Phil some money for an agreement that he'd use Jeff and Ellie again. This might have been the calling in of old favors."

The song that would become Phil Spector's watershed—"River Deep—Mountain High"—was written during an intensive week of collaboration after Jeff and Ellie joined Phil in L.A. The lyric was a pained and somewhat self-conscious attempt by Jeff to break out of his prosaic kiddie anthem mold; his florid imagery of love's pain, angst, and joy unfurled with an odd-sounding poetic and grammatical license from the opening line about a young girl and her rag doll. But the melody was actually a fusing of three different song ideas—each of the three writers had completely diverse riffs, and Phil was not averse to jamming them all together in a metrical hydra. He was after something striking: not quite R&B, not quite pop, amenable to both but on a higher plane. Though the song teetered and fought itself in spots—verse out of synch with melody, melody jumping too abruptly off the lyric line—Phil believed this was all to the good. It would be the Wall and Tina that would iron out and color the oddities, with pyrotechnic madness. In the end, it would be an eccentric and commercially viable entity—essentially a logarithm of Phil Spector himself.

"River Deep—Mountain High" needed five long sessions to cut. The first two came in late February, as Phil attacked the basic rhythm track. If Spector sessions had been large before, now they were gargantuan. Up to two dozen musicians were stuffed inside Studio A at a time, straining its capacity. Phil did run-throughs at the first two sessions, taking the tapes home and playing them again and again and always finding some imperfection that would require hours to fix. The third and final session for the rhythm track was on March 7, when twenty-one musicians and Jack Nitzsche occupied the studio floor. The cacophony included four guitars—Barney Kessel, Don Peake, John Ewing, Robert Gerslauer—and four basses—Jim Bond,

Carol Kaye, Ray Pohlman, Lyle Ritz. The rhythm sweeteners included keyboard players Harold Battiste, Larry Knechtal, and Michael Rubini; percussionists Frank Capp and Larry Estes; and a monster brass section—Plas Johnson and Jay Migliori on sax, Oliver Mitchell and Roy Caton on trumpet, Jim Horn and Lew McCreary on trombone. And for the first time, Phil went with two drummers, Earl Palmer and Jim Gordon. Running almost all day and night, Danny Davis would be paying bills for the session for the next year, at which time the tab came to over $22,000, which would have been an unthinkable cost for several *albums*.

When Tina came to that March 7 session, she was shocked at the assemblage in the studio. By the time Phil was ready for vocals, more than twenty background singers had entered the room. Tina, who never expected to sing in Grand Central Station, was not comfortable. She tried to do the lead vocal, but the song befuddled her. Phil excused her and set another week of rehearsal. Tina related so little to the bizarre song that she could not even sing it for Ike at home. When she went back to Gold Star, no one was in the studio except Phil and Larry Levine. Trying to sing it again while the immense rhythm track gorged her ears through headphones, she was constantly interrupted by Phil. "That's close," he would say. "Let's try it again." She had to inch up on the vocal, until, long after midnight, she was dripping with sweat and had to take off her blouse. Standing in a pitch-dark room in her bra, her head and her ears pounding, she took a deep breath and ripped it again, the veins in her neck bulging and her lower stomach in stabbing pain.

When she left the studio, Tina still did not know if she did it the way Phil wanted it, and neither did Phil. It took another week of mixing and dubbing strings before he had industry people listen to it. To his face, these people told him it was very likely a No. 1 record that would break Tina into the big time. Behind his back, some of the same people had doubts. As with the Righteous Brothers' records, the Gold Star echo chambers were used full crank, but where open space was kneaded into a mood before, now the echoes met an eddy of sheer noise. At some moments, the force was so monumental and eerie that it seemed to suck the listener into its core. At other moments, it was . . . noise. Then, even with Tina twisted into a knot, it was a flat emotional pancake. Ike Turner, hearing the track of Tina's vocal, loved it; when he heard the final mix, he told friends the record was overproduced and submerged Tina's voice. Jeff Barry thought it was muddy and sloppy, a botched job. That judgment was not uncommon, but in Jeff's case it only proved that he never comprehended Spector's music.

"There were always things that Phil looked for, because I know how he does it," Marshall Lieb said. "I know where the color lines are and I know his depth perception. Nothing is an accident. When you hear muddle from a Phil Spector record, he plants that.

"Phil was very crafty at getting as much power out of his records as he could. In the seventies producers were trying to get those kinds of levels and could not. Today, when you hear 'River Deep' it's still very powerful. I think it's wonderful, a stunning production."

What "River Deep" was, Phil Spector wanted it to be.

And in 1966, almost no one in America could deal with it.

As a synthesis of past rituals applied to a future formula, the outward impracticalities of "River Deep—Mountain High" doomed its subliminal brilliance. Even Vinnie Poncia, who thought he was tapped into Phil's genius, was torn. "There was absolutely nothing wrong with the record. It was at the wrong time," Poncia said. "See, Phil didn't care about the times. For him to work with an artist like Tina Turner, to fulfill what he set out to do in the studio, that was the heights. Phil was the general, but when it came to who put the final vocal on, he really sought something in the delivery, and that was the one thing he could not direct. It was something he could *find*, a Bill Medley, a Darlene Love, a Ronnie. So for him to get Tina in front of his microphone, that was a big thrill for him. Because now he had the crowning piece, the jewel that went on top of the whole thing.

"But at the time, those kinds of records were falling out of favor with the public. 'River Deep' was no different than 'Lovin' Feelin',' except that after that record they just weren't buying it any more. I also think the structure of the song hurt it. If you broke down the song—and it's a great song—the verse was so incredible. It's about the little girl and the rag doll, and that's what Phil loved. It was like Gene Pitney. Then the chorus was a different tempo, it takes you away from the verse.

"Phil knew that, because it happens all the time. Sometimes you do things and they don't come out great, sometimes you miss

⊙

by a mile. As long as you don't take it personally, you're okay. He took it personally."

Danny Davis's problem was that "River Deep" was too radical to call rock and roll. Even as an advance in black music it was out of step; Atlantic and Stax-Volt Records were reshaping soul with the Memphis pop-R&B of Aretha Franklin, Otis Redding, Wilson Pickett, and Sam and Dave. "River Deep" could not be called anything but a Phil Spector record. In 1966 that did not necessarily move vinyl. The trade papers, which once fawned on Spector records, reviewed this one with mild approbation. *Cash Box* tabbed it as a "Best Bet," a designation that generally meant let's wait and see. When "River Deep," backed with a Spector song called "I'll Keep You Happy," was released in late April, the L.A. radio station KRLA—to which Danny had given the bauble of breaking the record—put it right on the air, to a lukewarm response. Across the country, it was a hard sell. "In the office, we all loved that song, we thought it was a classic . . . and it was one of the toughest fuckin' records I can ever remember trying to get played," Davis recalled. "I'll never forget it. Bertha Potter, who was the music director at WDRC in Hartford, told me that it was 'a bunch of noise.' That was echoed by WMCA in New York. Everyone viewed it as a bunch of noise. I was tryin' like hell with that record. I flew out, I did big dinners, sent perfume to the wives. I was and am the best around and I could not get it played, man. It was one of the great losses of my life. But it was not my fault. Something was goin' on out there. Nobody wanted to be the first to budge on it."

The nadir of the crusade, and the epitome of how cursed it was, came when Danny went with Ike and Tina, who played a gig in St. Louis. Intending to promote "River Deep" there, Danny instead had to bail Ike out of jail. "He got arrested on a gun charge and I had to spend the whole time getting him out. Phil sent the money."

Trying to work with the volatile Ike as a comrade was like a bad dream. When "River Deep" didn't take off, Ike complained to Danny that the follow-up sessions Phil was doing with Tina were keeping the Revue off the road and that the record led to no new dates because blacks didn't like the song. Trying to rectify the situation, Ike began to release his own records, further undercutting "River Deep" among his fans. "Ike would say, 'This record ain't doin' anything and I got records all over. I got 'em on my mantel, I got 'em in my coat, and I got 'em in my closet. If nothin' happens I just put another one out on whatever label I can get,'" Davis said. "And Phil, of course, just got crazy when he heard that, but there wasn't much you could do. Ike was a little cokey to begin with, and you could say anything you want, he doesn't give a goddamn."

No other major record in pop music history was resisted for as many different reasons as "River Deep—Mountain High" was. It was a conundrum of discontent, with no one really knowing why it failed. Depending on who was the expert, it was too noisy, too black for white-oriented stations to play a Tina Turner soul record, or too white for black stations that played Tina Turner records. But the only plausible answer was that it was too Phil Spector.

"They didn't reject 'River Deep' because it was a bad record," Marshall Lieb said. "They rejected it because they had a vendetta for Phil. I remember it was very tough for him to get it played because of the way he had treated a lot of the program directors. Pop stations who were not used to playing a loud R&B act used that as an excuse not to play it, and that was a terrible shame because the music was very good and the artist was very good."

But "River Deep" *could* be resisted, for whatever reason. And when it became obvious that the record was in serious trouble, it was as if this one event was a mass catharsis of vengeance. Those whom Phil had wronged, directly or indirectly, banded together to gore the crippled beast by piling indignity on top of insult. On May 29, "River Deep" found the chart, at No. 88. The next week, as if swatted by a gigantic unseen hand, it *fell off!* No. 88! When "Walking in the Rain" went to No. 23, it was a letdown. What to make of *this?* "And it wasn't just an 88, it was a *tough* 88," Danny Davis said. This was so exaggerated a failure that it could only be considered a stoning.

Phil knew he was living on the edge of the blade. As he'd staked so much on this one record, he'd left no room to escape from failure. He was prepared to live with that, because he was too tired and too hostile to compromise any more. Still, the vicious personal backlash kicked him in the groin. That he should stand *in the way* of his record was not an irony to him; it was an injustice he could not live with. Angry at first, his insecurities made him think that maybe it *was* a bad and useless record. Paralyzed by the notion, he didn't just walk away from the business. He ran and hid. "He just couldn't

⊙

bear the shame," Davis said. "He was absolutely, thoroughly crushed by the rejection."

If there was salvation, it came from his friends in England. Tony Hall knew "River Deep" would be radical for the BBC and took the record to the ring of "pirate" radio stations that broadcast illegally from boats offshore in the channel. Begun as a protest against the conservative BBC playlists, these stations were run by young people with a sense of daring, and many of them were Spector buffs. "They were fantastic," Hall said. "I got them to love the record, and without any help from the BBC I think we took four weeks to get that to No. 1." Actually, "River Deep" went to No. 3 in Britain in mid-July. Sitting on his other Tina records up to then, Phil readied her cover of the old Motown song "A Love Like Yours (Don't Come Knockin' Every Day)" for British release. He did not think about releasing it in the U.S. That "River Deep" was a smash abroad only tied his stomach in knots. Speaking with Tony Hall about the fiasco at home, he was inconsolable. "It fucked his head completely," Hall said. "I could hear it in his voice over the phone. He was angry and hurt. He knew it was a fantastic bloody record. He thought, and rightly so, that it was the best record he ever made."

Cushioning himself, Phil did not wait for the "River Deep" verdict. Having caught the same bug that bit Don Kirshner, he was already looking to movies as a logical and estimable career turn. Phil had become friendly with actor Dennis Hopper, a coarse, hard-drinking man who offended almost every producer and director in Hollywood—and, as such, was yet another hip pariah with whom Phil could walk in step. When Hopper could not find movie work, Phil hired him as a photographer, and a Hopper collage was the front cover of the 1967 *River Deep—Mountain High* album that was released in England. But their big plan was to make an independent movie starring Dennis and his friend Peter Fonda—directed by Dennis, produced and financed by Phil—that they could sell to a studio. Poring over treatments, Hopper liked one by writer Steven Stern. Titled *The Last Movie*, it was an abstract parable as seen through the eyes of an American film crew shooting a Western movie in a Mexican village. On May 18, 1966, Phil made an oral agreement with Stern to option the treatment for $71,000 and to have Stern write the screenplay. The arrangement was for Stern to receive

$10,000 on completion of a script, $36,000 by December 31, and $25,000 or 12½ percent from the proceeds of the movie. Phil and Dennis began to scout Mexican locations and eventually settled on the rock-strewn landscape of Mazatlán. Phil guaranteed monies to Cherabusco Studios to use their facilities. Sets were built, crews assembled, and cinematographer Haskell Wexler hired as chief cameraman.

While they occupied themselves with this project, and "River Deep" became Spector's sacrificial lamb, Philles Records was dormant. "He told me after 'River Deep' that he was gonna close up the whole place," Danny Davis recalled. "He said: 'We're gonna go out of the business, we're gonna do other things.' It was comparable to what Kirshner told me on the ride to Penn Station; he was gonna go into the movie business. So I went through another crisis in that regard, waiting for the end to come."

But Phil did not close up. Instead, he sat around the office most days with Hopper and Fonda. The music hustings of Philles Records degenerated into a farcical amateur hour. "We had some beauts comin' in to see him, boy." Davis shuddered. "Oh, God, we had some guys who would walk in off the street and want to do a record. Phil would go to record studios or the clubs around town and people would give him records, and then they would follow up and he had no intention of doin' anything with anybody. But he would give 'em the sign that everything was good and the next day you would get these guys calling and it would fall to me to bob and weave and tell 'em no, because I'm good at that.

"Sometimes it looked like he was ready to go. He'd say, 'I want you to go in tomorrow and fire so-and-so,' whether it was the comptroller or whoever he had on the payroll at the time. But then he'd say, 'Oh, we still got product out, we're still waitin'. We'll keep him.' He was so fuckin' indecisive."

If Phil was getting off on his self-imposed asylum of idleness and loathing, he was given a fresh motive to wallow on August 2. That was the day that Lenny Bruce died.

The terrible irony was that things seemed to be looking up for Lenny. In the past months he had won all of his remaining obscenity cases and he waltzed through his lone outstanding narcotics charge with a small fine and probation. With the winds of change catching up to the laws of free expression, he could have gone back to work. And yet, stripped of the crutch of persecution, Lenny saw no reason to live. Now $400,000 in debt, he gained an alarming amount of weight and shot more heroin. As another token of solidarity with Lenny, Phil released an album of his stand-up material, *Lenny Bruce Is Out Again*. But Lenny went unrevived.

In the early evening of that Tuesday in August, Phil heard the morbid news on the radio: Lenny Bruce was found in his bathroom, a needle in his arm, dead of an apparent overdose. Hauling Danny Davis with him, Phil slid behind the wheel of his white Cadillac and, with Danny too scared to move or say a word, the car tore rubber all the way down the slinky roads to Lenny's house. After arriving in a great screech of brakes, Phil blew past the policemen at the door and scrambled upstairs to the bathroom death theater. In a showy outburst of grief, he threw himself to the floor next to where Lenny's body lay facedown next to the toilet, his jeans down at his ankles, a bathrobe sash tied around the arm from which the needle jutted. Looking up at the policemen all around, Phil screamed, "You killed him! All of you killed him!"

Leaving moments later with Danny, the Cadillac sped back down the same winding turns, which now were only vague outlines in the dark. Danny concluded that this was the end, that if Harold Kaplan was right about Phil, this was the time he had chosen to kill himself. But then Phil eased up and hit Sunset. And although Phil did a lot of mournful wailing about Lenny that night, this crisis had been a short one. Although he was madder at the world for it, there would be no suicide watch this time.

The very next morning, Danny was in the office when a strange man came by. "A nice-looking man in a gray suit," Davis recalled all too well. He gave Danny a card that identified him as a lieutenant in the LAPD, homicide. Telling Danny he had something to show him, he pulled out a proof sheet of pictures—the police photos of a dead Lenny Bruce, needle in his arm and sprawled on the floor. Taken aback by the gruesome pictures, Danny could only ask, "What'll I do with 'em?" With straight-faced sarcasm, the cop replied, "I thought you could use 'em for an album cover."

"I'll never forget it as long as I live," Davis said. "I looked at him and I thought the man was absolutely demented. I thought he had lost his mind."

When the lieutenant began talking price, a horrified Danny called Phil at home and informed him of the grotesque offer.

"How much does he want?" Phil wanted to know.

"Five thousand dollars. I told him we would have no interest in them."

Without pause, the phone was nearly blasted out of Danny's hand by Phil's bellowing voice. "*Buy 'em!*" he ordered.

Danny, though, would not draw out the money. "I sent the guy's card up to the house and Phil took care of it," he said. "I didn't want a thing to do with it. I thought it was one of the sickest things I'd ever heard of."

Danny preferred to believe that Phil wanted to hoard those ghastly negatives to keep them out of the hands of others who might exploit them. A decade later, when the movie *Lenny* was made, the death scene was re-created with Dustin Hoffman, vérité-style, in the manner of the photos. "The picture that came up on screen just before the end title was the superimposition of the real picture of Lenny Bruce," Davis said. "Phil sold that picture to the movie company and made maybe three times what he had purchased 'em for."

Phil paid for Lenny's funeral and gave the eulogy. In true Spectorian style, it was an ostentatious affair and almost all of Hollywood was invited—except many famous comedians who paid lip service to Lenny after his death. Fresh in Phil's mind was the night he took Lenny to The Trip and Bill Cosby and the Smothers Brothers avoided their table. "The Mort Sahls, Bill Cosbys, Buddy Hacketts—those are the people that really let Lenny down," Spector told *Rolling Stone*. "They're the ones who all said, when Lenny died, that they wanted to bury him—only they wanted to bury him when he was living, because none of them were there."

Danny Davis was not at the funeral either, by his own choice, turned off by what he perceived to be rites of feigned sorrow. Phil upbraided him for it. "He left me a note that ripped me a new asshole. He said that Lenny was our friend, we should pay him respect . . . but the respect he wanted to pay to Lenny was circus in nature."

By the end of 1966, Phil had released only two more records. One was the old Righteous Brothers' album cut, "White Cliffs of Dover." The other was the Ronettes' "I Can Hear Music," which came out of the Spector-Barry-Greenwich writing sessions for Tina Turner and was actually produced by Jeff Barry. Except for the early Lester Sill records, it was the only single ever issued on the Philles label not produced by Phil, and it taunted the Spector legend by tickling the chart at No. 100 in late October. Phil did cut one new record, Tina's "I'll Never Need You More Than This," also from the Spector-Barry-Greenwich pool. A slushy facsimile of "River Deep," it went unreleased.

"He started to show me signs of questioning his talent, and whether he really knew or cared what was happening in music," Davis recalled. "The things he said, the way he said it. About his records. He'd say: 'Jeez, Danny, I just don't know.'"

"He came down from that lofty perch where he truly thought he could make a hit record with anybody. All of a sudden he was down to reality," Vinnie Poncia reflected. "It started with Tina. That was the groundwork. Tina was the straw that broke the back."

The few hours Phil was in the studio were unpleasant. His head was not into music and his mood was truculent. "One time we got into a screaming thing," Larry Levine said, "because somebody had a pizza sent over and I said, 'You gotta give the kid a tip.' He said he didn't and out of that grew this thing where I was never gonna work with Phil again. So Phil wanted to take his tapes and I wouldn't give him his tapes until he paid his bill. So he's siccing the bodyguards on me, telling' 'em to beat me up. They didn't know what to do, they knew we'd been working with each other so long. I said, 'Have 'em do something and I'll sue you for everything.' It just got real ugly."

As always, things were smoothed out between them, but for Larry it was a sad time. He knew that the age of Phil Spector was over.

16

Phil was a very normal person at the beginning of his career . . .
but as time went on, they started writing about him being a genius
and then he said, yeah, I'm a genius. And then they would say he
was a mad genius, so he became the mad genius. I mean it was
anything they wrote about him: he's a recluse, so he became a re-
cluse. I think if Phil hadn't read anything about himself he would
still be the same. But that sort of destroyed him because he became
a replica of everything he read about himself. . . . I wouldn't say
he's mad. I think a lot of time he's pretending to be, because I've
seen him straight and I've seen him act that weird way of his. So a
lot of it is intentional, to let people wonder: what is this guy all
about? [Because] I think he's always wanted attention.

—RONNIE SPECTOR

The Ronettes, who in 1964 were one of the most popular rock-and-
roll acts in the world, could hardly book an appearance in 1966.
Always the only real spigot of income for the group, their road dates

☉   230

that year netted the three Ronettes under $10,000 each. As "family" with Phil, the act could have plodded on as a rock cliché for as long as Phil endured in that role himself. But when Nedra Talley married in March of 1966, it signaled the end of the bumpy road. The man she married, Scott Ross, had once been Murray the K's program director and then turned to religious broadcasting as a born-again Christian. For Nedra that meant new values and priorities. "I made a commitment to Christ and it turned my life around," she said. "I didn't feel I could continue what I was doing and really grow in any way. Because of the tensions we had with Phil, I did not feel, career-wise, that we could go in the direction we needed to go in with Ronnie emotionally involved with him."

The Ronettes sang together for the last time in January of 1967. It was an appropriate portent that in this new year—which would be rock and roll's apocalypse—Philles Records had gone dark.

Another symbol of foreclosure came from Larry Levine, who also chose January to change his status. With Phil not around, and Gold Star's antiquated facilities shunned by the new rockers, work had slowed to a near standstill. Seduced by Herb Alpert, whose records he engineered from the start, Larry accepted the job of chief engineer at A&M Records. A&M had recently bought the old Charlie Chaplin movie studio on Sunset and La Brea, and Levine supervised the construction of recording studios there. "By then Phil was out of it, so I didn't feel I was walking out on him," Levine said. "I went to Stan and Dave and they said I should do it."

At the Philles office, meanwhile, Danny Davis was still drawing paychecks for little more than turning on the lights. "It was ludicrous," he said. "Philles was in the toilet, it was no longer a viable entity. We weren't sellin' records and he was gone. I was doin' things in my office that were just . . . a guy who had a lock on all the industry awards, who had a lock on every radio guy in the world, who knew everybody, and I was sittin' there doin' nothing. He was just carrying me. He would leave me notes about things to do. Those notes he left me, God, it was disgusting. 'Call to get my car done.' 'Change my tires.' 'Call Minnesota Fats and tell him to come over.' I was like Sonny Bono, I was his gofer.

"And every time I wanted to leave he kept giving me more money. I was up to like a thousand a week. Everyone else was either fired or workin' on half-salary, but he didn't want me to leave. The fact is, Phil was always good to me. We had a genuine affection for each other."

But Danny began to worry that his industry clout might rust away in the Philles tomb. "He had taken my forte away from me, because he had no records to promote. It got to a point where if a Top Ten list came in on green paper, I would write, 'Love the shade of green,' just to stay in touch with guys. I was doin' nothing for him and he just didn't understand that."

Phil gave little thought to the hard realities of the business; just existing carried the pretense of influence. On that assumption, he began to reissue his old singles in compilation packages. In the spring of 1967 he sent out releases to the trade papers disclosing that he had signed Ike and Tina Turner to a new three-year deal; a new Ike and Tina single was to be out by June. *Billboard* ran this encouraging kernel of news in May with a headline reading "Spector Revives Push On Philles," but long after June no record had materialized.

Phil's illusions did nothing to prevent his imprint on rock from evaporating. On January 16–18, the Monterey International Pop Festival, which drew 50,000 to an outdoor concert featuring Janis Joplin, Jimi Hendrix, Otis Redding, and the Jefferson Airplane, rang in the new ethos of the late sixties, the music and culture of psychedelic rock. By the summer, when the Beatles' *Sgt. Pepper* album came out and the country was at war with itself over Vietnam and the generation gap, rock and roll weighed in on the side of enlightenment, dissent, and drugs. Phil Spector sat out the fray. He made no records in 1967 and—frightened by the runaway excess and false catechism of drugs within the music industry—he had no use for the wanked-out lunacy all around him. On only two occasions did Phil come into contact with LSD, one of those indirectly. That was when he picked up the phone one night and on the other end was a weak-sounding Annette in New York. That evening she had gone to a downtown rock club where, without her knowledge, someone spiked her drink with acid. Completely disoriented, Annette, who never had taken the drug before, did not know where she was and freaked out, screaming that her hand was gone. Taken to a hospital, she called Phil when her head cleared.

"He was incredibly angry, he just didn't believe it," she remembered. "He said, 'Don't worry, I'll take care of it.' He found out somehow who did it and I don't know what happened and I don't want to know. But Phil really came through for me. He always treated me like gold after everything was over. When I had some trouble he was there for me."

Phil's one personal experience with acid was just as terrifying for him. He took it under the guidance of a doctor, hoping he could better know what was at the root of his psyche. The problem was, he may have seen the answer all too clearly.

"He put himself under the influence of LSD prescribed by Dr. Kaplan and he told me that when he was under he saw his father commit suicide," Danny Davis related. "Phil always said he hated his father for what he did, for taking the easy way out. The acid went right to the heart of that hatred, to the pain, and it horrified him. That's why he was against LSD or anything that was ingested. He didn't care about a little pot every once in a while but he was very much against the acid, because it made him confront what he didn't want to."

Finally Danny decided that he could not go on. With four months left on his contract with Philles, he handed in a letter of resignation. Phil reacted badly.

"Don't think you can just get up and walk out," he told Danny.

"What do you hope to get if you sue me, Phil?" Danny laughed. "All I have is a Mustang and a color televison set."

Danny did not think anything of Phil's threat. Then, a few weeks later, he was served with legal papers. Phil was suing him for $250,000 for breach of contract. "Even Jay Cooper, Phil's attorney, didn't understand it," Davis recalled. "Cooper thought it was a godsend that I was gonna leave and save Phil all that money."

Coincidentally, at about the same time Phil became stuck in a legal row of his own, over *The Last Movie*. By mid-1967 expenses had swelled to over $1 million and the movie had not even been shot. At that point, Phil backed out of the project. Not only did Dennis Hopper sue him, so did Steven Stern, who still had not seen a dollar of his $71,000. Phil desperately needed someone to testify for him, to somehow prove he had reason to walk out. He realized he needed Danny Davis.

"He called and asked me would I bail him out of this thing," Davis said. "I told him, 'Listen, Phil, I'll do whatever you want, but you're suin' me for $250,000. If you drop the suit, I'll come to your aid.'" Phil agreed. He had to. "I mean, they were suin' him for millions, man. There were all kinds of monies that he had guaranteed. He had guaranteed the whole production. But when the above-and below-line figures came in at $1.2 million, Phil didn't want to live up to what he had said. It became a big imbroglio and there was all kind of heat from every quarter, from Dennis, from Steven Stern, from this one, that one. It looked very bad for him but with Phil it was 'Man, Dennis, I'll show you,' and I was to be his big weapon."

When Danny gave his deposition, Hopper's lawyers tried to prove that Phil had cared too little about the movie for it to have been made. "They said, 'Isn't it true, Mr. Davis, that during the discussions about this movie, Phil Spector sat away from the crowd reading a book on the care and breeding of St. Bernard dogs?' And I said, 'Yes, that's true'—which I understand was extremely damaging to Phil. But I said, 'Wait, you don't understand . . .' because, once again, you try and explain Phil Spector. That was exactly the way he wanted it to appear, that he had no interest in the movie, when indeed he wanted to make the picture, but he wanted to make it look like there was nothing important about the picture. Understand?"

In the end, rather than try to figure out Spector, Hopper settled with him. Phil paid $600,000, according to Davis, toward the cost of the aborted movie, including Steven Stern's fee. Incredibly, Phil and Dennis remained friends, the court case having been like a poker game of crazed nerve and dare between men too abnormal for mere logic. Davis, his part of the deal done, was free of Phil's legal claw when he found his next promotion job—back again with Don Kirshner, at Screen Gems.

Elliott Ingber, who had not seen Phil since "Bumbershoot," ran into him at Canter's Deli late in 1967. Elliott had moved far along the rock underground with Frank Zappa; writing songs in Zappa's bitingly satirical style, Ingber's "Don't Bogart That Joint" was a classic send-up of the drug culture. Observing Phil during his dormancy, ringed by bodyguards yet looking so alone, Elliott thought he had never seen anything sadder in his life. "He was weirded out," Ingber recalled. "He was dressed in his black three-piece suit and Beatle boots and a Tyrolean hat or something. It was like he was in a past life, but it was like no life."

Elliott tried to speak of his work with Frank Zappa, but Phil was indifferent. "Uh, that's good," he muttered at intervals. "The only way I could relate to him," said Ingber, "was the level I initially did, which was the guitar."

"You play anymore, man?" Elliott asked him.

'Nah, I don't play anymore," Phil told him. "I don't even think I got a guitar anymore."

"Well, come on down. We're playin' with Frank. I'll give you a fuckin' guitar."

"Nah, man."

Elliott then said good-bye and walked away, thoroughly bummed. If it was true that Phil Spector did not play and did not even *have* a guitar, that was the saddest thing of all.

One of the few people whom Phil permitted into his retreat was Gerry Goffin. Over the past year, Goffin's own life had turned upside down. He and Carole King wrote two huge hits, Aretha Franklin's "A Natural Woman" and the Monkees' "Pleasant Valley Sunday," and started a new label, Tomorrow Records, on which they produced a New York band called the Myddle Class. Gerry not only watched the label fail, he also watched Carole fall in love with the band's bass player, Charles Larkey, which led to the couple's divorce. King and Larkey formed a short-lived band called the City, recording an album for Ode, and King later played piano and sang backup on James Taylor's *Sweet Baby James* LP before recording one of history's biggest-selling albums, *Tapestry,* in the early seventies. In contrast, Goffin moved to L.A. and fell into a personal hell of drugs, a failed singing career, and a lack of songwriting success. Both he and Phil were riders on the storm during rock's changing times, which brought them together. Covered in leather, Phil on his Harley-Davidson and Gerry on his BSA, they biked up into the Santa Monica Mountains and wound through the arid hills all day. They just rode, burning oil, two men with no idea where they were going.

One day Phil wound out with Ronnie on the back of the Harley, Gerry with his girlfriend on the back of the BSA. "I remember saying to him, 'This is a little silly, man. We're gettin' older now, we're

235

not kids anymore. We're just riding around on motorcycles,'" Goffin recalled. "Phil didn't say anything, but Ronnie said, 'You're right.'"

Nedra's marriage made Ronnie want more from her relationship with Phil. When Ronnie used to tell Darlene Love that she was going to marry Phil, Darlene would try to talk her out of it. "You don't want that, child," she would say. "That's the last thing in the world you want to do." But now Ronnie began to push the idea on Phil, and while he knew the financial dangers of another divorce, possessing her legally made sense. Small and meek, Ronnie was no Annette; she was a little mouse in his presence and it was hard to imagine that she would want more than he was willing to give in marriage. On April 14, 1968, they married, in a ceremony attended by Ronnie's mother, Beatrice. The other two Ronettes were not invited.

"Only then did Ronnie admit she had not been married all along," Nedra Talley said. "It was like 'Oh, I was only joking.' It's hard to come out of a lie, but there was a competition thing with Ronnie and me. That's part of being close. If I was married, she had to be. Or if I had kids, she had to. There was also pressure on Ronnie for family's sake. She had not been raised to live with someone. Every woman wants to know that you respect and love her, and that the ring makes it all right."

Unlike what he had done to Annette, Phil tried to give Ronnie a great deal of attention after the wedding. Phil wanted children as much as Ronnie did, and when Ronnie did not conceive right away he had her take fertility pills. She was given the run of the house and the servants, and she thought it was neat that they bowed to her and said, "Yes, Mrs. Spector." Ronnie also expected, because Phil told her, that she would be in the studio as his top recording concern. But in addition to not making any records, he told her she had no reason to leave the house, that she had everything there that she needed to be happy. In time, even if Ronnie wanted to go to the market, the bodyguards would intercept her at the door. If Phil decreed that she could go out that day, a bodyguard would drive her, keeping her under constant watch; if Phil said no, she would be turned back inside the house and the bodyguard would fetch her what she needed.

"Phil had a habit of locking people in his house," Gerry Goffin said. "It was like a dumb little game. If he couldn't control the out-side world, he had to control the inside one. So, to say the least, the marriage was a little strange."

Phil may have assumed he could manipulate Ronnie into seeing his methods of repression as the fruit of Beverly Hills elitism; if Ronnie was sensitive that her background and intellect made her unfit for the social graces, it would be a giddy head trip for her that—as a lady of leisure—she need never touch the concrete be-yond the front gate and have her every need filled. Ronnie, how-ever, grew increasingly despondent.

"Ronnie would write me or call me and say, 'I can't go out of the house' and stuff like that, and I'd go out to her so she wouldn't feel shut off," Nedra said. "It wasn't like she felt she was a prisoner then. She would be trying to be happy, trying to make her marriage work. She wasn't miserable all the time. It was just certain sides of it she knew were not normal, like that she wasn't allowed to go out. The chauffeur was there not because he was a chauffeur. He was 'The Eye.'

"It was a whole lot of nonsense, but that was Phil. I really think the reason Phil didn't do any work then was because, with the mar-riage, it was more important to him to control her than it was to work. For Ronnie to even be in the studio all the time meant that she would be meeting people. So that was taken out of their lives. Ronnie was a singer and now it was like she was told to just forget that. That was the hardest part."

Along with the Stalin overkill, Phil tried to erase rock and roll as a reality inside 1200 La Collina Drive. Instead of rock, Wagnerian operas were the music of the house. Ronnie, it was said, was not even permitted to read *Billboard* or *Variety*, so as not to be dis-tracted by the industry bustle.

"I think Ronnie felt a little stupid," Gerry Goffin said, "because as soon as Phil married her he stopped producing records with her."

Timid as Ronnie was, it was only months before she cracked. Phil's regular tirades and verbal threats scared her and she became so nervous and fearful of him and his shoulder-holstered bodyguards that she had to be given sedatives by doctors. Ronnie managed to slip past The Eye and to get a lawyer. On August 1, just three and a half months after the marriage, divorce papers were filed in her name which read:

Since the marriage, defendant has been nagging plaintiff about everything including going out of the house. He has been acting too jealous towards plaintiff and has stated that he would not permit her to get a divorce. He has stated to her that if she seeks a divorce he will make sure she never smiles again. He has grabbed plaintiff by the arms and has threatened to stick his fingers in her eyes. He has used profanity to the plaintiff and her mother. He has stated to her that she would not be able to get a job in the entertainment world as long as he can help it. Plaintiff fears irreparable harm unless defendant is legally restrained from annoying and molesting her. Plaintiff is currently under a doctor's care for nerves.

In asking for $1,500 a month for expenses, Ronnie listed her net worth as "nothing," while estimating Phil's as "5 million." Phil quickly answered with a counteraction against her, charging Ronnie with "extreme cruelty," and on September 20 court papers were filed that said they were separated. However, Ronnie never moved out of the house, and days later Phil talked her into reconciling, mixing his avowals of love with fresh promises to record her.

Ronnie—whom Phil could convince of anything if he had her face to face—dropped her suit and went on, comforting herself with her doctors' medications and a new relief from the elegant rigor mortis of the house—alcohol.

To Phil, having a child was the key to keeping the marriage together. When Ronnie still did not conceive by early 1969, they adopted an infant boy. As Phil wanted it to appear as though his firstborn was of his own seed, he carefully found a newborn baby with mixed blood. Born on March 29, 1969, and named Donté Phillip Spector, he unveiled the birth of his son in announcement cards sent to friends. The announcement recited a heartwarming scenario of premature birth and uncertain incubation in the form of a three-act play. Act Three read: "Baby going home with mom and pop. Baby's weight 11 pounds. Parents believe it! *Ordeal over . . . Happy Ending.*" The bottom of the card bore the inscription: "The above is a Veronica and Phil Spector Production."

In early 1969 Phil came to an accommodation with commercial music and his place within it. "I know people expect me to come up with another 'River Deep' momentous production. But that's not where it's at," he told *Rolling Stone* later that year. "It's in pleasing yourself and making hit records. That's all that counts. That's the only reason people come to see you."* But he was also uneasy, at times agonized, about whether he *could* ride the commercial carousel. Frankly puzzled by what the market was, he said:

> *Everybody's a helluva lot hipper today, I'll tell you that. There's 13-year-old whores walkin' the streets now. It wouldn't have happened as much five years ago. Not 13-year-old drug addicts. . . . I tell you the whole world is a drop-out. I mean, everybody's a fuck-off. Everybody's mini-skirted, everybody's hip, everybody reads all the books. How in the hell you gonna overcome all that? . . .*
>
> *. . . I know I can make hit records. I don't worry about that. I'm apprehensive about certain people who don't have any standards but drug standards, really. If they're loaded at one time, my record will sound great; if they're not loaded, it may sound bad. I'm apprehensive about the kind of things that people expect. I mean, they don't really want hit records. . . . I'm apprehensive only to the extent that I don't know how to lose yet; I don't know how to say "fuck it" about my art. I get too involved. . . .*
>
> *I'm still involved with why "River Deep" wasn't a hit and what the fuck was . . . and am I that hated? Am I too paranoid? You know, you can antagonize people if they think you're not human, if you say, "Aw fuck, I ain't afraid." A lot of people will get very angry at that, disc jockeys in particular. . . .*
>
> *People put you down for really criticizing, but I can literally tear apart nine out of ten groups. I have to tell you something is desperately wrong with most groups. I mean really bad, bad news. . . .*
>
> *But I can't communicate with a lot of these [industry] people. I can't really bullshit with them, I don't have friends in the record industry. I don't talk with them. We don't jell; we don't communicate; because I'm too bitter I think.†*

*From the *Rolling Stone* interview, Jann Wenner (November 1, 1969): 23.
†From the *Rolling Stone* interview, Jann Wenner (November 1, 1969): 29, 28, 27.

The tragedy of Phil's two years in exile was that he was returning to a wayward and listless music scene more the outsider than ever, too removed now for his nonconformism to carry any creative sanction. Most centrally, his retreat had done nothing to preserve the concept of a record as a complete work. In the pale afterlife of the age of the producer, he could do nothing to change the state of rock. Only wistfully could he tell *Rolling Stone*:

> *I think Mick Jagger could be a lot of fun to record. It's not just the big artists; I think Janis Joplin leaves a lot to be desired recording wise. . . .*
>
> *But the one that really would be the most satisfying probably would be Dylan because I could communicate with him and justify what he really wants to say—no matter what it is—musically, which is something that you don't see very often happening today.*
>
> *Many of the artists today just sing, they don't really interpret anything. I mean the Doors don't interpret. They're not interpreters of music. They sing ideas. . . . [The Rolling Stones are] just makin' hit records now. There was a time when the Stones were really writing* contributions. *See that's a big word to me—"contributions"! . . .*
>
> *Now I'm getting a little tired of hearing about, you know, everybody's emotional problems. I mean it's too wavy. . . . I'm getting so fed up with it. No concept of melody—just goes on and on with the lyric. . . . They're making it a fad. If it had more music it would last, but it can't last this way. . . .*
>
> *They are going to really* kill *the music if they keep it up, because they're not writing songs anymore. They are only writing ideas. . . . They don't care about a hook or melody. . . .*
>
> *You see, I don't have a sound, a Phil Spector sound—I have a style . . . as opposed to Lou Adler or any of the other record producers who follow the artist's style. . . .*
>
> *My style is that I know things about recording that other people just don't know. It's simple and clear, and it's easy for me to make hits.** *

* From the *Rolling Stone* interview, Jann Wenner (November 1, 1969): 23, 25–26.

But if he recognized he could do little himself about the disemboweling of pop, what yanked him back in the end was the second death of black music. Acid, superbands, open-air rock masses, and black militancy had blown soul out of the pond. The seventies were about to begin with no real core of soul outside of the lazily corporate Atlantic and Motown. "I don't consider Motown black," Phil said in the *Rolling Stone* interview. "I consider them half and half. Black people making white music. The Monotones, the Drifters, the Shirelles, Fats . . . I mean, all those artists not making it, and around anymore. That's a big debt. But maybe it's only because nobody's doing it."*

Phil wanted to at least have a crack at paying back that collective white debt. Months before, even while still in his holding pattern, he signed his first new act in over two years. Steering clear of the torn denim and glazed eyeballs of the mainstream, he went with an integrated cocktail-lounge soul group, the Checkmates Ltd., a composite of refined Drifterish R&B and the self-contained backbeat of both rock bands and soul revues. The Checkmates, a guitar-bass-drum unit fronted by black singers Bobby Stevens and Sonny Charles, avoided the urge to fuse their emotive Motown-style blues with acid rock in the manner of Sly Stone. As a result, they had not climbed out of the narrow strobe light of Las Vegas stages. Although they were popular along the vestigial jazz and casino in–crowd, two Checkmates singles and an album released by Capitol did not do well. In a curious way, the Checkmates—Stevens and Charles, beyond whom Phil did not see—were an evolved form of the Righteous Brothers without the sawdust. They played well to black and white audiences, and Phil—who at twenty-eight was now the picture of Nehru-jacketed, aging hip—believed rock could still be embroidered with honest, decorous soul. Eventually Phil opened discussions with A&M Records, one of many labels that had been courting him since the Philles dim-out, about cutting a record with the Checkmates as the means of his return. Herb Alpert was one of the very few producers in the business with whom Phil did not erect a rivalry of the mind—Alpert's Tijuana Brass records were so extraneous to Phil's music that when Larry Levine had played them for him Phil thought Larry was pulling his leg. Through the years, the

* Ibid., 29.

two Fairfax High alumni were respectful of each other. A&M won high marks from Phil for bucking the trend of failed independent labels to challenge the majors by the late sixties. Of inestimable value, Herb also had Larry Levine at Sunset and La Brea, in a studio Larry set out to build in the acoustical image of Gold Star.

The A&M deal Phil made in late 1968 was a provisional one, and though the spoils of his past brought Phil a custom logo for his records—the label would read "A&M" and "Phil Spector Productions," the latter marked by a fiendish little man in a black cape and high hat—the fact that Phil would not be reactivating his own label meant the certain death of an era and an uncertain promise for the future. Phil himself raised no great expectations; disinviting any comparisons with his old hits, he told *Rolling Stone:* "I live off what I've done and my reputation is there, and it's unspoiled. I keep it that way." When word of the A&M deal was out, Lester Sill, from personal experience, did not believe Phil could ever be committed or dependable aiding someone else's empire. "My reaction was that he was just roaming and using," Sill said.

Phil's immediate concern with the Checkmates was finding new songs for them to record. Rock was now dominated by performers and bands who generated their own songs, and this trend had mandated the end of the great early sixties song combines. Out of that whole incredible confluence of music and hustling along Broadway, only Don Kirshner was left intact, but only because the boob tube had insulated him against rock reality. Kirshner made millions withstanding musical truth and honesty; his bubble-gum-music groups, the Monkees and then the Archies, were money-making machines of deceit (the Archies did not even exist outside of the studio) churning out songs by the likes of Jeff Barry, Goffin-King, Tommy Boyce, and Neil Diamond. For Kirshner, it was a satisfying if short-lived mirage of the old pecking order, and his lingering influence in that context brought Phil to New York for the first time in years. When he arrived, though, he found a Kirshner with little influence and few useful writers. But Spector still had charmed luck. While he was in Kirshner's office two writers, Irwin Levine and Toni Wine, walked in to pitch their material.

Levine, the son of prizefighter Benny Levine, had been around for a while, a lyricist without success, and he now was back with melodies composed by Wine, a top commercial jingle singer. Both thought they had walked in on a comedy act. "It was quite a scene," Levine recalled. "Kirshner was totally perplexed and embarrassed because there was Phil Spector calling him all kinds of names and jumping on top of the furniture like a crazy person." Phil, as he loved to do, was goofing on Kirshner, testing his slow-burn placidity; Kirshner, not having seen Spector for a while, had forgotten how far Phil could go. "He was calling Kirshner 'Golden Ears,' because they used to say Kirshner had golden ears for music, and Phil was makin' fun of that, sort of half joking, but Kirshner was very sensitive and was totally embarrassed. Toni and I were standing there hysterical and Kirshner was saying, 'You'll have to excuse me. This is a strange person.' I knew Donnie a long time and I never saw him in that position before. Phil could just unnerve him."

Phil liked Levine and Wine; they were a good audience for him and they were seasoned writers. The three of them went right from Kirshner's office to Wine's apartment and the pair played Phil some of their songs. "He told me, 'I'm gonna record the Checkmates and it's gonna be a smash, babe,' the whole routine," Levine said. They honed a few riffs into a working melody and then Phil left, telling them to work on it. When he came back some time later, Levine and Wine had words and music.

"I had this idea from a Sidney Poitier movie that was out, *For the Love of Ivy*," said Levine. "I was thinking of that maid and we came up with the 'black pearl, precious little girl' hook. Phil came in and he loved it."

The fairytalelike balladry of "Black Pearl" made it a song with great charm—an essential Phil had lost sight of with "River Deep"— and he made a split-fee deal with Herb Bernstein, an arranger whose publishing house employed Levine and Wine, and Herb Alpert's Irving Music. Phil then took that and several others of their songs back to L.A.

A well-rested Phil Spector—with hip new leather-and-suede duds and a large assortment of dark glasses and nifty, fashionable-length hairpieces—jumped out of the bushes in 1969 with the rush of a man determined not to let the sixties get away without a reminder of his place in them. First, his wombat face—snout-nosed, pebble eyes twinkling behind rose-colored shades, asparagus hair clumped under a corduroy cap—came before a multitude of theater audiences as a dope dealer in the opening scene of the movie *Easy Rider*. The film, co-starring and directed by Dennis Hopper, was made for $400,000 and grossed millions as a classic sixties' set piece of alienation. It also nearly bankrupted Hollywood studios when filmmakers followed its lead and left the lots to go on location. As such, it was the actualization of Hopper's dream of three years before. Phil was presented with the opening cameo by Dennis, and his dope pusher role was a ratchet in the film's smug amorality. Sitting in the back of a large white Rolls-Royce, Phil was a tightly framed rodent who sniffs Peter Fonda's cocaine, grins, nods, and says not a word as he makes the score that finances Hopper and Fonda's motorcycle odyssey into the Hades of America. Phil saw it as accreditation of the hip perversity he always craved—just so no one missed it, he sent out Christmas cards composed of the movie's still shot of him in the Rolls, coke spoon going noseward, with the greeting: "A Little 'Snow' At Christmas Time Never Hurt Anyone!!" However, the ineffable Hopper may have had an ulterior motive: an ace card in the arcane poker game with Spector.

"The real point of it was that Dennis Hopper could put Phil Spector in a movie and not let him talk," related Danny Davis, who by knowing both men was hip to the in-joke. "That was Dennis shutting up Phil Spector, which of course was something nobody could ever do. It's true, believe me, you don't know these two guys. Something like that would turn on Dennis immensely."

Phil's next winning hand was getting Dennis to rent an office next to his at 9130 Sunset; he bragged all over Hollywood about that. But Dennis had a royal flush in 1970 when he made none other than *The Last Movie*, without one cent from Phil.

More important was the March release of the first Spector-produced records on A&M. The debut single was the Checkmates' "Love Is All I Have to Give," written by Spector and Bobby Stevens, a mordant blues wail made glacierlike by an overload of mandolins, guitars, and strings. An inauspicious miss, it was a hardly noticed No. 65 in mid-May, offering no clue as to whether the radio blockade of his records had lifted. A second March issue was the Spector-Levine-Wine "You Came, You Saw, You Conquered," sung by Ronnie but released, amazingly, as "The Ronettes Featuring the Voice of Veronica"—the very phrase that once turned Ronette against Ronette. Produced in early Ronettes style, Phil may have hoped for nostalgic uplift or else was still frozen by his failure with Ronnie as a solo. If it was that he was simply not willing to give her any autonomy—during the sessions Ronnie sat forlornly in the back of the booth when not recording, allowed nowhere else—he ran her off the rails hard; an engaging record, "You Came" never charted.

In truth, Phil gave neither of these records a second thought once they were released. These were A&M obligations, and even Phil seemed to shrug his shoulders as he described his work with the Checkmates to Rolling Stone: "Very commercial records. Good records. Easy records. Soul records. Some have depth, some don't have."* However, he made one vital change for the second Checkmates single, which was to be "Black Pearl." Needing sugar-plum soul for the song, he went with Sonny Charles on lead vocal. A huge man with horn-rimmed glasses, Charles's high and sweet trill was normally a counterpoint to Bobby Stevens's blues burr. But Phil loved Charles's voice and released "Black Pearl" under the name of "Sonny Charles and the Checkmates Ltd.," which did not please Stevens.

Seeing how well "Black Pearl" congealed in the studio, Phil rushed the record out in April, now the explicit thrust of his comeback. Irwin Levine and Toni Wine, in New York, knew he had cut the song but had not heard anything from him. When they heard an early dub, they were dazed. "It was incredible," Levine said. Spector had made changes; he also kept the song unaffected. Above all, Sonny Charles was monumentally convincing as a sensitive and prideful man throwing off the pain of the ghetto in a way Mann and Weil would never accept—"No more servants baby; they're gonna serve my queen," Charles laid down, softly and firmly on a record that may have been Spector's finest of all. "Black Pearl" shimmered like topaz, certainly recorded and mixed more diaphanously than any of the others. The effect was so soufflé-light that the Wall of Sound was more like a floating cloud of strings, woodwinds, and electric pianos that played off funky keyboard runs and a stately, sinewy bass line. Extending R&B into a romantic Formica, it showed the way for the synthesizers and stringed hooks of soul in the seventies and eighties.

---

*From the Rolling Stone interview, Jann Wenner (November 1, 1969): 29.

It also showed that an earnest Phil Spector still could not be touched when it came to the art of making a record.

"Black Pearl" hit the chart on April 10. At the beginning it stalled, stuck in the old mucilage about whether it was too black for white radio. But as the record's soothing charm made its impression, the same crowd that pilloried "River Deep" became swept into the rapids of Phil Spector's suddenly hot comeback. Top 20 in six weeks, "Black Pearl" eased up to No. 13 pop and Top 10 soul in July. Though it went no higher, the song would not leave the chart for another seven weeks; while it might not have been bought in overwhelming numbers, it was surely a song that people wanted to hear.

This was a victory almost as much for Larry Levine as for Phil. By no rights should "Black Pearl" or the other new Spector records have recalled the symphonic splendor of the vintage Philles songs. Although Larry built the A&M studio to the dimensions of Gold Star, the ceiling at the old Chaplin studio was higher, the acoustics tinnier, the echo chambers far inferior. "It didn't sound like Gold Star; it never could," Levine said. "And the Wall of Sound was indigenous to Gold Star, to the studio, the chambers, the walls." Moving to a different studio, and in his post-Philles head, Phil did not come in wanting or thinking it possible to resurrect the Wall. Complicating the Spector style further, Phil cut in stereo for the first time at A&M, although he recorded and mixed the rhythm track completely in mono.

"I feel that 'Black Pearl' was less Wall of Sound and more Detroit anyway," Levine said. "Phil was out of that old thing. Once he left Gold Star it was over. But Phil always wanted bigness, the echo, so even though the chambers were not what I wanted them to be, you work at it. That's what an engineer does; you search and work to get it right. Somehow we mixed it to what it was. I remember this one producer at A&M used to get on me for the chambers, that I couldn't get a good echo. So I played 'Black Pearl' for him and said, 'You mean like this?' And he said, 'Yeah, you could never get an echo like that here.' "

With "Black Pearl" a hit, Phil brought Irwin Levine and Toni Wine to the coast for writing sessions during the summer. But now, his statement made, Phil was only marginally interested in A&M work. "He would waste a lot of time," Levine recalled. "He had pinball machines all over the place and it was hard to get any work done. Sometimes we would get in his car and he'd drive down Sunset and torment the hippies. He'd have American flags up all over his antenna and Phil and the hippies would be hollering through the window and they'd be throwing things. It wasn't that Phil was ideological, he just likes to torment people."

It was during this time, in fact, that Phil apparently fell out with Don Kirshner when he went too far in tweaking the uptight songmeister.

"Phil had the largest dog on record, this Russian wolfhound named Olga or something," Levine said. "Donnie was visiting Phil one day and Donnie was deathly afraid of dogs, any dog. The smallest dog in the world Kirshner was afraid of. So Kirshner was sitting in a chair and Phil brought in this dog, which I'm telling you was as big as a horse, and he had him come up to Donnie and put his paws on Donnie's chest. Donnie almost had a heart attack. I don't know if Kirshner ever spoke to Phil again after that."

Phil had cut several tracks for a Checkmates album, but problems had developed with the group. Despite "Black Pearl" and the national attention it brought, Bobby Stevens's discontent about Sonny Charles's sudden prominence was still a bleeding wound. "He was having a problem with them all because of it," Levine said, "and it was driving Phil crazy. He was disgusted. I remember he told me, 'I could walk down the street and find a bunch of black guys on any corner and make 'em stars.' It was like, who are these guys to fight like this when I made 'em famous? It got to the point where he couldn't get into the rest of the project."

Phil left the completion of the album, including a truly pretentious "*Hair* Anthology Suite," a medley from the Broadway play, to producer Perry Botkin, Jr., who arranged "Black Pearl." In the late fall the Checkmates LP, *Love Is All We Have to Give*, was released and sold poorly—though, ironically, Spector's booming cover of "Proud Mary," the last Checkmates single, gave Ike and Tina Turner the idea to cut their own smash cover a year later, breaking them out to the public the way "River Deep" did not. The album and the single hardly mattered to Phil, now for a specific reason. He had gotten a higher calling.

17

Everyone was saying, "Oh Beatles, don't break up, give us some-
thing to remember you by," and you give it to them and then the
critics just knock the shit out of it. "It's awful, it's this, it's that."
But it's your Beatles, your great Beatles! Forget my name . . . if
my name hadn't been on the album there wouldn't have been all
that. George told me that, John, everyone. That's the dues you have
to pay. It was nothing to me. I had my reputation before the Beatles
were around. . . they knew that and I knew that. I knew who I was
and what I was before I met the Beatles.

—PHIL SPECTOR, 1970

If the final and climactic year of the sixties tied up the loose ends of
an exhilarating and hideous decade, the first year of the new decade
peeled back the pages of the calendar in search of old comforts.
Although they had changed the world, a battle-weary generation now
looked for the solace and immunity of innocence—ironically allied
with a Phil Spector scornful of late sixties' rock. "I feel like an old-

⊙

timer wishin' for the groovy young days," Spector told *Rolling Stone*, "but I listen to the Beatles' album and I know they're wishin' for it too, because you can hear it. 'Lady Madonna' was such a groovy old-time thing." Now, early in 1970, it was written by fate that Phil Spector would be in London seeking to create a fundamental rock-and-roll perspective for the great merchants of social change in the sixties. Sequestered in a basement studio in the Apple Records office building at 3 Savile Row, he sorted through almost thirty hours of unmixed recording tape trying to find some way to make it the last testament of the Beatles.

This hellacious and thankless task was taken with almost no help from a sundered Beatles. By the fall of 1969, the Beatles were finished as a group, wrecked by internal strife, jealousy, and rampant mismanagement within their Apple Records business structure. Hastening their demise, John Lennon had begun to release solo records with Yoko Ono as a way of abrading his already nasty personal and business feud with Paul McCartney. John, who was playing concerts and promoting the peace movement with the Plastic Ono Band, had made up his mind to quit the Beatles flat that fall but was persuaded by the group's recently named American manager, Allen Klein, to hold off until he found an equitable way to divide their assets—an impossible wish since Klein was the bone of contention between Lennon and McCartney; Paul, who had pitched his father-in-law, show-biz lawyer Lee Eastman, as manager, wanted Klein removed before any dissolution.

A year before, as this situation began to presage the group's undoing, Paul convinced the other three Beatles to record what was intended as a musical *rapprochement:* a documentary movie and soundtrack album of their recording sessions and final public concert. Paul believed the Beatles had to set aside their separate music directions, which had soured the *White Album,* and "get back to their roots." When the sessions went on in January 1969, the project was given the working title *Get Back.* But the whole episode sank the Beatles further into a morass. Over three weeks they cut a number of disjointed tracks, some new, some covers of oldies, in a malaise of bitter feelings and raw nerve endings during which George Harrison briefly quit in a huff. For the grand finale, the farewell concert, they climbed to the roof at 3 Savile Row and on an icy-cold day reflective of their spirit of frozen loathing sang several songs before 16-mm cameras and a few puzzled spectators on the street below. Without looking at or relating to each other, the Beatles were eternally captured on film disintegrating in open fratricide. The wonderful single of "Get Back," produced by George Martin, came out of the sessions, but the film and the album—eventually retitled *Let It Be*—were nothing more than ungainly reels of tape and film. No Beatle cared enough to go back and complete songs or choose any for inclusion on the album, and for that reason Martin refused to even begin mixing the tapes, which sat on a shelf at Apple. "Nobody could look at it," John Lennon later said of the stomach-turning project. "I really couldn't stand it."

John himself was much more concerned with his solo work. Although the Beatles did put aside their differences over the summer of 1969, recording the ingenious and intimately beautiful *Abbey Road* in one last breath of unity for art's sake, John's personal and artistic feelings were reserved for his own records, such as the brutally honest "Cold Turkey." After the turn of the new decade he wrote "Instant Karma," a rollicking caveat to the enemies of his world that they better get themselves together or they were gonna be dead. However, he was not eager to produce the song. John was not turned on by the intricacies of record-making; getting in front of a microphone and singing rock and roll was all he ever wanted to do, which is why he could record "Give Peace a Chance" in a hotel room bed. In producing "Cold Turkey," he became frazzled running back and forth from the studio to the booth. John did not want a repeat with "Instant Karma," and in discussions with Allen Klein the name of Phil Spector came up.

Phil had stayed on good terms with the Beatles through the years, in the form of communiqués that felt out the possibility of Spector producing an occasional Beatles record. When Phil released the *River Deep* album on A&M the previous fall in a limited American run, he obtained a cover blurb from George Harrison that gushed in praise: "'River Deep—Mountain High' is a perfect record from start to finish. You couldn't improve on it." John also loved Spector's records. "If we ever used anybody besides George Martin," he once said, "it would be Phil." Now John and Klein agreed that bringing in Phil to produce "Instant Karma" was a terrific idea. Phil, who was aroused by the bid, didn't think there could be any other choice.

Ironically, Phil had publicly bad-mouthed Allen Klein only

months before as a show-biz viper. A rumpled, fast-talking New York accountant with a vast knowledge of the tax laws, Klein had wormed his way into the management of both the Rolling Stones and the Beatles. Despite the fact that he was one of the most powerful men in the entertainment industry, many in the business shared Phil's stated opinion that Klein was "not a very good cat." "Phil could read people and he knew the guy was shady," said Pete Bennett, the Beatles' American promotion man whose testimony later helped send Klein to prison for two months on tax evasion. "Klein may have wanted a piece of Phil too, but Phil kept away." Beyond Klein, Phil saw a distinct parallel in Lennon's musical head and his own. These were the two most headstrong and idiosyncratic geniuses in modern music, yet despite their divergent rock paths Phil and all the Beatles were walking on the same tracks now—conservators of the prologue to rock's seventies' identity, yet unsure of where they stood in new and unpredictable territory.

From his point of view, "Phil needed that association with Lennon and the Beatles," Vinnie Poncia said. "He acquiesced to the thing he should've acquiesced to with the Lovin' Spoonful. He thought he couldn't possibly fail if John Lennon was with him. He didn't particularly want the association, but he needed it."

Phil went to London in late January. He moved into a large suite at the Inn on the Park Hotel, sharing the room with the garrulous and uncomplicated Pete Bennett. Phil's menagerie of hairpieces occupied an entire closet. His longtime bodyguard, George Brand, a beefy ex-federal marshal, was one adjoining door away. The "Instant Karma" session was held at the EMI studio on Abbey Road, where the famous album was recorded. Pulling a small but mandatory Phil trip, Phil showed up late, keeping Lennon and a version of the Plastic Ono Band that included George Harrison on guitar, Klaus Voorman on bass, and Alan White on drum waiting for an hour. John began the session, then Phil came in and got a take of the song on tape. But that was just the start. He fattened up the rhythm by overdubbing John on one piano, George and White on another, Voorman on an electric keyboard. Then he overdubbed a muffled drum that sounded like hands slapping a mattress.

Expecting something like the scratchy pop funk of "Cold Turkey," John was impressed with the broad, richly textured sound Spector created. What was accentuated in this four-man Wall of Sound was not spare noise but the bare blues elements: the pile-driving rhythm and the authentic bite of John's hoarse and cracking voice. Many of his Beatles records had been mixed unevenly, and rarely was the rhythm toughened like this. John was delighted, but Phil was not satisfied. He told John he wanted to take the tape back to L.A. and add strings. Lennon said no and the disc was released in early February in England. Weeks later, when released in America, the record was different, cleaner and tighter. Without John knowing, Phil had remixed it again, and in an updated symbol of the Phil Spector past the disc was inscribed "Phil & Ronnie."

John minded none of this. He had no trouble giving Phil his due. The record, his biggest solo hit so far, went to No. 3, selling over one million copies in the U.S. alone. Phil had done so well that John and Allen Klein asked him to take a crack at the dormant *Let It Be* tapes. With no restrictions on his judgment and work, Phil took to the Apple basement. Day after day in February and March, he tried to find the germ of art in all those hours of raw tape, under a vow of secrecy in case the album was unsalvageable. "I didn't even know Phil was in England," said Tony Hall, his closest contact across the water. "It was done very hush-hush. He did a lot of the album before I heard he was here."

The only other George Martin–produced song suitable for release before Phil arrived was the *Let It Be* title cut, Paul's gospel plea for redemption from Mother Mary. It came out in early March, but only a month later Paul issued his first solo LP, *McCartney*, with an accompanying announcement that he was done with the Beatles and that the group had ceased to exist. Against this noxious backdrop, Phil rushed to complete *Let It Be*, which was now beyond any question going to close the Beatles' legacy. Amassing strings and choirs, he coated the urchin tapes with aristocratic heavy cream. Most of the songs in the tapes were blues-flavored rockers and Phil could have gone with the taut rhythm of "Instant Karma." Instead, he felt obligated to send the group off with great sentimental joy and sorrow. If the Beatles were averse to that, none of them made it known. George, who was soon to begin his own solo LP, attended some of the overdubbing sessions and thought that Spector's tumbling, dreamlike éducements would perfectly suit the eastern mystic motif of his own music; right away George got a commitment from him to produce the album.

Phil did not want *Let It Be* separated from the chain of Beatles progression. There had been gossip in the music papers that this album was going to be an aggregation of "lost" Beatles tracks, a novelty rather than an important new work. Shunning any novelty interpretation, Phil avoided oldie covers like "Save the Last Dance for Me" and stuck with original Beatles tunes. To sustain the Beatles' musical versatility he let stand some of the raw tracks, in leathery, trenchant contrast to the rest. One of these was the original "Get Back," which had funkier Billy Preston keyboard riffs and John's immortal spoken closing: "I hope we passed the audition." When the album was ready, Phil sent an acetate to each Beatle, and each sent him a telegram of approval.

Still, Phil had no delusions about *Let It Be*. He knew he could not win, that no matter how well he did with the album there would be those Beatle worshippers who would look at an outsider—an American outsider, and one with a legendary ego—and see only desecration. In England Spector's vast popularity was confined to his own music. If Phil needed the ego trip, he was sure he would not need the approaching storm of dissent—a dark omen of which came mere days before the album's release when Paul suddenly changed his mind, disquieted because of what Phil did to his song "The Long and Winding Road." The album's first single, this languid and mawkish ballad was originally cut only with an acoustic guitar, and now Paul hardly recognized it in a Spectorian slew of swelling strings, harps, and background singers. Repulsed by what he heard as shlock, Paul vehemently told Phil and Allen Klein that he wanted the song pared down to size. But by then the album was already in the pressing shop. When Paul sued Klein and the other three Beatles months later, he cited "The Long and Winding Road" in his court papers, claiming it was evidence that the group had conspired to "ruin my career artistically."

Paul's ire was a prelude. When *Let It Be* was released on May 5 and the extent of Spector's influence was known, the critical inquisition was "River Deep" revisited; Phil was punished just as universally. Spector, wrote *Rolling Stone*'s John Mendelsohn in a typically mean-spirited review, "whipped out his orchestra and choir and proceeded to turn several of the rough gems of the best Beatle album in ages into costume jewelry. . . . One can't help but wonder . . . how he came to the conclusion that lavish decoration of several of the tracks would enhance the straightforwardness of the album. . . . To Phil Spector, stinging slaps on both wrists." Mendelsohn judged "The Long and Winding Road" to be "virtually unlistenable" and "an extravaganza of oppressive mush."*

As difficult as his job had been, and given the fact that he had no part in the original recordings, Phil felt no reason to be anybody's whipping boy. With the carping at a fever pitch—including some stinging criticism by George Martin—Phil angrily told British journalist Richard Williams: "It was no favor to me to give me George Martin's job because I don't consider [him] in [my] league. . . . He's an arranger, that's all. As far as *Let It Be,* he had left it in deplorable condition, and it was not satisfactory to any of them, they did not want it out as it was. So John said, 'Let Phil do it' and I said, 'Fine.' Then I said, 'Would anybody like to get involved in it, work on it with me?' 'No.' . . . They didn't care. But they did have the right to say, 'We don't want it out,' and they didn't say that. In five years from now maybe people will understand how good the material was."†

Looking back through the tunnel of time, it is preposterous that so many people could have believed Spector "ruined" *Let It Be.* In a moving victory of the proletariat, the album sold over two million copies in its first two weeks, setting an American sales record for an album at that time. It stayed at the top of the album chart for five weeks and was on the chart for fifty-four weeks. With sales of over four million worldwide, *Let It Be* outsold the Beatles' *Revolver* and *Yesterday . . . and Today* LPs. Though it was obviously a Phil Spector production—it simply could not have sounded like anything else— the character and essence of the Beatles was present in every groove. Indeed, the reviled "Long and Winding Road" became a letter-perfect parable of the Beatles' adieu, a sentimental journey through an epoch now run out of time, and a No. 1 song. When *Let It Be* won a Grammy for best original score in a motion picture, the award was accepted by none other than Paul McCartney, apparently aware that his career was not ruined after all.

Phil went into the studio with George Harrison in late May. Off and on for the next six months they recorded an ambitious twenty-three-

*From *Rolling Stone,* Records, June 11, 1970:35.

†Richard Williams, *Out of His Head: The Sound of Phil Spector* (New York: Outerbridge & Lazard, 1972), 156–57.

song, three-record boxed set album philosophically titled *All Things Must Pass*. It was a converging of two studio fanatics; George rearranged and Phil overdubbed so many times that Allen Klein gave up trying to set a release date. However, Spector and Harrison could not have been better tailored to each other.

Harrison's material was essentially a profusion of mantras that swayed in much the same anesthetizing manner as "To Know Him Is to Love Him." Taken on its face, Harrison's preachy Krishna litany seemed a stupefyingly unappealing concept. But George's ideas, his nasal twang, weeping guitar, and humility were sharpened by Spector, who also deepened the metaphysical feel. Phil's rhythmically pounding basses and drum feels sutured George's sentimentality with cheerful energy and made Indian asceticism into dance music. As with John's "Instant Karma," Phil worked with a small but powerful rhythm section that included superstar musicians Harrison, Eric Clapton, and Dave Mason on guitar, Ringo Starr on drum, the American keyboardist Billy Preston, and Rolling Stones horn player Bobby Keys. Polished as they were, these top sidemen—whose monster jam session formed the third record of the LP—had never played the way they did under Spector's direction.

"He was unique the way he worked," recalled Billy Preston, who was also a major contributor to *Let It Be*. "He would use a lot of keyboards playing the same chord to make it big and strong. We would do it several times in different octaves and it was monotonous as hell. But he was making it the Phil Spector sound. Myself, I never really was a fan of his sound. I thought it worked on the Ronettes' stuff, it worked on certain things but not on others. But with George's stuff it was perfect."

The collaboration worked well all around. "It was a lot of laughs," Preston said. "Phil didn't seek to overtake George or anything. He would hold court and all you could do was laugh 'cause he had the floor and Phil looked like a cartoon to me, a funny little guy with a funny little voice, loony but a lot of fun. And he was brilliant. I still don't know how he got the echo like he did; he'd record with an echo in the room and that was the only time I ever saw that, man. He had every machine going all at once and he knew what every one was doin' in relation to the others. It was a circus and he was the ringleader."

Astounding almost everyone in the industry, *All Things Must Pass*, released in late November 1970, became the No. 1 album in

England and the U.S. inside of two weeks. Its first single, the two-sided "My Sweet Lord"/"Isn't It a Pity," held the top spot for five weeks; the second single, "What is Life?" went to No. 9. While with the Beatles, George, allotted two songs per album, saw only one of his songs become a hit single, "Something." *All Things Must Pass* did not just enhance Harrison as an artist—it propelled him beyond Lennon and McCartney. With invaluable aid from Spector, he also forged the seventies first new rock idiom.

Almost obscured in the buying frenzy of George's album was the release only ten days later of Lennon's first solo LP, one that was nothing short of an exorcism. This record, *John Lennon/Plastic Ono Band*, produced by Phil out of a series of harrowing sessions in the fall, was as stridently negative as George's work was spiritually optimistic. It surfaced because the impressionable and tortured Lennon felt he needed to sort out his post-Beatle life and who he was. John's whole life had been a quest for meaning and knowledge, but he could never make sense of the man underneath. His solution, temporarily, was the sneering program of "new wave" California therapist Arthur Janov. Janov had written a book called *The Primal Scream, Primal Therapy: The Cure for Neurosis*, the theory of which was that human beings repress negative emotion rooted in childhood. Taking therapy directly from Janov for three months, John was put through agonizing sessions in which he lay spread-eagled on the floor and cried and screamed in anger as he recalled his tragic childhood—his frightening apparitions not unlike those seen by Phil while on his LSD trip. Although John eventually spurned Janov and primal therapy as a panacea, he thought he had found and could express his inner self. He wrote songs that were jarring in their naked honesty, and Phil produced them as "primal rock"—the Wall of Sound cropped to exact the image of a bare room with one harsh light bulb. As Lennon screamed and raged in anguished self-pity, his guitar, Ringo's drum, Preston's keyboard, and Klaus Voorman's bass played a madrigal that cut to the bone. A No. 6 LP in December 1970, nearly two decades later the album is as compelling and important a work as any in rock, pricking the ears with John's seething rejection of his mother and his scalding précis: "The dream is over."

As Apple Records broke into pieces, most of its side acts sent packing and its grand show-biz aims dashed, it fell to Phil to hold together the business order of what was left. Named head of A&R, he chose releases by the group Badfinger and held spending in line, with an orderliness that worked to the Beatles' benefit since Allen Klein's shadowy investment practices thrived on chaotic, indecipherable account books. Phil also tried to make inroads into the new British blues band scene. He produced a song called "Tell the Truth" for Eric Clapton's group Derek and the Dominoes. But Clapton did not like how the mix sounded and refused to issue the record. This, however, was a mere diversion. In early 1971 John wrote and Phil produced "Power to the People," the final anthem in the Lennon political trilogy after "Revolution" and "Give Peace a Chance." If John was deadly serious about the sledgehammer doggerel, Phil had the wisdom to temper it into more like a tickling feather. Despite the sinister-sounding marching feet of the intro, the hard and honking rock arrangement made militant protest amiable enough to make it a No. 11 record in March.

Phil bounced back and forth between London and L.A. so much that he spent very little time with Ronnie. In August of 1969, before the Lennon and Harrison gigs came about, he had another divorce alarm when Ronnie again filed court papers, but Phil was able to get her to back down as he did the first time. Now he made good on his soothing promises by taking Ronnie to London early in 1971 to record a song that Harrison wrote for her called "Try Some, Buy Some." Though the song was cut and released on the Apple label, it was completely wrong for her—another of George's mystic chants, it forced Ronnie to try to appeal to the spirit instead of the flesh and it was ignored.

Two months later, in more serious business, Phil produced the Harrison single "Bangladesh," a song that identified the first of rock's humanitarian causes: the starving refugees of civil war-torn East Pakistan. George and the Indian sitar player Ravi Shankar organized a relief fund, into which royalties from the record were routed. "Bangladesh," an emotional plea to "feed the people," was a big hit, and that prompted George to make rock-and-roll altruism a grand spectacle. On August 1 he gave two benefit concerts in Madison Square Garden with a lineup of guest musicians including Ringo, Eric Clapton, Billy Preston, Bob Dylan, and Leon Russell, the one-time Spector session pianist who was now a major force on his own

257

and in the sessions and performances of Dylan and Joe Cocker. Stationed in a backstage trailer, Phil recorded the shows for a live album—a three-record set called *Concert for Bangladesh*—that was released in the fall and won a Grammy.

When Phil arrived in New York for the concerts, he sent a ticket to Annette Merar so she could attend the year's major rock event. "I had the best seat in the house, like third row center," she recalled. "But I never could find him and then after the show was over I went backstage and was informed that he had left with George and Ringo about a half an hour before. That was shitty. He knew I was there. He's the one that called me and asked me if I wanted to go." Actually, Phil almost didn't make it out of the arena in one piece that night. During the evening show he became agitated and got into a loud confrontation backstage with security police who proceeded to pound him with their clubs. "I'm Phil Spector!" he could be heard screaming. "Don't you know who I am!" When they began to hustle him out, George Harrison yelled to Pete Bennett, "They're beating up Phil!" The obedient and bull-like promotion man wedged himself through the ring of uniformed bodies around Phil and pulled him free.

"George Brand was just sitting there, he didn't make a move to save Phil," Bennett said. "I got in there and I grab him and put his head under my arm so they couldn't beat on his head. I said, 'What are you doing? He's our producer!' and one of the guys says, 'I don't care what he is, he's a nasty son of a bitch.' He was just bein' Phil, a little wild, but he's a genius and you don't treat a Phil Spector like that. I said to 'em, 'Come on, try anything and I'll kill youse all!' And they just walked away. I think they woulda killed him if not for me."

The incident was a minor irritant for Phil, who was euphoric and drunk with power when he left the Garden, two years of propping up two kingly thrones in rock now capped by the historic Bangladesh triumph. At the post-concert party at Jimmy Weston's restaurant, an incredible conglomeration of rock superstardom jammed on the restaurant's small bandstand—a group made up of Ringo, Preston, Keith Moon of the Who, Keith Richards of the Rolling Stones—and Phil on piano. The last time Spector openly performed had been at The Trip with the Modern Folk Quartet, when he was bent on sinking into the sod of a new rock world. Now he seemed

⊙

to own the mixing board of that world. As the superstars jammed, the soft-pop singer Andy Williams came into the restaurant. Looking for a meal, Andy unknowingly stepped into Spector's intimidating line of sight. "Look! It's *Andy Williams!*" Phil burbled. "Hey, Andy, come on up here and sing us a song!"

Billy Preston remembered, "I mean Phil was really shouting at him. He was just in a good mood but Phil is a wacko and Andy freaked out, man. He got scared, he didn't know who these weird rock-and-roll guys were and whether Phil was gonna go on like that. I looked up and Andy was running out the door. Phil could do that to you."

After *Bangladesh,* Phil produced John Lennon's *Imagine* LP, a delightful work that showed a happier John facing his romantic and whimsical side, still irascible (mainly in John's slap at Paul McCartney, "How Do You Sleep?") but sensitive to popular tastes. The album sold 1½ million copies and went to No. 1 in October on the strength of the marvelous Top 10 title single—a hypnotic and unaffected daydream of a future with nothing to die for, no heaven and no hell. As close to ecclesiastic as a rock-and-roll song could be with its echo-diffused, almost watery vocal and string arrangement, "Imagine" was a stunning example of a minimal Spector production with maximum impact.

By September 1971, when John tired of the stale cultural diversions of London and he and Yoko resettled in New York, Phil had virtually become a spoke in John's wheels. When John moved into an apartment on Bank Street in Greenwich Village, Phil rented an apartment on Seventy-second Street and Central Park West. At the time, John's lawyers were fighting to overturn a U.S. Immigration Department ruling to deport him because of a marijuana bust three years before. Phil saw this as Lenny Bruce–style persecution. He wrote long and impassioned letters on John's behalf—citing his artistic achievement—to politicians and newspapers. Sickened by the rock-and-roll world's apathy to John's cause, he fumed to music writer Robert Hilburn of the L.A. *Times:* "Where is Lennon's own generation? Where are all the rock stars who owe so much to Lennon's influence? Where are all the people whose lives were so enriched by the Beatles' music? Why aren't they demanding that this outrage be stopped?" After a three-year wait, the U.S. Court of Appeals struck down the deportation order and Lennon received permanent resident status.

Acclimating themselves to the oblique and more than slightly offensive underbelly of politically active Village nudniks, John and Yoko fell in with the superstars of the radical chic underground in Greenwich Village and began to join in all sorts of bizarre leftist causes, everything from prison reform and Indian rights to the Black Panthers and gay lib. They made avant-garde films, such as the one that displayed assorted bare bottoms. Phil, by contrast, could muster no zeal for the self-possessed New Left, its buffoons like Abbie Hoffman and Jerry Rubin and its screwball artists, poets, and axe-grinding street bands. He would make the rounds on the rad-chic party circuit, but not as a proselyte, only as a ray of John's sun. The new Village was the same for Phil Spector as the new Strip had been years before: nights of stepping out in long limos, women on each arm, and kept nice and warm by ankle-length fur coats. It was the chic of money and power and attention, not politics. To be sure, Phil had made sure to blunt John's strident political pretensions to keep his records marketable. As John got more into ear-curdling, hard-core posturing, Phil saw less of a place for himself. When he produced John's "Happy Christmas (War Is Over)," a pleasant holi-day song that was backed by the young voices of the Harlem Com-munity Choir, it turned out to be the last of Lennon's "Imagine"-style naïveté for years to come. His next album, *Sometime in New York City*, was acridly political, a Lennon relapse into dejected vi-triol. A two-record set—the second being a live and chaotic jam session with the Mothers of Invention—the LP contained titles like "Attica State," "Born in a Prison," and "Angela," after Angela Davis. The single release of "Woman Is the Nigger of the World"/"Sisters O Sisters" was a Lennon disaster, going no higher than No. 77. The album, its cover fashioned like a *New York Times* front page and emblazoned with sayings such as "Ono News That's Fit to Print" and "Don't think they didn't know about Hitler," sold an embarrass-ing 164,000 copies, and its mindless squirts of bile rendered Phil helpless and ready to jump off John's treadmill.

Phil's work with Lennon and Harrison had been vital, cauter-izing the emerging individual identities of the two ex-Beatles. But now he wanted to get back his own identity, to start recording again in L.A. with his old imperial authority. And the truth was, he had

⊙

260

little other choice. George was doing his own producing now, with none of the Spector guile—in George's hands, the mystic beat became a harangue, and it would cost him the gains of the past two years. John, meanwhile, was an alcoholic, drug-abusing wreck. The Nixon White House and the Senate Judiciary and Internal Security Committees labeled him a security threat because of his left-wing affiliations. Under surveillance, his phones tapped, and his apartment bugged, John grew so paranoid that he thought most everyone he saw was following him, and for a time he conducted his business in the backseat of his limousine. Unfortunately for Phil, the rub was that he had no frame of reference other than the free ride he had with the two superstars. For one thing, he had lived for nearly three years solely within the restrictive girders of their music. For another, Phil the chameleon had taken on some of John Lennon's more unsavory traits. He began to drink and his already-substantial paranoia worsened.

Hoping that he could stave off his own descent, Phil looked to shore up his domestic life, which had sagged under the weight of neglect and chained love. Phil, who was big on symbols of family unity, got no closer to Ronnie but he did adopt two more children, twin six-year-old blond boys, Gary and Louis, in December 1971. Musically, though, he was at a standstill. His contract with A&M expired with the last Checkmates single in 1970, and though he cut a number of instrumental tracks with Larry Levine, there was no thread to his work nor acts to sing over the tracks. If he was going nowhere, he was getting there even slower when the new boys did not keep his marriage from crumbling and Ronnie filed yet a third set of divorce papers. That set off a mudslide of retribution that occupied his attention almost entirely for the next two years of court battles.

The final unraveling of the marriage was a carnival of irrationality. It began on June 9, 1972, when Ronnie got into her Chevy Camaro. According to her court papers, Phil "took the keys away from me and refused to return them to me. . . . My husband locked me out of our bedroom and told me to stay out." Ronnie spent the next two nights sharing the room which her mother was using in the house. Then, on June 12, she said, "My husband came to my mother's room, told me I should get a lawyer to get a divorce . . .

and yelled and screamed at me. My son Donté was present in the room at the time and began to cry. In an attempt to get away from my husband I ran downstairs to the kitchen where the governess and cook were present. I was followed by my husband, who grabbed my handbag out of my hand and the contents were strewn over the floor. My husband then pushed me out of the house through the kitchen door. When I left the house, I had no funds or assets of any kind."

Ronnie spent that night at a hotel, then stayed with her mother for three more nights. Once more she tried to get into the master bedroom so that she could gather up her clothes, but the door was locked and Phil refused to let her in. The next day Ronnie hired Beverly Hills lawyers Jay Stein and Daniel Jaffe, who called Phil and informed him that they had filed, and that Ronnie was seeking custody of Donté. "Thereafter, my mother and I [went to] a hotel," Ronnie said. That same day Phil told her he had dumped all of her clothes "in a garbage can on La Cienega Boulevard."

Phil, who had recently been slightly injured in a collision while driving his Rolls-Royce, apparently felt healthy enough to swamp and terrorize the switchboard at the Beverly Crest Hotel for weeks trying to speak to Ronnie, and several of the operators testified that he threatened them when they complied with Ronnie's request not to put him through. In July the court ordered Phil to pay her hotel bills and to allow her visitation rights to see Donté (she was not interested in the twins), but Ronnie claimed he was slow with the payments and was cutting short her time with the boy, and in addition refused to return her wallet, driver's license, and her "full-length mink coat."

Over the summer, Ronnie gave testimony in divorce proceedings that Phil had "imposed his will on [me] by the use of force and threats." Pressed on her drinking by Phil's attorney, Jay Cooper, Ronnie said that she had used alcohol only since her marriage, "usually only with [Phil]," and did so to "shut out his continuous stream of shrieking." After being deposed by Stein and Jaffe at the Santa Monica courthouse, Phil screamed epithets at them in the corridor, then ran after them as they walked to their car in the parking lot and continued to shower them with four-letter words. Ordered to pay temporary support to Ronnie of $1,200 a month, he sent a Brink's truck to Stein and Jaffe's office and three Brink's guards delivered one of the payments—all in nickels.

On the advice of Stein and Jaffe, Ronnie entered several hospitals for psychiatric evaluations, including a six-week stay at St. Francis Hospital in Lynwood during which she was kept under sedation. When she went back to the Beverly Crest in September, her mother had gone home to New York and Ronnie was alone. Her first day there the hotel manager found her wandering around, apparently drunk. Then, days later, she fell asleep with a cigarette in her hand and her bed caught on fire. Ronnie was narrowly rescued when a hotel employee smelled the smoke. After being taken to UCLA Medical Hospital, she said she wanted to go to New York to be with her mother, and she flew there on September 21. In the meantime, Stein and Jaffe hired an accountant to audit Phil's business interests, bank accounts, and trust funds, and established community property of "at least $225,000," not including $375,366.68 in royalties from Phil's records with Lennon and Harrison. (Phil claimed there was no community property.) They had just filed the motion when Ronnie sent them a curious legal-sounding letter written in a childlike scrawl abruptly discharging them: "You are no longer to represent me in any legal actions what so ever. Any and all agreements I have signed with you are cancelled."

Stunned by this weird turn, Stein and Jaffe wrote to Ronnie asking to meet with her. Instead, she filed a notarized affidavit accusing them of keeping her hospitalized and drugged in order to confuse and lead her. "All [they] were doing was just trying to obtain a large sum of money for themselves . . . from Mr. Spector and myself. . . . It was [their] idea to pursue a legal battle . . . against my wishes and best interests." In more of the same strangely stilted English she said: "I definitely feel and have always felt that I can settle the divorce matter between Mr. Spector and myself very amicably and in no way do I want to fight. In fact, I really do not want nor did I ever want anything at all from Mr. Spector. Nor do I want to see Mr. Spector pay out sums of money for things he knew nothing about and were not authorized by either him or me," apparently referring to the enormous hospital bills she had accrued.

Stein and Jaffe obviously felt all this was Phil's doing, once again getting to Ronnie with his sweet talk and promises—this time, possibly, of a generous settlement if she would keep the lawyers and Donté out of it. "We believe the fact that we have ascertained . . . substantial community property constitutes a threat to [Phil]," they told the court, "causing him to renew his effort to reach [Ronnie] and by reason of his domination and control over her, to get her . . . to discharge us." Even Ronnie's mother, they pointed out, was now receiving $400 a month from Phil. The two attorneys implored Ronnie to reconsider, notifying her that in the event of termination she was immediately responsible for over $4,000 in legal fees. They also went ahead on the community property issue. Ronnie first told them not to. Then, months later, early in 1973, she had a change of heart. She had moved to New York by then and may have felt she was out of Phil's range for abuse and manipulation. In any case, she went ahead with the divorce and custody battle.

That meant Phil would have to fight again in court. Held in the fist of the divorce war, Phil entered a new phase of depression that exacerbated the self-abusing tendencies he had acquired from John Lennon. He began to drink now himself, though because of a bad stomach and a congenital anemia it would make him sick. "Phil can't really drink," Vinnie Poncia remarked. "I've seen him throw up on one drink. But he had to show people he could drink." At the same time, he began to walk around with a gun protruding from a shoulder holster, just like George Brand and the other bodyguards. Combined with his drinking and his foul temper, the combination was ominous.

18

People call me a genius. Well, Phil Spector is a genius.
                    —BOB DYLAN during a concert at the L.A. Forum,
                                                    November 15, 1978

The decision of whom Phil would produce in L.A. was made for him—by John Lennon. Just months after Phil had stepped a continent away from Lennon, John himself came to the West Coast. Yoko had become so tired of his misery-laced booze and drug binges that she virtually kicked him out of their apartment and sent him to L.A. in hopes that the separation would do John and the marriage good. Arriving in October of 1973 with his young Japanese travel and bed partner, May Pang, John had little else to do except look up Phil and do an album.

John's music was more wayward than ever. Recently he had taken refuge in the empty commercial pop of his *Mind Games* LP, and in contemplating what kind of album to do now he figured he could regenerate his sense of purpose by going back to the place he found it: old-time rock and roll. John made up his mind to cut covers of oldies. "I just wanna be like Ronnie Spector," he told Phil in placing the production entirely in his hands. But if this idea sounded good to John, it was a stick of dynamite to hand Phil on his own turf during this trying period. An excessively avaricious Spector immediately paid for the sessions himself, thus wresting official control from John, Apple Records, and his American label, Capitol. While *Mind Games* was the name of his last album, it soon came to characterize Phil's design for this one. John could not get through the A&M studio gate unless he told the guard he was there for the Phil Spector sessions. Booking scads of his favorite musicians for the dates, Phil conceded John only his guitarist friend Jesse Ed Davis, Plastic Ono Band drummer Jim Keltner, and John's New York engineer, Roy Cicala.

In the past, John could be firm if he thought Phil went on too long with tracks or took the Phil trip too far. Now sessions were held in an air of unbearable tension as Spector tinkered and did runthroughs until dawn and generally treated John like one of the help. At one session, Phil kept putting off John's vocal until John asked him, "When are you going to get to me?" Phil, not even looking at him, mumbled, "I'll get to you, I'll get to you." In the next instant, John smashed a headset against a console and yelled, "You'll get to me!"

An added and ugly complication was that John and Phil were drinking—and John was in such bad shape that he appeared bent on killing himself with booze, downing fifths of Courvoisier and Remy Martin in one swallow. "You have to understand, with Phil, drinking isn't the bottom line, it's just an anger cushion," said Dan Kessel, who with his brother David—the two sons of Barney Kessel, all three of whom played guitar on the sessions—had become Spector acolytes and quasi-bodyguards, "just being real bugged about a lot of things and wanting it to sort of cushion the nervous system, as opposed to where John got wild and out of hand. John was good in the studio but outside it he got weird."

The combination of snail-like sessions and tapwater-free booze was deadly. For long hours, John, and some musicians, had little to do but drink. John got so sloshed and violently out of control late one night that Phil and George Brand hustled him into their car and took him home. There, they bound John's wrists and ankles with neckties because Phil said he didn't want John to hurt himself. They left him like that, tied up like a steer, with John yelling "Jew bastard!" at Phil as he and Brand left.

"Phil *had* to handcuff John because John would have killed himself," Dan Kessel said. "Yoko really blew John's mind when she threw him out, and he was raging out of his head and threatening suicide. John would sleep at Phil's house and Phil would have to lock the door on him when he'd get too crazy. But when he woke up and it was all over, it was kinda like, you know, 'Thanks a lot for doing that.'"

John recorded around a dozen tracks, including outrageous versions of "Be My Baby" and "To Know Her Is to Love Her." But when the sessions did not get any easier, and Phil continually picked fights with a variety of people in the studio, John became disenchanted with the album. He spent much of his time on wild and destructive drinking binges with Harry Nilsson, whom he met when the singer/songwriter dropped by the sessions. Twice a disorderly Lennon was asked to leave nightclubs—the second time when he and Nilsson heckled and disrupted a show by the Smothers Brothers and were unceremoniously dumped on the street by the bouncers.

Phil went on with the album, but he was reaching his breaking point as well. Stories had been coming out of the La Brea studios, of equipment damaged, of studio rooms trashed, of people defecating in hallways and elevators. Because the Lennon sessions were so turbulent and besotted, A&M officials assumed it had to be Spector's gang and ordered them out. "That was a raw deal," David Kessel said. "I can tell you that Phil and his crew had nothing to do with any of that. He really ran a disciplined ship. I know how it went down and Phil got framed." Rather than pleading his case, Phil silently fumed at Herb Alpert for this opprobrious treatment and moved operations to L.A.'s Record Plant. "He didn't want to dignify the whole thing. He didn't know if it came down from Herb but there was some scuttlebutt to that effect and it was like 'If you believe that, fuck you. I'll go somewhere else. I don't need this hassle.'"

Only days later, he snapped. Not getting what he wanted during a stormy session, he drew his gun, pointed it over his head, and fired a shot into the ceiling. John—who had assumed that Spector kept his gun unloaded and on his hip only for effect—was startled. His ears ringing from the shot, he said, "Phil, if you're gonna kill me, kill me. But don't fuck with me ears. I need 'em."

Said David Kessel: "There was heavy burnout goin' on in there, a lot of raw nerves on edge. In a position like Phil's, he walks in and forty musicians come up and wanna ask questions or talk about the old days or offer advice on how to arrange and mix. And Phil doesn't really need or want to hear any of that. He gets to the point where . . . it's a way of saying 'Leave me alone! I'm makin' the record!' Granted, shooting a gun is radical, but so is Phil Spector. These aren't your normal sessions when you're in and out in three hours. These people are in there hour after hour after hour."

Already tainted, the sessions were brought to a halt when Phil, facing a custody hearing, could let nothing else enter his mind. He even got John to come to domestic court with him as a character reference, but as soon as Ronnie came into the courtroom Phil spat streams of obscenities at her. John tried to restrain him but he was a maniac, and when he refused to stop screaming the judge found him in contempt. Phil was so deranged that he did not notice John get up and leave the courtroom. Never again would they be in the same room.

John did not want to deal with the abandoned album, but he was shocked that he could not even get his hands on the tapes—Phil, claiming ownership, took them from the studio and dropped out of sight. Whenever John called him, an underling would give a different reason why Phil was inaccessible. Then, in early February, Phil had another accident in his Rolls. After jamming on the brakes, he went through the windshield and was taken to the emergency room at UCLA Medical Center bleeding from severe facial cuts. Suffering from multiple head and body injuries and burns, he underwent surgery.

The accident, in typical Spector fashion, was cloaked in secrecy and mystery. *Rolling Stone,* failing to run down any details, speculated that Phil might simply be incognito after having a hair transplant. Lennon, calling to get his tapes again, was told, "Mr. Spector died in an accident." That was when he gave up trying and left it to Capitol to retrieve the tapes. John cut a lightweight album with Harry Nilsson, *Pussycats,* and went back to New York, calling his eight months in L.A. his "Lost Weekend." In June 1974 Capitol came to a settlement with Phil and paid him $94,000 for the irksome tapes. They were brought to John in New York, where he looked at the metal cannisters holding the tapes and cringed with memories of L.A. and Spector; unable to force himself to listen to them, he later gave the raw and unmixed tapes to a music publisher as a payoff in a plagiarism lawsuit. John, who had begun to remix and recut the songs for a compensatory album, was mortified when seven untouched Spector tracks were suddenly released along with eight redone ones as a television mail-order album called *Roots*. That led Capitol to issue five unremixed tracks as part of Lennon's *Rock and Roll* album. A myriad of lawsuits ensued, the result of which was that John—in the sweetest of ironies—won $140,000 in damages from both parties over an album he regretted ever doing.

Phil came out of the hospital under medication and his hair spray-colored gold and silver to divert attention from the hideous cuts on his face and scalp. He also wore a gigantic cross around his neck. "He'd just seen *The Exorcist* and he said he wasn't taking any chances," Dan Kessel said. "We told him he looked like a circus freak but he thought it was normal in Hollywood." Outside Canter's one night, Phil got into a big argument with a man he did not know was a plainclothes cop. Phil was ready to have a Wyatt Earp showdown until the man pulled out his badge. "This cop had seen Phil's holster," Kessel said, "and on a guy with gold hair and a cross around his neck, he thought we were a Charles Manson weirdo gang." The policeman put Phil, Dan, and David up against a car and yelled, "Where are the guns?" Though all three of them were licensed to carry their weapons, they spent that night in the West Hollywood jail.

Guns, in fact, were becoming a major part of Phil's identity, which he seemed to enjoy. Giving cues in the studio to each segment of the orchestra, when he would come to the Kessels he would call out: "Gun section." When Phil and the Kessels went to Las Vegas to see Elvis Presley in concert and then went backstage so that Phil could meet the King, there was an uneasy moment while the two armed camps checked each other out. Finally, when all seemed cool, everyone took off his holster in a kind of modern show-biz peace ritual.

The growing industry talk about Phil's instability, his guns, and the horrifying Lennon sessions did not stop Warner Brothers Records Chairman of the board Mo Ostin from signing him to a thee-year deal that included the formation of the custom Warner-Spector label, the logo for which looked like a large crystal ball—a fitting imprint given that no one could even guess what Spector would do for the label. Worked out by Phil's new heavyweight show-biz manager Marty Machat, he received an advance in the high six-figure range. Playing all sides to Phil's advantage, Machat took the rights to Spector's new product from Warners and licensed them to England's Polydor Records under the name of Phil Spector International—letting Phil pocket another chunk of advance money. Under this arrangement, Phil had baronial powers; he cut however many records he had to for Warners but released only what *he* wanted to in the United States.

Ostin willingly accepted these conditions. Phil Spector was the prize moose head on his office wall, and he feted Spector with a round of welcome parties and a media blitz. None of the movie stars in the Warners lots received more attention, and the result of all this fawning was that Phil did not have to move a creative muscle. Ideas and acts were pushed on him, with assurances that whatever he did would be boffo. No one forced him to go into the rock woods and come out with something fresh and profound. Phil had no sooner arrived when Ostin prevailed upon him to produce another of his new superstar signees, Cher, the onetime Spector session singer turned queen of Vegas and television bathos. Cher—whose lone pantsuit from the old days was long gone, replaced by an array of the world's most brazenly immodest and unsightly show gowns—had several solo hits in the early seventies, but now that she was divorcing Sonny Bono their popular variety series was in a ratings dive. Her career in decline, Cher had dropped into the John Lennon sessions as Phil was cutting a cover track of the Motown song "A Love Like Yours (Don't Come Knockin' Every Day)" and in her pushy way tried to talk Phil into using her vocal on it. He had to scream "No!" over and over as she kept bugging him about it. Now, at Ostin's urging, he relented, doing the tune as a duet with Cher and Harry Nilsson. He also cut Cher on "A Woman's Story," a brooding lament of a prostitute (written by Phil, Nino Tempo, and April Stevens), and a slowed-down cover of "Baby, I Love You." These sessions did not go smoothly—at one date Phil punched out

⊙   270

Cher's manager, David Geffen, who he thought was badgering him. Looking up from the floor at Phil and his bodyguards and their arsenal of guns, Geffen pulled himself to his feet and silently left the studio, nursing a split lip. At another, an engineer, Steve Katz, became so unnerved by the guns that he refused to do the session, leaving Phil to scrounge around for an engineer.

Ostin then shoved another faded star Phil's way: Dion DiMucci, the former teen idol who like the title of one of his old hits had been a wanderer in the sixties before kicking a heroin habit and attempting a seventies rebirth with Warners. Phil saw Ostin's logic about recording Dion: working with a fellow survivor might be revitalizing and a nice sales gimmick. When he went into the project he was as serious as Lennon had been about finding lost roots. Phil assembled a full orchestra, this time at his old shop, Studio A at Gold Star, and with Stan Ross on the control board for the first time since the Paris Sisters. He cut an album of eight songs called *Born to Be with You*, co-writing one of its songs with Dion and two more with Gerry Goffin; pulling up more roots, he used a song by Mann and Weil, "Make the Woman Love Me," and both Barry Mann and Jeff Barry were credited as musicians on the album jacket.

Also present at one session was a young Bruce Springsteen—a Spector disciple and legatee whose dense and pounding teen rock operas like "Born to Run" had won him simultaneous, if premature, cover stories on *Time* and *Newsweek*. With an avowed affection for both Spector and Bob Dylan, Springsteen's records were essentially a blue-collar, axle-greased Wall of Sound. Brought to the studio by Robert Hilburn, Phil had the awed Bruce sit alongside him in the booth. At one point Phil opened the intercom and playfully growled for everyone to hear, "If you wanted to steal my sound, you shoulda gotten me to do it!" The facetious remark broke up the room and Springsteen laughed out loud, but it also contained a poignant truth: Bruce Springsteen's records were cast in the image of Spector's music, yet Phil Spector was doing nothing close to their impact and promise.

Although Phil was recording, his personal travails always beckoned outside the studio door. The custody and divorce war was bad enough, but he had to contend with a new legal headache when Barbara Owen brought suit in September 1974 to evict him from the mansion he loved but could never commit himself to purchasing outright. Owen, now seventy-four years old, widowed and ailing, agreed to sell the house the year before to the Concord Investment Corporation, but when Phil's lease expired in February he did not move out, as requested, claiming a ninety-day right to match the sale price of $255,000. Concord at first tried to ignore that Spector was even there; workmen began to tear down the barbed wire and fencing around the house. Seeing his security barriers torn down, a shaking Spector filed suit against Concord, saying the renovation was "causing me considerable anxiety, nervousness and grief." Concord then began to amass its own legal ammunition against Phil, calling him a "nuisance" and that his guard dogs' "loud and raucous barking disturbs the surrounding neighbors, and whose vicious demeanor has terrorized neighbors . . . assaulted and attacked by the dogs." In the end, though, Spector and Jay Cooper fought the sale so long and hard that Concord eventually renewed Phil's lease, at $6,500 per month.

Phil fought Ronnie just as hard as one court motion after another formed a quilt of battle strategies. When Ronnie and her mother came back to L.A. in April for hearings and stayed at the Sunset Marquis, Phil sent George Brand over with Donté for Ronnie's visitation period—but instructed George not to allow her mother to see the boy, because it had not been specifically stipulated. Seeing Beatrice Bennett in Ronnie's room, Brand yanked Donté's hand from Ronnie's. When Ronnie and Donté were together, the intimidating bodyguard would pull up a chair and sit in the doorway. At one point in the drawn-out affair, Phil agreed to pay psychiatric bills for Ronnie, who twice checked into hospitals—and Ronnie agreed to set community property at a mere $50,000.

"Phil is a very smart man and he constantly played mind games with Ronnie," Nedra Talley said. "Mind games, that was Phil Spector. He allowed her to go into the best hospitals in L.A. and say, oh, this is 'chic' to go to these exclusive hospitals for a week, and then he turned around and used it against her in court."

That seemed evident when Phil quickly filed papers saying he was "deeply concerned because of [Ronnie's] alcoholism and drug problems for which she has sustained multiple hospitalizations." Ronnie, he said, had been "taken by ambulance" to hospitals, had "repeated commitments to psychiatric wards," and "an emotional breakdown." In the end, the case appeared to come down to which of them was in worse shape mentally. Both Phil and Ronnie, as well as Donté, were examined by psychiatrists. "Trying to be objective about it, it was not all Phil's fault. Phil had his problems and Ronnie had hers too," Nedra said. "My cousin Ronnie is a trip. She had an ego. She was not in love for love, like it should be with a man. She knew she could not drink and still she drank. Actually, neither of them needed Donté."

In December, terms of the divorce were finalized. Phil was ordered to pay $2,500 a month to Ronnie for thirty-six months, in addition to community property that was a tiny fraction of what Jay Stein and Daniel Jaffe once projected. For Phil, who had won around $1 million on the Muhammad Ali–George Foreman fight (betting heavily on the underdog Ali), the money was irrelevant. By far more important, he was given custody of Donté.

Unshackled, Ronnie dried out at Scott Ross and Nedra Talley's suburban Virginia home. It was many months before she could even think about returning to the business on her own.

"Darlene and I saw Ronnie after the divorce and we were shocked at how she looked," recalled ex-Blossom Gloria Jones. "She was not the same person. We looked at her like 'What happened?' Ronnie was like the cheerleader in the old days, happy-go-lucky. Phil took that away from her."

The divorce was Phil's lone victory of 1974. In November Warner/Spector issued two singles within two days: Dion's "Make the Woman Love Me" and Cher's "A Woman's Story." Both ballads, they were swept aside in the middle seventies' disco craze. The Dion redux, which was doubly hurt by the somber and maudlin mood of both artist and producer, was actually doomed weeks before when Phil quarreled with Dion's manager, Zach Glickman. "Zach was wearin' his manager's hat, getting too pushy for Phil's taste," David Kessel recalled. Among other things, Glickman demanded that Phil turn over the album's tapes—which for Phil Spector, like the tearing down of his barbed wire, was akin to a declaration of war. "Phil doesn't like to be pushed," Dan Kessel said. "He had it all goin', there was no reason why it couldn't go on the way it was. And Dion was freaked out because of the inability of Zach and Phil to get it goin', but that could've only happened one way—Phil's way. If it's not gonna go

Phil's way, there's nothing in it for him. He does it his way or he doesn't need to do it at all." Having arranged with Dick Clark for Dion to go on "American Bandstand" and break "Make the Woman Love Me," Phil spited Glickman and killed the gig. Then, when the record did not sell, he released the lugubrious and depressing *Born to Be with You* only in England rather than risk more rejection at home. If Dion was bewildered and disillusioned by the experience, the fact that the debut Warner/Spector album was to be unavailable in the United States disgusted Mo Ostin and ended his special interest in Spector.

Although Phil was freed of the divorce albatross, the torment of 1974 levied a toll on him, and his work fared no better through the next three years. Disappointed by the failure of "A Woman's Story," a record he put a lot of thought into, he seemed to give up trying to influence popular tastes. The idea that he would have to compete with people making inane disco pulp no doubt made Phil shudder more than anyone who thought about that numbing anomaly. Riding out the era as a detached spectator, he proceeded to fulfill his contractual obligations by signing two acts he cared nothing about. The first was a disco group called Calhoon and the other a singer/guitarist named Danny Potter. "With those," David Kessel remembered, "Phil threw up a couple of mikes and said, 'Go,' then we left the studio. He didn't produce them but he made sure they were recorded, in order to justify the label." In between unsuccessful singles by these acts, Phil did commit to an act he thought might please him and the mass market, singer Jerri Bo Keno, a white girl from New York who had sung in disco clubs. Thinking she could be a Vickie Sue Robinson–style diva of dance music (Robinson had a smash disco hit), he cut the closest thing the Wall of Sound ever deigned come to the shamelessly syncopated disco beat. Spector announced her to be his comeback vehicle, but when a single he had written called "Here It Comes (and Here I Go)" failed in the fall of 1975, "it was sort of like vaporization," said Dan Kessel. "He said hello and good-bye to her." And to disco, none too soon.

The Warner/Spector label was closed out almost as a Phil Spector rock postscript. In July 1976 two old tracks by Ronnie, "Paradise"/"When I Saw You," were issued with no other purpose but as an exercise in Spector mockery. This was followed in February 1977 by a new track cut with Darlene Love, "Lord, If You're a Woman," backed with her unreleased Poncia/Andreoli track "Stumble and Fall." To fulfill his album commitment, Phil released a Lenny Bruce retrospective, a two-record greatest hits compilation, and a reissue of the Christmas album.

The sessions Phil ran during his Warners playout were a far cry from the studio spectacles of the past. Kim Fowley, who had gone on to produce Johnny Winter and Warren Zevon and had songs recorded by the Byrds, Cat Stevens, and many others, had never sung lead in his life when he got to make a record for Phil during this time. "I had used the Kessel brothers on an album called *Vampires from Outer Space*," said Fowley, "and these guys are like the sons Phil never had. Wonderful guys. They dress in black, they know karate, they carry guns. I suppose if Phil Spector and Sly Stallone had twins, it would be the Kessels. So they said they were recording and I should bring my songs and some beer. I said, 'Who's producing?' and they said Phil was. I said, 'Phil Spector producing Kim Fowley the vocalist! Now I can die and go to heaven.'

"So we went to this shitty studio across from the Chinese Theater which was horrible, a toilet. Guys were sitting around in urine-stained underwear and it looked like a junkie shooting gallery. I go in this dirty room and Phil appears—God, I'm in there the same way Bobby Sheen and all those poor bastards were, and he thanks me for coming and says, 'I wanna make sure you guys get into this and make a great record. No matter what, just keep singing.' So I begin and you know what he does? He sets off the fire alarm and seals the doors and leaves with the Kessels. Every fire truck in Hollywood came, guys with axes to rescue us. I didn't know if there was a fire or not, and while they're crashin' the doors down I'm singin' my ass off, man. So that was Phil Spector letting all the noise and hysteria make a vocal better. One of my tracks came out on a Spector album in England and I never got a royalty from him. Phil, if you're reading this, you owe me something."

Soon after the Darlene Love record, with the early fanfare forgotten, Warner/Spector quietly folded. It left Phil with no reason to record. He closed up the Sunset office—the succeeding occupant was David Geffen—and Phil Spector Enterprises became no more than a Hollywood box number. Rather than look for acts, Phil stayed in the house, the windows covered with tarpaulin, his music activity limited to playing an album of Johnny Cash's greatest hits. "He loved the old Sun Records' sound, the tape delay, the ominous-sounding deep voice," Dan Kessel said. "It soothed him." The only way Phil would get back in the studio was if the right person talked him back. The first who qualified was Marty Machat, his manager. Machat also managed Leonard Cohen, the Canadian poet/novelist/singer whose existentialist, often suicidal reflections of sorrow set to sparse music had begat a cult following. Machat, whose wife Ariel promoted Cohen, believed that with strong musical arrangements Cohen could find a broad audience. As a favor to Machat, and because he was lost in his own melancholia, Phil agreed to produce Cohen's debut Warners album.

Doc Pomus, the great old songwriter, happened to be in L.A. on business when Phil began working with Cohen. Phil, Doc's one-time Hotel Forrest protégé, may have loved Pomus more than any other person in the business; when Doc, who was now confined to a wheelchair, was down and out a few years earlier, Phil sent him a blank check (Pomus made it out for $3,000). Now Phil was the one who appeared to need help. Doc spent a month hanging out at the house, wincing as he watched Spector drink and act erratically. "He would change clothes four times a day," Pomus recalled, "and each time he'd have a different gun on, to match the outfit."

In this Fellini-esque cuckoo's nest, Spector and Cohen wrote songs, planned the album, and wallowed in booze. "They were really gettin' loaded," Pomus remembered. "They were like two drunks staggerin' around." So pained at seeing Phil this way, Doc practically dragged him out of that demented house each night. "He hadn't been out for so long, they told me it was like a year, year and a half, and he was pale as a sheet. I got him to start goin' out, but his drinking made it impossible. My driver and I never carried guns in New York but we did in L.A. because we were nervous about goin' out with Phil. 'Cause he would walk over to the biggest guy at the bar and say, 'You're a faggot.' He'd start with everybody and we'd have to save his life a few times, and then he'd go to the bathroom and throw up. He'd pull out sixty credit cards at the table and order whole lobsters and he'd eat none of it, 'cause he was drinkin' and he didn't know what he was doin'. God, it was so sad.

"See, he gets a kick out of it too, because he likes to play parts. But I knew he was unhappy. He made me spend every night at the place because he's lonely, he doesn't see anybody. When I had to go home he said if I left he never was gonna talk to me again."

The Leonard Cohen sessions were typically unpleasant. Cohen, like John Lennon, was pushed aside and ignored. Phil was so paranoid about the tapes that he took them home each night with an armed guard. And there was yet another violent scene in the studio when violinist Bobby Bruce began to joke with Phil by speaking with an affected, faggoty lisp. Phil, who was always sensitive about his own lisp, thought Bruce was mimicking him and ordered it to stop. "Yeth, Phil," Bruce replied, whereupon a maniacal Spector tore out his gun, aimed it in Bruce's direction, and ordered him out of the studio. Larry Levine, who had left A&M and engineered the Cohen sessions at Gold Star, was shaken by the incident, and he and the rest of the musicians could not go on with the date.

"It scared the shit out of me," Levine said. "Phil was crocked and I was trying to talk to him, because you hear about accidents, and it was the scariest thing when he got like that. It was the booze. When Phil started drinking, he was out of his head. That was not Phil. That's not the Phil I knew."

Released in early 1978, the album, *Death of a Ladies' Man*, bombed, heard by few ears except those of the rock critics it offended—the lone dissenter being Robert Hilburn, the *Los Angeles Times* music writer, who called it the year's best album. In fact, the lyrics—a primer of a hopeless romantic caught in the warp of modern feminism—may have been the poet's most trenchant to date. But Cohen himself led the attack on the record, which disastrously set fey lyricism, backed on some tracks by Bob Dylan, against the Spector sound machine. Despite their shared depression, Phil's hyperbolic bombast clobbered Cohen; and when Cohen heard the mix he publicly renounced the album even before it was out. *Ladies' Man*, Cohen told *Rolling Stone*, was "the collaboration of an Olympian and crippled nature." Spector, he said, had "taken the guts out of the record. . . . I think that in the final moment, Phil couldn't resist annihilating me. I don't think he can tolerate any other shadows in his own darkness.

"I say these things not to hurt him," Cohen concluded. "Incidentally, beyond all this, I liked him. Just man-to-man he's delightful and with children he's very kind. But I would also like him to know . . . that he was urged to reconsider his approach to recording by a man who knows him well and who has suffered because of his failure to allow things to breathe."

Dan and David Kessel were the next to divert Phil from what Leonard Cohen called a "Medici pose" of living death inside the cold and dark house. Dan and Dave were hanging around with the New York punk rockers and the Ramones when the group was on tour in L.A. With disco now dead and the new wave mudpie of British and Lower East Side assault rock seeping into the mainstream, there was a clear rationale for suggesting that Phil get involved with a punk band. The leather jacketed and dour-faced Ramones, fronted by the endomorphic six-foot-nine-inch lead singer Joey Ramone (the same surname was used by the four nonrelated band members, which also included guitarist Johnny, bassist Dee Dee, and drummer Marky), the Ramones were probably the most talented of all the bands out to subvert a rock world gone soft around the middle. Playing in the punk idiom of feverish rapid-fire guitar chords broken into two-minute bursts, they also fused many rock influences, including Phil Spector's records, and the satiric humor of mock shock song titles like "Blitzkrieg Bop" and "Now I Wanna Sniff Some Glue." One of the first and few punk acts to land a recording contract, they self-produced three modest-selling albums for Sire Records, a Warners subsidiary label, but the frantic excitement of their hugely popular live shows was lost on vinyl and they had not yet broken through to the masses.

Dan and David took Phil to a Ramones show at the Whisky-a-Go-Go, and his interest in the band was indicated not by his words but by the fact that he went backstage later. The first thing he said to them was "My bodyguards wanna fight your bodyguards." Then, announcing his availability, he said, "You wanna make a good album by yourselves or a great album with me?" Phil's main interest in the Ramones was really Joey, whose melodically sharp, New York-sounding inflections was nearly a male version of Ronnie's voice. Phil wanted to record Joey solo. "He said he was gonna make me the next Buddy Holly," Joey recalled. Informed that the group was the act, they both committed to an album and Marty Machat made a deal with Sire president Seymour Stein. A song-plugger along the old Broadway, Stein went way back with Phil and knew what it would require to get an album out of him to benefit the Ramones: he gave

Phil carte blanche and then left him alone, knowing no one would see an album for long months. In return, Phil agreed to produce one of Stein's pet acts, the Paley Brothers. Spector immediately cut a handful of tracks with Andy and Jonathan Paley before, through no fault of his own, they split up as an act.

Turning to the Ramones, pulling the Phil trips and control games on a ripened and off-the-wall band set in its own ways, his manic presence at once divided the group and obscured the rock-and-roll bond they shared. At an early idea meeting Phil insulted drummer Marky Ramone's girlfriend. As they drove to Phil's house for the first time, they thought they were entering a compound. "You drive in there," Joey said, "and you see all the signs about dogs and electrified fences . . . the barbed wire, the mine fields. I'm sure a good portion of it's a put-on, part of the persona, the psychosis, but it can be intimidating. It's like when you went there, you were there; you can't get out until he's ready to let you out, and he's never ready, 'cause I guess he didn't have company too often and I guess he likes to keep you around. You'd say, 'Well, Phil, it's time for us to go now,' and he'd disappear. Then he'd come back and he'd want to show you his terrarium or some of the hideous-looking things he had in there. The night had to belong to Phil, just like the studio does. . . . It was just too weird. One time I opened a closet door in his kitchen and this St. Bernard dog jumped out of the dark. It was locked in, just hangin' out in there."

While the other three Ramones had misgivings, Joey held them in line. "I mean, I was excited about it, because Phil Spector was a major inspiration to me and because we were both pioneers. When the Spector sound came around there was a void, there was Pat Boone and then there was Phil Spector. He was a reaction to all that superficial whitebread crap. When we came out there was a gap too; it was the beginning of disco, of the corporate sound, Journey, Foreigner. There was no exciting rock as we knew it, the music we grew up on. I think Phil liked that aspect of us and I think it was important to him in a lot of ways to get involved with us.

"But there was a lot of shit in the beginning. Phil obviously had a real bad drinking problem and he made it difficult. John was pretty okay about it. Dee Dee was . . . well, Dee Dee was goin' through his own period, he had his demons. And L.A. is the kind of place you can get into trouble, especially if there's a lot of waiting around.

We were based in L.A. already at that point for about two months 'cause we had just finished the movie *Rock 'n' Roll High School*. And then we were doin' the album with Phil and it's like Phil would run down the songs like a couple of hundred times before he'd even do one take; he was listening for something. We were used to goin' in and knockin' 'em out in one take. We like it to be spontaneous, you like to capture that. It takes us like a month to record an album. But with Phil, this album took forever. It was like a crazy Chinese water torture and Dee Dee started crackin' up."

Phil was not far behind. Even though only two tracks necessitated outside musicians—a full orchestra for a cover of "Baby I Love You"; Steve Douglas and former Electric Flag keyboardist Barry Goldberg on "Rock 'n' Roll Radio"—the sessions at Gold Star were laborious and wounding. Producing the title track of *Rock 'n' Roll High School,* Spector took eight hours mixing the long opening guitar chord to his satisfaction. On every song he overdubbed the Ramones' guitar, bass, and drum parts long into the night—but when he felt unsure about how to deal with this new style of music, he would stop the session and do the old routines with a beleaguered Larry Levine. "Or if a stranger came in and Phil didn't know about it," said Joey, "work would cease and Phil would get weird, do his tantrums or he'd have . . . guys would bring him these little white cups of Manischewitz and after a few of them Phil would start bangin' on the floor and screamin'. . . 'piss, shit, fuck. Fuck, shit, piss!' He would just go on, he started freakin' out, and there would be no reason to go on any longer with the session."

As Dee Dee Ramone and Phil came closer to going over the edge, the studio became a collision course waiting for an accident to happen. At one crisis point, Joey and the band's musical director, Ed Stasium, warned Phil his drinking was killing the album and he eased off. "We wanted Ed there to oversee," Joey said, "but then pretty soon Phil was plyin' him with daiquiris and they were hangin' out havin' candlelight daiquiris." Finally, provoked by a drug-blitzed Dee Dee, Phil snapped in his usual manner—brandishing his gun.

"He held his gun to Dee Dee's head," Joey said. "Dee Dee was kinda fucked up on Quaaludes or something and he told Phil he was gonna kill him. I guess Phil felt he had only one way to respond."

This latest gun incident turned off Dee Dee further, and it may have also helped send Larry Levine to the emergency room. Larry, smoking almost without end despite suffering a heart attack six years before, went home one night and had stabbing chest pains. He got to the hospital in time to live out his second heart attack.

"The Ramones, Jesus, that was a terrible experience." Levine flinched. "It was a contributing factor to my heart attack. The night before it happened, Phil and I had this . . . we had gone around. He wasn't doing any work. He was drinking and he was procrastinating and we couldn't get any work done. The Ramones were in the studio, they were there all night and I couldn't get him . . . he wouldn't focus. He'd sit there and he'd be in a stupor. It was really that bad."

Convinced that he had caused Levine's heart attack, a distraught Phil did not visit him in the hospital. "He wouldn't even talk to me until years later. I'm sure he felt responsible. I tried to assure him he wasn't. I was due for it anyway, with the smoking. . . . But it was very difficult when he was drinking. I would go back and forth with him as a gag because Phil would put people on and it was an effort to try and communicate. But it just got impossible to move ahead. We were stuck."

"Phil was frustrated by the fact that we make our own decisions," Joey Ramone suggested. "We're our own band, we have our final say, and Phil's not used to having that. So I don't know if working with us was his dream come true or his nightmare come true."

It seemed more like twenty years when, eight months from the start date, the Ramones' *End of the Century* was released in February 1980. For a budget-busting $200,000—the average Ramones LP was made for around $70,000—Seymour Stein bought himself the Ramones' best work. Critical reaction was favorable, and it became the first Ramones album to go Top 50 on the chart. As he did with Lennon and Harrison, Phil did not alter the basic idiom; rounding and widening the punk beat, not one ounce of the raw energy was sacrificed. The entire record bristled with a dynamic range and clarity the Ramones did not know was possible. Kurt Loder of *Rolling Stone* called it "the most commercially credible album the Ramones have ever made [and] also Phil Spector's finest and most mature effort in years, undoubtedly his most restrained production since his work with John Lennon. Surprisingly, *End of the Century* doesn't sound like the end of the world overdubbed on twenty-four tracks in some airless Los Angeles studio. . . . [Spector] has created a setting that's rich and vibrant and surging with power, but it's the Ramones who are spotlighted, not their producer. More than ever before, Spector has managed to conceal his considerable art and thus reaffirm it."*

"I personally loved the album," Joey said, "but I'm probably the only one in the band who felt that way. See, I had a sort of decent rapport with him. Sure he's difficult and yeah it was hell. I mean there are things about Phil . . . he's not the nicest guy in the world. But you just accept what he is to work with him. And I thought he did a great job. There were a couple of things that made me cringe, but 'Danny Says' is a fuckin' classic and 'Rock 'n' Roll Radio' sounds great. What he did with the opening chord of 'Rock 'n' Roll High School' is like 'Strawberry Fields,' the way it fuses into the drums."

Joey had been home in New York for months when Phil called him one morning to play him the album's first single, the "Baby, I Love You" cover, over the phone. "It was like six A.M. in L.A. but he never sleeps. He doesn't sleep and he doesn't eat. He just mixes records all night." Unfortunately, the choice of the song as a single—another of Spector's conditions with Seymour Stein was that one of his songs would be the first release—was a bad one. The only overtly Spectorian tune on the album, with its glutinous and stabbing string line, it may have directly merged the rock and roll of Phil Spector and the Ramones, but it failed to grab air play. In some quarters it was held as a joke, though not in England where the song went to No. 2.

As a Phil Spector album, it presaged a possible return to the wars for the world's top record producer, but the discord and horror stories surrounding it was a deterrent; though Spector's contract had an option for a second Ramones LP, even Joey rejected that idea. Phil considered hooking up with the new wave band Blondie after seeing them open for the Ramones one night, but that band's leader, Chris Stein, told Joey there was no way he could work with Phil.

Maybe that is what Phil really wanted, to be just left alone.

Jack Nitzsche, who had not seen Phil in years, showed up un-

* From "The Ramones and Phil Spector in Radioland," Kurt Loder, *Rolling Stone* (March 20, 1980):26.

announced at the front gate late in 1979. Nitzsche had blossomed during and after working with Phil—he produced, among many others, Bobby Darin, Rick Nelson, and Jackie DeShannon, and recorded four solo albums; one, *St. Giles Cripplegate,* in 1972, utilized the London Symphony Orchestra. Nitzsche had been in the thick of the seventies' soft-rock wave, co-producing Neil Young's first LP and producing and writing for Young's backup band Crazy Horse, for a time joining the band on the road as their pianist. He also produced the Neville Brothers and the first two Mink Deville albums. Branching out into films, he scored the Mick Jagger movie *Performance,* then *The Exorcist* and *One Flew over the Cuckoo's Nest.* However, Nitzsche was in a bad way now. Recently he had been arrested for assaulting his girlfriend, actress Carrie Snodgress, who said that Nitzsche, in a drunken rage, raped her with the barrel of a gun, kicked and beat her, and threatened to shoot her and her small child.

Seeing Nitzsche, Phil thought he was scary. Rather than let him in, Phil leaned out of an upstairs window and was said to have aimed a gun at his onetime arranger and ordered him off the grounds. Nitzsche fled back down La Collina Drive and into a wasteland of his own misery, but the real question about Phil Spector now was whom if anyone he would welcome inside that dark house.

19

Where is his son,
That nimble-footed madcap Prince of Wales
And his comrades, that daff'd the world aside
And bid it pass?

—WILLIAM SHAKESPEARE, *Henry IV*

At 10 P.M. on the night of January 23, 1980, ten-year-old Donté Spector walked into a West Hollywood police station and told police he had lost his bicycle. Asked by a deputy sheriff if his parents knew he was out so late, Donté said that he had run away from home that morning. He had been staying with his nine-year-old girlfriend since school let out and he did not want to go back home.

An hour later a police detective and a probation officer called Phil and informed him that his son was at the station house. Refusing to come over and get Donté, he told them, "I don't care what you do with him."

When Ronnie was notified, she immediately petitioned for custody, and Phil allowed Donté to move to New York to live with her. Ronnie's singing comebacks in the seventies had failed and a recently signed recording deal only provided her with a $2,000 advance, but she stated she could give Donté "the opportunity of living with a loving parent." In April, with Phil and Ronnie in attendance and at a safe distance, the court gave her custody and ordered Phil to pay child support of $850 a month—"by check or money order," the judge warned a sneering Phil, "no pennies, nickels or quarters."

Phil's lawyers, fearing that Ronnie was still on the sauce, asked for attorney's supervision over her in New York. "I'm satisfied the mother's a good mother," the judge replied. "They can spend their time supervising people who really need supervising, not Mrs. Spector."

"Thank you," Ronnie said.

Maliciously, Phil made out the first four support checks in Donté's name, not Ronnie's, and was again found in contempt of court.

By the mid-eighties Ronnie had remarried, to a show-biz manager named Jonathan Greenfield, and had her first natural-born children—ironically, they were twins—but rather than stability, Donté felt more alienation. He went back to L.A.—not to live with Phil but with an elderly Bertha Spector. "Donté got into trouble," Nedra Talley related, "because neither Phil nor Ronnie did right by him. Getting Donté was a threat to Ronnie, I think. She may have felt he was a challenge to her new life.

"I was trying to see about getting Donté to live with me. I was willing to do that because I've given myself to raising my children and one more to love would not be a problem. Donté needs that kind of love. He's sort of caught in the middle of two crazy situations. The last time I was out there, about five years ago, I went to the house about Donté and Phil didn't want me to let Donté know that I had come. I said, 'Phil, I'm not gonna play games. I don't know what game you and Ronnie are playing but don't include me in the middle.' My only angle was that I loved Donté and that the last time I saw him he told me he wanted to be with me.

"But that was the last time I saw Phil and nothing more was said about it. Now Donté's a big boy, he can do whatever he wants, and you just hope he's okay. But I think with Phil and Ronnie, they were more afraid that it would look like a failure on their part if Donté lived with me. And Phil never liked to admit failure."

At forty years of age, Phil Spector was retired from rock and roll. Either the distilled techno-pop of the eighties was not worth his time or he was too insecure about being able to find a place in it on his psychopathic terms and would rather deny that he had to try. His only active involvement over the first half of the decade, with Yoko Ono in 1981, seemed like yet another postscript. This was after the murder of John Lennon, when Phil could not bear to live with the karmic demerit that John went to his grave with the bitterness of 1973 unresolved between them. Right up until his death, John had not forgiven him. Only weeks before, when Doc Pomus mentioned Phil's name to him in idle conversation, John tensed and said, "I don't wanna talk about him." Following John's assassination, Yoko became locked in litigation with the producer of the Grammy-winning Lennon-Ono *Double Fantasy* LP, Jack Douglas. Phil, who still had a financial stake in the Lennons' account books, flew to New York to testify on Yoko's behalf. If he could not make up with John, this at least broke down the barrier with Yoko, who had never liked Phil and had spoken unkindly of him in a recent *Soho News* interview. When she went into the studio to commemorate John with her *Season of Glass* LP—which featured John's shattered and bloodstained glasses on the front cover—she hired Phil to produce. Yoko, however, needed to have unstinted authority to express and dictate the deepness of her personal loss, and she told Phil he could go home after about half the record was complete. The parting was in no way acrimonious, and she later gave Phil one of John's guitars. For Phil it was like a conciliatory hand reaching to him from the beyond.

One recompense of Spector's seemingly permanent seclusion was that, with no other comparative work, his classic hits crystallized as his only legacy. The body of that work, so daring, so inscrutable, and so listenable two decades later, was intrinsic to the man who made a new rock and roll and then vanished into a dusky netherlife. Spector's hits enjoyed tremendous rediscovery in the eighties, and a 1983 BBC documentary ran on many public television stations. This sixty-minute film by producer Binia Tymieniecka, done without Spector's cooperation and employing a where-have-you-gone theme, was a surreal knife that both sculpted his art and cut his heart out. Probably the most indelible scenes belonged to Dee Dee and Johnny Ramone, who had their revenge for an eight-month sentence with Spector. "He seemed more positive and able," Dee Dee said. "When I got to the studio, I found him to be a helpless little boy, like a helpless person. . . . He seemed like a man walkin' his last mile." Though *End of the Century* had outsold all the Ramones' eighties' albums, Johnny said: "Phil seemed to be frustrated with us, but I think he's frustrated with himself really. Times have changed and most producers from the mid-sixties haven't really grown. There's a new sound and he doesn't have it. His time has passed."

Now Phil lent credence to that assumption himself. He evidently considered his role in music mostly as a conservator of a bankable legend—the Spector sixties' catalogue. While almost no one could reach him directly, only go through intermediaries, the use of his old songs in movies, television, and commercials—with Spector himself choosing who should have these rights—made up a thriving business. "His organization says he will decide what is best for the 'Spector situation,' " Dan Kessel said. "He runs his business like a general runs an army. Phil had had a whole lot of different incarnations, but he is completely in control of his rock and roll."

To his amazement, Danny Davis, whose relationship with Phil wavered through the years but never broke, found that he was deputized as an emissary to Spector simply by virtue of their long-ago association. "It's unbelievable; every day I started getting calls from people wanting to get to him," Davis said. "He makes a point to tell people, 'You would have never gotten in here if it wasn't for Danny Davis'—he once told people in my company that he only talks to Danny Davis and Nino Tempo. I mean, I felt like a golden oldie myself when he said that. But the fact is, he added to my luster in the business. He has been a great door-opener, even after I left him. Everyone says to me, 'Jesus, you worked for Phil Spector, tell me about this and that.' He's been an experience in my life money couldn't buy, but at the same time, through all of the years, the only people he knew he could count on and who really cared about him was me and my family."

By the middle eighties, Danny, doing promotion for Private Eye Records, saw that the Spector legend would prove profitable to him. He hooked Phil up with pleople pitching screenplays and Broadway shows based on his life, with the understanding that Danny would be executive producer, but while Phil initially consented to these projects, nothing ever developed. Trying again in late 1986, Danny thought he could talk Phil into producing LaToya Jackson for the Private Eye label. The oldest of Michael Jackson's singing siblings, and prettier even than Michael, LaToya had not gotten anywhere on her own. With the Jackson name as the lure, Danny approached Phil with the idea. "She can't sing and needs somebody to really do her in the studio," Davis said. "He said 'Jeez, yeah. I like her. When can you bring her over?' "

The next night, Danny drove LaToya to 1200 La Collina, trying somehow to explain to her on the way about Phil Spector—"because she doesn't have a clue. She's heard about him but she didn't know how he is." Entering the house, winding past the bodyguards and into the mausoleumlike living room, Danny could see that LaToya did not know what to make of the dementia all around her. After making them wait for half an hour, Phil made his appearance. Seeing LaToya, "he was absolutely mesmerized by this woman," recalled Davis. "He was completely taken with her. And he goes into a thing I know is indigenous to his insecurity. He is extremely shy and it is obvious he doesn't know how to talk to LaToya. So he starts with all kinds of . . . he says, 'I got Barry and Cynthia doin' songs just for you'—which I know is an absolute lie. Barry Mann doesn't wanna talk to him and Cynthia doesn't like him. But he's desperately tryin' to tell her things. Then she wants him to go to the piano so she could hear what he's got, and he says, 'No, no, no,' he did all kinds of bobbin'. I thought he was Dan Dailey tryin' to get out of it. He didn't play anything 'cause he didn't *have* anything to play. So he says, 'Well, listen, we'll meet again. I got a lot of ideas.'

"So now we're driving back and LaToya says, 'Jeez, Danny, I don't think so. He's a little too weird.' And I said, 'Let me tell you something, Toya. He's weird, he's unique, he's bizarre, he's off the wall. But, believe me, you work with him and he will give you the hit record you're seeking.'"

Two days later, urgent messages were waiting for Danny all over town, to call LaToya Jackson. Ringing her up, a terribly distraught LaToya related a horror story about her return visit to Phil's house the night before. As she told it, Phil came into the room, sat down uncomfortably close to her, pressed a key into her hand, and murmured, "Would you like to go there with me?" Looking at the key, LaToya saw the words "Bates Motel" scrawled on it. "LaToya is a Jehovah's Wit-

⊙   288

ness," said Davis. "She doesn't go to the movies or drink or do anything untoward. She didn't know what it meant."

Getting no reaction, Phil asked her, "Don't you know what that is? That's the motel in *Psycho* where they killed all the pretty young girls."

Phil was apparently drunk, and LaToya did not know if he was trying to make her laugh or freak her out. "She became absolutely frantic," Davis said. "She spent the next four hours trying to get out of his clutches. And he is now doing all kinds of outrageous conversation. He's doin' lines like 'I don't need your fuckin' brother,' things that had nothin' to do with what she was there for. He goes into these tirades every fifteen minutes and he leaves and comes back each time with a brand-new personality, either one that's vitriolic or entertaining or up and down. And she tells me he made a couple of moves on her."

Several times LaToya made up excuses that she had an early-morning meeting and had to go, but Phil would say, "It's all right. The people you're supposed to meet just called and said it's cancelled." Finally, on the verge of screaming, LaToya got out. Then, all through the night, Phil kept calling her house in Encino and badgering her, so much so that Joe Jackson, the austere father of the clan, had to get on the phone. Phil supposedly was abusive and insulting to him. For a few tense hours a very real confrontation loomed between the Jackson and Spector compounds.

"I don't have to tell you, at the end of this, how bad I was made to look to Joe Jackson," said Davis.

Later that morning, Danny got a call from Phil. "Danny, you shoulda protected me," he said innocently.

"Phil, you had no business doing that," Danny told him.

But Phil had no qualms of conscience about his treatment of LaToya; instead, he made it into a loyalty test for Danny. "He started putting me on the defensive. He said 'She's a cunt' and this and that. I said, 'Phil, you're saying things to her she doesn't know about. She's a Jehovah's Witness, they don't know about that stuff.' And he goes, 'Oh no? Well, she was no Jehovah's Witness when I fucked her.'

"That's Phil. There's no way to explain Phil, no way to understand him. There used to be a time when I really understood why he could say things like that and that kind of hatefulness, when I tolerated it. Now I just can't fathom it."

When Danny would not go along with Phil's acocunt of the incident nor his attacks on LaToya, Phil tried to placate him. "He ended up telling me he wanted me to go to work for him again. More bullshit. I know him. I know when he's bullshitting. When he pulls that crap on me I tell him. 'Hey, Phil, this is Danny, remember?' "

Danny continued to stay in touch with Phil, but never again bothered to take acts over to him. "I don't think he *wants* to go ahead on anything," he said. "I don't know if it's insecurity. He didn't seem afraid to tackle the LaToya project, but it was like he did all that shit to turn her off. He's so agonizing. That's why nobody brings him a project anymore, nobody wants him to produce 'em. I think he wanted the LaToya thing more than his right arm. I think he is desperate for work. But he . . . he just turns people off. Who knows why? He is a case history in Psych 1. I could talk from now until next Thursday and I could not explain Phil Spector."

Phil broke his drought of inactivity in 1987, but his trips to the studio were fleeting and furtive, the projects immaterial. Seymour Stein at Sire got him to remix tracks by the British band Depeche Mode. As an introduction of eighties' rock, it might have been the means of another Spector rising. But when Phil consumed more time than the group could stand, they took it out of his hands. "That was another example of people having no conception of what he is," Dan Kessel said. "They got all excited that they could get him and then expected it to be a one-day thing. That's one reason Phil doesn't work. Sure, Phil doesn't want to come back and have a flop. There's a little stage fright. But in his mind, he's been doin' it for so long that he's not tied up in knots saying, 'Can I do it?' He's older, he's mellowed, the business thing is great. He doesn't need hassles, by monstrosities like Depeche Mode."

Staying on safer and more edifying ground. Phil's other job was to record redheaded teen actress Molly Ringwald singing the lead vocal over an old instrumental track of the Ronettes' "(The Best Part of) Breakin' Up" for a movie called *The Pickup Artist*, a banality that was gone from theaters after one week. This was both a business decision and a reward to Ringwald, whose teenage heartache movies have exposed Spector's old tunes to another new teen generation.

Up until the mid-eighties Spector had played hide-and-seek with people to advertise that he was still viable. There would be phone calls at all hours to favored old intimates, to Doc Pomus, to Irwin Levine, to Bobby Sheen, bidding them to be ready to join him on some massive project. He called Gerry Goffin and wanted him to get back with Carole

King after a decade, for a project that was going to be that momentous. "He said he was gonna make a big comeback and he was gonna make another $100 million," Goffin said. "He wanted me and Carole to write with him again." Gerry went to the trouble of getting Carole's approval, then never heard another word from Phil. "I remember that he told me, 'I may have to produce Frank Sinatra before I get to produce anybody who can sell records.' I think he felt it was hard for him to be accepted again by important people."

But then the calls stopped. Rather than feeling he had to have people at the ready in case he did find a way back—or con them into thinking he would—he apparently decided he would be happier not even trying. His longtime and much overburdened personal secretary, Donna Sekulidis, who was Phil's voice on these phone forays and in all other aspects of his existence, was fired in 1987 after she and Phil argued over which of them owned the typewriter she used; her stomach free of Maalox after ten years, Sekulidis then concentrated on a rock band she managed but had never told Phil about, fearing he would want to get involved and make them crazy. With Donna gone, Phil's connections with the business began to dry up. In the past that would have made him panic; now he didn't care.

When Marty Machat died in early 1988, Phil hired a new man to handle business matters—and it was none other than Allen Klein. This was a message to the industry that Spector intended to settle old business disputes right away. For years, Spector had been squabbling with Leiber and Stoller's Trio Music over back royalty splits. Immediately, Klein put Trio on notice that he would get every cent due Phil. Spector had also been close to issuing his old hits in a gigantic compact disc package through Rhino Records. At one point, Klein was said to have gotten Phil to take that potential gold mine away from Rhino so that it could be released on Klein's ABKCO label.

For years Phil had lived with a woman named Janice Savala, a thin brunette who once worked as a secretary for Lester Sill at Screen Gems. When she moved in with Phil, her friends were prohibited from calling her because Phil did not want her talking to outsiders; in time, she lost almost all outside contact. She evidently did not mind the sacrifices she had to make in order to be with him. "Janice is positively clonelike," Danny Davis said. "She is completely devoted to him, an absolute lackey." The years that she remained loyal and submissive did her well. When Phil reached his mid-forties and felt it was time for a new round of domesticity, he began telling people that he and Janice had married and that she bore him a second set of twins. Hounded again by his landlords, Phil finally moved to another palace of a house, but in the prosaic suburban grotto of Pasadena. There the industry couldn't touch him.

"He's definitely on the progressive Howard Hughes plan," Dan Kessel said.

Three decades after "To Know Him Is to Love Him," the rock-and-roll world had little appreciation for the fact that when Phil Spector invented modern rock he did so when the music industry treated rock and roll as a poor stepchild. While Spector's bruising confrontations, his ruthlessness, and his bucking of convention helped usher rock to a dominant role in modern pop, even some of those who most closely aided his cause—and theirs—grew to believe that he damaged them. Barry Mann and Cynthia Weil, their words and music immortalized by Spector, still bleed from the woulds inflicted over twenty years ago. "There are just too many things I'd rather not talk about, about the collaboration," Weil said. The industry is still intolerant. No Spector record was ever nominated for a Grammy award, nor does it seem possible that he could be considered for a lifetime award for producing or songwriting.

"He deserves an award, he really does," Lester Sill said. "In spite of whatever he is, he's certainly a genius. I think if he just didn't let that crazy ego get in his way, he would still be an incredible producer today. It's a shame too. He became such a dark, morbid person. That black cloud is all around him.

"I hurt for him because he's such a talented guy and he needed help a long time ago. There was a kind side of him that people never saw. I remember the late Paul Case, and how Phil couldn't do enough for Paul, and how Phil once gave everyone in the office Polaroid cameras that cost him $150 each. There was that side to him. But he never allowed it to flourish and it hurt him."

"I'm on the board of the Music Hall of Fame and two of the last six years I've brought up Phil's name for an award of some sort," said Marshall Lieb, whose long footpath from the Teddy Bears was pocked with his own destructive tendencies and withdrawals before he was reclaimed by motion picture scoring. "But they've gone somewhere else. There's a lot of opposition to Phil on the Grammys too. His name comes

⊙   292

up, and it's nice to know it keeps coming up, but it doesn't get much further than that. It's just automatic; mention the name and people just sort of say 'What a bonebrain.' It all has to do with the past, and right now it's not far enough in the past for some people to overlook some of the things Phil has done on a personal level.

"But, with me, there's enough time gone by where when I run into somebody who knows him I'll say, 'Tell Phil that Marsh said hello, give him my number, tell him to call me.' The scars and wounds are not there any longer. Like veryone else, there was a time I was bugged at him for something or other. But you put that stuff aside. Life is too dang short.

"I would really like to put Phil on a picture. I gave a lot of people their first jobs in film, in a new medium other than recording, and that would be great for Phil, get him away from the bullshit and pressures of that industry. I have fought to offer Phil a picture project, but you mention it to movie people and they get scared; you're not sure that he's gonna show up and how he's gonna act—which is also a fear of the awards people. I could make it work, though, I know I could. He would know I wasn't like the Mo Ostins of the world, that I cared about him as a person."

Marshall had not seen or spoken with Phil in many years when, with no warning, their paths crossed in the summer of 1987. It happened in much the same way they first came together, among the people who all began adulthood equally unsure—at the thirtieth reunion of the Fairfax High graduating glass of '57. Walking into the bar of the Santa Monica beach club where the reunion was held, Marshall never even imagined that Phil would come out of his seclusion and be there. As he ordered a drink, one of his ex-classmates asked him if he had seen Phil at the other end of the bar. Springing around, Marshall looked through the dim light and saw the large-nosed, weak-chinned face he knew so well. Phil, black shades hiding his eyes even in the darkened room, sat at a corner table with two bodyguards, drinking but looking fit and natty in a three-piece suit.

"I'm going to go over there and say hello to Phillip," Marshall said to the other guest, who cautioned him, "Don't bother. He won't even recognize you." That was the prevailing attitude there that night. Some of Phil's old classmates had tried to make conversation with him, only to be dismissed by his wordless inattention. Harvey Goldstein, the jilted Teddy Bear, would not make any effort at a greeting. "I wouldn't play his game," said Goldstein. "That's exactly what he wanted and there was just no way I was gonna give this guy any satisfaction at all."

Marshall, though, felt he had to make contact. "I walked over and put my face in his face, I demanded his eyes, because he doesn't look at people; that's part of his little trap. I could see into him, man, even with the dark glasses. I just know that this guy was hurtin' in some way.

"I said, 'Marshall Lieb,' and while he was sort of surprised and sort of not happy, it meant something to see me. I think he acknowledged me beyond all the rest of the people. He stood up and grabbed my hand with both of his. I said, you know, 'How you doin'?' and I had to wait for an answer and I just felt, 'Oh shit, I'd like to talk with him.' I mean, we are so beyond all that stuff in the past. But he's sort of in his own kind of . . . I think he would have liked to say some things but he couldn't."

Marshall, reaching blindly, told Phil that he had made some attempts to reach him. He talked about Stan Ross for a minute. "But it almost seemed as if it wasn't recording and some disassociated sentence would pop back. I could say that he looked drugged out but it's not fair. I just felt really bad, because Phil is always in my heart, his pictures are all over the walls in my home. I mean we raised this guy, my mother and me—and he did ask about her, he said, 'How's your mom?' That was really the only coherent thing he said.

"I told him I'd see him later in the evening, and a lot of people during the evening said, 'Why don't you go over and talk to Phil?' and I just didn't want to any more. It was too sad, for me too tragic."

The more Marshall thought about that night, however, the more he thought he knew about the Phil Spector he lost. "He needed to be there," Lieb said. "He needed for those people to pass by that table and say 'Hello, Phil,' and even though he would not acknowledge them he needed to them for know he was there. If it was just for the ego, he would've left early. But he stayed at that table the whole night, he was the last to leave. He made up his mind he was going to stay with that class, as a family. He came to be with those people who consider him just plain old Phil; this is his one identification with real life. Because, right now, what he's living is not real life. He's living some sort of death.

"It was the same as it was with Elvis. I was a close friend of Elvis, I watched him deteriorate as a person trying to kill himself, and when I saw that happening it was very difficult to watch someone who is strong and aggressive become so weak and troubled. When you are king and you are it, some people are frightened by it. That's what they've worked for, to be it, and when they get there they think there's more to go when there isn't. Mick Jagger became it and enjoys being it. Phil became it but he isn't quite comfortable with it.

"As frightened as Phil was when we were kids, he knew he was going somewhere. Now he has nowhere to go and that probably scares him a hell of a lot more."

20

I am trying to get my life reasonable. I'm not ever going to be happy. Happiness isn't on, because happiness is temporary. Unhappiness is temporary. Ecstasy is temporary. Orgasm is temporary. Everything is temporary. But being reasonable is an approach. And being reasonable with yourself, it's very difficult, very difficult to be reasonable.
  —PHIL SPECTOR, *London Daily Telegraph*, February 1, 2003

You can't get rid of him. It's like gum on your shoe. You pull at it and it doesn't come off. That's how I feel about him. He can't quite let me go. And it's scary, too. Maybe we do have a bond, but he's gotta be put away.
  —RONNIE SPECTOR, 2003

By the 1990s, the legend, if not the story, was complete. The Phil Spector model of dark, demented, isolated, creepy-cool had crusted into a virtual background soundtrack for a legion of artistes, auteurs, authors, and music industry social climbers. The most notable of the last, David

Geffen, for example, began his climb as the post-Spector Spector by landing a job in the William Morris mailroom, propelled by the fib that he was actually related to Phil Spector.

For others, the soundtrack was literal. Witness Martin Scorsese's opening-credits mood setter for *Mean Streets,* "Be My Baby"—Phil's intended love entreaty to Ronnie Spector, which was now an undercurrent of their brooding and pain, and like them more of an echo of the Marquis de Sade than the Brill Building. This was obvious even in the mid-seventies, when the enigmatic line about "humming a song from 1962" in Bob Seger's haunting plaint of long-spoiled innocence was revealed to be a reference to "Be My Baby," never mind that the tune was from 1963.

Indeed, the Phil and Ronnie psychodrama had become the postmodern *Love Story* for the whacked-out, anything-but-innocent generation that had come of age in the sixties. That is, it was a story that sucked the life out of its protagonists. Such was the plotline of James Robert Baker's *Fuel-Injected Dreams,* the 1986 roman à clef of "rock's greatest legend" Dennis Contrelle and his love/prey, the erstwhile teenage sex kitten and lead singer of the Stingrays, Sharlene Contrelle. Sought out years later by a disc jockey haunted by the disappearance of a girlfriend at the time the last Stingrays album came out, Dennis and Sharlene are found in a *Satyricon* hell of sex, drugs, and sado-masochism. But, alas, no music, which for both of them died long ago.

Better still was an unpublished novella by the singer/songwriter Josh Alan Friedman, who after befriending Ronnie told her story in her voice as "Bonnie." Recounting a time when Phil went off to London, leaving her locked in their Beverly Hills house, she recalls:

We would sleep together over the phone—not talking, but keeping the phone line open on our pillows all night, so he could hear me breathe. Once he paid off a doctor to put my leg in a cast when nothin' was wrong, so I had to stay in a wheelchair for weeks. His jealousy got crazier as he became impotent. By then he had me in my little pixie Santa getup, crawling along the floor on a dog leash, makin' me bark on command.*

*Al Aronowitz, "Column Forty-Seven" (unpublished article, July 1, 1999).

If Phil had plenty of secrets still intact, there were none left unearthed from his sick liaison with Ronnie. Indeed, Ronnie herself exhumed any last remains in her 1990 autobiography, mandatorily titled *Be My Baby: How I Survived Mascara, Miniskirts, and Madness*. The irony of the Phil and Ronnie amalgam was that they became inseparable in pop culture even as both moved on to other, increasingly barren pastures.

After their divorce, Ronnie tried to cash in on what Phil had made her, but she couldn't keep from hitting the skids hard. And evidently, she couldn't keep from falling for strong-willed types. When she remarried in 1983, it was to show-biz manager Jonathan Greenfield, with whom she had two children. With him running interference, she tried to carry on a semblance of a singing career. The last passable imitation of Ronnie Spector was her backing vocals on the two Eddie Money sides, "Take Me Home Tonight" and "Who Can Sleep," in the mid-eighties.

That Greenfield was pulling strings—or, more accurately, clutching at straws—on her behalf seemed evident when he called me about a year after this book was originally published. Ostensibly, his purpose was to laud the work and hint grandly at some sort of writing project in which I would collaborate with Ronnie. At his request, I gave him my address. The next day, I opened the door to a process server handing me a summons. Incredibly, Ronnie, to whom these pages are very kind, had filed a multimillion-dollar libel suit against me. If Greenfield had hoped to squeeze out a settlement or judgment, he was magnificently inept. The case, having been filed exactly one day after the statute of limitations had expired, was summarily tossed out of court. (Spector, incidentally, also had sued for libel but quickly settled out of court, agreeing to the recision of a few sentences incidental to the book's content.)

With all the horror that Ronnie had endured while married to Phil, she still kept his name even after she remarried, and Phil still exercised a certain psychological hold on her. From where Phil sat, that was a monumental victory, something he hinted at in a January 2003 interview:

> Not to get on a dissertation about ex-wives and shit like that, but wife and marriage isn't a word, it's a sentence; and wives last through our marriage, ex-wives last for ever, and all that other bullshit. But she can still get up 40 years later and sing "Be My Baby"

⊙

and get applause. I made her famous, and she resents that. "Oh, but he's a control-freak." If you come down to what people really hate about Phil Spector, it's that he controls everything. But it's funny, you hear such negative shit about me but there isn't anyone in this business who has touched me who hasn't achieved some sort of success with me. There isn't anyone who hasn't made money. Not that that means anything, but it's interesting.[*]

On a more tangible plane, the official epoch of Phil Spector, elder statesman of rock and roll, began on March 18, 1989, when he crawled out of the woodwork and into the brightly burning spotlight in the main ballroom of the Waldorf-Astoria Hotel in New York for his induction into the Rock and Roll Hall of Fame. As a member of the Hall's fourth class of honorees, he was in splendid company, joining the Rolling Stones, Otis Redding, the Temptations, Stevie Wonder, and Dion. Yet upon learning of his induction, Phil was barely moved. Having been snubbed for decades by the industry—his sole Grammy being for his reclamation of *Let It Be,* with not a piece of hardware to show for the Wall of Sound—he had paid scant attention to the Hall of Fame. He had no objection to the actual edifice that had been built lakeside in Cleveland. It was those annual induction rites that had begun in New York in 1986 that made his skin crawl. Phil, and not a few others, cast off the ritual as an exercise in self-congratulatory flummery, its "winners" proclaimed by an alarmingly small papacy—mainly *Rolling Stone* publisher Jann Wenner and Atlantic Records founder and industry lion Ahmet Ertegun. MTV, with its growing fixation on pond-scum rappers, was bad enough. Did music really need an awards show for *altercockers,* making him feel as old as they were?

What's more, for a new kid on the block, this Hall of Fame was awfully haughty. For one thing, Wenner had made it known that rock's implicit hegemony stopped at the Waldorf-Astoria's doors, where he took over. It was for this reason that the three surviving Beatles had refused to attend their induction in 1995. To wit, they had been told that *Rolling Stone,* and not they, would own the cherished and ineffably valuable videotapes of them on stage together for the first time since John

[*]Mick Brown, "Spector and the Devils," *London Daily Telegraph,* February 1, 2003.

Lennon's murder. For Phil, of course, such an infringement—especially where tapes were involved—was a call to war. He'd rather die than cede an inch.

Spector was far more accommodating when it came to other industry fetes. He'd had no hesitation attending Blues Foundation dinners for Ertegun and Jerry Wexler in Los Angeles in the mid-eighties. He also had gratefully accepted an award in Nashville in 1988 after a cover of "To Know Him Is to Love Him" on the album *Trio,* by Dolly Parton, Linda Ronstadt, and Emmylou Harris, had become the most-played country song of the year. On the latter occasion, he was humble, funny, and generous with his praise of country artists who respected music. Still, if Wenner could use those shallow huzzahs at the Waldorf-Astoria for his own purposes, so could Phil Spector. He conceived his appearance at the Hall of Fame ceremony to fit with the question sure to be percolating in the crowd: after all these years in the music gulag, what was the old *meshugenah* going to do to embarrass himself—or us? His answer was that they were going to get him as is, unbowed and unchastened.

Among the now wheezing Broadway mob, pulses raced in anticipation. Phil also was excited, knowing they'd all be there: Ahmet, Seymour Stein, Mo Ostin, Berry Gordy, Lester Sill, Johnny Bienstock, Jean Aberbach. About the only member of the now gray and bald cognoscenti who would be absent was Donnie Kirshner, who apparently had been enjoined from the Hall of Fame's honor roll for grievances dating back to when he'd usurped power from the now *really* old guard. How ironic—and preposterous—that on a night when Phil would receive his props as a legend, Kirshner, without whose patronal funneling of hit material there may never have been a Phil Spector as the world knew him, was still waiting in vain for his.

Many of the people who had grievances against Kirshner had similar grudges against Spector, but no one could seriously prevent him from receiving this honor. All they could do was hope that he wouldn't be a total asshole—which, of course, only made that notion all the more tantalizing to Phil. In any event, he flew to New York knowing that at the very least, he would send those people home humming another Spector tune. The problem was, he was also so scared—in a cold sweat right down to his bones—about standing up there alone and metaphorically naked that he truly had no idea what would happen. He made a few cursory notes, but he knew he would wing it according to the vibe.

☉   300

Phil's stomach hurt too much for him to sit at his VIP table and watch the segments of the ceremony that preceded his. Instead, he laid low outside the ballroom as the audience watched a brief film that included a medley of his greatest hits. When the film ended, people began looking around and murmuring "Where is he?" Ertegun took to the podium and assured them, "Ladies and gentlemen, he is here."

Tina Turner, who had been touched by his genius only briefly, at the locus of his biggest failure, had been chosen to introduce him. Sizzling the grill, she delivered a few encomiums, then cooed with breathless urgency, "I'm glad to say that the Rock and Roll Hall of Fame welcomes Phil Spector!"

As "Be My Baby" was piped in through the loudspeakers, the sea of darkness parted, and there he was, an elf in a tux and a red cummerbund and kerchief, his toupee stylishly bobbed and banged in front and blown stringy down the back of the neck. Huge, aviator-shaped, red-colored shades covered half his face, which was pale and cherubic. He seemed happy—a little *too* happy, half-walking, half-wobbling toward the lectern, wedged between three tuxedoed bodyguards who steered him in the right direction. He was met on the way by Ertegun, and the old allies/foils threw their arms around each other. Phil kissed Ahmet on the cheek. When he got to Tina, he kept trying to find her hand and missing, until she grabbed his left arm and wrapped her hand around it. Then he bowed, whereupon his glasses nearly fell off. After he flicked them back on with his index finger, Tina handed him the silver obelisk-shaped Hall of Fame trophy. He reached for it and missed, and she placed it in his left hand. By now, everyone on stage was fighting to maintain a smile, and they all held their breath as Phil steadied himself in front of the microphone, squinted through his shades, fumbled through his note cards, and began his address. The old lisp was there, but the high-pitched, boyish timbre was now the guttural bark of a confused cocker spaniel.

"I don't get it," he croaked as he cradled the award amid nervous laughter. "I'm very sorry to have missed the inauguration. Mr. Bush, I think that you did very good, and I'm going to vote for you next time . . . . Tina Turner is the best. Don't believe the things they say about her because they're all true."

It was the kind of dry, ironic bon mot Phil loved to deliver, fancying himself a hipper, cooler Noel Coward, martini in hand, but it got lost in the general disjunction and fell flat, invoking silence. He tried his first theme again—"Where is the inauguration?"—but went no further when it hung out there like a big matzo ball. Now the audience was restless. He uttered a few more incoherent sentences. By the time the show's producer Bill Graham stuck a note on the podium ordering him off, he and the audience were finally on the same beam: both had had enough.

As the band pointedly began to strike up a tune, he said, "God bless you," before adding a final, oblique beat: "The credibility factor has really changed."

Once more, there was a germ of what Phil really wanted to say—that for him to be feted in such a fashion meant the recording industry had put aside its long tradition of carrying a grudge. But no one was in the mood to break the Phil Spector code, and there was a sigh of relief as he stumbled out of view, nearly taking a header on the steps.

For some, the aftermath was not unlike the scene in *The Producers* after the "Springtime for Hitler" number, when the audience sat silent, mouths agape. Others, who knew well of the delight Phil always took in unnerving stuffed shirts, enjoyed every minute of what may have been his tour de force. Doc Pomus, who knew the act for what it was, roared with laughter. "That," he would say later, "was the best imitation of a drunk since Marcia Manon in [the silent movie] *Stella Maris*." But then it was Pomus who always liked to tell people who asked him if Phil was a recluse, "Not recluse—reckless, baby. Reckless!"

Darlene Love, who'd also observed the Spector spectrum of affected psychodramas, explained to those at her table that Phil may have been drunk, scared, or both, but in any case, "what he was saying didn't make any sense. But that's Phil Spector. It probably wasn't supposed to."

Ertegun and Stein tried to yuck it up, having expected some such lunacy. But they were relieved they'd never have to go through it again—or so they thought.

A different Phil emerged afterward as host of a low-key party in his suite on the thirty-seventh floor of the Waldorf-Astoria. Here, mingling with a handful of invited guests who guzzled the Dom Perignon he paid for, Phil was sober, clear-eyed, smooth-tongued, and more charming and garrulous than anyone seemed to remember he could be. He professed bewilderment about the honor he'd received. At one point, he asked Darlene Love, "What does this award mean? What is it all about?"

She recalled, "I told him, 'This means that your peers care about you.' But he doesn't believe that people care about him. He really thinks they don't care. Phil is just so very alone."

Another guest, Gerry Goffin, asked Phil whether he might want to get back in the studio. "I don't work. I don't have to work," he replied.

Near the end of the party, as Mick Jagger approached him, Phil bellowed mirthfully, "You old motherfucker." Jagger, just as grandly, responded by calling him "an even older motherfucker."

All was good again in the Phil Spector circus. Throughout the night, he found himself exchanging war stories with the Broadway Brahmins, like an old soldier reliving battles that changed the world. Although he still held personal grievances against many in this crowd, the overall effect was one of amelioration, making him feel like one of the old lions of rock for the first time in his life. In the after-hours afterglow, it must have felt good being Phil Spector. There was even reason to believe that there might be a future in it.

Phil let it be known that night that he was open to taking an active role in the Hall, which could claim a remarkable coup when he agreed to become a member of the Nominating Committee. This was a repository of genuine industry heavies (Seymour Stein, Clive Davis, Al Cafaro, Al Teller), wheezing relics (Ertegun, Jerry Wexler), and social-climbing musicians (Patti Smith Group leader Lenny Kaye), A&R men (Danny Fields), promoters (Frank Barsalona), producers (Jimmy Iovine), and publicists (Bob Merlis), as well as perhaps the biggest concentration of rock journalists this side of a free backstage buffet: Dave Marsh, Jon Landau, Kurt Loder, Lisa Robinson, Anthony DeCurtis, and Robert Hilburn. Among this regiment of mostly middling figures, Phil provided an immediate spike in credibility, obscuring the tacky *Rolling Stone* patronage club that the committee was. (Startling by their omission were movers such as Tommy Mottola, Sid Bernstein, Lester Sill, Leiber and Stoller, Quincy Jones, and Bill Graham—who was given the job of producing the Waldorf-Astoria show), producers such as Giorgio Moroder and Phil Ramone; and more venerable rock writers such as Greil Marcus, Lester Bangs, Robert Christgau, and Al Aronowitz.)

Although Spector still took comfort by lurking in the shadows, he made it his business to come out of them to take calls and answer correspondence about the workings of the committee. He also would make the flight back to New York each March for the awards ceremony and gladly fork over $2,500 for his plate at the dinner. In 1991, he began hosting an enormous party in Suite 37A at the Waldorf-Astoria, and this shindig would become *the* party of the Hall of Fame festivities throughout the nineties. In truth, these affairs were bankrolled by Allen Klein, the canny overseer of Spector's legend and mountain of royalties. Klein gladly paid up and remained in the shadows waiting for Phil's reemergence on the public scene to return the investment. He didn't have to wait long. In 1991, ABKCO released the eagerly awaited Spector four-CD box set, *Back to Mono,* which contained sixty-three classic tracks, including the entire Christmas album. Sales were brisk.

That year at the Hall of Fame ceremonies, Phil returned to the stage where two years before he had freaked everyone out. He was there to introduce Tina Turner upon her induction, and this time he played not the fool but the elder statesman. He ascended the stage unsupported and upright, not tanked up (or pretending to be). He wore a three-piece, black and charcoal, crushed-velvet tux; a white bow tie; a gold watch fob; graded purple shades; and a red and white "Back to Mono" pin in his right lapel. When he spoke, it wasn't to steal the scene from Tina or to seek any revenge for "River Deep—Mountain High." Rather, he soldiered on, with perfect pitch and perspective, in a few soft-spoken and heartfelt sentences.

"She's the closest thing to a diamond I've ever seen," he said. "She has the roughness and rawness, the beauty. She shines, she's bright, she's priceless. Did not receive the recognition due to her until much too late in life. Ladies and gentleman, Tina Turner."

He then stepped back, receding before Tina's bright and shiny presence—willingly, for a change. And if his words were playing back in his mind with himself substituted as the victim of a recognition too long delayed, he kept the thought to himself. Bitterness didn't become a rock statesman.

Being an elder had its perks and advantages, and it provided effective cover for a life gone horribly wrong. At home, in the darkness, Phil had engendered no enduring family bonds or long-term friendships. The person who had been with him the longest, bodyguard George Brand, quit in the early nineties after twenty-seven years of service. George, who may have introduced Phil to guns, had been more than Phil's muscle. He'd also been a stand-in father to the children Phil seemed to care little about, including the twins he'd had with Janice Savala in 1982, Phillip Jr. and Nicole, his only natural-born children. For all of those twenty-seven years, Phil had never given George a raise. The last time he refused, George walked.

The birth of the twins had finally led Phil to vacate the electrified gate and barbed wire–surrounded, tarp-shrouded mansion on La Collina Drive. Still spooked by the commitment and finality of owning property, he again rented, this time a Colonial house in a somnolent parcel of Pasadena called Arroyo Seco, the quintessence of suburbia. The house bred no heartwarming "Father Knows Best" plotlines, however; indeed, the Spector family was more like the Addams family, only weirder. There were no father-and-child softball games, no PTA meetings or swap meets. Rather, Phil pretty much recused himself from Janice save for the time they spent together during the day in the office of Phil Spector Productions—of which they were the only employees. Janice's job was to answer the phone and tell nearly everyone who called, "Mr. Spector is not interested." Phil rarely left the house for industry events, and when he did, he went unaccompanied or with a bimbo on his arm, blatantly sending the message that he was not married to Janice, as the rumors had it.

Phil's relationship with his children transcended mere neglect, it was pathologically disordered and cruel. It seemed to suggest that his self-hatred was so spectacular and unconfined that he was compelled to strip the dignity from anyone bearing his name. His "firstborn," Donté, whom he'd adopted to shore up his counterfeit virility and for whose custody he'd fought Ronnie so tenaciously, was thereafter nearly forgotten, as were his erstwhile "Christmas presents" to Ronnie, the adopted twins, Gary and Louis.

Years later, when Phil's life would be ripped open and its secret horrors spread out like a rancid buffet in the media, Donté and Gary would go on record with shocking revelations. "I lived in a mansion and went to school in a stretch limo," Donté told the British newspaper the *Mail*. "But when we went home, we would be locked in our rooms. I didn't have a toilet, just a small pot in the room. It was humiliating." Gary added, "We were locked in our separate rooms by our governess, let out for breakfast, then taken to school by guards." They went even further in a "Biography" episode that first aired in September 2003.

DONTÉ: We were told by the help, "Get ready, your father wants to go somewhere." We'd get all excited, and we'd get dressed up. We'd sit on the stairs from maybe six o'clock at night to twelve, one, two in the morning. And then the help would come—my father wouldn't even come himself. And they'd say, "Your father changed his mind."

GARY: The only time I spent Christmas with my father was when we spent Christmas at our next-door neighbor's house. He came over unexpected and started playing the piano. The problem was, he had too much to drink. And he was embarrassing himself as well as us. We spent most Thanksgivings with George [Brand's] relatives. George was more of a father to me. He taught me how to swim, how to ride a bike.

DONTÉ: I guess I have to give my dad credit. If he couldn't be responsible enough to take care of us, he put somebody in our lives that could.

GARY: The one time I did go to the studio with my father, when Joey Ramone was there, I would sit next to him watching him do the controls, on the console, and I thought it was the greatest thing. I was spending time with my father. . . . I'm [his] biggest fan still. I separate my father from the producer. And as a producer, he's one of the best I've ever heard. And so for that I will always honor and respect him.

DONTÉ : I love my dad with all my heart. Yes, I have resentments because he wasn't the father I wanted him to be. I'm still going to therapy to figure out why he trusted his friends better than he trusted his family.

Far more disturbing were Gary's claims that Phil had brought him and Louis into his bedroom during amorous encounters and ordered them to perform simulated intercourse with women. He said that this had occurred when they were as young as nine. They told the *Mail* of being blindfolded and handcuffed for Phil and the women's "amusement," and of Phil lifting them onto the women himself. According to Gary, Phil told him this was a "learning experience."

Whether Janice knew about any of this is unclear, but apparently there was much more of a familial bond with Phillip Jr. and Nicole. By the time of the move to Pasadena, Donté, Gary, and Louis were gone

⊙   306

from Phil's purview. Phil had told them that he wouldn't pay for college, so they had left to fend for themselves. Louis studied art, and when he gave his first exhibition at a Los Angeles restaurant, he invited Phil, who never showed. Gary enlisted in the military as an Army cook, then enlisted in the Air Force with an advanced rank. The other officers somehow knew who his father was and sniped that Phil had bought him his stripes. Wearily, he could only repeat that he hadn't seen a dime from Phil in years.

Donté, who had not learned he was adopted until Ronnie told him in the eighties, fared worse. He married and had children, but heroin addiction cost him his marriage. He spent years alternating between the street and rehabilitation clinics, never speaking with Phil about his problems. In 2003, when Donté finally revealed that he was homeless and HIV positive, he said that he had asked Phil for money. Spector, who by then was starting to line the pockets of a legion of lawyers, had turned a deaf ear. "He just hung up," Donté said.

Sometime in the late nineties, Phil sent Gary a letter, apparently in an attempt to clear the air, and possibly ease his guilt, about his failures as a father. The letter, full of mawkish self-hatred, read in part, "My writings are nothing more or less than the ramblings of a diseased mind and soul. And sometimes I am such a manic-depressive, I wish my dear sweet mother had been on the pill."

As for Phil Jr. and Nicole, there was no repeat of the grotesqueries Phil had played out with Donté, Gary, and Louis. Indeed, Phil tried to morph into a family man for their benefit, and for the benefit of those on the outside to whom he wanted to prove the point. Although the process did not include marrying the twins' mother, he did seem to soften around the edges. No longer confining his forays out of the house to night-crawling visits to Sunset Strip eateries and VIP rooms, he began throwing afternoon parties at, of all places, the Montrose Bowling Alley, a quintessential suburban family-oriented venue. Invitations went out to old allies and acolytes to come and enjoy a day of pins falling, pizza, and Wall of Sound tunes piped through the loudspeakers.

At the Montrose, he assumed a paternal identity, parading Phil Jr. and Nicole around the bowling alley as he glad-handed the crowd—easily kibitzing, signing autographs, and posing for pictures. Veteran Spector watchers could hardly believe their eyes. One of the guests, Larry Levine, had been estranged from Phil for more than a decade.

(Levine's heart attack during one of the horrific Ramones sessions had caused Phil so much guilt that he had been unable to face Larry.) After receiving the startling invitation out of nowhere, Levine eagerly drove to Montrose and found Spector in a let-the-good-times-roll mode, an apparition that was worth the trip.

"Phil didn't need to say anything about the past or be apologetic about anything, and I didn't need to hear [an apology]," Levine recalled. "In fact, I always wanted to tell him my heart attack really wasn't his fault. But he obsesses over things like that, so he wouldn't have listened to me anyway. And it was implicit that by having me there, he wanted to make it up to me and get back to the way it had been between us. He didn't say much, but I could read it in his eyes that he was genuinely happy I'd come over.

"This was a Phil I'd rarely seen before. I'd seen him in very normal, down-to-earth situations before—he only got that crazy look in his eyes when he thought he had to put on an act and be the mad genius—but I'd almost never seen him *happy*. He told me, 'Larry, I'm enjoying my life for the first time.' That never seemed to be an option with Phil; he never let himself be happy. I sat there at a table in the bowling alley with Hal Blaine, and we [said], 'Who's that guy pretending to be Phil Spector?'"

Blaine had seen the new and improved Spector at closer range, having been invited to Phil's house on what became periodic visits. During those times, he said, "we never spoke about music, or about getting back in the studio. Never. I don't even know if he had any interest in music. I was there because Phil liked my jokes; he thought I was the funniest fucking guy in the world. He had me believing I was Shecky Greene or Buddy Hackett. I'd do a stand-up act, and he'd fall on the floor laughing."

The laughter stopped all too soon, likely leading Phil to wonder if there was any point to feeling good about life after all. It happened in mid-1991, when he suffered the second great wound in his life after Ben Spector's suicide: Phil Jr. was diagnosed with terminal childhood lymphatic leukemia.

In many ways, this was a far crueler tragedy than his father's death, which came with no warning and the circumstances of which were kept from him for years. Now he had no choice but to stand by helplessly as his son slipped away, all his wealth and status of no use. After futile attempts at chemotherapy, Phil Jr. died on the day after Christmas.

It was Phil's fifty-first birthday. This seemed to be particularly coarse timing.

It wasn't just that Phil's son died on his birthday, but that it occurred so close to Christmas. Phil had not officially renounced Judaism, but he had long been a lapsed Jew who sometimes wore a cross around his neck and celebrated Christmas instead of Hanukkah. Indeed, Phil fancied himself some sort of renegade saint for having birthed an updated appreciation for Christmas music with his 1963 Christmas album, *A Christmas Gift for You*. Masterpiece that it was, it had flopped in its original release, crippled by the Kennedy assassination, but had been resurrected in successive years as the most popular album of seasonal music ever recorded. For Phil, it became no less than a metaphor of faith tested and rewarded—a tip of the cap from the heavens.

Each year Phil would dutifully decorate his house with great gobs of Christmas lights. A life-size, acrylic Santa Claus and his reindeer traipsed about the lawn. But all the accoutrements of this ersatz Christianity had done nothing to protect him from the cruelties of fate that seemed to plague him. Phil Jr. was nine when he died, about the same age Phil had been when Ben Spector had caught the last train for the coast.

Wracked with guilt on many levels, Phil toughed it out on his own, unable or unwilling to share his grief with anyone. He retreated deeper into the darkness and for a time fixated on death. Just three months later, in a state of melancholia, he went to New York for the Rock and Roll Hall of Fame dinner. He hadn't spoken of his son's death to more than a few people in the industry crowd, the funeral and burial had been private affairs, and the news had been kept out of the media. When called on to give a brief speech at the dinner, however, he inserted a couple of sentences that again brought murmurs in the audience.

"The most vulgar and obscene four-letter word in this language is 'dead,'" he said. "It is indecent. It has no redeeming social value."

Death would come around to haunt him again and again in the ensuing years. Within just four years, in fact, he suffered another family loss—this time of the woman he called, part mockingly and with intensely conflicting emotions, "my dear mother." The ambivalent love and loathing Phil had for Bertha Spector—the latter a factor of his unshakable conviction that her hectoring had caused his worst character traits—had not crimped his familial obligations. Overseeing the residential and financial conditions of Bertha, as well as those of his sister,

Shirley—whose periodic stays in expensive sanitariums had meshed into a permanent confinement by the eighties—was his karmic wishing well, a bounty he could pay to avoid having to look inside himself for the roots of his failings as a man. It was easier to blame a maternal influence and at the same time purge the guilt of doing so with a few bucks. As Oedipal as he was, this was the very same way he saw women in general. The danger sign was that after years and years of therapy, that complex only seemed to get worse.

Bertha remained sprightly into her eighties, and Phil indulged her wish not to be confined to a retirement home, instead paying the rent for a comfortable apartment she lived in for many years in Hollywood. There she industriously cared for herself, shopping for her own groceries and taking daily walks. One day in 1995, when she was out on one of those walks, she tripped on a loose board on the sidewalk of a construction site. With the same litigious spunk of her son, and possibly with his advice, she immediately filed a personal injury lawsuit against the construction company. Sadly, however, weakened by the accident, she died two weeks later at age eighty-four. That ensured more solitary grief and tortured emotions for Phil, and perhaps a return, after a long latency period, of privately railing at the father whose suicide had begun his unyielding lifetime of pain.

Phil carried on, stoically but unsteadily. He continued the bowling parties, out of a desire for normalcy, but Phil Jr.'s death in particular seemed to take the life out of him and caused him to rebuild the old shell. He went back to being a trespasser in his own world.

"People would be asking, 'Where's Phil?'" Levine said. "You'd see him in flickering moments at the bowling alley. He'd show up very late, and he'd sit outside in his limo in the parking lot. Occasionally, he'd stick his head in, but he didn't feel like mingling. It's really sad when he gets like that. And these parties became big shindigs. They grew every year. Everybody would look forward to them. There were huge crowds of friends and hangers-on. And Phil didn't even know who a lot of them were. It was just too much for him to deal with at that point. He was going the other way, in terms of sociability. When he lost his son, it hit him very hard. It devastated him."

Spector made an effort, however. He'd invite Larry to sit with him in his VIP Lakers seats at the Forum, where he'd often taken Phil Jr. Eerily, for the entire game he wouldn't say a word and at times would get weepy. There was little Larry could do other than suggest that Phil do something that had been previously taboo—recording once again. He didn't think Phil would take him up on it.

Soon after Phil Jr.'s death, Janice, unable to reach Phil through the shroud of grief, moved out with Nicole. Phil reacted as he usually did when a woman turned her back on him. He filed several small-claims lawsuits in which he accused her of stealing a computer, a television, and a video recorder and not performing work he had paid her to do.

This, of course, had the same ring to it as his firing of his personal secretary Donna Sekulidis over an allegedly stolen typewriter. It had nothing to do with recovering those items and everything to do with Phil exerting his control over women. Janice wouldn't be intimidated. Like Ronnie, she fought back, answering each suit by successfully arguing that Phil had given her the merchandise to keep. Rather than pout, Phil threw a Machiavellian curveball, keeping Janice on as his assistant. This served him well for two reasons. It meant not only that he'd retain her valuable services as a skilled screener but also that she would be kept returning to Arroyo Seco. It was a small victory, but those were about all he had left.

Seeking control over women was an ongoing obsession. However frequent and satisfying his sexual encounters were, the prime motivation for these adventures seemed to be acquiring the total fealty of the women he diddled with, no matter how fleetingly. Evidently, there were many of them, few of which endured beyond a single fling. Phil often would become enraged and abusive after being rejected either in response to a sexual advance or merely because the woman wanted to leave before he was ready to let her go. During these encounters, a number of women experienced something like what La Toya Jackson had when Phil had pulled his "Bates Motel" riff on her, although for some of them, the consequences were more serious and frightening.

The most foreboding aspect of these incidents was that an alarming number of these women found themselves face-to-face with the wrong end of a gun.

Spector's reputation as a desperado gunslinger had, of course, become wedded to his legend, in no small part because of the "O.K. Corral" moments of the studio sessions with John Lennon, Leonard Cohen, and the Ramones. And yet few seemed to be genuinely concerned that anything untoward might come of it. Like Elvis and his guns, Spector and *his* guns had set into the fiber of rock. As a consequence, seeing him with a gun—or, as Doc Pomus had noted, with any number of guns he would rotate to match his outfit—very nearly became a *requirement,* something one would expect. No one saw any harm in it. For all his attempts at macho posturing, had he ever actually hurt someone—physically, that is, as opposed to psychologically? As much of a schlemiel as he was, if he ever did take a shot at anybody, he'd surely shoot himself in the ass and wind up the schlimazel as well.

As the gun tales grew, no one seemed quite to grasp the concept that by accepting it as "just Phil's shtick," they were enabling his dementia. Worse, the enablers included the very people who should have taken it the most seriously, the law enforcement authorities in Beverly Hills, Pasadena, and the Los Angeles County Sheriff's Department. This man with a history of pathological behavior who had amassed what seemed like an arsenal was able easily to renew his gun permits, seemingly with no questions asked.

As for the victims of his gun reveries, court records show that only two ever pressed charges against him for physical abuse. The first case, in January 1972, involved an unknown woman who called Beverly Hills police after Phil—wearing a maroon jacket with a karate emblem, court papers note—pointed a loaded revolver at her in the Daisy Club on Rodeo Drive. In the second case, in November 1975, two parking valets at the Beverly Hills Hotel heard a woman scream at him, "Get away from me!" When they asked Phil what was going on, he pointed a gun at them, then drove away with his manager, Marty Machat, in a silver Cadillac before being caught and arrested. Both times, he pleaded guilty to a misdemeanor of brandishing a firearm and was given a small fine and probation—one year and two years, respectively—with the condition that he not possess any deadly weapons.

Apparently, when Phil pulled a gun on Leonard Cohen in the studio in 1977, he violated probation—only no one reported it, an all-too-common response in the years to come in incidents like these:

1978: When TV producer Alan Sacks and his assistant Cathy Henderson visited Phil to discuss music for a new pilot, Spector confronted them, yelling, "You only came over because you want to go back and say I drink and like to play with guns!" He then obliged his own stereotype, pointing a gun at Sacks several times, leading Sacks to push the muzzle away from his face. He continued "playing" in this manner for hours, refusing to let Sacks and Henderson leave the house. They finally got out after midnight when another couple arrived, but they filed no police report.

1988: When one of his personal assistants, Dianne Ogden, wanted to leave his house, a drunken Spector pointed a gun at her face. Terrified, she agreed to his demand to spend the night with him. Ogden let it slide and two weeks later was a guest at a dinner party at his house. When she refused to spend the night and was walking to her car, a drunken Spector ran after her, carrying what she later described as an "Uzi-type assault rifle" and banging on her windows with it as she drove away. Ogden would not return to the house, but she did not file charges. Even so, at Phil's request, she agreed to organize a bowling party for him in 1989.

1991: Incensed when Melissa Grovesnor, whom he had met in New York and flown out to L.A., said that she wanted to leave his house, a hammered Spector left the room, then returned wearing a shoulder holster and holding a gun. He pointed the gun at her head while he swore at her. In fear for her life, she sat in the same chair for hours and cried herself to sleep. The next morning, Phil, acting as though nothing had happened, asked her if she wanted to go home, then drove her to the airport. Grovesnor, a waitress in a restaurant Phil frequented when in New York, maintained a social friendship with him and kept the gun-pointing interlude quiet.

1993: After Dorothy Melvin, a personal assistant to comedienne Joan Rivers, began seeing Phil romantically, she awoke one morning and saw him outside pointing a gun at her empty car. She went outdoors and asked him what he was doing. He hit her on the head with the gun and screamed, "Get the fuck back in the house!" He forced her at gunpoint into the foyer, where he ordered her to take off her clothes. When she pleaded with him to let her go, he again hit her on the head with the gun and thundered, "I told you to take your fucking clothes off!" Melvin took off her jacket, but then Phil began going through her purse, accusing her of snooping around his house and stealing from him. Then he told her, "Get the fuck out." She asked for her purse, but he refused to give it to her. She ran out of the house but couldn't drive away because the security gate was locked. Sitting in her car trembling and not knowing what to do, she heard the "pump" of a shotgun being "racked." Then Phil ran toward the car with the shotgun, yelling, "I told you to get the fuck out of here!" She told him the gate was locked, and he went back into the house and opened it.

Unlike the others, Melvin did go to the police, and soon after returned with two cops to recover her purse. As the cops searched the house for the purse, Phil mouthed off and had to be hand-cuffed. Melvin did not press charges, wary of the publicity. Amazingly, she also saw Phil socially thereafter, but only in groups and only in public places.*

Another episode of note happened in 2001 at the Polo Lounge of the Beverly Hills Hotel, witnessed by Carol Connors, the ex-Teddy Bear. The erstwhile Annette Kleinbard had through the years become one of pop music's top lyricists, writing, among other standards, "Gonna Fly Now" for the movie *Rocky*. She and Phil had not spoken in more than thirty years, and Connors had never gotten over his crude remark—"Too bad she didn't die"—after her near-fatal car accident in 1959. Phil, who may have subconsciously resented her because her songwriting career had outlasted his, saw her in the lounge but said nothing. After he became intoxicated, a woman friend of Connors's remarked that his hair, or wig, looked like a "Brillo pad." Spector snapped, whipping out a gun and aiming it at her.

Carol went numb at the knees, petrified that Phil's quaking hand would discharge the gun. For a few tense moments, he held his "Philly the Kid" pose. Then, looking green, he put the gun back in its holster and went running for the bathroom, where he violently threw up. No one pressed the gun-waving issue. (The hotel's management may have intervened to protect Phil, a big-spending regular at the Polo Lounge.)

Connors, still shaken years later, said that she couldn't speak about the Polo Lounge episode. "I can't," she said. "Maybe someday. Not now."

Then there was the time when a Japanese record company execu-tive shared a limo ride with Phil to an industry event in L.A. According

---

* Cases cited in Motion to Admit Evidence of Other Crimes filed by the District Attorney's Office in Los Angeles Supreme Court on February 17, 2005. Dept. 106, Case No. BA255233, pages 12–24.

to a 2003 *Vanity Fair* article, "Spector, who'd been sampling the limo's liquor supply, pulled a piece from his tux, took aim at the executive, and snarled, 'You fucking Japanese! You attacked our country!'" In a familiar ending to the story, the magazine reported that "before things got out of hand, the driver dropped Spector at the Peninsula, where he walked into the lobby and threw up."

Rumors of incidents such as these, rather than alarm those who knew him, were passed off as jokey manifestations of the Spector "legend"—even of his madcap wit—the "man's man" flip side of his droll Noel Coward verbal panache. That his psychotic impulses were almost exclusively directed at women raised few if any eyebrows. No one—not even the victimized women themselves—seemed to anticipate that his full-blown misogyny portended something horrible, either for the man behind the gun or those in front of it.

Spector's out was that he always pulled back and reholstered his gun before pulling the trigger—a rationale frequently stressed by his point men, Dan and Dave Kessel, in making the case that Phil was always in complete control during these "Phil being Phil" performances. In this light, his behavior wasn't malicious as much as it was a harmless burlesque act, one in which he could go over the top, be really shitty to people, and make a fool of himself. It was always Phil who felt the worst afterward, and in the end, it was no harm, no foul.

Phil, to be sure, could charm or talk his way out of trouble merely by switching gears and acting "normally" moments after scaring the tar out of someone. Or he would point out that he'd forgotten to take his lithium or Prozac, which his psychiatrists had prescribed for him. It's debatable that he ever really forgot; as he would admit, he would simply refuse to take his meds. Perhaps this explains why he would disappear after a psychotic outburst and come back placid, rational, and, possibly, sedated.

All this begs the question of whether Spector should have been permitted to keep guns at all. That issue aside, he would keep on pushing his luck with both his guns and his rotten attitude toward women. If he ever wondered whether his luck would run out, he likely didn't care. Or maybe he couldn't stand that he did.

21

In my next life, I want to come back as either a proctologist, so I can deal with all the assholes I meet, or as a matador, so I can deal with the bullshit.

—PHIL SPECTOR, *Esquire*, September 1999

Whether it was a therapeutic exercise following the death of his son or the inevitable consequence of living with his own legacy, by early 1993 Spector began to reconsider Larry Levine's suggestion that he get back into the studio. To be sure, Phil had left the door open a crack throughout his post-Ramones exile, seemingly stalking the right moment and the right project, but perhaps not wishing to find either. Or maybe he was seeking the right sucker, since it was a given that his price—not money, which he had always rejected as anything close to his motivation for a return—would be steep.

Even as pop music divided amoeba-like into numerous organisms in the eighties, Spector's legend bled across yet another generation.

⊙

Numerous acts, even rappers, would sometimes ask his representatives about hiring him to produce a session. Phil sat back at a kingly distance, pronouncing them all unfit for his attention, providing effective cover for his own insecurities. Yet such entreaties required that he keep himself informed about industry trends and studio innovations. Playing the part of the genius who never really left, he could discourse impressively on the good (practically nothing) and the bad (practically everything) in rock.

Still he had no real intention of getting back into the studio grind, since doing so would mean doing more than pontificating about music. He'd gotten close with Depeche Mode, but after that band flinched at the actualities of the producer-prisoner dynamic, he felt no compulsion to punch the clock anytime soon. It took until early 1993 for a real, viable victim to emerge. The episode began innocently enough when Phil happened to see the Canadian diva Céline Dion belting out an ear-splitting rendition of "River Deep—Mountain High" on the "Late Show with David Letterman." Impressed with the twenty-five-year-old light pop singer, who had achieved some success mainly for Disney soundtracks such as the Grammy- and Oscar-winning title song from *Beauty and the Beast*, he put out a feeler to her. Not only was he flattered that she had an appreciation for gritty blues rock—and for him in particular, he assumed—but he equated the experience with that of "discovering" Tina Turner at "The TAMI Show" in 1965. It was, he must have reckoned, another epiphany in rock-and-roll history, even if the instrument now was a G-rated French Canadian chanteuse who spoke only broken English.

An emolument was that the concept of turning Dion into a kind of power-pop princess was apparently shared by her manager, René Angélil, who was only slightly younger than Phil and trying to break out his young protégé (and love interest; they would marry the next year) into a serious mainstream bracket. As an old-timer in the business, the white-bearded Angélil had an innate appreciation for Spector. More important, as a Canadian and an outsider among the jaded American industry cliques, he was perhaps less prone to be scared off by the can-you-top-this Spector horror stories.

When Phil met with Dion and Angélil, he was careful not to descend into "Bad Phil." On his best behavior, he was charming and effusive about her talent and crossover appeal. She could, he swore, become the next Tina Turner, with a few tweaks. The fact that Angélil

317

had a good bit of leverage with Dion's label, Sony Music, having already established a custom Sony Music Canada label for her, 550 Music, also appealed to Spector. Indeed, having a worldwide corporate giant under his thumb may have turned Phil on more than any other aspect of the deal. And Angélil thrilled to the prospect of having Dion's muscular voice fronting a rebuilt Wall of Sound, just as long as Spector understood who the star was.

Of course, Phil had no doubt who the star was. Working with Marvin Mitchelson, the famous palimony lawyer, he drove a hard bargain, turning the Angélil-Sony connection into an extraordinary coup: an agreement to produce an unspecified number of sides for Dion on the condition that the sessions would be under the aegis of, and paid for by, Phil Spector International. The arrangement may have seemed acceptable, and even advantageous, to Angélil, since Phil was picking up the tab for the sessions and had sweetened the pot by renouncing up-front money to take roughly a 15 percent royalty split on the back end. Angélil may even have believed that he had gotten one over on Spector, playing him at a time when he was desperate to record Dion as his comeback project.

Phil, as ever, knew better. Angélil had evidently lost sight of the real import of Spector's paying for the studio time. It wasn't the time he was buying; it was the tapes that came out of the sessions. Tape ownership was standard operating procedure for Spector, dating back to John Lennon's L.A. sessions, and Sony, if not Angélil, should have been aware of the hellacious repercussions of Phil's tape tangos in the Lennon, Leonard Cohen, and Ramones sessions. The deal can only be explained by Angélil's own desperation and his sway over Sony. It's also possible that the agreement was sanctioned by Sony Canada and that the parent company didn't even know about it or sign off on it.

Whatever the underlying factors, by the time the ink was dry, Phil Spector was relevant again. The beast was back in clover.

Having pulled off this coup, Phil was still nervous—one might even say gun-shy—enough not to rush into a public announcement of the deal. Instead, swearing everyone he told about the project to secrecy, he turned with purpose to the business of making music. His first exigency was finding an arranger. He would have loved to have called Jack Nitzsche, who could always commit the sounds and impulses in Spector's dog ears to notes on lead sheets as if by antennae. But Nitzsche was still besotted and unstable. Seeking a similar mind meld, Phil called on an even longer-termed ally, Don Peake. Now fifty, Peake had spent the past few years touring with Ray Charles and scoring Wes Craven horror movies. He hadn't seen or spoken with Phil since the Lennon sessions. Then the phone rang, and the raspy voice that he knew so well was laying it on thick.

"He said, 'Don, you're the only guy I can trust,'" Peake recalled with a laugh. "All of a sudden, after all those years, I was the only guy he could trust. Only Phil can bullshit you like that. He's the best at it. I mean, he went on about this new secret project he was doing, and it was as if we'd never stopped talking. He just comes out of nowhere like that and makes you believe he can't live without you. And, I confess, I got a tingle up my back. It's like I was being entrusted with a state secret, which it was. At least to Phil it was."

Invited to come to the house a few days later, Peake found himself a central player in a dream scenario that few, including himself, ever thought would happen.

"He said he was doing an album—he didn't say with whom—and he needed me to do the notations, work out all the musicians' parts like Jack used to do," Peake said. "You can't imagine how flattered I was to perform that role. I had a few days off between Ray Charles gigs, and I just dropped everything and went up to Pasadena."

When Peake entered Phil's house, the first thing he saw was Lennon's pristine white guitar, which Yoko Ono had, in the name of absolution, bequeathed to Phil after John's death. "It was right there in the foyer, with Yoko's note reading, 'To Phil, John would have wanted you to have this,'" Peake recalled. "My God, what a piece of history! Something like that stops you in your tracks and gets you in the mood to make great music."

That vibe was enhanced by a no-nonsense Spector, who dispensed with the usual unnerving "Phil Trip." "He was perfectly normal," Peake said. "We got right down to it. Then, too, we went back too far for him to play with my head. I mean this. I never saw Phil do anything crazy through the years. I'm not saying he didn't, just not with me.

"That day, it was just me and him. The only other people in the house were a housekeeper and a girl named Paulette who was working for Phil. And he started playing on a little electric keyboard. He'd written some songs, and I was well aware that these were probably the first new Phil Spector songs in like twenty-five years and that I was really the first person in the world to get to hear 'em.

"They were quite good, too. He had no titles for them, just numbers, like Number One, Number Two. But there were some very distinctive grooves. One of them seemed to me to be influenced by Django Reinhardt, the great Belgian jazz guitarist of the forties and fifties, who had a band called the Hot Club of France Quartet that played some amazing swing music. All guitarists know about Django Reinhardt. And Phil knows anyone who ever laid down a note anyway. When I heard the chord progression, I said to him, 'Whoa, that sounds like an old Django Reinhardt piece,' and he kind of smiled and nodded. That told me he wasn't settling for the same commercial crap. He wanted something very special and put a lot of thought into it. I just wish he would have told me who the hell the singer was. I never found out it was Céline Dion until the gossip circulated months later."

In planning the project, Phil eased his anxiety by steering away from the contemporary music crowd he barely knew and reaching for the comfort of old cronies. Not surprisingly, he enlisted Larry Levine, who was thrilled that Phil had taken him up on his advice, although for him, too, working with Phil after all those years was a daunting step.

"Of course I was going to accept, but I didn't know if my chops were ready, so I did it as a consultant," Levine said. "We brought in Boris Menart, who finished the Ramones album when I got sick, as the lead engineer, but Phil wanted the mixing and overdubbing to be in my hands when the recording was finished."

It all seemed wrinkle-free to Levine, but for the fact that the Céline Dion sessions were going to be billed to Phil. "I just couldn't understand how that happened," Levine said. "I thought, 'How the hell is that going to work?' I assumed Phil was smarter than everybody and would just make it work. But I'd seen the same thing wreck the John Lennon sessions, and here we were again. With Phil, some things never change."

Taking it slow, lest the songs and Peake's arrangements not be completely to his liking, Phil wasn't ready for his grand reentry into studio life until well into 1994. Finally, getting back into general mode, he booked the 7 to 11 P.M. block at Ocean Way Recording Studio One at 6000 Sunset Boulevard in Hollywood for June 20, 1994. Before he could go in, though, he needed another arranger, as Peake had gone back out on the road with Ray Charles. He called on yet another familiar face from his past, Jimmie Haskell, who'd had zero contact with Spector since producing *The Teddy Bears Sing!* in 1959. Haskell had since enjoyed a plentiful career far from Phil's orbit, doing arrangements for a wide range of acts and winning Grammys for "Ode to Billy Joe," "If You Leave Me Now," and "Bridge over Troubled Water."

"One day I get a call from his girl saying Phil wants me to be at the Beverly Hills Hotel at 8 P.M. the next night," recalled a still nonplussed Haskell, who though semiretired couldn't resist the mysterious entreaty. "After all, this is Phil Spector, so you go."

At the hotel bar—the future scene of Phil's gun incident involving Carol Connors's woman friend—Jimmie was greeted by a Spector who seemed not very different from the brash, demanding teenager he'd met in the studio so long ago. Phil arrived with Marvin Mitchelson, greeted Haskell, and sat down with him at a back table. Jimmie ordered milk and cheesecake, and when the waiter said the kitchen was closed, Phil crooked a finger at the help. "My guest wants a piece of cheesecake and a glass of milk. Accommodate him," he told the maître d', who replied obediently, "Yes, Mr. Spector," and made tracks for the kitchen.

Jimmie was duly impressed, but not as much as when Phil described the project, which he said was with "a singer" whose name he wouldn't divulge. He told Jimmie that he needed him to do the charts. Later in the evening, they went to Phil's house, where Haskell sat just as transfixed as Peake had been, dutifully charting the notes as Phil played songs on his electric keyboard. Even at that stage, Haskell didn't know who the singer was. "It was all hush-hush," he recalled. "Then, late in the evening, he put on a tape of the David Letterman show and said, 'That's her.' And I barely knew who Céline Dion was. But to him, it had to stay a big secret. He said, 'I don't want to see her name on any music sheet. I don't want anybody to know.' I guess he felt if people knew, it would be more pressure on him to come through."

Phil's final task for Haskell was to have him book the musicians for the Dion sessions. For a man with Haskell's credits, it was an odd, even an insulting, request. Jimmie tried to beg off. "Phil, I don't really hire musicians anymore," he said.

Spector became agitated. "If you don't call the musicians," he sputtered, "you're off this gig!"

"Now, I don't know if he really meant it or not, but instead of being offended, I found myself intrigued," Haskell recalled. "I didn't know why he picked me, but it made me feel as if he needed me to do this thing that was greatly important to him. And maybe he did need me.

This was at a time when some of his old studio hands were falling by the wayside. Nitzsche was wasted; Steve Douglas had just died [on April 19, 1993]; other musicians weren't active anymore. So I swallowed my pride and said, 'Okay, Phil, I'll hire the musicians.'"

Still, as with anything else with Phil, it wasn't as simple as that. "He went through the guys he wanted, then he said he wanted to pay them scale," Haskell said. "I told him, 'Phil, not for these guys. They all get double scale.' He blew up and said, 'Either they play for scale or they don't work for me!'

"So now I had to start calling up these legendary musicians who hadn't played for scale in years. I thought they'd turn it down flat, and some did, but when they heard it was Phil, they got excited. One guy, a trumpet player, said, 'I don't work for scale, but I'd sure like to come watch.' Most of them wanted in. Don Randi, Phil's old piano player, said, 'If this is what Phil wants in his old age, it's okay with me.' And we assembled a terrific orchestra, and they all played for scale. I really don't know why he did that to his guys. The best answer, which applies to Spector in many ways, is that he just thought he could, so he did. He didn't get to be as wealthy as he is by throwing his money around."

It may not have been loyalty on either side that reunited some of the foot soldiers in "Spector's Army," however. It may have been simple expediency. Keyboardist Mike Lang, a sometime Spector's Army stringer, believed he was the sole exception to the scale rule. "I would have to bring in $100,000 worth of custom-made synthesizers for string and voice sounds, so he told me he'd list me as the session leader to bump me up to double scale," Lang said. "But the reality is that with the others, he could pay scale because, frankly, a lot of them were no longer that busy, and they were probably happy to get session work again."

There was a typical Spector mob of twenty-three musicians for the June 20 session: Nino Tempo, Don Menza, and Jay Migliore on sax; Bob Findley on trumpet; Dick "Slyde" Hyde on trombone; Dan and Dave Kessel, Craig Stull, and John Kurnick on acoustic guitar; Steve Carnelli on electric guitar; Chuck Berghofer and Max Bennett on bass; Jim Keltner and David Kemper on drums; Lang, Randi, Mike Rubini, and Pete Jolly on keyboard; Julius Wechter, Gary Coleman, Terry Gibbs, Frank Capp, and Bobbye Hall on percussion.

Haskell, not used to working in a conglomeration of this sort, ran out of the masking tape he was using to bind the lead sheets for the musicians to turn through on their stands, leaving piles of loose paper all around, including Phil's set in the booth. Just as Jimmie was about to give the downbeat on the studio floor, Phil held up his stack of sheets and yelled through the open microphone, "Jimmie, Jack was on dope. What's your excuse?"

Jimmie didn't flinch, although his son, who was watching the session, took offense. "Look, you have to be prepared for cutting, sarcastic remarks from Phil," Haskell said. "I just went right on with what I was doing."

The session bore some classic Spector trademarks, including a coterie of cronies who crowded into the booth and liberally partook from the buffet table. These included some former heavies who had seen better days but still had cachet—Bob Dylan, Brian Wilson, Chris Isaak; one certifiable generic leech—Kato Kaelin, on loan from the O. J. Simpson trial; and one very intriguing old soldier who had definitely faded away—Ike Turner, whom Phil had once paid to stay away from his studio. Since then, Ike had lost Tina, his band, and his career, and he had done a stretch in a California state prison on drug-related charges. Phil, who had helped Ike get out of jail and aided him financially, had made Ike's rehabilitation into a cause, unmindful of the irony that the cleaned-up Ike was likely less fucked-up now than Phil was.

Fancying Ike and himself the same kind of serious outlaw, Phil puckishly announced during a break, "By the way, everyone, I want you to know Ike and I have something in common. We both wear"—he pulled open his jacket—"beepers!" It was a funny riff, most of all to Phil, who figured he could always get a laugh from his well-known gun charades.

For now, the gun remained out of sight, as did the bottles and cups of booze on the console. According to Haskell, "He looked great, and he was completely clearheaded. I'll tell you this, at the Beverly Hills Hotel he sounded like he'd been drinking, and there was a bottle of vodka in his limo. But in the studio, I saw none of that."

Like all Spector sessions, this one ran long, until around 2 A.M., to get tracks for two songs in the can, for which Céline laid down the vocals after the orchestra was dismissed. Although the songs were untitled on the sheets, a usual Spector custom, Larry Levine remembered one was called "Is This What I Get for Loving You," which Phil foresaw as a single release. Both tracks were cut with dispatch, with Haskell marveling that "we cut the rhythm section so fast, the guys told me it was the fastest they'd ever worked."

And yet Phil cut no corners. Working flawlessly in 60-track stereo, the old mono spatial image was re-created. As Levine put it, "You can split a sound into a thousand tracks, but the essential Wall of Sound process remains the same—it's a room of people playing live." The guitars and basses played identical chords in unison, forming the bottom. Lang's synthesizer put the top on, although Phil would add strings later. Levine rechanneled through overdubbing, clever miking and echo the old "slab." The Wall was there, just like that. "On the first playback, Phil knew he'd got it," Haskell said.

Phil was indeed satisfied. Three days later, there was another session at Ocean Way, with twenty-five musicians, and one more track was cut. Levine doesn't recall the tune, but according to the charts he kept from the sessions, Phil also cut an instrumental track for "River Deep—Mountain High" over a couple of sessions in June 1995 at Ocean Way. When Spector and Levine took all their tracks to the mixing phase, they hunkered down at a variety of studios. "We just bounced from one studio to another," Levine recalled. "Royal Tone, A&M, Studio 56, Mad Hatter. We just kept mixing and overdubbing, sometimes for hours with only one instrument—mainly Mike Lang's keyboards—and adding background voices no one would hear anyway. Phil wouldn't finish anything. He was never happy with that he got."

Neither, apparently was René Angélil and his Sony benefactors, who lived under Spector's thumb for all of two sessions before the inevitable split. Hastening their dissension was the unexpected complication that after they had made the devil's bargain with Spector, Dion's 1993 album *The Colour of My Love,* produced by soft pop meister David Foster, had become a runaway hit, selling twelve million copies. This meant that Angélil and Dion were no longer as desperate for a breakout project, as they already had it, nor as anxious to follow Spector so blindly. Acquiescing to his whims didn't seem as cool anymore, especially when he would keep her waiting for hours before getting to her vocals. To Dion, this seemed no more than a gratuitous show of who was boss, and she took it as disrespect.

Mike Lang observed that "Céline and her husband were from a different world. She's a very easy person to work with, a very nice woman, and they've worked successfully on huge projects without any problems. I think it just never occurred to them that Phil was going to do *everything* his way, with no input from them. And you could see that, basically, he was treating Céline like a Ronette, a tool at his disposal, and at some point they got tired of that. You could see where they'd say, 'I don't want to do this anymore; I'm not having a good time'—not having realized that *nobody* has a good time with Phil."

Jimmie Haskell confirmed how miserable Céline was. "We had booked a session at Ocean Way to add strings, but nothing got done because a Sony executive came in, and he and Phil were in the booth arguing. So while that went on, I went into a side room for coffee, and she was in there and she just looked lost. I think her husband had gone back to Canada on business, and she felt all alone and caught between these powerful men. I tried to commiserate with her because that's how everyone there felt about it.

"Eventually, a guy from Sony came into the room looking extremely frustrated and said, 'Mr. Haskell, we're having difficulties with Mr. Spector over who owns the tapes of these sessions. Can you help us?' That amazed me, that they thought I could do something. I told him, 'When it comes to business, Phil is his own man.' It's just hard to believe they didn't understand that from the beginning and that it would become a sticking point."

That day, Haskell believed, was for all purposes the end of the project. "It became a stalemate: Phil owned the tapes, but he didn't own the voice. And that's how it stood. The tragedy of it is that those songs were guaranteed hits. If they were released today, they'd be hits. And Phil legally could have released them; he still could. But he's afraid they'll fail and that he doesn't have the option of failing."

Which is why, despite the legal tangle, Phil didn't give up on somehow getting those tracks to his liking. He would, at his own pace, return to the studio for yet more mixing and dubbing. As late as March 1996—making it three years since he had made this his reclamation project—he was back at Ocean Way for two more dates identified as Céline Dion sessions on the Professional Musicians Local 47 contract sheets. Once again, Mike Lang was the session leader, but by then he had grown less enchanted with the product.

"He was still mixing the same tracks, but they didn't sound like they did when they were originally recorded, when I thought they had an amazing feel to them, really hit home," Lang said. "They put Céline in a different place—more raw, more basic. But as he kept on adding all of this stuff to make them sound like his old records, it got too much for my taste. On the playback, I was hearing too much ambience, not the feel of the band, which was submerged in that Wall.

"Keep in mind, these were not final mixes—I don't think he ever got to that. They were monitor playbacks. But I could see where he was going with it—all the echo, tape delay. It wasn't nineties music; it was sixties music."

Dion and Angélil apparently had no part in these renewed sessions, which involved cutting instrumental tracks. If they did, their input was ignored. But when word got out—possibly leaked by Phil's adjutants to the rock press—that Spector was in the studio working on a Céline Dion album, they were forced to address the rumors. Certainly, it seemed pertinent that these Spector sessions preceded, and threatened to step on, the release of another Dion album, *Falling into You*, which though co-produced by David Foster, fueled speculation that Phil had produced some of its tracks. Coincidentally, one of these was another version of "River Deep—Mountain High," fueling the rumors even more.

This silly distraction was the last thing Angélil needed as he went about pushing the album and quashing any notion of an alliance with Spector to *Entertainment Weekly*, although he did it with great care. In the March 29, 1996, issue of the magazine, rather than confront or insult Phil, he fibbed that Dion's recent European tour had prevented completion of tracks Spector had produced with her. More soft-pedaling came from Dion's Sony Canada A&R man, Vito Luprano, who said, "We all had our fingers crossed to the point of cutting off our circulation, because it could've been so magnificent. It was a great idea, but it didn't work out." Dion, for her part, waxed wide-eyed about Phil's sessions with "hundreds of people," including a sixty-piece orchestra, but also cut into the shank of the problem by noting, "We needed to get a record out. Phil wanted more time. He wanted two years."

The album's producers, Foster and Meat Loaf's piano player, Jim Steinman, added to the confusion about Phil's role in the album. Foster, who also produced the likes of Whitney Houston and Barbra Streisand, blistered him for "coming out saying" he'd "chosen" the album "for his comeback, as if the rest of us have nothing to do with it." Steinman ridiculed the Spector sessions as "turbulent" and a "pretty hilarious, nightmarish experience. They just had problems, I'll leave it at that. They ended up with nothing they could use."

Yet if either Foster or Steinman had been present at any of Phil's sessions, Lang, Haskell, and Levine don't remember it, and there's no trace of it on paper. Union contracts show that the two Spector gigs in March 1996 were followed by those paid for by Sony, with completely different musicians. Presumably, these were the Foster and Steinman sessions, though no producer of record is listed. Certainly, neither of them had been anywhere near the original 1994 Spector sessions, of which they seemed unaware. Clearly, then, *Falling into You* was solely the work of Foster and Steinman—including the new "River Deep— Mountain High" track—and the album obviously had been developed after Dion had become disenchanted with Spector.

Ignoring the fact that he had contributed to the confusion about his role in the album, Phil felt trashed by Foster and Steinman, of whom he knew little and cared less. When the *Entertainment Weekly* quotes were read to him by the magazine's fact-checkers, he responded with a three-page fax to the editors insisting that he was the one who had backed out of the Dion project. Taking pains to praise "the extraordinary talent of Ms. Céline Dion," he saved his fire for certain unnamed people— implicitly, Angélil, Foster, and the Sony crowd—whom he said "simply wanted to record 'hits' even if they were contrived or repugnant—or nothing more than Whitney Houston– and Mariah Carey–rejected soundalike songs. . . . It became apparent that the people around Ms. Dion were more interested in controlling the project, and the people who recorded her, than [in] making history."

He insisted that had he been able to complete his work, Céline might have landed "on the covers of both *Time* and *Newsweek*," à la the nascent Bruce Springsteen. He also twitted Sony further, blustering that since he owned the original masters, "should you wish to hear the amazing and historic recordings I made with Ms. Dion, have no fear, because you will. I am presently finishing them up, and since I paid for them, and own them, I am planning to release them on my label, for the entire world to hear, and compare to her current recordings, or whatever you call those things they've released."

With the most relish of all, he slagged "amateurs, students, and bad clones of yours truly"—implicitly, Foster and Steinman—then administered the ultimate smackdown: "The one thing they should have learned a long time ago, you don't tell Shakespeare what plays to write, or how to write them. You don't tell Mozart what operas to write, or how to write them. And you certainly don't tell Phil Spector what songs to write, or how to write them, or what records to produce, or how to produce them."

Given a chance to respond by the magazine, Steinman, a Spector devotee who with Meat Loaf had turned *Bat Out of Hell* into a Wall of

Sound tribute, issued a semi-facetious surrender: "I'm thrilled to be insulted by Phil Spector. He's my God, my idol. To be insulted by Phil Spector is a big honor. If he spits on me I consider myself purified."

Although Phil must have loved being able to turn reality upside down with his condemnation of Dion's people as too controlling, he probably knew he'd never make good on his threat to release his tapes, though even Dion agreed that the songs she'd made for Phil were "incredible" and "just unbelievable." For one thing, he lost his leverage when *Falling into You* went on to win Grammys for best album and pop album of the year. Anything of his would now have an impossibly high bar to clear—that is, if he could actually put anything out. Unsaid but obvious as well was the certainty that Sony would sue to keep a competing product off the shelves.

Just as significant was Phil's fear that the songs might fall short as a comeback masterwork and draw inevitable critical fire. So the tapes sat in his vault, under lock and key, along with master tapes by Leonard Cohen, the Ramones, and God knows who else, to be unheard by human ears maybe forever. Even so, the tapes, which had always served a symbolic purpose, did so now by reifying his now hazy legend. As long as he had them, he could pretend they were hidden gold, a mere unlocking away from changing the world yet again. It was another one of those small victories that for him, and only for him, meant everything.

Given the gross imbalance between past and present achievement, he had done astoundingly well living off royalties from his sixties hits. The truly astonishing part wasn't the amount of his wealth as much as the oh-lucky-man knack he had for supplementing it. To be sure, he was a millionaire many times over, though not, as he wanted people to believe, in the same category as Quincy Jones or Lou Adler, fraternally rooted producers who unlike Phil had aped the Donnie Kirshner formula and crossed the border into movies and television. But neither did Jones or Adler ever win a cool million on a boxing match, as had Phil with Ali-Foreman. Nor were they able to live for years in a Beverly Hills mansion at a flophouse rent by pestering its owners into compliance. Or to command $6 million for selling the rights to one song in their purview, such as Phil did when he leased "Be My Baby" to the producers of *Dirty Dancing*, as well as that and other Ronettes hits for use in Levi's and American Express commercials.

Quincy Jones may have had an east wing full of Grammys, Emmys, and Oscars, but only Phil could play stickup with every bit and piece of his legacy. What's more, he used this implicit embargo not just for profit but for revenge. For example, he reeled when he heard Ronnie Spector's excerpted "be my little baby" riff in Eddie Money's "Take Me Home Tonight," for which she and Money needed no permission, since it was merely a few bars from a song and thus not copyright protected. However, when she began a nightclub act to cash in on the short-lived Ronnie redux in the late eighties, Phil's lawyers gave her and her pseudo-Spector husband, Jonathan Greenfield, notice enjoining her from performing any Ronettes song in anything but medley form. That pretty much killed the act.

At the same time, pointedly, he allowed the Righteous Brothers full license to their Wall of Sound hits at their oldies concert gigs, and he allowed all of his tunes co-written with Ellie Greenwich to be used in her kitschy musical *Leader of the Pack* (featuring Paul Shaffer for a time in an affectionately twitting Spector role, with the name changed to Gus to avoid offending Phil). He also didn't make trouble for Darlene Love when she reprised her Bob B. Soxx and solo hits, as well as, endlessly, "Christmas (Baby Please Come Home)," a song that had become fused into the fiber of the season as much as any ever recorded.

All this was, of course, a clear message to his onetime leading lady and now perpetual victim: this wasn't business; it was strictly personal.

The Ronettes were not content to go through life as Spector's doormat. In 1988, they tried to fight him on his own turf—in the court room—by joining a long roster of fifties and sixties singing groups who were filing retroactive lawsuits against music industry heavies for getting fat on their old songs. Most of these suits were initiated in the eighties by the Artists Rights Enforcement Corporation, headed by former music agent Chuck Rubin, which would win a huge victory when an appeals court in Nashville ruled in 1994 against two recording companies for stiffing a number of groups, including the Shirelles, out of a combined $1.2 million. Three years later, Darlene Love would beat Phil in such a case, but only for a pittance, when she was awarded a $268,555 judgment against him dating back to 1987. The amount she received was limited by the statute of limitations, which prevented her from going back farther in time. Given that restriction, the priority of the Rubin group wasn't the original record royalties but instead latter-day commercial uses of those oldies but goodies, which typically paid a 50 percent royalty.

Nonetheless, the Ronettes shot for the moon in their suit, asking no less than $12 million for breach of contract, purloined royalties from unauthorized use of their work, and, gilding the lily in a way certain to tie Phil up in knots, possession of all their master tapes. In question here were both forms of licensing fees extant in recording industry contracts. One was mechanical rights—found in the "universal use" or "compulsory mechanical rule" clauses—dealing with in-store sales and number of radio plays based on a set contractual royalty rate. The other was synchronization rights, covering re-recording or in-person performances of old songs (which Phil had legally enjoined Ronnie from doing), as well as resale of the songs for commercial use—the kind of use that pays off at rates up to 50 percent.

This was a serious challenge to Phil's pride, hegemony, and fortune, and he girded for yet another royal rumble in court with his favorite mascara-caked foil.

When the case began in a New York district court, his first move was to claim, with the famous Spector chutzpah, that there'd never been a written Ronettes contract, and thus he owed them not a cent beyond his generous charity. During the trial, however, the Ronettes produced a contract dated 1963. (Not by coincidence, a similar contract for Darlene Love had turned up in her case against Spector after Phil had denied that any existed.) Still, Spector claimed that the Ronettes' demands were moot because Ronnie had personally signed over all rights to the group's records in their 1974 divorce—in effect, releasing him from future claims and lawsuits. The case would drag on for thirteen years, as lawyers on both sides did a minuet, filing papers and asking for postponements.

At the same time, Phil assumed the role of plaintiff in making the same claim of onerous behavior against a record company in London. In early 1997, he filed suit to get the British publishing rights to "To Know Him Is to Love Him" away from Bourne Music, which had purchased the song's British copyright from its original license holder. Intriguingly, the original copyright holder was Warman Music, a company owned for years by the anti-Spector polka bandleader Lawrence Welk. Warman had sold the copyright to Bourne in 1986. Now the copyright, having expired after 10 years, should have reverted to him as the song's composer. But Bourne balked, on the highly technical grounds that Phil hadn't given them six months' notice that he was taking the copyright back. In May 1997, a judge ruled that the copyright was his—a signal victory for American artists whose songs had been tied up for years by British publishing houses. Phil was given his due; *Billboard*'s story of the ruling was headlined SPECTOR CASE PROVIDES CRUCIAL PRECEDENT.

The trial also provided an opportunity for a homecoming party of sorts in England, where he was still treasured far more than he was at home. Each day outside the courthouse he was mobbed by the British media, just like in the old days, though not without some typical English sniping in the newspapers.

"Press photographers crowded around the small, cadaverous 56-year-old [Spector]," wrote Jonathan Glancey in the *Independent* of one such mobbing. "Passing Spice Girl and Oasis fans would have wondered what the fuss was about."

Not that he was about to be pushed into the rock-and-roll old-age home by any latter-day act, least of all the Spice Girls. In fact, in the late nineties, when Christian conservatives skewered the jiggly group, saying that watching them perform was, like watching a pornographic film, Spector had chimed in, brightly and memorably. Seeming to defend them, he began, "There's a big difference." Then came the punch line: "A porno movie has better music."

Because Phil was assumed to have a vast cult following, it seemed obligatory that someone would make a movie of his life. For years, treatments and scripts had regularly arrived over Hollywood studio transoms, including one by screenwriter Jerico Stone (*My Stepmother Is an Alien* and *Matinee*). All faced the same obstacle: Phil's lack of commitment, meaning, in practical terms, his permission to use songs for a soundtrack, an essential element of any Spector biopic. Knowing that he held the power to actualize a movie that portrayed him the way he wanted or thwart one that didn't, he merely sat back and played the field.

The closest any project came was when the first edition of this book was optioned in 1990 by a Washington, D.C., production company called Powerhouse Entertainment. While the book itself was, and still is, unauthorized, and provoked Spector's quickly dispensed libel suit, the producers tried to curry his favor by offering him script approval, with the proviso that the movie would not be a whitewash. As Phil, through intermediaries, toyed with the notion of sub rosa cooperation on a movie homage he clearly wanted to be made, the project went into preproduction. Haskell Wexler was hired as cinematographer, directors were interviewed, and casting was begun. Then, mercurial as ever, Phil issued another of his habitual threats to sue if the production went ahead. With no chance at securing the songs, the project died right there.

Phil did make it to the screen (sort of) in 1993, when actor Rob LaBelle portrayed the 1966 vintage Spector briefly and unremarkably in the Tina Turner biopic *What's Love Got to Do with It*. Unlike Paul Shaffer's itchy, weasely, and volatile Phil—that is, the *real* Phil—LaBelle's Phil was a serene, near-silent, sunglasses-wrapped, *tall* sphinx lost in genius thoughts. Evidently, this was how Phil saw himself, or wanted to be, and the wildly inaccurate image was delivered, perhaps in appreciation for his granting the producers rights to the "River Deep—Mountain High" master tapes. The flick, which was a runaway hit and garnered two Oscar nominations, allowed him to take a bow, justifiably, since it might not have gotten made without his forbearance.

If that wasn't enough of an ego rub, by the mid-nineties some heavyweights were wooing him to relent on a Spector biopic. British rock journalist Roy Carr, who had some degree of access to Phil, was recruited as a conduit for no less than Al Pacino, who had become interested in the role, regarding himself as the perfect Spector analogue given his snubbed stature and ease in playing psychotic characters. Carr flew to Pasadena and spent some time at Phil's house trying to hammer out a treatment, but he got nowhere. The one tangible outcome of the trip, Carr recalled, was Phil's giving him "a very fancy and beautifully engraved Magnum .44 pistol" and memories of Phil "shooting trees in his garden."

Next up in the Spector movie derby was the A-list team of Tom Cruise and rock writer turned director Cameron Crowe, fresh off their *Jerry Maguire* collaboration. The pint-size actor took his interest directly to Phil in 1997, hanging out with him at Spector's house and studying his moves. Soon Cruise was talking and looking just like the real item, scaring small children and dogs. This must have flattered Phil to no end, but once more the project came to nothing, possibly because Phil was scarier playing himself. The official postmortem from Marvin Mitchelson in the Spector camp was that "Phil wasn't all that pleased with what Tom and Cameron had done." Thereafter, Spector and Mitchelson tried to forge ahead on their own. All they needed, Mitchelson said, was a happy ending.

22

*Phil Spector has definitely got an extremely high opinion of himself,
which he deserves, obviously. But there are a lot of people I admire just
as much, like Bruce Springsteen or Michael Stipe, who . . . are still quite
humble. And that's what we wanted to do on this album, to record like
Springsteen did with the E Street Band. You listen back to those records
and you think 'Fucking hell! They were having a good time there, really
enjoying themselves.' And we just couldn't have done that with Phil
Spector.*

—JAMES WALSH, lead vocalist, Starsailor

More and more now, Phil shed his cadaverous shroud and skipped down
the cobblestones. When Nino Tempo cut a jazz CD for Atlantic Records
and did a gig supporting it in a Sunset Strip club with Mike Lang and
several other session cats, Phil came to see them and later indulged in
happily riotous conversation with the band and Ahmet Ertegun. All he
needed was a Nehru jacket, and it could have been 1965 all over again.

On June 10, 1997, when he was inducted into the Songwriters Hall of Fame and feted with Joni Mitchell and three others in the Imperial Ballroom of the Sheraton New York Hotel, it was as if he had just come in from the borscht belt. Giving his speech, looking fit and neatly tucked into a black tux with a déclassé "Back to Mono" pin, he was everything he had wanted to be at his Rock and Roll Hall of Fame induction. The one-liners came fast and furious.

"They told me to keep it short, which is what I've been all my life."

"Why does New York call an opera house the Metropolitan and a prison Sing Sing?"

"Some of you have weird interpretations of me. I can only tell you, in a world where carpenters get resurrected, you get me."

Twitting his own ego with hyperbole only he could get away with, he explained his "artistry and rage" by comparing it favorably with the bloodcurdling Borgia dynasty, since he, too, had sparked a renaissance after all. He even lightened up about death, saying that his daughter, Nicole, who attended the ceremony with him, "can't wait for me to pass on so she can get all the money and copyrights."

"When I get inducted anywhere," he closed, "you always think, 'Obituary.' This will look good in the obituary."

The *New York Times* article about the event, headlined HONORING FAMOUS AND INFAMOUS AT THE HALL OF FAME—with Phil qualifying on both counts—led with writer Jon Pareles reprising Spector's habit of "waving a gun in the studio" but segued to describing his "jovial" performance. It also ran with a shot of Phil beaming on stage in his shades as he held the award aloft, a retrocool cat with not a care.

Two years later, back at the Rock and Roll Hall of Fame dinner, he was still mewling. Indeed, Phil's thirty-seventh-floor suite at the Waldorf Towers was *the* place to be. The gala he hosted there drew the cream of the industry crowd, interrupted only temporarily by the ceremony in the ballroom downstairs.

It was, as the rock archivist Michael Ochs mirthfully called it, "the Phil Spector Fuck You–Fuck You–Fuck You Party," as Phil greeted each guest with that mandatory rock term of endearment, which always seemed to roll off his tongue and could turn in a second from clubbily collegial to gratuitously cruel. That would normally happen after he'd drained glass after glass of anything hard and straight up. After doing so on this occasion, he was urinating in the john when he was met by the son of the epochal disk jockey Alan Freed, who had been enshrined posthumously that night. The son was a huge Spector fan but said something that caused Phil to snap, "You're an asshole!" then storm out, leaving the startled Freed red-faced and speechless.

For the most part, though, the vibe was swingin', man, as Phil made the rounds, described by the veteran rock journalist Al Aronowitz as "mischievous and elfin" and "looking for all the world like Jiminy Cricket in a white suit, with a red AIDS bow on his left lapel." He was accompanied by a new bodyguard, a beefy ex–Los Angeles Police Department detective sergeant named Jay Romaine, who spent most of his time lighting Phil's cigarettes and shielding him from the hard-charging, unwanted advances of industry-related women with whom he had apparently consorted in the past.

One such woman, nearly falling-down drunk and crammed into a low-cut black dress, began ranting to no one in particular, "I'm gonna blow them all up!" and "You have to fuck every time you want to get ahead!" Phil hardly blinked, safely screened as usual, this time perhaps from the consequences of a promise made in the heat of a moment long since forgotten.

He was even able to handle with grace an awkward scenario when, getting into an elevator downstairs, he suddenly found himself eye to chin with an exiting Paul McCartney, who was being inducted that night for his solo career. The two lions of the sixties hadn't spoken in a good thirty years, and unlike when Phil had run into Mick Jagger a decade before at this event, there was no reserve of old kinship here. For an uneasy minute, they stood rooted, the wounds of the ancient Beatles–Allen Klein–Spector fissure still unhealed, eyeing each other warily, wondering what to do or say. Sir Paul made the first move, showily throwing his arms around his old enemy—"a music business hug," as Aronowitz perfectly described the obviously strained and empty gesture—and nearly knocking Phil off his platform shoes. Both of them went along with the charade—locked in the dance, exchanging some fleeting pleasantries—until, with great relief, they moved quickly back to their own orbits.

Later, for his guests upstairs, Phil performed a mocking re-creation of the interlude, oozing in a dead-on imitation of McCartney's Scouse dialect, *"Ow ya been? It's been a long time, y'know. I looooove ya!"*

Then, returning to own voice, the kicker: *"Love* me? He hates my fucking guts!"

Left unsaid: If only I could've told him how much I hate *his* fuck-ing guts!

By 1998, Spector decided that he needed to fortify his status as a cap-tain and king of the industry by transplanting himself to an appropriate "castle," a palatial aerie fit for a king. The common, nonregal splendor of his confinement in Pasadena, he confessed, had never made it for him. Writing in a bylined compilation of existentialist musings in the "What I've Learned" section of the September 1999 issue of *Esquire*, he explained, "I decided to move out of my other place, the Tarantula Arms, where I had a nice furnished web. It was located in Pasadena. . . . If I owned both hell and Pasadena, I'd sell Pasadena."

Having commissioned high-end real estate agents to bird-dog new digs that would allow him to live high at a low price, he wound up with the ultimate handyman special: an early Spanish manse at 1700 S. Grandview Drive in Alhambra, with ten bedrooms and eight baths, minareted archways, and three sprawling, pine-forested acres encircled by a steel death match cage—or at least that's what the wrought-iron palisades on six-foot white stucco walls seemed to resemble.

This was the pretentiously dubbed Pyrenes Castle, built in 1926 when the neighborhood had been an upscale bedroom community for high rollers of the silent film industry. At one time, the place had been an ornately appointed hotel. Now it seemed to be the only such estate left intact, looking down on rows of unassuming homes in a now mainly middle-class, predominantly Mexican area. For Spector, Alhambra offered what its ancient namesake city in Spain had to the Moorish kings who built their manors and moats there. It was the perfect fortress for the man who had everything, including high-tension wires and Keep Out signs for the gates and yards of tarpaulin for the windows.

Inside the front gate, a concrete stairwell climbed eighty-eight steps to the front door, winding through an obstacle course of trees and thick brush. Phil would make this route a mandatory excursion for visi-tors, who would have to ascend it on foot, often in the dark, instead of being permitted the ease of driving up the horseshoe driveway that led to the back door. By doing this, he let them know what a royal pain in the ass he was, and how in control.

Phil felt that he was finally "home" here, insulated from any ple-beian staining. As he noted in his *Esquire* piece, "I've bought myself a beautiful and enchanting castle in a hick town where there is no place to go that you shouldn't go."

Despite his new public image as an upstanding elder of rock, however, Phil's psychotic and misogynistic tendencies had not abated. That very winter, when Phil was brought by a friend to a Christmas party in Bel Air, for no apparent reason he began flicking ashes from his cigar onto the host's golden retriever. When the owner's girlfriend, Deborah Strand, told him to leave the dog alone, Phil whipped out a gun and pressed it against her cheek. "How does this make you feel, bitch?" he hissed, doing his tough-guy bit.

While partygoers silently stood and stared, Spector put the gun away, then Jay Romaine grabbed him and ushered him firmly out of the house. Neither Strand nor anyone else notified the police. Strand was told that the lunatic with the gun was a powerful music industry figure and calling the police might make trouble for the mutual friend who had brought him. (The friend's father was the president of Warner Brothers Records.)*

To Phil, such incidents probably seemed magnificently trivial. Much more important now was the Phil Spector royal train, which made stops to let him show his face at the Rock and Roll Hall of Fame and other industry backslapping exercises, as well as backstage at Springsteen, Stones, and U2 concerts. He also made it back into the studio, this time to satisfy a hankering to cut some country tracks. According to Larry Levine, who again was at the engineering board, "He brought some musicians in from Nashville, and he was really excited by it."

The session was held in mid-1999 at Studio One on Santa Monica Boulevard. But the real news was that the gig served as a rapprochement between Phil and Jack Nitzsche. That happened when Phil said what the hell and called his old right-hand man to ask him to arrange the charts. For Phil, it was little more than a mercy hire, as Nitzsche had nearly died of a stroke the year before and needed work and validation. Distant now were the skills and the ear that had won him an Oscar for "Up Where We Belong," stoked his movie scores for films such as $9\frac{1}{2}$

* Cases cited in Motion to Admit Evidence of Other Crimes filed by the District Attorney's Office in Los Angeles Supreme Court on February 17, 2005. Dept. 106, Case No. BA255233, page 25.

Weeks and *Stand by Me,* and production work for Mink DeVille and Graham Parker. His last important work had been scoring the otherwise forgettable 1990 Dennis Hopper film *The Hot Spot,* on which he collaborated with John Lee Hooker and Miles Davis. In recent years, the only time many had seen Nitzsche was when he popped up on an episode of "Cops" after being arrested in Hollywood for waving a gun at some teenagers who stole his hat.

In addition to his poor health, Nitzsche apparently was still blitzed on coke and booze when he came in for the Spector session. As Levine put it, "Jack was out of his skull. He was loaded up and he got the charts all wrong, and Phil couldn't fix them. We had all these people in the studio, and it was a very small studio, so everyone was on edge waiting around. Phil was really pissed off at Jack, too, because the session never got off the ground. It was a total waste of everybody's time.

"I just remember feeling very sad seeing Jack like that. As bad as Phil got sometimes, he never got fucked-up like that."

Within a year and a half, on August 25, 2000, a withered Nitzsche suffered cardiac arrest brought on by a bronchial infection and died. He was sixty-three. The funeral at Hollywood Forever Cemetery was a mass unburdening of guilt by the music crowd, which showed up in force to mourn a man whom they'd stood by and watched destroy himself.

As Nitzsche's top banana and model of errant behavior, Phil may have had the most to rue. But he reckoned he'd paid his debt with the Studio One session and promptly agreed to deliver the eulogy. After a service conducted by the bass player Jim Bond, Spector stood beside a casket draped in roses (bought by the hundreds by Neil Young) and began quoting from the lyrics of "To Know Him Is to Love Him,"—linking, implicitly at least, Nitzsche's lost soul with that of Benjamin Spector's. In so doing, Phil, for the first and perhaps only time, exposed that core of his own soul hardened and inspired by Ben's suicide. The familiar elegiac tone of the song and the high emotional investment that gave it life brought many in the crowd to tears.

His newfound stand-up skills lifting the veil of grief, Phil went on to tell of a long-ago session at Gold Star. The session had run two days, and when Nitzsche finally went out to the parking lot to go home, the shoeshine guy who used to hang out there had sold his car. Phil concluded the eulogy by generously crediting Nitzsche with altering the course of music every bit as much as he had. Afterward, he stayed around, greeting admirers right next to Nitzsche's son Jack Jr., as if he had earned a place in the Nitzsche family. All who heard him on that day spoke with wonder of his touching and amusing descant.

Indeed, he was getting quite good at this sort of thing, the toastmaster general of rock award shows, banquets, and funerals. Not that he was any less unfeeling toward those whom he'd ceased to recognize existed. For example, still peeved that George Brand, his underpaid bodyguard and houseman, had walked on him, Phil injected himself into a legal tangle over a vintage sports car he had bought used then sold to Brand for $1,000 in 1964 after nearly wrecking it in numerous traffic accidents. Brand had restored the car—a Cobra Daytona Coupe, one of only six built by racing legend Carroll Shelby—and his daughter had kept it in storage for thirty years. After she committed suicide in 2000, Brand sold the car for $3 million, and it was later resold for $4 million.

The sale sparked a lawsuit by a friend of Brand's daughter, who claimed that she'd given the car to him. When Phil saw the story in the paper, he jumped into the fray. Maintaining that the car had been his all along, he sued for the car or the $4 million. This comically clumsy attempt to stick it to Brand was quickly dismissed in courts, but not before an unenviable but priceless try by Spector's latest big-shot lawyer, Robert Shapiro of O. J. Simpson infamy, to explain with a straight face Phil's contention that he hadn't known the car was missing for thirty years.

"This isn't a man who gets in his car every morning and checks his oil pressure and drives it to work," Shapiro intoned. "He is the most prolific producer in the history of music, and he's extremely focused on his work. He delegates most of these things to other people."

To anyone cognizant of Phil's firm grip on all aspects of his financial interests, that thesis was worth $4 million in laughs alone.

Then there was Marshall Lieb, whom Phil had ignored since the breakup of the Teddy Bears, except for their fleeting contact at that forlorn high school reunion in 1987. Lieb had had a mildly successful career in the seventies and eighties scoring motion pictures and had become a major organizer of classic automobile shows in Southern California. On March 15, 1999, he was en route to a car show in Northridge when he had a massive heart attack and died before help could reach him. He was fifty-nine. Phil, who'd acted as if he didn't know Marshall was still alive, now acted as though he didn't know he was dead, passing up the funeral at Hillside Memorial Park in Culver City.

Still, in the solipsistic sphere of Phil Spector, he was on a roll, with the new millennium delivering a climactic confirmation: the National Academy of Recording Arts and Sciences dropped its ancient grudge against him and announced that he would be getting his long overdue Grammy—the Trustees Award for "outstanding contributions to the recording industry in a non-performing capacity," which had previously been bestowed on the likes of George Martin, Count Basie, and George and Ira Gershwin.

Apparently, this wasn't good enough for Phil. Still embittered by decades of expatriation by the Grammys, he wasn't mollified by an award that was more sop than genuine tribute. Spector was upset by several things. First, he thought he should be getting a Lifetime Achievement Award (which was being given to Harry Belafonte, Woody Guthrie, John Lee Hooker, Mitch Miller, and Willie Nelson). Second, he was pissed that he would have to share the award with Clive Davis. And finally, there was the matter of his not being allowed to speak on the nationally televised show. A brief compilation of video clips would have to suffice. This was, after all, Phil Spector, who had acceded to being shut up in public only once, as the inside joke of his cameo role in *Easy Rider*, and he had no intention of letting the Grammy crowd, which he still detested, zip his lip.

When the February 22 ceremonies rolled around, he was nowhere to be found. His award was given in absentia. And while the focus of those festivities was the sarong not quite worn by Jennifer Lopez, Phil succeeded in getting more useful attention for his no-show stunt than for being honored—something he may have prefigured. At *E! Online*, a series of "Best and Worst" of the Grammys had at the top of the page an item headlined WILL HE OR WON'T HE? which read: "Nope, he won't. The reclusive Phil Spector was the only recipient not to make any kind of appearance accepting his Trustee Award." The old recluse label still had its benefits, especially when the opportunity to reprise it played to his ego.

If his snub of the Grammys was calculated, it may explain why he had brushed off his estranged son Gary, who had planned to come to L.A. to watch him accept the Grammy. Now living in Colorado, Gary had called Phil hours before he was to catch a Greyhound bus, asking if Phil could get him into the auditorium, that it would mean the world to him to share that glorious moment. Phil was unmoved; he told Gary to stay away, calling it a "personal" moment for him and him alone. If Phil

⊙   340

knew at that point that he was going to stand up the show, this may have been the most "Phil-like" way of dealing with the request.

So now he had passed another milestone. When the Trustees Award arrived by mail, he had all the hardware a rock elder could want. Now if only he had a life.

Clues about where Phil Spector was, and what he was, could be gleaned from his streaming wit and wisdom in *Esquire*. His misanthropic "What I've Learned" tract careened from strained aphoristic drollery—"Most people should be obscene and not heard"; "If you talk to God, you're praying. If God talks back, it's schizophrenia"; "If the average man is made in God's image, then Mozart was plainly superior to God"—to topical riffs showing he'd been paying attention to the outside world—"I wonder how Michael Jackson started out as a black man and ended up a white girl"; "The main problem with the Christian Right is that it is neither." As an impeachment antiphon, he wrote that the "bloated, sexist, prissy, pompous, unsmiling, and unthinking accuser and huge bantam cock of a man, Henry Hyde," proved "it is far better to keep your mouth shut and let everyone think you're stupid than to open it and leave no doubt." (Hyde headed the House of Representatives committee that recommended the impeachment of President Bill Clinton in 1998.)

The sharpest barbs, though, were aimed at his own pathological defects. To wit:*

"I am dysfunctional by choice, and I love my attitude problem."

"I am constantly trapped in my own freedom, environment and heredity."

"I prefer life on the outskirts of hell, located east of a rock and west of a hard place."

"Today I find my life in a gloomy region, where the year is divided into one day and one night and lies entirely outside the stream of history. . . . However, I guess my life is better than that of a poor, thin, spasmodic, hectic, shrill and pallid being."

*Phil Spector, "What I've Learned," *Esquire*, September 1999.

"Since I'm one of those people who are not happy unless they are not happy, it's comforting to know that mental health doesn't always mean being happy. If it did, nobody would qualify."

The most intriguing sentence of the article, for those who really cared about the author, was in the accompanying text, which told of Spector being "currently at work on a number of projects—he won't say which ones—for Atlantic Records." If that was so, they never reached the critical mass of a studio session. Indeed, his only real music business activity at the time was in a purely passive role—as the defendant in the amaranthine back-royalty lawsuit by the Ronettes, which finally reached a conclusion in 2000.

By then, the trial judge apparently had heard enough to be less than pleased with Phil's lack of candor about the Ronettes' 1963 contract and on June 22 came down hard on him, ruling that his sale of Ronettes songs constituted "non-contractual exploitation." Worse for Phil, this ruling applied to both the mechanical rights on record sales and the synchronization rights covering those million-dollar commercials paying royalty rates up to 50 percent. All told, the judge placed back royalties and damages at a hefty $2,971,272.96 dating back to 1981, the statute of limitations cutoff point.

Although Phil should have been relieved that the judge didn't grant the trio's demand for the original master recordings—which would have tripped his nuclear wire—the judgment figuratively kicked him in the nuts. Wasting no time, he took the case to an appellate court, which on December 17 unanimously dismissed his arguments, calling them "unavailing" and the judgment "proper."

Phil now appeared to be dead meat, driving a delirious Ronnie to some uncharacteristic trash-talking. As if believing his hold on her was finally lifted, she giddily pronounced the case "practically over, and so is he."

In fact, Phil had only one thin reed left to cling to: reappealing in the appellate court, since the first appeal had been dismissed without prejudice. It was surely a long-odds proposition, but this time his arguments found some traction—and he was bailed out by the very contract he'd denied existed. On October 21, 2001, another five-judge panel overruled the lower court on the premise that the contract was in fact binding and that the Ronettes had no dibs on the lucrative synchronization rights, although they were entitled to back royalties for the mechanical rights, which the panel sent back to the lower court to figure out. At a 3 percent royalty rate, Phil knew that the figure would be a fraction of the original $2.9 million. Ronnie would also be able to claim money Phil had withheld from her on the grounds that she'd given up her rights to future royalties in their 1974 divorce settlement, which the judges found specious.

It wasn't total victory, but close enough for Phil to assume the role of justice's avenging angel as he stood on the courthouse steps and let his lawyer, Andrew Bart, floridly praise the court for "sending a clear signal that we're a system of law."

As poor Ronnie had said, it was indeed over, and so was she. The headline in one of the New York papers after the decision was RONETTES VS. SPECTOR: PHIL WINS. But for all it mattered, it was really "Ronette," in the singular, because for Veronica Yvette Bennett, there was no way out of that recurring drama.

That said, Phil, too, had been lacerated by his marriage to Ronnie, leaving him immune to one of his own creeds, as stated in his dolorous *Esquire* article: "The dread of loneliness is greater than the fear of bondage, so we get married." Incredibly, in his own delusions, it was *he* who had been held in bondage by that union, and he'd be damned if he'd ever do *that* again. But if his victories over her were tangible, in matters of the heart, he was a perpetual loser.

As a consequence, he lurked in the shadowy middle ground between his polar ends of loneliness and marriage. It was enough, apparently, to be not quite lonely, not quite married. What that amounted to, at least since his relationship with Janice had ended, was a conveyor belt of one-nighters with (sometimes very) bad endings. Now, elder statesman that he was, he figured he was up to giving a real relationship a go. Toward that end, in mid-2000 he began a liaison with Nancy Sinatra, Frank's famous, vivacious daughter. They'd known each other since the sixties, when she'd had a brief but glorious career with "These Boots Are Made for Walkin'," "Sugar Town," and a duet with her father called "Somethin' Stupid." Her musical roots also crossed with Phil's. The producer of most of her work had been Lee Hazelwood, whose studio wizardry with Duane Eddy had so influenced Phil and who was one of the first industry heavies Phil had pissed off.

Sinatra was a different bird as Spector women went: bright, snappy, tough, six months older than he but still hot enough to have posed nude in *Playboy* in 1995, and rich. All in all, a "kick-ass broad," as he said, admiringly. She'd call him on his bullshit, with a knowing laugh that disarmed him. But she also knew how to boost his ego. Phil had idolized Frank as the paragon of cool, and if he was never quite able to fake that quality himself, it was a kick when Nancy would tell people, "He's very much like my father."

Moreover, her status as a professional daughter was a boon to the royalty theme he craved for his own life. They seemed perfect for each other, the pre–baby boomer power couple, bedecked in jewels, big cars (Phil's latest acquisition was a white Rolls-Royce with the license PHIL-500), and history. And with Nancy dragging him out of his dungeon, they made the scene at all the right Hollywood parties and restaurants, with one newspaper noting that they were "arm in arm at the 30th anniversary of the Los Angeles jazz club The Big Potato. . . . Friends say the couple have [*sic*] been together for a while and appear to be extremely happy." Clearly, Phil liked the novelty of bending to a woman as strong and controlling as he was. Things were going well, even with Nancy getting static from the extended Sinatra clan, who constantly told her that getting involved with a man with Spector's past abuses was stupid.

Stupider still, Phil couldn't handle the good thing he had going. Although there may have been other reasons for their breakup, the suspicion was that Spector's jealousy—not of another man, but of another producer, after Nancy made good on a long-held aim of cutting her first album in three decades—did them in. It surprised no one that Nancy reunited with Lee Hazelwood for the project and went off to cut the album with him in Nashville—no one, that is, except Phil, who may have assumed that she would want to utilize his expertise, if not using him outright as producer. Acquaintances of Phil's insist this was not the case and that he actually lent valuable counsel to the album—knowing all along that he had no business stepping on Hazelwood's primacy with Nancy and that given his thorny history with Phil, the hoary producer's head might have exploded if he saw Spector in the studio again. It indeed seems plausible that Phil had some effect. When the album, *Nancy Sinatra,* was released in September 2004 to excellent reviews, much of the content recalled the lush Spector sound applied to songs penned by Bono, Steve Van Zandt, Jarvis Cocker, and others.

⊙

Whatever the circumstances, long before the album was out, so was Phil, who by early 2002 had a music project of his own in the works, and probably had had enough of the "royalty romance" theme. And so he let his boots do some walking all over her, in the process removing an important ballast and once more leaving himself aimless in matters of the heart. After ending the relationship, he acted as if it hadn't been a very meaningful one, despite what everyone assumed, later calling her "a waste of fucking time."

Perhaps Nancy's response appeared on her album. One of the tracks was a Jarvis Cocker song with the title—"Don't Let Him Waste Your Time."

Boorishness aside, there were times when Spector seemed to have grown sentimental in his old age. When Joey Ramone died of lymphatic cancer on April 15, 2001, at age forty-nine, Phil felt immense grief and the requisite guilt about outliving yet another restless rock soul. They were dropping like flies, it seemed, and although Phil hadn't seen Joey since the hellacious *End of the Century* sessions, Joey had always cut him slack for his behavior, leaving Johnny and Dee Dee Ramone to sling the hatchet. The latter two, Phil believed, were no more than rock-and-roll chaff, a verdict few challenged when Johnny woofed "God bless President Bush" at the band's 2002 Rock and Roll Hall of Fame induction and Dee Dee tried an embarrassing stint as a rap artist.

When Dee Dee and Johnny died within two years of each other, in 2002 and 2004, Dee Dee as a result of a hardly unexpected heroin overdose, Phil made no public comment. Joey's death, however, moved him to write an emotional, epitaphic open letter to the lead Ramone that appeared two days later on rock photographer Bob Gruen's Web site. The letter read, in part, "It is not often in a lifetime that one meets such a beautiful and free Spirit, as you, who so loved life and music; and who did things in his own life, and his own way. And who, when we were working together, taught me that it is only with the heart that one can see rightly. . . . I shall be sustained by your gifts Joey. And even though I am crying for you, I know if the eyes had no tears, the soul would have no rainbow." He even broached his own personal loss, writing, "I would be remiss if I did not mention to you that my little boy Phillip Jr. is up there waiting for you. So look for him, Joey. And you'll know him right away. Just look and listen for the loudest little angel and that's him. I know the two of you will take good care of each other." He concluded by paraphrasing Antoine de Saint-Exupéry: "In one of the stars you shall be living. In one of them you shall be laughing. And so it will be as if all the stars were laughing when I look at the sky at night." He signed the letter, "Your devoted and loving friend, Phil Spector."

If this was a tad much for what had been a fleeting and bumpy relationship, it probably could be explained by Phil's contemplating his mortality and all that he had lost of human value along the way. And if three of those things were all three of his sons, he could at least salvage one child who hadn't gotten away—his daughter, Nicole, who turned twenty in 2002. Phil had not scrimped on her needs, paying for her to attend college in New York and putting her up at the Castle on her breaks. It was during one of those stays that, old softie that he was, he heard her out when she began raving about a British pop band called Starsailor. He even agreed to go to a gig the group had at the Troubador in late 2001—a major concession, given that he had virtually tuned out music, convinced that rock had gone so far afield from its roots and divine calling that there was nothing in it for him.

But Starsailor had possibilities. That their debut album the year before had sold more than a million copies worldwide (though they were practically unknown in the U.S.), had been named England's best new band by *New Musical Express,* and had opened for the Rolling Stones was immaterial to him. Instead, it was the portentous, aching voice of lead singer James Walsh that intrigued him as the latest entry in the succession of Spector vocal protagonists. Walsh's pipes were soul deep and tremulous, driving the group's open-scab themes of confused young manhood, the usual fodder for British bands of the day, such as their better-known stablemates on the U.K. EMI label, Coldplay and Radiohead. Walsh gave testament to Jeff Buckley as his songwriting muse, but Phil heard his lyrics as a vague echo of Leonard Cohen, and he agreed with a common critique of the foursome that they lacked a certain artiness—a perfect candidate to be buffed by a good Wall of Sound.

Phil had Nicole run interference for him by arranging through pro-motional intermediaries for her to go backstage at a subsequent Star-sailor show to tell them that her famous father was a fan and ask if they wanted to meet him. As it happened, Walsh had recently heard and loved the 2001 reissue in the U.K. of Dion's *Born to be with You* album, with new tracks produced by Steve Barri and Michael Omartian, which

☉   346

had won album of the year votes in the British rock press. The entire band was floored when Nicole identified Phil Spector as her father, and they were even more impressed when she proffered an invitation to meet Phil that very night.

This was a scene reminiscent of 1978 and the Ramones: a Sunset Strip bar pickup meant to change the world. Like the punk rockers then, before reality could set in, the British popsters were in a limo headed for the spooky Spector mansion in the hills, a little terrified but unable to resist. When they got to the Castle, the full-court press was on. At the gate, the car doors were opened, and Jay Romaine led them up the long stairway to the door—the pitch dark broken only by red-lit security cameras, the silence only by undefined animal noises. Once in the foyer, they saw the autographed pictures of the Beatles and Frank Sinatra and Lennon's guitar. After the mandatory half-hour wait, in came the host, dressed in a velvet pajama suit with "PS" embroidered on the breast pocket, looking like a half-pint Hugh Hefner.

"I love your stuff," he said. "I wanna produce you."

Barely able to breathe, the group realized that *they'd* been hired, not the other way around. Still, at his age and theirs, it wasn't as if he was a demon spirit, but rather an eccentric uncle telling tall tales at the family picnic. As Walsh recalled, "There was definitely some sort of pomp and circumstance about him," but he seemed grateful to have an audience to play to and spent the time recycling war stories about John, George, Mick, and others, striking Walsh as a "great conversationalist," "pretty charismatic," and "very open." Any weirdness was kept sheathed, as were any guns. Hooked, they agreed to another meeting, to which they brought demo tapes. Phil was again courtly and down-to-earth, oafish even. Rather than caviar and quail, he served ham sandwiches, and when Phil began choking on his sandwich and turning blue, the band's drummer, Ben Byrne, leaped up and performed the Heimlich maneuver, saving his life. The thought may have occurred to the group that if they didn't give him the job, he might not survive his next step.

The suits at EMI and its U.S. label, Capitol were not so sure. Concerned that Starsailor didn't realize what they were getting into, EMI would agree only to a trial week of Spector sessions, during which, with palpable irony, Phil would have to "pass the audition." And the sessions would take place not in L.A. but in London, which EMI hoped would let Spector know whose turf he was on. Finally, although he never asked for it, there was no chance that he would have ownership of the master tapes.

Phil was bemused by the conditions, as all he really wanted was to have a little fun in the studio for a change, working with a fresh-faced group and not a big-name act that had to have a chart-topping hit or else. When he landed in London two months later, in March 2002, the scene became an acid flashback of 1971, with Phil immediately frothing about re-creating the vibes of his last recording sessions in town. "We'll do it at Abbey Road," he said, "just like *All Things Must Pass.*"

He soon discovered, however, how true that old album title was. Trying to line up veterans from those ancient sessions, he rang up the engineer, Jeff McDonald, who told him that he hadn't been in a studio for twenty years and was now working as a masseur. Phil then had Boris Menart fly in from L.A. to man the board. However, according to Larry Levine, who heard it from Phil, Menart was barred from the studio, as EMI went about establishing the band's authority to dictate their own engineer and the recording venue—not Abbey Road but the band's home base, Metropolitan Studios. It's quite possible the report that Menart was stopped at the studio door was apocryphal, suggesting that Phil came to London expecting full control, and when he didn't get it, he felt slighted. With Phil, that usually meant an exaggerated story.

And yet once the sessions commenced, he had little trouble assuming command. Starsailor had no choice but to adhere to Phil's studio methods, archaic as they were to them. They watched him bypass the studio's computerized equipment and work for hours on end in the old-school way of isolating and sound checking each instrument one by one. Since the room sometimes held more than sixty musicians, sessions that began at 6 P.M. stretched into the wee hours of the morning before the first take of a song could be done. When he got the sound balanced right, though, he could make the earth move. "To listen to the drums like that—the classic Wall of Sound—was a magical moment," Walsh marveled.

Those revelatory moments were many, but so were some senior moments when Walsh swore that Phil made "little mistakes," such as overlooking out-of-tune guitars. "We sat there thinking this guy's supposed to be a perfectionist and he's either completely lost it, or he's going to get a 64-piece orchestra to drown it out."[*]

[*]"Surviving Spector, other Starsailor tales," *Boston Globe,* January 15, 2004.

⊙ 348

Of course, neither was the case. Spector, to put it charitably, simply heard things they didn't, or couldn't, in the framework of the overall sound he wanted. As it turned out, that sound was not a full-blown Wall, which Phil knew to be inapt for their songs' mattress-on-the-dorm-room-floor imagery. In poring over songs, in fact, Phil decided that the hit would be "Silence Is Easy," which Walsh had written about the angst of impending fatherhood, but which Phil construed as a raw nerve in general. He was floored by a hook line that could have come from his own pen: "Silence is easy, just becomes me/You don't even know me, all lie about me" (alternately ending with "why do you hate me?"). Upon hearing the demo, he had exclaimed, "This should be the fucking national anthem!" and "I'm gonna take this to number one!" Undeniably, the song was strong. When Walsh heard the track, he thought of "Instant Karma," with its spare but lively rhythm line, hand claps, and swelling choir on the fade-out.

Similarly, the second track cut, "White Dove," an ethereal, violin- and cello-driven ballad, was self-consciously reminiscent of "Imagine," featuring a yearning vocal and a fragile, dewy elegance. But therein was the rub. The songs were technically as perfect as music could get, but they summoned Spector's past rather than Starsailor's future. Listening to other, unfinished tracks, Walsh felt that "all had the same drumbeat, the same Wall of Sound thing." The songs' eclecticism, he said, was "sucked out of them," yet the group was powerless to do anything. Sitting idly by as Phil tarried for hours on end getting the sound, it was as if the album was all about Phil, not them.

If they had it in mind to challenge him, they demurred, unsure whether he would even remember the next day, given his radically different personalities each time he came in. One day he'd be collegial, the next overbearing, the next distant. Walsh recalled his getting "mad ideas" for songs. Scrupulously, he didn't descend to bottom-barrel Spector. There were no guns, no boozing, no crazy scenes. And outside the studio, he was a gracious companion. In his suite at the Lanesborough Hotel, he introduced them to a visiting Bruce Springsteen. In return, they took him to a Coldplay concert.

But the experience was overwhelming for the band—and it had been only a week. Even when Phil left for home and returned for a second round of sessions a few months later—at Abbey Road this time, in a bow to him—the respite did nothing to recharge them, and exhaustion set in quickly again. Not incidentally, even after his "audition" had stretched to six weeks, Spector still hadn't completed any song beyond those first two tracks. Even under orders to get the album done, he was never satisfied enough to wrap up the tracks.

That's when Starsailor decided maybe they weren't ready for their "Spector album" just yet, lest their own identity be compromised. In this, they came to the same logical conclusion that many others had before them: wanting a Spector album was not worth putting up with Spector himself. That became the unanimous verdict when they voted on letting Phil go at a band meeting. Appointed to give him the bad news, the band's bass player, James Stelfox, needed two brandies before he could face him and say, "Phil, it's been great, but we feel we need to carry on."

Though stung, Phil kept his calm. "I understand," he said. "This is your baby. It's your dream; go live it." A few days later, after discussing it with Allen Klein, he became offended. Calling a meeting with the band in his hotel room, he bared his fangs. Ignoring his six weeks of picking lint from his navel when work had gone undone, he focused on how the band members had occupied themselves during the endless waiting around until he had them do something.

"All you're interested in is playing PlayStation!" he howled. "You're not prepared to work!"

If he thought he could bully or shame them into taking him back, he had wasted his time. They held firm, and he went home for good in September 2002, his "comeback" having been limited to the two tracks on what became the *Silence Is Easy* album, which they completed on their own with another producer. Using the first Spector track as the title cut and first single release was an acknowledgment that they could not come up with anything as good on their own. Indeed, although they had become fatigued by the Spector sound, they cut the rest of the album trying to imitate it. Even without him, it took until January 2004 for the album to come out. "When you work with Phil Spector," Walsh said, rather sheepishly, "he inevitably leaves his mark." He also said, with a certain amount of pride, "We got two tracks out of Phil Spector, which is more than anyone else managed in twenty-three years."

In the end, though, the Starsailor thing did little good for either side. In spite of the Spector connection—which leaked after his dismissal and then recalled in the media ad nauseam when the album was released, eleven months after February 3, 2003—*Silence Is Easy* failed to move the band beyond its parochial core of fans or break them out in the U.S., although it would sell more than a million copies around the world and debut at No. 2 in England.

As for Phil, he seemed almost marginal to the album, his two cuts hardly qualifying it for consideration as his comeback—or, as seemed more likely by then, his farewell—opus. In *Rolling Stone's* February 5, 2004, review, Christian Hoard failed even to mention Spector in decrying the album as "Coldplay covering Barry Manilow, melancholy pop rock admirable for its swooning beauty but plagued by generic heartache. . . . Prettiness comes easy to young British poppers; the hard part is finding something to say."

In fact, the entire Starsailor juncture did significantly less for music than it did in edging Phil closer to the abyss. Closer still, perhaps, because of a seemingly small but theoretically fateful incident on the trip home. When Jay Romaine opened his suitcase at customs, in it were numerous soaps, shampoos, and other toiletries taken from the Lanesborough Hotel. It was hardly a capital offense, but Phil, aware that some people might think that Romaine had taken the items for him, fired Jay on the spot. With Nancy Sinatra already gone, the firing removed one more ballast and reliable shield against trouble.

Actually, shedding the bodyguard was something Phil had had on his mind, believing he was at a life stage when he was finally able to confront his pathological lesions without a safety net to catch him if he fucked up. By way of preparing for this, he began shying away from booze, at least at gatherings where people would be watching him. Attending a Christmas party in Bel Air with his faithful adjutant Marvin Mitchelson in 2002, Phil was by all appearances the square in the room, a glass of Coca-Cola in his hand. By contrast, another VIP at the party, astronaut Buzz Aldrin, seemed to be somewhere in orbit. As Mitchelson would later point out, dirtying Aldrin to defend Spector, "I think [Aldrin] was a little drunk, but Phil was totally sober."

Further self-therapy for Phil was to air some harsh truths about himself. In November 2002, he acquiesced to an interview request from music writer Mick Brown of the *London Daily Telegraph,* who flew in from London to sit down with him at the Castle. What emerged from the interview was an amazing harvest of Spector self-imprecations that made his *Esquire* ponderings seem upbeat, although the object clearly was to court sympathy for the devil. Indeed, the horned incubus occupied his thoughts as he sat in his living room, Bach and Brahms playing softly in the background. Brown described him as "a hunched, small figure on a large white sofa," his hands trembling, and he was "drinking something that might be wine, or cranberry juice, or who knows what else."

Brown's 5,700-word article began like this:

> "I have not been well," says Phil Spector, choosing his words carefully. "I was crippled inside. Emotionally. Insane is a hard word. I wasn't insane, but I wasn't well enough to function as a regular part of society, so I didn't. I chose not to." He pauses. "I have devils inside that fight me."[*]

The article even included the dirty family secret, now confirmed by Phil himself, that his parents had been cousins, which he posited might explain "who I became." He also mentioned his fear that heredity might curse his daughter and render her, like him, "a very tortured soul."

At the same time, he noted, he was seeing a shrink again, confronting "something I'd either not accepted . . . or [was] not prepared to accept or live with in my life." He also said that he was on his meds, at least "to an extent," for insomnia and schizophrenia, though he clarified, "I wouldn't say I'm schizophrenic. But I have a bipolar personality. . . . I'm my own worst enemy."

But maybe not so much now, he implied. Throughout his life, he said, "I was different" and "had to make my own world," giving people reason to "hate my guts." But he claimed that he was "a completely different person" now, trying to "get my life reasonable." He did, however, admit, "I'm not ever going to be happy. Happiness isn't on, because happiness is temporary. Unhappiness is temporary. Ecstasy is temporary. . . . Everything is temporary. But being reasonable is an approach. And being reasonable with yourself, it's very difficult, very difficult to be reasonable."

In the three-month interim between the interview and its publication in February 2003, Spector evidently relapsed. He grew depressed, as he usually did around Christmas, with its reminders of his son's death. He had a spat with Janice Savala, whereupon he fired her again as a sometime office assistant, a job she had been splitting with Hal Blaine's

---

[*]All Spector quotes from Mick Brown, "Spector and the Devils," *London Daily Telegraph*, February 1, 2003.

music agent daughter Michelle. Away from notice, he began to reach for the bottle more often.

When the Mick Brown article appeared on February 1, Phil's self-inflicted verbal stigmata were less cathartic than cautionary. The devils were rumbling inside him again.

And then, as if with bells tolling in the dark tower of Babel, it was February 3.

23

I continue to try to live up to the standard of one of my heroes, Henry VIII, who perhaps came as close to the ideal of perfect wickedness as the infirmities of human nature will allow.

— PHIL SPECTOR, 1999

In the early evening on Sunday, February 2, the devil aroused Phil Spector to rise from the lonely crypt of the Pyrenes Castle; put on a black silk shirt, a white linen sport jacket, black slacks, and three-inch Cuban boot heels; and commit some sins of the flesh. After walking through the foyer and out the back door at around 7 P.M., he slunk into the back of one of his snazziest trophy cars—a brand-new black Mercedes S430 limo, still with its dealer plates—and headed eight miles east, into the bowels of L.A.

His driver for the night was Adriano De Souza, an illegal Brazilian immigrant who'd been working for Spector as a backup driver for several months. Phil instructed De Souza to take him first to Studio City in the San Fernando Valley, where the driver had taken him before, to pick up his date, Rommie Davis, a caterer who provided the food for his bowling soirees in Montrose each year. Then it was on to Beverly Hills, where the pair alighted at a restaurant called The Grill on the Alley. Following a two-hour dinner, they got back into the car, and Spector told De Souza to drive back to Davis's home, where they dropped her off. He then had De Souza return to the Grill.

On the sidewalk outside, a Grill waitress, Kathy Sullivan, was waiting for him. She got in the Mercedes, and they drove to Trader Vic's restaurant at Wilshire and Santa Monica boulevards in Hollywood. They were there for an hour, then moved on to Dan Tana's restaurant on Santa Monica, one of Spector's favorite stops, where a private booth was held for him. They arrived there around midnight and ordered prime rib from the menu. Mainly, though, Phil drank. In fact, over the three stops, he downed three, possibly four, daiquiris and two navy grogs, each containing three shots of different kinds of rum.

Could this really be the now famously sober Phil Spector drinking all that booze? The bartender at Dan Tana's, having poured him only soft drinks in recent months, must have wondered that. Getting an alcohol order from the waiter, the bartender walked over to Phil's table to make sure he wanted liquor. His answer—affirmative—would have stunned some of those in his inner circle who had fallen for the sobriety act. One, who believed he could see through Phil's deceits, was his childhood schoolmate Harvey Kubernik. In an unpublished manuscript written at the time, Kubernik wrote of being impressed by the fact that when he was with Phil, he no longer felt in "danger of being hit by a stray bullet. The mind games and bodyguards have been replaced by a lone driver. I am really happy to see him function like this around town the last few years." But in the early hours of February 3, Phil was already zoomed, increasing the potential for a stray bullet to fly.

Phil settled his check at Dan Tana's at around 1 A.M., putting the $55 dinner on his Diners Club card and adding a $500 tip—not an inordinately high amount for a notoriously big tipper like him. As he and Sullivan returned to the car, he nearly got into a dustup with two young men standing outside the restaurant smoking. When one of them said something to him, Phil—who used to sic his bodyguards on people like this—just glared at the man before entering the backseat of the Mercedes. Sullivan calmed him down, and he ordered De Souza to take them to the House of Blues music club a few minutes away on Sunset.

Sullivan wasn't into it, saying she had to work the next morning. Spector, now slurring his words, became snappish and she agreed to go.

They got to the club at around 1:30 A.M. and made their way three flights up in the elevator to the top-floor, members-only VIP hideaway called the Foundation Room. Judas Priest lead singer Rob Halford was on stage on the crowded ground floor, but Phil was more interested in the quietude of the sparsely inhabited lounge.

When he tried to enter through the wrong door, the statuesque blond hostess at the right door to the room instinctively thought he was a crasher and tried to shoo him away. Phil, offended about being treated so indecorously—not to mention going unrecognized—threw a loud and ostentatious hissy fit until a longer-tenured club employee intervened and clued in the hostess, who had been on the job only a few weeks. "Treat him like Dan Aykroyd [the famous ex–"Saturday Night Live" star who had co-founded the club]," she was told. "Like gold."

When she apologized, Phil stopped his fluttering. She introduced herself as Lana and smiled, her eyes dancing. To Phil, it was a moment. She escorted Sullivan and him to a dark table in the more exclusive area called the Buddha Room. When she walked back outside, his eyes feasted on her from behind. He then ordered a Bacardi 151, straight up. When Sullivan ordered only water, he picked another fight with her.

"Get a fucking drink!" he snarled.

When she refused, he had had enough of her. "That's it—you're going home," he barked. He summoned Lana and told her to walk the mystified Sullivan to his Mercedes and instruct De Souza to drive her home. In the meantime, the waiter brought the drink order, whereupon Phil told him, "Take the fucking water away."

Drinking alone, he proceeded to hit on a couple of waitresses but was rebuffed. He then settled his $8.50 tab, leaving a $450 tip, excessive even for him. As he was paying, he asked for another drink, but was told the bar was closed.

It was around 2 A.M., and there was one chance left for a pickup score—the long-legged hostess who again caught his eye when she returned from walking Kathy Sullivan out. Phil had had her in his sights for the past hour. Now, with the clock running out, he asked her to join him at the table. She asked her manager if she could. He said she could sit, but just in case Spector had made the invitation to get around the bar closing, he made it clear that Phil couldn't have any more drinks. For about twenty minutes, she and Phil were engaged in animated conversation. He may not have made much sense, but he surely got even higher just seeing how he held the attention of this attractive blonde.

Lana was long and cool, more than seductive even in her conservative club "uniform": black skirt, black nylon jacket, dark stockings, black flat shoes. At age forty, she had a few age lines but mostly pristine skin, a large mouth and large eyes, and high cheekbones. She was just his type. Indeed, it was not unusual that such a woman would gravitate to him (witness Nancy Sinatra) or that such a woman, who was old enough to know better and smart enough to be more selective, would be disarmed by the glow of power—even faded power, which Lana Clarkson in particular could relate to.

Born in Long Beach, California, on April 5, 1962—by which time Phil Spector had already produced two chart-topping records—Lana Jean Clarkson grew up in upper-middle-class comfort in California wine country, attended prep school, and quickly gravitated to modeling/acting pursuits. She accrued a good number of credits as a prototypical "starlet," with the requisite bit parts in TV fare such as "Three's Company," "The Jeffersons," "Happy Days," "Laverne and Shirley," "The Love Boat," "Fantasy Island," "Hill Street Blues," and "CHiPs," and made a memorable, if fleeting, film debut when she landed a one-word role ("Hi") in the 1982 smash teen farce *Fast Times at Ridgemont High* as the sex kitten wife of science teacher Mr. Vargas. *Fast Times* served as a launchpad for eighties movie icons such as Sean Penn, Jennifer Jason Leigh, Nicolas Cage, and Judge Reinhold, and for a time Clarkson seemed to be on a hard upward thrust, with a meaty role in *Blind Date* and blink-and-miss-her parts in *Brainstorm, Scarface,* and the prophetically titled *Deathstalker.*

By the mid-eighties, however, she was generally typecast as a brainless bimbo, the only lead roles accommodated in "B movie king" Roger Corman projects—with the usual Corman elements for profitable camp: skimpy budgets and plots, and skimpily clad women. The first Corman movie she appeared in was *Barbarian Queen,* which transported Corman's fare of horror, gore, and sex to the Roman Empire, with Lana taking a bloody toll on the Romans for torturing, raping, and murdering her bridegroom. Her contribution to celluloid history was the seraphic line, "I'll be no man's slave and no man's whore! And if I can't kill them all, by the gods, they'll know I've tried!"

Similar vehicles followed: *Amazon Women on the Moon, Wizards of the Lost Kingdom, Vice Girls,* and, inevitably, *Barbarian Queen II:*

357

The Empress Strikes Back. She attained a sort of cult status with a poster of her in her *Barbarian* outfit, wearing a hat with ivory horns and slinging a long sword, a popular item in Hollywood emporiums and on the basement walls of more than one schmo with a penchant for big, dominant women. Appearances aside, Clarkson was nothing like the poster. She was more victim than barbarian, having by the nineties been fairly discarded in the Hollywood starlet derby. She'd done some more TV shots, taking the sex siren thing as far as she could before hitting forty, by which time she was living paycheck to paycheck in a prosaic, rundown house on a canal in Venice, California, with her pet cat Midnight. Recently, she had begun her own production company, called Living Doll Productions; put up a Web site with sexy images of her and a hopeful listing of her contact information; and worked as a presenter at comic book conventions, including one at which pinup girls and former Playboy Playmates signed autographs.

None of it could stem the decline of her career, which had been hastened by a freak accident in 1991 when she was dancing for children at a charity event and tripped on a throw rug, breaking her hands and wrists in twenty-six places and taking her further out of the game for three months while she wore a cast up to her elbows. She was still gorgeous, still hot, but so was every other tall blonde in Hollywood who wasn't over forty. Like Phil, the clock was running on her. They were, in fact, more alike than they knew.

For one thing, she had battled deep depression. In 2002, upon turning forty, she had been faced with mounting financial troubles, forcing her to borrow money from friends, one of whom became worried when Lana sent her an e-mail message that read, "I am going to tidy up my affairs and chuck it, cuz it's really all too much for just one girl to bear anymore." However, she'd gotten herself together and made an effort to give up booze and an overreliance on painkillers. She was happy, dating again after some painful breakups. The job at the House of Blues, which she had begun on January 14, 2003, had eased some of her money woes, leaving the days free for her to go on auditions. Giving some thought to her career, she planned to segue from sex symbol to comedy roles. She'd done some of that in summer stock plays around town, and the reaction from critics had been positive. She had the talent; what she needed was a break.

"I am going to meet people," she had told a friend recently. "They will remember that I am here, and it might get me another job."

That doesn't sound like someone who was ready to cash it in. In fact, she had just accepted invitations to two social events, a March ceremony in which friends were going to renew their marriage vows and another friend's birthday party. The day before, she'd sent the latter an e-mail message that read, "Can't wait. XOXO Lana."

It's unclear what Lana Clarkson may have believed a faded record producer could do for her career, or what he may have told her he could do for it. Whatever promises, if any, had been made, she apparently thought she'd met a beneficial person in Phil Spector. She was last seen by her co-workers at the House of Blues clocking out at 2:21 A.M. and leaving with him—amusingly, or pathetically, towering above him and helping him stagger out of the Foundation Room, to the elevator, and then to his car.

Outside the club, it was a cool and humid morning. Phil stumbled into the backseat, according to later testimony by De Souza, reeking of booze. He offered Lana a lift to her car in the employees' parking lot a block away on La Cienega Boulevard. She agreed and got in. During the short hop, he made his move, asking her back to his house for a nightcap. Politely, she declined. But whether it was something Phil said or something that intrigued her about the invitation, she changed her mind by the time they got to the lot. As Lana was picking up a few items from her Cougar, a contented Spector also got out, unzipped his pants, and urinated on a stairwell. They both got back into the Mercedes, with Lana hedging for just a moment. Standing by the driver's window, she felt compelled to tell De Souza, "This will be quick. Only one drink."

Phil was irritated. "Don't talk to the driver," he said sternly.

They said little on the ride to Alhambra, with Phil playing a movie on a portable DVD player. When they pulled up to the gate at around 3:30, her eyes must have widened at the massive, minareted mansion framed by the cylindrical turrets rising at either end. A working girl could feel like a princess in this brooding fairyland; how could she not have been consumed by the wonder of it all: an hour ago she was working a door, and now she was entering the portal to a castle.

They got out inside the gate so that Phil could take her—or rather, be taken, with her assistance—up the stairway to heaven to the front door. De Souza drove to the motor court outside the rear entrance and parked. Within fifteen minutes, Phil came out the back door and collected the DVD player and some cell phones bundled into a brief-case, then went back inside. De Souza turned off the engine and waited, listening to music until he fell asleep. An hour and a half later, he was jolted awake by a shrill *pow,* as he would later describe it. He got out of the car and walked around the motor court in the dark. When he saw nothing amiss, he returned to the car.

A minute later, the back door opened, casting a sheaf of light into the blackness outside. Against the brightness of the doorway, a silhouet-ted figure appeared. De Souza got out again and walked toward the door. When he got closer, he saw that it was Phil, still wearing the white sport jacket, looking disoriented and disheveled. He held a revolver in his right hand, placed across his stomach.

"I think I killed somebody," he blurted out.

As Spector matter-of-factly delivered this stupefying news, De Souza peered around him into the foyer, where he saw the woman slumped motionless in a white antique chair, her legs outstretched, blood on her face. Horrified, he said, "What happened, sir?"

Phil could only shrug, and De Souza had no intention of asking again. Not knowing if he might be the next one Spector "thought" he'd killed, he tore back to the car and reached for his cell phone, but his fin-gers were trembling too much to tap out 911. Seeing Phil still in the doorway, staring at the woman on the chair, De Souza managed to start the car and drive it halfway down the driveway, where he stopped and got himself together enough to dial the phone. But he didn't call 911. Instead, he called Michelle Blaine, leaving a frantic message when there was no answer. He then drove to the front gate to double-check the street number of the house and made the 911 call—the only 911 call made from the Castle that night, despite what Phil would claim later.

Within ten minutes, eight Alhambra Police Department officers arrived at the open front gate and peered up the walkway through the trees and bushes. Not knowing how many people were in the house or if any might be armed, they proceeded slowly. Lead officer Michael Page ordered a jacket placed over a surveillance camera at the front of the house so the cops could approach unseen. He decided against going right to the front door because there was no cover. Four cops were inspecting the garage at the back of the property when they saw some-thing moving inside the house. Moments later, Spector appeared at the back door, having taken off his jacket but still wearing his black shirt, his hands in the pockets of his black pants.

Officer Brandon Cardella faced Spector. Cardella, who was carrying a bulletproof shield three and a half feet high and two feet wide, ordered Spector to raise his hands. Spector complied briefly before returning them to his pockets.

"You got to come see this," Spector told the officers enigmatically.

As the officers moved closer, Spector went into the house. He kept his hands in his pockets, despite Cardella's repeated orders to raise them. Officers feared he might be armed. Page leveled his Taser at Spector. A dart struck him but had no apparent effect.

"Go!" Page ordered the others. "Let's get inside the house."

With Cardella in the lead, the four officers, including Jim Hammond and Beatrice Rodriguez, ran into the house. Cardella knocked Spector to the side, and Page set upon him, hitting him point-blank with the Taser. Two dartlike, 50,000-volt probes hit Spector in the chest, the brute force blackening his eyes and buckling his legs. As he writhed and wailed in a quivering heap, Page pressed his knee into Spector's back and held down his arms. Noticing that a submachine gun Page had strapped to his back was slipping off, another cop grabbed it before it fell within Spector's reach. He turned to make sure his Taser also wasn't nearby. Page then shoved Spector against a staircase that ran down into the foyer and forced him to the cold marble tile floor, pinning him there until he was satisfied Spector was unarmed.

Moments later, in the dim light of the foyer, music blaring through the house, Page noticed the dead woman on the chair. Having regained his bearings, Phil became agitated. Page remained with him, covering the adjacent stairwell with his pistol, while the other cops began clearing the ground floor. While doing so, Rodriguez, a few feet from where Page held Spector, heard Phil say, "What's wrong with you guys? What are you doing? I didn't mean to shoot her. It was an accident," which jibed almost exactly with what De Souza said he had told him.

Shortly after, Page activated a microcassette recorder he had tucked into his shirt pocket. Phil, not noticing (or not caring if he did), continued running off at the mouth, his words slurred and often incoherent as he repeatedly cursed the cops. At one point, he said, "The gun went off accidentally. She works at the House of Blues. It was a mistake."

Lana Clarkson was still wearing the black nylon jacket, nylons, and shoes, but her dress had been removed, and she had on a black slip. A 2-inch, blue steel Colt Cobra .38-caliber six-shot revolver—a classic ".38

Special," and apparently the gun Phil had been holding when he had made his avowal of guilt to De Souza—was on the floor under her left leg. Oddly, her leopard-print purse was slung over her right shoulder, leaving the bag dangling upside down against her right side. It was an altogether unnatural death pose, bearing obvious signs to the cops that someone had perhaps rearranged things in a hurry.

The Colt had five live cartridges in the cylinder. Under the hammer, there was a spent cartridge—the one that had, by all appearances, caused Lana Clarkson's lower face to be nearly blown off by a single entry wound to the mouth, leaving a gaping hole in her face and the back of her head. The power of that gunshot could be seen in the gruesome carnage around the foyer. Blood was spattered on the floor, walls, and stairway; pieces of her broken teeth were scattered all around, some as far away as the stairs. Someone, it seemed, had tried to wipe the gun clean, but hastily, and not thoroughly enough to remove a few encrusted splotches of blood on the steel shaft.

The gun wiping struck the cops as an amateurish attempt to clean off fingerprints, and the gun looked as though it had been placed under her after the fact. The question was if anyone else could have been involved beyond Spector and Clarkson. By now, the cops had begun searching the thirty-three rooms for anyone who might be hiding or who might have seen or heard anything. After the Alhambra police acknowledged that the case was far too big a deal for them to handle, teams of detectives were dispatched from the Los Angeles County Sheriff's Department homicide bureau.

Spector needed to be taken away, as his actions and words had identified him as the prime suspect and he showed no willingness to cooperate with the cops. Within twenty minutes of their entering the house, he was hustled out the door, hands cuffed behind his back, and into one of the cruisers for a trip to the Alhambra City Jail to be booked and questioned. It was now around 5:45, and word of a woman's death at Phil Spector's house had spread to newspaper night desks and to media stringers covering the L.A. crime beat. Thus, when Spector was dumped into the backseat of the cruiser, early press arrivals were already in the driveway. Among them was *Los Angeles Times* photographer Lori Shepler, who was standing fortuitously close to the cruiser and was able to preserve for posterity the image of a slimy and scrawny Spector—wig unkempt, shirt dirty, eyes black—uncomfortably leaning forward to find a way to sit with his hands behind his back. Media savvy as he was, Phil may not have objected to being dragged out into the public eye crocked and thrown about like a rag doll, possibly expecting commiseration for the indignity of it all. In Shepler's shot, a beefy young cop seated just to Spector's left looks into the camera lens, a smirk on his face, seeming very much to be enjoying Spector's humiliation.

Within hours, this "money shot" would be picked up by the Associated Press and run in papers around the globe, titillatingly accompanying the breaking news that the legendary rock-and-roll producer had been arrested on suspicion of murder. The noirish, *Hollywood Babylon* feel of the photo, which made Jack Nitzsche's bleary, gun-pointing cameo on "Cops" seem like "Sesame Street," would be supplanted in later editions by Spector's similarly bedraggled mug shot. At the Castle, meanwhile, dozens of warrant-armed detectives streamed onto the grounds over the next forty-eight hours. More blood was found on the inside knob of the back door, a banister on the stairway, and the sleeve and lapel of Phil's white sport jacket in an upstairs dressing room. A blood-soaked diaper, of all things, was found on the floor of a powder room off the foyer—suggesting that someone had used it to soak up some blood and possibly thrown it into the room when the cops began banging on the door.

Looking in Clarkson's purse, they found her rolled-up skirt. How it had gotten there was a mystery, but Phil had clearly set the mood for getting more comfortable. On the living room fireplace mantel, two candles were still burning. There was an empty Jose Cuervo tequila bottle and a can of Canada Dry soda on the living room coffee table. Two brandy glasses with trace amounts of alcohol also were found, one on the coffee table, the other on the powder room sink. Rummaging through the upstairs rooms, detectives located ten handguns and a shotgun. Some of the weapons took the same unique ammunition as the Colt did. This pointed to Spector as the owner of the Colt, as did the discovery of an empty holster fitting the Colt in the open top drawer of a bureau in the foyer.

Once the house was deemed secure and empty of other people, paramedics removed the shrouded body of Lana Clarkson. Her fairy-tale adventure at Phil Spector's Castle on the hill had ended not in paradise but in the morgue.

Phil, meanwhile, was fingerprinted, booked, and held in the booking area of the Alhambra jail. He was still agitated and refused to tell jailers his name or address. They were certain he was drunk, as his speech was slurred and his breath stank of alcohol. He was clearheaded enough to summon Robert Shapiro to bail him out, and he refused to answer inter-rogators' questions. He even tried to get some information, asking one cop "What happened?" three times. Each time came the same answer: "I don't know. I wasn't there." Officer Derek Gilliam was assigned to sit with Spector until he calmed down enough for the booking to proceed. Gilliam sat with him for about an hour while Spector rambled about the music business and the "dead girl in my house."

Spector told Gilliam that the girl had taken a gun from him and, waving it lariat-style above her head, had begun singing "Da Doo Ron Ron" and "You've Lost That Lovin' Feelin'." He insisted that he had told her to put the gun down, but instead she had placed it against her right temple and pulled the trigger. To demonstrate, he raised his right index finger to his head and dropped his thumb as though it were the hammer of a gun.

"It went like this—bang!" he said. Then he hung his head straight back and stared silently at the ceiling for five seconds, as though he were dead. Twice more he demonstrated, each time letting his head hang back in silence for a longer time. The third time, Gilliam said, he thought Spector might have had a seizure. Then, with an expression Gilliam would describe as a "half-slanted smile," Spector added the final beat chillingly: "Nobody takes a gun from me."

At around noon, Alhambra detective Esther Pineda visited Spector in jail to see if he wanted to talk to the sheriff's homicide investigators. Phil had left messages for Shapiro to come bail him out, but Shapiro didn't show. So Phil decided that he might as well talk to the detec-tive, and with Pineda's tape recorder turned on, he launched into a near-spastic verbal eddy:

> This is nonsense. You people have had me here for six fucking hours, maybe nine hours. And you have me locked up like some Goddamn fucking turd in some fucking piece of shit. And you treat me—and then while this person eats and shits and farts. And you have me jerking around. And when somebody comes over to my fucking house who pretends to be security at the House of Blues— remember, I own the House of Blues. Where this lady pretended to work, okay? And just blow her head open in my fucking house and then comes and—and then—and then you people come

around and—and arrest me and bang the shit out of my fucking ass and beat the shit out of me and then you pretend and arrest me and then pretend like you're fucking Alhambra. . . .

I don't know what the fucking lady—what her problem is, but she wasn't a security at the House of Blues and she's a piece of shit. And I don't know what her fucking problem was, but she certainly had no right to come to my fucking castle, blow her fucking head open, and [unintelligible] a murder. What the fuck is wrong with you people?*

This magnificently moonstruck fulmination seemed well suited to an insanity defense—how else to explain Phil's whacked-out claim that he "owned" the House of Blues and that Clarkson didn't really work there? But for Phil it had a purpose: to blur the sharp details of the cops' recollections and create a different reality. His reality was that a woman hell-bent on killing herself had succeeded and brought indignity and infamy to him and his Albion. That was his story, which he had decided on before discussing it with a lawyer, meaning he was stuck with it.

He should have saved his breath, much as he did when asked to take a Breathalyzer test, though every cop who saw him believed that he was seriously drunk. He was able to put off an official determination of that for hours, creating further delay when he began to complain of injuries he'd sustained from the Taser attack and was taken to San Gabriel Valley Medical Center to be checked. While there, at about 5:30 P.M.—a full twelve and a half hours after the shooting—during a routine sexual assault examination, he finally gave a urine sample. Tellingly, even after all that time, his blood alcohol level was at .08, indicating that he was still legally drunk. No serious injuries were found, mainly just some bruising on his arms, and he was returned to the Alhambra jail at around 7 P.M.

The entire time he was in custody, Phil was shut off from the world outside and vice versa. When neither Shapiro nor Marvin Mitchelson

---

*All details and descriptions of Spector's activities and statements on February 2–3, 2003, and of the crime scene were taken from testimony by Detective Mark Lillienfeld of the Los Angeles County Sheriff's Department's homicide bureau in an affidavit request for a search warrant granted in Los Angeles County Superior Court on February 25, 2003, and unsealed December 10, 2005; a transcript of grand jury testimony, unsealed by Superior Court judge Larry Paul Fidler, November 11, 2004; and the District Attorney's Motion to Admit Evidence of Other Crimes filed in Los Angeles Superior Court, February 17, 2005.

showed up at the jail, Phil dumped the whole process of getting him out on Michelle Blaine. Stunned by the mushrooming drama, she rang up her father for guidance.

"I was in the studio that day, and Michelle called me, crying, saying she didn't know what to do," recalled Hal Blaine, who was himself agog. "I could only think of one thing. I told her, 'Call Bob Shapiro.'"

But rather than hightail it to Alhambra, Shapiro began dickering with Michelle for money. As Hal Blaine heard it, Shapiro said, "I'll need a million and a half." Having been trained by Phil to tightly control the purse strings, she blanched and said, "Sorry, we're going to have to get somebody else."

Shapiro thought for a moment and said, according to Hal Blaine, "I'll do it for a million," as though that would mean penury for him. It got him the gig.

After Shapiro arranged with Phil's accountants to stake a $1 million bail bond, as set by a judge that afternoon, Alhambra police told Phil that he'd made bail. By 8 P.M., he was out the door, snaking past reporters in a limo sent for him by Shapiro. With investigators sifting through the Castle, which was now cordoned off with yellow police tape, he would stay at Shapiro's home for several nights while starting to hatch a defense. According to one acquaintance, Phil was no doubt anxious to check out the story on the tube. "I'd be willing to bet you that Phil posted his bail and got to a TV that night to see his own media coverage," the acquaintance said. "And he had to wait 20 minutes into "Entertainment Tonight" to see himself pop up briefly as 'Sixties Beatles producer Phil Spector.' I'm sure he was watching, and I'm sure that destroyed him."*

"Entertainment Tonight" notwithstanding, the tabloids in both the U.S. and England lapped up the sordid elements of sex, death, and money, reprising old O. J. Simpson headlines with a new name. Abetted by the unbelievably timed Mick Brown interview in the *London Daily Telegraph,* the media template was established early, seen through the prism of Phil's vices. PHIL SPECTOR: GUNS, MADNESS, AND MAYHEM was the headline of a treatment on rock writer Robert Fontenot's Web site. This headline was abridged by *Newsweek*—GUN CRAZY; protracted by the *Austin (Texas) American-Statesman*—SPECTOR SURROUNDED BY

*"Phil Spector with a Bullet," Steve Pond, *Playboy,* June 2003, p. 158.

MUSIC, MYSTERY AND MURDER?; and overstuffed by the ever-hammy *New York Post*—MURDER AT THE MANSION: MUSIC GENIUS PHIL SPECTOR ARRESTED IN L.A. GUN SLAY. Rarely was the story framed from the victim's perspective, although such headlines were no less panting. ACTRESS KILLED WANTED STARDOM—FOUND FAME IN DEATH, read one. Across the pond, the Fleet Street tabloid the *Mirror* ran with the banner LANA'S LAST BOOZY HOURS; EXCLUSIVE: SHOT ACTRESS DRANK BUBBLY AND BOURBON WITH SPECTOR.

If Spector was in fact tracking media coverage, he was likely gratified that the story was being played out as a pulpy, melodramatic burlesque—the better to turn Lana Clarkson into a cartoon, drained of humanity, while at the same time seeing himself invested with super powers. The *New York Post* story, for example, used a recent Reuters photo of him that was captioned "Rock God: Phil Spector produced countless hits." In it, Phil wore a sporty burgundy fedora, a matching open-collared shirt, wraparound shades, and an Alfred E. Neuman grin. The shot reflected his attitude now: confident and unperturbed about beating the rap.

Steeling for yet another fight—this time for his life—he was lean, taut, and mean. He had no room for remorse for Lana Clarkson, much less any contrition for her death. At best, it was incidental that a human being had died before his eyes so violently. The issue now was his life, not the "fucking lady." And his insistence that Clarkson had blown her own brains out was already a matter of concern to Robert Shapiro, who would have preferred that Phil had kept some options open by way of a defense, such as an accidental death claim that could yield a plea bargain, if need be. What's more, the misogynistic undercurrent of Phil's claims was patently obvious. Combined with Spector's abominable history with women, it would make suicide a hard sell to a jury. For Shapiro, having his hands tied in this manner no doubt brought back some unpleasant memories of O. J. Simpson, whom Shapiro had quit in mid-trial. At least with O. J., however, there had been a built-in advantage in the enormous popularity he had as a former football player. In this case, Shapiro was stuck with a legendary madman.

Remarkably, Spector did get support from the woman who until February 3 had been his most famous victim. Appearing on "Good Morning America" the day after the shooting, a visibly shaken Ronnie Spector, admitting that she was "still in shock," said, "My heart goes out to the woman and her family." This of course was quite believable, since, as she noted, when she'd fled from an earlier Spector mansion, "I knew that if I didn't leave at that time, I was going to die there." But then she said, "I don't think he would murder anybody." Several days later, a *New York Daily News* reporter reminded her that she had in the past spoken about how Phil had threatened to kill her. She responded, "Not personally, though. That was with a hit man." That couldn't have been of much comfort to Phil.

Weeks passed with neither Spector nor Shapiro issuing any public statements, choosing to hold back until they could get some feel for the way the investigation was going. It was left to surrogates to speak on Phil's behalf, even though no one could get a call through to him and had no idea how he was planning to defend himself. This included Marvin Mitchelson, who when he was queried by the media could only wing it. He would tell of Spector's recent sobriety phase—which he creatively stretched into three and a half years—throwing in the Buzz Aldrin Christmas party story to help make the case. As for the shooting, he called it "inconceivable" that Phil could kill somebody. After all, he noted, Spector had never actually "shot at anyone," and "if he even did it," it was "untoward and unlikely he'd do this without some reason we can't understand yet." That didn't help either.

Nor did Mitchelson's postmortem of the movie script he and Phil had been working on. "We thought we had a happy ending to the story," he said in the February 9 edition of the *New York Times*. "After all these years, a happy ending. Now I don't know what's going to happen, but it doesn't look like it's going to be a happy ending."

Throughout February and early March, the media rehashed the old Spector horror tales—the guns, the women, the weirdness, the beyond-dysfunctional marriage to Ronnie. Spector's hushed-up abuses were not known even to his confidants at this point, but a British tabloid located a woman named Barbara Nichols who claimed to have dated him in the mid-nineties. She recalled that Phil carried two guns, and told of his hitting her. During what she called a session of "kinky" sex, she said that Spector had pointed one of his guns at her and said, "I could kill you." He subsequently sent her a crude letter, which read, "I remain mad, bad and dangerous to know."

This account was quite similar to another late-coming recitation by a Spector victim, a former topless dancer named Sandy Kane, who told the *New York Daily News* in December 2003 of her "horrible" encounter with Phil twenty-five years earlier, when she was twenty-one and had met Phil at The Improv comedy club. Later, riding in his limo with Nino Tempo, April Stevens, and comedian Kenny Kramer, "he showed us his gun," she recalled. Then, taking her for a romp in his hotel suite, he "held me down and started kissing me." When he demanded oral sex, she said, "'I don't do that," whereupon he pulled out the gun again.

"You better," he supposedly replied.

"I did what he wanted," Kane admitted. "When your life is in danger, you do what you have to." She said that she hadn't reported the episode because "I was scared. I was a topless dancer. I felt they would blame me." Now she said, "I want justice done."

Phil also had to endure the slings of his estranged sons, who poured out their painful memories of neglect. The shocker, of course, was Gary Spector's revelation of the twisted "coming of age" rituals in which he and his brother Louis had been thrown on top of Phil's girlfriends in a sexual kabuki. It was Donté Spector, though, who was the most pitiless. "While we don't know if Dad killed this lady," he said, "he should be locked up. He's a sick man." He also made it known that when he'd heard the news of the shooting at the Castle, he thought "Dad had finally made good on one of his threats."

Through all of the pillorying, Phil kept himself hidden. About a month after the shooting, Los Angeles County Sheriff's Department detective Robert W. Kenney, one of a team of eight pairs of homicide investigators assigned to the case, told me that Spector was "keeping his mouth shut," and that when lead detectives Paul Fournier and Rich Tomlin had gone to the Castle to interview him in depth, he had told them, "I'm not gonna say anything, and I'd appreciate it if you wouldn't either." This, of course, was his right, but it rang hollow with the detectives.

"Ask yourself," Kenney said. "If you're living with your wife or girlfriend and something happened to her, and you had nothing to do with it, we wouldn't be able to shut you up. You'd want us to know every little detail in the hope of getting to the truth. Anyone would."

But Phil Spector wasn't just anyone.

24

. . . O, how wretched
Is that poor man that hangs on princes' favours!
There is betwixt that smile we would aspire to,
That sweet aspect of princes, and their ruin,
More pangs and fears than wars or women have:
And when he falls, he falls like Lucifer,
Never to hope again.

—WILLIAM SHAKESPEARE, *Henry VIII*

Spector has a continuous history of firearm-related violence that begins
in 1972 and continues essentially unabated through November 2003,
some nine months after the Clarkson homicide. He knows that his con-
duct is against the law. Moreover, he knows that it is against the law
because it is dangerous and puts the lives of victims at risk. That is pre-
cisely why he resorts to it again and again: because it causes people—
reasonably—to fear for their lives and forces them to do what he wants.

—DOUGLAS SORTINO, Deputy District Attorney,

Los Angeles County, Motion in Limine to Admit Evidence of Other
Crimes, filed in California Superior Court, February 17, 2005

Whether [Spector] is a good person or not, is not the issue.
—LESLIE ABRAMSON, May 7, 2004

Lana Clarkson was buried on February 23 after a funeral service attended by 250 people at the Henry Fonda Music Box Theater in Hollywood—ironically, the same venue Phil had booked for Lenny Bruce's funeral in 1966. Two days later, the Los Angeles County Sheriff's Department went to court and obtained a new search warrant to subpoena Phil's cell phone and credit card records, as well as his e-mail and Internet history. Their objective was to determine whether Phil had perhaps trolled Clarkson's Web site and downloaded any of her pictures. If so, it might mean that he had known of her before he went to the House of Blues on February 2, contradicting what he had said, and his trip there may have been a form of stalking.

As various plots thickened, L.A. district attorney Steve Cooley postponed an arraignment hearing that had been scheduled for March 3. Aware of the pitfalls encountered in the Simpson case, with its cast of inept cops and forensics people, the authorities decided to take their time on this one—to secure every scrap of evidence and build their case meticulously. Deliberately, the investigating teams used the time to seek out anyone with a Spector connection who might have a clue, including those in the New York crowd he hung out with at places such as Elaine's and the Shark Bar. They also interviewed Sandy Kane.

They wanted, of course, to talk to Ronnie, but she had hired a lawyer and, like Phil, refused to talk—a move that to the cops seemed more than coincidental. "If I had to guess," Robert Kenney said, "I would say that the Spector camp got to her. You know, keep your mouth shut, and maybe we'll work something out. She's been relatively outspoken about him in the past. The only reason I can think of for her not to talk is financial." It wouldn't have been the first time that Phil had "gotten to" Ronnie in a legal matter. But she would be able to remain silent for only so long. "She's going to be subpoenaed whether she talks to us or not," Kenney promised. "We're going to make her come to court as a witness."

Almost anyone was liable to be questioned. One day Hal Blaine answered a knock at his door and saw two detectives staring at him.

371

"They spent three hours asking me about Phil, about guns, drinking, the whole schmear," the drummer said. "I said I never saw Phil with a gun—because I never had. Listen, I was in the service, and I was a police officer once. I carried a badge for five years in San Bernardino as an undercover cop. I know about guns. They said, 'You used to hang with Phil.' I said, no, I never hung with Phil. I worked on and off with him for thirty years, but I never even had dinner with him, drinks, nothing.

"Then it was like, well, your daughter works for him; you must be close. I said she works for him because she's been in the business for twenty years and knows what she's doing. She's been an assistant director, a production assistant, an agent. I had nothing to do with it. I was shocked when she told me she was working for him. They asked everything. The only thing they didn't ask was if I knew whether Phil Spector was circumcised or not."

As Phil had hoped, there was a subtle shift in the wind as the weeks passed with no official action by the DA. Gone were the daily Spector stories in the tabloids, replaced by the faster-moving Michael Jackson child molestation story. Gone were the Spector jokes and song parodies ("And Then He Shot Me," for example) on the drive time radio shows. The delay itself seemed newsworthy only for the assumption it bred that maybe all wasn't going as planned in the investigation and that a homicide rap was not open-and-shut after all. Marvin Mitchelson played this angle, theorizing, "There's no motive. I think the police are having trouble with that."

Then, on March 10, came more trouble. That day, L.A. radio station KFI, citing "sources in the L.A. County Sheriff's Office" and "toxicology reports," broke the ennui to report, shockingly, that Spector had been cleared and would face no charges. This startling bit of information caught the investigators completely unawares, sending them scrambling for answers.

"I heard it on the radio and I said, 'Where did they get this crap from?'" a bewildered Bob Kenney said a few days later. "How could it be? The toxicology reports aren't in. If we'd made that determination, we would be bound by responsibility to make an announcement; it wouldn't be leaked. But if we cleared him, then why the hell am I still working night and day on this thing?"

Sewing the pieces of the "scoop" together, the detectives traced the story to a "media source," presumably someone at KFI, who Kenney said "had access to our crime lab during a press tour of the facilities and took some pictures of stuff they weren't supposed to, evidence in the case on a table. From that they made a conclusion that had no basis in reality."

Actually, there was one other possible source in the affair—the elfin man holed up in the Pyrenes Castle. It seems that a few days before, when detectives returned his computer to Robert Shapiro, Phil misconstrued it—as apparently only he could—as a kind of surrender. Michelle Blaine later told the press that Phil's reaction was to yell *"Yeeahhhh!"* He then told her, "Okay, Michelle, let's compose an e-mail," which would be a declaration of victory, sent to a select few. Marvin Mitchelson was one of the recipients, and when he got the message, he forwarded it to KFI, either on his own or on Phil's instructions.

The message was cringingly cavalier. Gleefully and inappropriately, he burbled in self-aggrandizement, saving his only hint of anguish for the dead woman for his breathless revelation that he had been "cleared of this horrible tragedy"—which he explained away by conflating a brand-new legal defense term: "accidental suicide." There was Spector chutzpah galore, never more oily than when he wrote, "I hate to use the words I told you so. But I did tell you so. After seven weeks of silence, we can say with certainty, this will speak for itself, and boy, does it speak volumes."

Actually, that the story had gotten this far *did* speak volumes— about sham journalism. The tabletop "evidence" and Spector's triumphant e-mail message, based on nothing but his own delusions, had apparently been all the corroboration KFI's news editors needed to air a fable as a breaking story. And yet, bogus as it was, the story's impact was seismic. Throughout the day's news cycle, it was reported over and over that Spector was in the clear. Suddenly, the Gothic atmospherics of the Castle, the frightful picture of Spector in the police cruiser, the cause-and-effect linkage of his past with the murder of an angelic woman—all of it was being purged in a media firestorm.

Finally, it occurred to the AP's veteran court reporter Linda Deutsch to do what KFI had not: call Robert Shapiro's office for confirmation. Shapiro's first public statement about the case was neither a confirmation nor a denial. Instead, he postured vacuously in legalese that "a thorough and accurate investigation of the evidence will prove that Phil Spector is innocent of any crime." This wasn't just lawyerly circumspection; it was another way of saying that Spector had *not* been cleared. Obviously, if he had been exonerated, Shapiro would have already flooded the airwaves with jubilant proclamations. By the end of the day, when Deutsch's story hit the wires, the fire was being doused. Despite all the excitement, nothing had really changed.

This fact was officially confirmed by the sheriff's department the following day, when the *Los Angeles Times* ran a disclaimer by Captain Frank Merriman, the head of the department's homicide division, that the department had specifically ruled out suicide. Although Merriman could not avow that Spector would be charged with homicide, that was the implication. Merriman also made it clear that the department held Spector responsible for the spurious leak. "Someone is trying to plant seeds of doubt with potential jurors," he said, leaving no doubt about whom he meant. "Someone wants us to go back and forth on this. We're not going to play that. We're going to let the ball bounce a few times on our side of the net."

However, that thinly veiled "someone" still wanted to play. And for him, the game was just beginning.

Many of those who'd had a positive relationship, at least on balance, with Phil were having their own crises about what to make of the "horrible tragedy." Most couldn't get calls through to him. Larry Levine, for one, felt Phil's sting when he sent him an e-mail message meant to be light-hearted. Figuring that Phil could use a laugh and knowing his sense of humor, Larry included a graphic depiction of balloons exploding, with the punch line, "All it takes to ruin a good day is one little prick."

As Levine explained, "I'd gotten it in an e-mail from Hal Blaine, and I thought it was a funny joke that he would appreciate given the circumstances. I mean, Phil loved those kind of jokes. He loved it when Hal said things like that. But then I get an e-mail back from Phil that says, 'I know all these things you've been saying about me'—and I don't know that I've ever said anything derogatory about Phil—'and now you send me *this*?! Don't ever talk to me again.' So I guess I'm persona non grata with him. That's the last communication I had with Phil.

"Looking back, had I thought about it, I wouldn't have sent it. Maybe it was not a good time. But obviously Phil thought I was calling him a prick, and I wasn't. I'm still all for Phil. I love Phil. But once he puts you off the list, you're off it. And if that's how he reacted with me, a guy he loved, for something like that, I imagine the list is quite long by now. He wants blind loyalty from everybody, but he doesn't trust anyone now. And I don't know who he has left as a friend."

Had Phil not overreacted to the e-mail—an ironic twist after the KFI e-mail affair—he would have known that Levine believed in his innocence. "Oh, yeah, I know he didn't kill her," Levine said. "No way he could have. When I saw him hold a gun to Bobby Bruce's head during the Ramones' sessions, there was no way he would have hurt Bobby. He was just showing off."

Of course, Lana Clarkson's friends just as adamantly expressed their belief that she could not possibly have put a gun to her own head—not a woman as bright and together as she was, they all said. The difference between the two protagonists was that in Spector's case, as Levine acknowledged, a disaster always lay just a twitch of a finger away. "That was always the worry with Phil," he noted, "that someday an accident would happen."

This sort of ambivalence ate away at Spector's pals. Although they wouldn't have recognized him without a gun, they'd never believed he would fire one at anybody—unless, of course, he did. The conundrum made them dizzy. "The whole thing is going to get unraveled," Don Peake said. "I'm sure it was an accident. They must have had some kind of a struggle, and she tried to grab the gun, something like that. That's the only way it could have gone off."

Marky Ramone, the surviving Ramone from the *End of the Century* album, had his own vision, telling Connie Chung on CNN, "I'm assuming it was either an accident or it could have been a life-threatening situation." If this was meant to imply that Spector may have killed Lana Clarkson in self-defense, it was a crackpot notion by any stretch. He also broached comic relief by describing Phil's past behavior as "a little rambunctious," his gun follies as "bravado," and his locking the Ramones in his house for days as "eccentric." The lone Ramone was even ready now to dismiss the gun incident in the studio with Dee Dee, whom he insisted had "exaggerated the point a little." The truth was that Phil "didn't hold it to anyone's head. He was just waving it around." Marky's myopia may have been topped only by that of Marvin Mitchelson, who insisted in interviews that Phil was "great to his children" and "a terrific father."

Gene Pitney, forever joined to Spector through the ligature of "He's a Rebel," offered a harsher take. Pitney, who was in Wales on one of his many international tours the day after the shooting, wondered if

Spector had been on "antipsychotic drugs and alcohol" when the gun went off. "He probably doesn't even know what happened," Pitney said, "doesn't even know where he was."

Living in the strange ennui surrounding the case, Phil acted as if being the prime suspect in a murder case was a flea he could brush off his shoulder. Acting as normally as that meant when applied to him, he attempted a seamless transition to doing the kinds of things he would have if none of this unpleasantness had happened. Doing so, he may have thought, might contribute to making the disturbing images of February 3 seem contradictory and even blunt any charges. Thus he didn't stay holed up in the Castle for long. In June, after flying to New York with his new bodyguard, an ex-cop named Bill Pavelic, he wasted no time making the scene at Elaine's—where he was thrilled to no end to meet Hall of Fame catcher Yogi Berra—and wheeling around town, at times accompanied by a still loyal Paul Shaffer.

One night, bounding into the East Village nightclub Route 85a, he caused such a commotion that it made the *New York Post* the next day. "For a subject in a murder case, Phil Spector could use some manners," the item began. According to the *Post*, the "bewigged, beshaded producer" crashed a private party in the back room, barking at the people to leave because he had the room reserved. "He just sat down and ruined my party," said the woman who'd booked the room. A toadying manager took Spector's side and evicted the party, leaving one of the guests shuddering. "I was afraid he had a gun," the guest said. "I hope he goes to jail."

Continuing to spread goodwill, Spector, while riding in his Mercedes in November 2003, told his driver to stop at a Starbucks in South Pasadena. He went in and, appearing drunk, shouted at the manager, "Where's the pisser in this place?" After being directed to the bathroom, he stumbled back outside and was recognized by a man sitting at a sidewalk table with two friends. The man invited Phil to sit with them. When the driver intervened, saying no, the man cracked, "I guess your bodyguard says you can't join us." At that, Phil lost it.

"You shit," he barked. "This interview isn't authorized." Then, too drunk or too arrogant to realize it was the worst possible thing to say, he raged on. "You fat fuck, I'm gonna go get my gun and blow you fat fucks away."

He got back in the car, and the driver began slowly circling the parking lot, as if preparing for a drive-by shooting. One of the men got nervous and left. A few minutes later, so did Spector.*

His boldest shot from the lip, however, played out in the spring when the July 2003 issue of *Esquire* hit the stands with an interview Phil had recently given to writer Scott Raab. This was another seeding in his cultivation of the media, and he went in ready to go on the record about the circumstances of February 3.

If Phil chose his forum based on the credulousness of the interviewer, he did well with Raab, whom Phil had let ride on the private jet he'd hired for his trip to New York. Slavishly fawning, unctuously calling him "Phillip," Raab's first-person swoon to Spector's majesty, "Be My, Be My Baby," cast him as a benign knight—not a "recluse-zombie-maniac dwarf . . . dragging his chains and baying at the moon" but merely a "very nice man." Phil's j'accuse moment came when he had his say about his arrest.

"It's 'Anatomy of a Frame-Up!'" he foamed. "There is no case, they have no case. I didn't do *anything* wrong—I didn't do anything. I called the police myself. *I called the police.* This is not the Menendez brothers. They have no case. If they had a case, I'd be sitting in jail right now.

"She kissed the gun. I have no idea why—I never knew her, never even saw her before that night. . . . I don't know where or how she got the gun. She asked me for a ride home. Then she wanted to see the castle. She was loud and drunk even before we left the House of Blues. She grabbed a bottle of tequila from the bar to take with her. I was *not* drunk. I wasn't drunk *at all. There is no case.* She killed herself."

Almost every word of this was horsefeathers, since he had not called the police or been anything close to sober that night. On its face, the demented woman/suicide claim made no sense. But the way he put it was pure genius: *She kissed the gun.* These four words, delivered with Raymond Chandler–like fistiness and offhand sexual innuendo, turned the gun into a phallic symbol that Lana Clarkson had gone all the way with—and turned Clarkson herself into not just a madwoman but a *loose* madwoman. (Raab did his part, denigrating Clarkson as "a chronically aspiring buxom blond B-movie actress/model/comedienne/hostess—a type always common in Hollywood and not unknown at the castle.")

---

*Cases cited in Motion to Admit Evidence of Other Crimes filed by the District Attorney's Office in Los Angeles Supreme Court on February 17, 2005. Dept. 106, Case No. BA255233, pages 25–26.

There were also some interesting sidebars in the piece, such as that Phil was unhappy with Marvin Mitchelson for talking out of turn and with Nancy Sinatra for not standing by him. (He claimed that her first comment to him had been, "My mother told me *Omigod—Nancy,* it could've been you!") Robert Shapiro couldn't have been comforted by Phil's ranting that Shapiro had overcharged him by demanding a $1 million retainer. Shapiro, he insisted, should have gotten him out of jail "as a courtesy—not for seven figures. As a courtesy, I've taken him for *three hundred thousand dollars'* worth of gifts and rides and plane trips. I wasn't a referral—I was his best friend. Nancy Sinatra, Marvin Mitchelson—they all proved to be fucking wastes of time."

Spector actually was twice blessed that summer by the high-gloss rags. A month before, *Vanity Fair* had presented its Spector story, "Legend with a Bullet," by Robert Sam Anson, who in lieu of participation by Spector took at face value some, ahem, questionable sources to muddy Clarkson's name. The grimier parts, many unattributed, trashed her as a queen not of barbarian hordes but of self-indulgence: a jet-setting, gun-toting, martial arts–practicing, tequila-tippling floozy who'd been "chummy" with powerful Hollywood movers such as Jack Nicholson, Warren Beatty, Lou Adler, and Robert Evans. An unnamed "co-worker" noted that "Oriental guys loved her, even with the height, because they love blondes" and that "she was the type who'd get booked in a second on a $10,000 Paris deal."

Although Anson didn't say that she had actually slept with any of these wealthy men to support her extravagant lifestyle (one that she would have had to live without her closest friends knowing about it), he did say that she had been a whore in the past. "For a time in the early 1990s," he wrote, citing another mystery source, "she was a $1,000-an-hour call girl, working under the name of 'Alana' for Beverly Hills madam Jody 'Babydol' Gibson."

To anyone who knew Clarkson, this article was an outrageous lie. She was, if anything, rather prudish about sex and wasn't known to carry a gun or have a clue about the art of self-defense. As a piece of journalism, it was only slightly less egregious than the KFI "scoop." But for Spector, it provided welcome backup in the smearing of Lana Clarkson. Given that Phil had hired a private investigator to dig up dirt on Lana, could the more salacious slanders even have come from his camp? Or did they come from former Clarkson publicist and boyfriend Edward Lozzi, who was quoted in the piece, but only about her alleged gun prowess: "She could shoot the eye off a fly at a thousand yards." Something Anson never mentioned was that Lozzi was now working for a lawyer representing the very madam in question, who happened to be trying to sell a tell-all book about Clarkson.

No one was saying. And, mercifully, the wormy chronicle was largely ignored as the case took a new turn, moving beyond wild speculation and routine slander and into the justice system—though this would begin an even longer and more labyrinthine journey.

On September 15, 2003, the Los Angeles County coroner's department officially ruled on Lana Clarkson's death. While the report was kept sealed at the behest of the sheriff's department, it was revealed that she had died of a gunshot wound to the head and neck that had severed her spinal cord, with the bullet lodging in the back of her skull, and that she had been "shot by another." Captain Frank Merriman surfaced to confirm his original statement after Phil's e-mail fiasco. "It wasn't an accident," he told the *Los Angeles Times*. "Phil Spector shot her."

With this determination certified, the sheriff's department could finally do what it had been itching to do for seven months. It presented the case to District Attorney Steve Cooley, who assigned it to Assistant District Attorney Douglas Sortino for review. Formal charges were filed at a November 20 arraignment in Alhambra before Los Angeles Superior Court judge Michael Pastor. Two counts were filed. The first was described this way: "The crime of MURDER . . . a felony, was committed by PHILLIP HARVEY SPECTOR, who did unlawfully and with malice aforethought murder LANA CLARKSON, a human being." The second related to the use of "a firearm(s), to wit, Handguns . . . causing the above offense to become a serious felony [and] a violent felony."

What this meant, in light of the penal code statutes cited in the complaint, was that Spector faced fifteen years to life on the main charge and up to ten years more for committing a violent crime with a gun. If he hadn't spent much time dry lately, it must have been sobering indeed when he heard the charges read in the airless courtroom that day, although he wasn't about to lose his composure. Having been notified by Robert Shapiro of the arraignment, he chose his wardrobe with care and arrived—in his newest chic wheels, a white stretch Hummer—wearing a conservative black suit and shirt, gray shades, and, as the AP observed, a "fashionably long wig."

He was a far cry from the black-eyed hair ball the world had last seen in the police cruiser, and he acted with appropriate dignity. Standing erect beside Shapiro, he spoke only when addressed by the judge, responding with a throaty "yes" twice to acknowledge the charges and waive his right to a speedy trial, and to enter a plea of not guilty. Avoiding the media on the courthouse steps after his bail was extended, he exited from a basement garage, returned home, and shut the door.

Now his recently burnished public profile dimmed. There'd be no more boastful e-mails, slick media manipulation, or carousing road trips and public spectacles. Having previously convinced himself that the sheriff's department gumshoes had gotten nothing on him in their endless picking, he must have felt as if the wind had been knocked out of him. Still, all it really meant was that a new phase had begun. It was go time now; he'd have to crack some nuts in the DA's office. No longer was it sufficient to be cocky. From now on, he'd have to be scary, not giving an inch. To do that, he decided, he needed not a mouthpiece but an attack dog.

The punctilious Shapiro knew that he wasn't built for that kind of guerrilla lawyering. Already butting heads with Phil about his unyielding suicide strategy, and displeased by Spector's caustic remarks about him in *Esquire*, Shapiro informed him in late January 2004 that he was withdrawing from the case. Phil, who evidently believed he could insult anyone as long as he paid them, didn't take it well. One could hardly blame him, since preliminary hearings were rapidly approaching and he'd have to start over with a new lawyer. It ate at him for months, and in July he filed a civil suit against Shapiro, whom he said had done "very little" or "incompetent" work, had acted in an "unprofessional, unethical and unconscionable" manner, and had taken "advantage" of Phil's "legal plight" to "line [his] pockets" with the retainer (which Phil said had been $1.5 million). He claimed that Shapiro had "coerced" him into paying such a high price at a time when Spector had been "under a tremendous amount of mental stress that comes with being arrested for murder." He demanded that $500,000 plus damages be paid back.

In truth, the Spector-Shapiro cleft came down to the same thing it always did with Phil—control. He simply never let Shapiro be the lawyer, leaving him with little room to make a deal with the DA. But then, was there a lawyer alive who could accept Phil's contradictory "accidental suicide" defense strategy?

In mid-February, Phil thought he'd found that entity when he hired Leslie Abramson, who was as incendiary and obnoxious as he was, and as schooled in the art of unnerving people with calculated boorishness. Abramson, at once recognizable for her flossy blond mane and cheese-grater voice, had gone where no female trial lawyer had gone before, shepherding the defense in big-name trials, most famously those of the pestilent Menendez brothers in a far more hopeless case than this one (as Phil himself had noted in *Esquire*). Then, all she'd had to do was sell a jury that the brothers, who had killed their parents in their bed and then lived it up on the insurance money, had acted in self-defense. Although they were eventually convicted of murder, the initial jury deadlock and mistrial had made her famous.

Abramson's shrill and abrasive style would now be applied to winning a first-ever case of "accidental suicide." She seemed eager to dive right in. At a February 17 preliminary hearing, she met the press with a smile and a genuflection to her client, insisting she'd postponed her retirement to take the case. "I was about to hang it up when I got the call," she said. "No other defendant would get me to give up my freedom." She then cooed that Phil was "my idol" and "the definition of cool," although it was unclear whether she knew the Crystals from Cristal champagne. Not that Phil cared; if she was a liar, what was important was that she be a good one.

The jazz and fluff aside, Abramson understood that she was there to play hardball. And she and Phil had quickly decided that their high hard one would be the very coroner's report that had been the determinant in charging him. It was a daring move, one that might backfire. But Phil had no other viable choice in winning his gambit than doing the O. J. thing: turning the case on its head to make it all about incompetence, malfeasance, and hidden agendas by the cops and prosecutors. Besides, a high-stakes game was better than no game at all. As it was, Phil had had to sit back and watch the sheriff's department leak selective tidbits from the coroner's report almost from the start. Indeed, the report had been compiled and completed on February 7, 2003, but it had been nine months before Phil's team had finally had a chance to peruse it, after he was formally charged. These leaks included that Lana Clarkson's blood had been found on Spector's jacket, on the cloth used to clean the gun, and around the house as far as the knob on the back door.

The spin game had gotten worse for Phil when in November 2003, after the *Los Angeles Times* won a request to unseal the police report and search warrants. Spector's first comment to Adriano De Souza—"I think I killed somebody"—became as prominent in the case as the one about Clarkson's kissing the gun.

But, as Abramson pointed out after she had released the coroner's report, there was more to the story. She and Phil had found a number of inconsistencies in the official version of the February 3 events. The most profound ones concerned the gun, which, unlike the others taken from the house, was not registered. (Of course, the matching ammo in the house was still a problem.) Not only was Clarkson's blood found on the inside and outside of the barrel—suggesting that it must have been inside her mouth, symptomatic of a traditional suicide—but gunpowder residue had covered both of her hands, indicative of her having held it. Indeed, it was manna to Phil that the coroner himself seemed ambivalent about who had fired the gun, writing that Clarkson "may have discharged [it] or had [her] hands otherwise in an environment of gunshot residue." Hence, he would argue, it wasn't the coroner but the cops and the DA who had made the ultimate determination of homicide.

In addition, although Phil's blood alcohol level—admittedly, twelve and a half hours after the fact—was a legally drunk .08, Clarkson's was .12, and she also had "therapeutic" levels of the prescription painkiller hydrocodone (Vicodin) in her system. Such a mix of booze and painkillers could produce seriously impaired senses and, accordingly, seriously erratic behavior.

Then there was the little matter of a fingernail, or rather a sliver of a fingernail. The autopsy report showed that an acrylic nail on Clarkson's right thumb was broken off. Spector and Shapiro had known about the nail since the summer, when in a weird turn, a former homicide investigator for the sheriff's department, hired by Shapiro to search the Castle after the cops were done, supposedly found the nail—a fact that came to light after he told his old buddies about it at a department barbecue in July. Word got back to the DA's office, and they asked Shapiro to turn over the nail. Shapiro coyly sat on the request without ever saying whether he had it or not. The nail, if it existed, and even if it had traces of gunpowder on it, was not definitive evidence that Clarkson had committed suicide. An argument could be made either way: that Clarkson had had the gun in her hand and the recoil of the shot had broken the nail, or that it had been blown off as she'd tried to shield her face from the shot. The same range of interpretation, in fact, applied to the residue on Clarkson's hands that Phil and Abramson found so compelling.

Of greater importance to them, the elusive nail—and the DA's assumption that it was in Phil's possession—gave the Spector team leverage. Now they had a useful straw man, given that Shapiro's private detective was connected to the sheriff's department, thus raising conspiracy theories. And by being noncommittal on the issue, they could force a delay while the DA's office tried to get its hands on that damn nail.

These classic diversionary tactics were put into play the day before a May 7 preliminary hearing, when as part of their strategy, the Spector team preemptively released the entire coroner's report to the media, on the premise that the DA had hidden important details that they said supported Phil's innocence. Hoping that the media would take the bait, they would not be disappointed. The next day, before Spector and Abramson had even gotten to court, an AP story headlined ACTRESS MAY HAVE SHOT SELF IN SPECTOR CASE reported that "an actress killed at music producer Phil Spector's home was shot with a gun inside her mouth and had gunshot residue on both hands, indicating she may have fired the weapon." It also noted the broken fingernail, "which defense attorneys are expected to argue came from firing the gun."

The release of the coroner's report immediately threw the prosecutors back on their heels. When stories began to break with this angle, DA Steve Cooley was forced to send out a spokeswoman, Sandi Gibbons, to try to redirect the focus to the sections of the report inculpatory to Spector. In addition to the blood on his jacket and the cloth used to wipe the gun, these sections included curious anomalies, such as the gun being in Spector's hand at the back door, as witnessed by De Souza, then found wiped clean under Clarkson's left leg—this despite the fact that she was right-handed, which at least circumstantially pointed to an effort by a frantic, blood-spattered Spector to dispose of evidence and clumsily stage a suicide scene.

As investigators had construed it, the amount of blood on the floor near the back door proved that Clarkson had been shot there, possibly after washing out the brandy glass found in the sink and trying to get to the door to leave. Had Phil at that point gotten in her way, pulled his gun, and done his "you're not going anywhere" shtick? Had there been a physical confrontation? Was that why there was a contusion on Clarkson's skull? Although that piece of the puzzle was missing, the DA was positive that her lifeless body had been moved—thus the awkward, unnatural positioning of the corpse on the chair—leaving blood and tooth fragments across the foyer floor. And in the end, the coroner had concluded—somewhat contradictorily given the other, evenhanded observation that Clarkson "may have" pulled the trigger—that her "male companion" had had possession of the gun when it was discharged.

Gibbons also pointed out that Phil had gunpowder residue on *his* hands (a smaller amount, insisted Abramson, who had not released those results in her document dump) and explained that the residue on Clarkson was due to a three-foot "cloud" that would have dusted her hands, even if they were in her lap. Gibbons didn't add the obvious corollary—that this "cloud" could explain the residue on Phil's hands as well.

Finally, the investigators had used a bit of generic mindreading to come up with anecdotal evidence indicating that Clarkson had not shot herself. As a blunt but perfectly serious Robert Kenney put it, "Pick up any homicide investigation book. When women commit suicide, they don't shoot themselves in the face. Chicks aren't like guys. They're thinking about how they'll look at their funeral. They don't want to mess up their face. "

At the May 7 preliminary hearing, Phil, dressed in an all-black pin-striped suit, plum-tinted shades, and a fashionably short and shaggy auburn wig, squirmed in his seat and looked outraged. Abramson, as always, sounded outraged. They had to be pleased that the hearing was taken up with discussing only one issue—the one that had already thrown the case off the rails: the "partially blackened, gunpowder-covered thumbnail," as a Reuters story put it.

Clearly, the DA had become distracted, even obsessed, by the notion that the Spector camp was hiding evidence, which Abramson did nothing to dispel. Court watchers knew that this kind of thing was old hat for her. During the Menendez sentencing hearing, it had been revealed that Abramson had had a psychologist hide potentially incriminating information against one of the brothers, although no charges had been filed against her after the yearlong investigation into the matter. Now she was only too happy to let the matter fester, at first grandly denying that she had the nail—"If I did," she quipped, "I'd blow it up poster size and put it on every billboard in Los Angeles County"—then cagily insisting to Judge Carlos Uranga that she couldn't speak about the matter in open court. After agreeing to meet with both sides in chambers, Uranga took back his order that Abramson produce the nail, putting off a decision until a future hearing.

With this small tactical victory, Abramson and Spector could vent with great moral umbrage about how they were standing up to a bullying DA. Phil had made the point in the courtroom, scowling and at one point rubbing his nose with his middle finger while Deputy District Attorney Doug Sortino, the lead prosecutor of the case, was speaking—obliquely but clearly flipping Sortino off.

As soon as Phil reached the corridor outside, he was cracking wise. "He's the one who proves you can have children through anal sex," he chirped, referring to Sortino.

Making a wan attempt to shush him, Abramson purred, "Phil, I get to be nasty; you don't."

But in this, his first en masse meeting with the press, there was no chance of that. As Abramson conducted an impromptu question-and-answer session, she began by laboriously drawing conspiracy theories—such as that Shapiro's private eye was a "plant" and a "spy" and that the coroner had reached his homicide ruling because of pressure from the sheriff's department and "political pressure from whatever source" to make justice in L.A. seem blind to status and wealth. But she could barely finish a sentence without Phil interjecting some catty remark. At one point, when she brought up how he had been Tasered and roughed up, he interrupted, saying, "Broken nose and two black eyes, and 50,000 volts of electricity shot through me, unarmed, inviting the police into my house."

Another time, Abramson insisted that Adriano De Souza had misunderstood what Phil had told him because he was from Brazil and "is not perfect in his English. I will not say he's illiterate; he is not. I will not say he is stupid; he is not—"

"But he *is* illegal!" Phil chimed in.

"Well, that's a different issue," she said, not wanting to go there.

"Yeah, he's an illegal alien," he went on. "And he was being threatened with deportation."

"Exactly," she assented, no longer reticent, going on to claim that De Souza was supposed to be deported, but the DA "interceded" to make sure he would be around for the trial.

A few times when Phil broke in, Abramson mock-chided him, "Phillip, please, darling." He looked pained and backed off temporarily, only to start in again. Not able to keep him quiet, she pardoned him for

vare of his case" and then observed, "You can't stop a star-
from being a starring talent—you just can't!"
ie, he asked, "I should stop now?" to guffaws from the crowd.
rning to the subject of her delayed retirement, Abramson said,
"If I'm going to end my career on this case—nobody wants to go out a
loser." Then, with a smirk, "Frankly, guys, it's a winner."

They left the stage that day with their spin and their talking points established, and with the fingernail snafu a pleasant complication. Playing
with house money, Abramson could even suggest breezily that although
she didn't have the nail, Robert Shapiro might, pulling him back into the
case. Indeed, the Spector team seemed to be set up nicely. Early on,
Shapiro, dipping freely into Spector's bank account, had retained the
services of the same duo of forensics experts he'd imported into the O. J.
Simpson case, former New York City medical examiner Michael Baden
and former L.A. County coroner Henry Lee. Veteran trial watchers had
seen these two mercenaries—each with a price tag of around
$100,000—manipulate evidence to fit a predetermined conclusion ben-
efiting a defendant's case, no matter how dubious, and be believed
because of their "impeccable" credentials. During the Simpson trial,
Lee had been an embarrassment, at one point identifying "new" foot-
prints in O. J.'s driveway that had in fact been left embedded in the
cement by the workers who paved the driveway years before. And yet
the fatuous judge, Lance Ito, amazingly had warned prosecutors not to
challenge Lee's credibility.
      Phil wanted that kind of star power on his side. Baden had even
been allowed to observe the Lana Clarkson autopsy, after which Shapiro
had parroted Baden's "independent" opinion that the evidence was "not
inconsistent with suicide"—a weaselly way of not saying that it *was* a suicide but nonetheless a finger in the DA's eye. Which was really the
Spector agenda now: blame the case against him on prosecutorial dirty
business.
      "They can fling as much mud as they want, but the mud won't
stick," Abramson huffed for reporters, although this was exactly her own
strategy.
      If it did stick, they knew, some of Phil's explanations of what had
happened at the Castle—at least as they stood now—might be laughed
out of court. For example, it was unimaginable that he believed he could
get away with claiming that the blood on his clothes—*Clarkson's*

blood—had come from being Tasered and tackled by the cops. That blood was, of course, also on the jacket he had taken off and thrown in the upstairs powder room before the cops had arrived. In fact, the only DNA of Phil's to be found anywhere was the semen on one of Clarkson's breasts. And if De Souza had "misunderstood" him, he would have to claim that Officer Beatrice Rodriguez had, too.

More problems arose when the DA's office let it be known that it had numerous depositions from women whom Spector had allegedly terrorized using a gun. Fearing this all along, Abramson got even nastier, sneering at the procession of victimized women. "Every rock that gets turned over, another one crawls out," she observed. Anticipating any damaging testimony from Ronnie, she indelicately mentioned her several psychiatric confinements, no matter that Phil had caused them.

Whether or not it was coincidental, around this time, in the spring of 2004, Phil patched things up with Nancy Sinatra. No longer a "waste of time," she was seen with him at their old haunts. That led some to wonder if *she* needed a psychiatric confinement, and according to a tabloid report, the Sinatra family was "furious that Nancy is rallying to Phil's side when they remain scared to death of him."

Nancy, though, was stolid. "He's a wonderful man," she gushed to a reporter. "I don't know what happened on [February 3]. I've never asked him. But I never for a minute believed he could do such a thing."

If Phil liked the sound of those words, he'd like them even better from the witness stand.

By midsummer, it looked more and more as if he'd need that sort of character witness. In July, Judge Uranga finally called the Spector team's bluff about the illusory fingernail, reinstating his order to Abramson to turn it over to the DA or be forbidden to use it in the case. No longer able to equivocate about the nail, she scrambled into full retreat, even offering to bring in Henry Lee, who, she said, had done his own search and found only a piece of white thread tinted with blood. She may have wanted to dazzle Uranga with the very name of Henry Lee, but he wasn't buying it. Ending any further discussion of the issue, he set a preliminary hearing for October 20 to decide whether there was enough evidence to go to trial.

Spector and Abramson saw this as another opportunity. Such a hearing would allow them to hear the prosecutors' case and challenge it point by point—fortified by the star power of Lee, Baden, and their latest six-figure forensics expert hire, former Allegheny County (Pennsylvania) medical examiner Cyril Wecht, all of whom would reliably testify that Lana Clarkson's wounds were "not inconsistent with suicide." Long shot though it may have been, they figured they could at least demonstrate to the DA that he had another O. J. Simpson nightmare in the making.

Cooley, however, had other plans. No doubt thinking along with Spector, Cooley and Doug Sortino weren't about to show their cards in open court, where the media would be sure to eat up the O. J. trope, with Spector in the starring role. Secretly, Sortino impaneled a grand jury to hear the evidence, knowing full well that he could pull an indictment out of his hip pocket at any time. This was the DA's high hard one, and it would soon whiz under Phil's chin. When it did, however, Abramson's chin would be nowhere in sight. All along, their dueling egos had presaged an inevitable breach in their united front. It always seemed a question of how long, not if, Phil could abide a strong, manipulative woman who made him seem weak by comparison—or accept that any woman could really crack nuts in court without seeming shrewish instead of tough.

Eventually, he decided that the task required a man. A real man. A damn near *made* man. Before hiring Abramson, he had diddled with the idea of taking on Bruce Cutler, who'd made a celebrity (and nuisance) of himself in winning acquittals for crime family boss John Gotti in three federal trials. He might have won a fourth, when Gotti in 1990 was charged with conspiracy to murder after rival don Paul Castellano was whacked on a Manhattan street, but the feds had Cutler disqualified on the grounds that he was "in-house counsel" to the Gambino crime family and thus a possible witness.

As a cog in the Mob's mechanism, Cutler was appropriately feared, and this was something he seemed to enjoy. Looking more bouncer than barrister, he was a peculiar but regular sight on the New York celebrity scene, a barrel-chested, bullnecked, bald-pated Mussolini look-alike with a taste for expensive suits and an eye for the nearest television camera. In court, he dripped with contempt for prosecution witnesses during his "Brucifications," as observers called his brutal cross-examinations. What Cutler did best was evince that government witnesses, who in many cases were turncoat Mob guys, could be bigger creeps than *his* creep.

⊙

This was precisely Phil's plan, with the DA to be made into a bigger creep than himself, and he had apparently entered into some kind of representation arrangement with Cutler in January before going with Abramson as his choice in the courtroom—in part because he thought a woman would seem less bullying when confronting female witnesses. But with Abramson having won no rulings favorable to him, he had buyer's remorse. Now it was brass knuckles time—a metaphor made for Cutler, who had not only defended convicts but also was one, having been sentenced to ninety days' house arrest and three years' probation after the 1992 Gotti trial for violating a court order prohibiting lawyers on both sides from making public comments about the case.

Phil apparently didn't bother to tell Abramson that he was making the switch to Cutler as the point man in court. It happened in July when, with Abramson out of the country, Cutler filed a motion to take over the case in her absence. For Abramson, who increasingly had been squabbling with Spector over tactics, Cutler's entrance had to sting. If Phil wanted her to stick around but be second banana to Cutler—perhaps at a greatly reduced fee—it was an offer she could refuse. She and her co-counsel, Marcia Morrissey, withdrew from the defense, complaining abstrusely, "We were put in an untenable position and we were forced to resign. If we wanted to be ethical and competent, we had to resign."

No one really knew what this meant, and she didn't explain. Was she inferring that she had resigned not because of an ego clash with Cutler but because Spector had wanted her to do something unethical? Whatever the underlying facts, Cutler, already in tune with Phil, closed the door on Abramson with a descriptive allegory: as Spector's "personal attorney" since before Abramson had arrived, he'd had to step in when she had "jumped ship and I had to take control of the ship and bring it into port."

Abramson, for once, had no glib comeback. All she could do was return to her interrupted retirement and try not to think about her "idol" and the "winner" of a case she couldn't get away from fast enough.

Needing to familiarize himself with the viscera of the case, Cutler sought and obtained a three-month delay in the scheduled preliminary hearing, until December 16. However, Steve Cooley's grand jury—which the Spector team didn't know about—made its decision in early September, and Phil's lawyers were notified on the 22nd to appear in court on the 27th. That's when they knew they'd been outmaneuvered by the DA and there would be no hearing on the evidence after all.

Cutler—who was not licensed to practice law in California and thus had to become co-counsel with Roger Rosen, his co-counsel from the Gotti trials, who now practiced in L.A.—had left much of the grunt work to Rosen. He now hurried out to be with Spector and Rosen at the Los Angeles courthouse on September 27 for what they fully assumed would be the reading of an indictment for murder one, with the special circumstances of committing a felony with a weapon. Phil arrived at the courthouse looking smooth and grinning, his long wig artfully highlighted with blond streaks. Clad all in black, broken up only by a gold cobra lapel pin and a gold bauble stickpin, he also had on his arm a pointedly symbolic tall, striking blonde—Michelle Blaine. Towering over him in her low-cut, shocking pink dress, with her short-cropped platinum hair and Wayfarer sunglasses, Blaine was clearly playing to "type"—the Lana Clarkson "type"—visual testament to how common it was for such alluring women to accrue to him, precluding the scenario that he would ever need to threaten or keep such a woman from fleeing his presence. His buoyant bounce and blasé expression seemed to mock the very notion.

When he entered the courtroom, however, the grave atmospherics peeled away the front. He seemed especially irritable and at times looked faint. When the indictment was read, his knees went soft, and he grabbed Rosen's arm to steady himself. He said nothing beyond entering his not guilty plea and intoning "Yes, Your Honor" when Judge David Wesley asked if he was waiving his right to a speedy trial. Wesley then set a tentative trial date—the same December 16 on which the preliminary hearing was to be held—and agreed with both sides to hold the trial in L.A. instead of the smaller county courthouse in Pasadena (closer to Alhambra), which was at risk of being overrun by the media.

The weakness had left Phil's knees by the time he appeared on the courthouse steps. Stopping to address the media, he obviously had a lot to say. Whereas Abramson could at least pretend to rebuke him while allowing just enough of his taunts to complement her tirades, there was no holding him back now as he waded knee-deep into a blistering personal attack on "the Hitler-like District Attorney Steve Cooley and his storm-trooping henchmen." He called the prosecutors "reprehensible, unconscionable, and despicable" for "secretly, as fascists would," going to "a secret grand jury to seek and get an indictment."

Pointing out that Lakers star Kobe Bryant had been granted a preliminary hearing in Colorado despite not being a resident of that state, while Phil had "voted and paid property taxes here for the last some fifty-odd years," Spector asked, "Does [Cooley] have something to hide and fear? I think so." That "something" was that "the judge and the public will see that no crime was committed at my home on February 3, 2003, . . . and that the district attorney is pursuing a personal vendetta." There were also the mandatory slanders of "the deceased," whom he made sure to remind everyone "was legally intoxicated on the drug Vicodin and alcohol at the time she took her own life." He ended with a plea to "a fellow artist, Governor Arnold Schwarzenegger, to step in and grant me my California constitutional rights and stop this miscarriage of justice . . . so I can get on with my life."

So contented was he with his harangue that a few days later, he e-mailed a transcription of his remarks to the media, with the request, "I would appreciate if you'd print as much of this as possible." Cutler, however, may have told Spector to leave the "storm trooper" language to him, as Gotti always had to great effect. Indeed, Cutler was not shy about using that sort of incendiary language, nor about admitting that he was going to play hard to sway the public.

"Our aim," he said, "is not only to win this case but also to win it in the court of public opinion." Steve Cooley, he warned, would know "this case never should have been brought."

However, Cooley was also playing to the public—and to potential jurors. In early October, he asked Judge Larry Fidler, who would be presiding at the trial, to allow him to release the grand jury transcript. The Spector team, which had been emphatic about the public's right to know in regard to the coroner's report, was now less so. They wanted to keep the lid on the witnesses whom they hadn't been able to cross-examine and demanded that Fidler seal the transcript. They said that the transcript was "full of lies" and would be prejudicial because Spector's peculiar legacy was so widely known by the public, who would accept the worst as fact. Fidler downplayed the latter supposition, confessing that he, a middle-aged man, had never heard of Phil Spector before this case. That may have been the unkindest cut of all.

On November 11, Fidler sided with the DA, and all of the horrid details of February 3 began flooding into the media a month later. The most damaging segments were Spector's own self-crucifying words to Adriano De Souza and Officer Beatrice Rodriguez—"I think I shot somebody" and "I didn't mean to shoot her. It was an accident"—and the stream of accusatory testimony from women he'd terrorized in the past.

However, simply because the transcripts were made public didn't mean that the Spector team would stand by and allow every word in them to be repeated from the witness stand. Implementing a strategy of legal coitus interruptus, Cutler began raising issues that needed to be settled before a trial could take place, which worked to get the trial put off numerous times, from December 2004 to April 2005 and then to September 2005, throwing it on Fidler to decide the admissibility of certain grand jury testimony.

The most important ruling came on May 23, 2005, concerning the women from Spector's past. The grand jury had heard from ten of them, dating back to 1972. Sortino had made his case to admit their testimony and that of victims of Spector's gun antics in a Motion to Admit Evidence of Other Crimes filed on February 17, retelling the nightmarish experiences of Dianne Ogden, Melissa Grovesnor, Dorothy Melvin, Deborah Strand, and others, including the men threatened at Starbucks months after February 3. Tying together all the previous incidents with the shooting of Lana Clarkson, Sortino wrote of Spector's "continuous history of firearm-related violence" and turned psychologist, darkly explaining that Phil persisted in behavior that he "knows is against the law" and that "puts the lives of victims at risk . . . because it causes people to fear for their lives and forces them to do what he wants."

Sortino continued, "Prior to each crime, Spector consumed alcohol [and] displayed [a] weapon . . . in a threatening way [and] pointed it at the victim at close range [sometimes] touching the victims' faces with the weapon." He concluded that "the similarities between the uncharged assaults . . . and the charged murder of Lana Clarkson . . . disprove [Spector's] assertions that Clarkson's death was self-inflicted, caused without malice, or accidental. These incidents explain what really occurred in the rear foyer of 1700 S. Grandview Drive on the morning of February 3, 2003."

Phil, in a brazen display of nerve, had already gone on record with a blanket denial that these incidents had ever happened, insisting with a straight face that he had "never pulled a gun on these women" and that their stories were "the first I've heard of it." Bruce Cutler, looking to open fire figuratively on the women's credibility, called them, "sycophants and parasites." This was a weird charge since it might have actually explained why they hadn't pressed charges against Phil in the first place. It also raised the question of whether Spector had ever paid them to keep quiet. Playing off of Cutler's "bad cop," Roger Rosen gave a softer answer that didn't vilify the women or challenge their stories but only questioned whether they were relevant. "It makes for interesting reading," he said, "but why don't we try this case based on the facts of the case? Who cares about something that happened thirty years ago? He's not on trial for any of those things. He's on trial for what happened to Ms. Clarkson."

Knowing how crucial the ruling would be, Phil arrived in court that day clad in another black suit, adorned with a dragonfly brooch and big brass buttons, and escorting an attractive blonde young enough to be his daughter. Identified in press reports as Rachelle Marie Short, she had first cropped up in a Fox News story in March, referred to there as "a thirty-something blonde" seen accompanying Phil and "sporting a big diamond ring mounted on a platinum band on her left hand." Later in the year, she would be identified by name and age (twenty-five) in a report that Phil said he would marry her, but only if he beat the murder rap. In that story, Short's mother, Karen McDonald, was quoted as being "ecstatic" about Phil's becoming her son-in-law, calling him "a good man [who] wouldn't murder anyone" and saying that "he wouldn't harm my daughter."

Whether it was true love or an extension of the Michelle Blaine role for show purposes only, at least through the rest of 2005, he and Rachelle were seen both in public and in the courtroom holding hands and cooing. If it was love, it wouldn't hurt a bit if anyone on the fence about his innocence could see how gentle and loving, even how sub-servient, he could be with a beautiful blonde.

Fidler, however, wasn't swayed by the sideshow. Although he acknowledged that allowing the evidence was "a dangerous path to go down," he concluded that the incidents seemed to illustrate the state's theory in the case and ruled that the prosecutors could present as evidence four of the ten incidents, striking the other six, including the two misdemeanor convictions from the 1970s. This wasn't a total loss for the defense, as the trial wouldn't be a carousel of accusing women and tales of previous convictions. Still, if Phil had any illusions of having the trial revolve around the narrow and restrictive parameters of the gun residue evidence, the unregistered gun, and Lana Clarkson's "shady" character, Fidler's ruling must have felt like a mortal blow.

Phil did succeed in one respect at the hearing—adding another "mad genius" reference point to his long résumé of whacked-out public appearances. This one was unveiled as soon as he walked into the court-room. Atop Spector's jowly, now matronly face was a wildly blown-out, sprayed, poofed, and teased wig—blond, no less—reminiscent of Tom Hulce's Mozart in *Amadeus*. Was this intentional? Was he trying to reestablish his legacy as America's Mozart? Was it a goof? Was he going for an insanity defense? He didn't say, for once fighting the urge to speak to reporters outside. But the wire service pictures of him spoke volumes, and the images of him under that mushroom cloud of hair— reproduced with abandon in newspapers and on the Internet—quickly replaced the picture of him in the police cruiser as the definitive shot.

Among old allies who once thought they knew him well enough to get inside his head, there was only bewilderment over this Spector stunt and the rather foppish way he had come to dress in court appearances: the knee-length jackets, the clanging brooches, the rainbow collection of shades to cover his eyes. "I don't understand why he continues to dress and look so strange," Larry Levine said. "Phil was always a sharp dresser, very hip and stylish, but not effeminate like this. And the day he had the big hair—why would he do that? You'd want to convince poten-tial jurors you're not totally idiotic."

Other housekeeping had to be done before a trial could go forward, including determining the admissibility of Officer Rodriguez's devastat-ing statement. At a hearing on the matter, Cutler tried to convince Judge Fidler that Rodriguez's testimony was "only the bare recollection of a woman doing her job, with all of this chaos and danger and violence around her," as if this was somehow unusual for a cop. He suggested that what Spector had really said, or at least meant to say, was, "I *didn't* shoot her. It was an accident."

Fortunately for Phil, as Cutler also noted, none of the other cops with Rodriguez had heard Spector say what she claimed he had. And what they did hear him say at other moments was very different, and not at all incriminating, such as, "I'm sorry there's a dead woman here," and "If you're going to arrest me, just tell me what happened." Perhaps cast-ing the most doubt was Officer Michael Page's tape of him saying, "The gun went off accidentally. She works at the House of Blues. It was a mistake."

⊙ 394

"We deny in the clearest terms that he shot that lady and it was Mr. Spector's gun!" Cutler boomed, his fist pounding the defense table. "We also deny in the clearest terms that Mr. Spector ever *admitted* that he shot that lady!"

In the event that Fidler believed that Phil had admitted it, Cutler tried a backup argument. He reminded the judge that the cops had "crashed" into Phil's home like (what else?) "storm troopers" and had attacked, "hog tied," "Tasered," and "figuratively punched him until he said something." (Cutler did not define what a figurative punching was.) Moreover, he said, the cops hadn't read Spector his Miranda rights. Needing to maintain Phil's position that he hadn't been drunk on February 2 or 3, Cutler said that he had instead been "experiencing symptoms of withdrawal" from medications, which may have included "hallucinations, forgetfulness, serious fatigue, and/or slurring." He noted that Spector had been prescribed a veritable pharmacopoeia, including two different antidepressants, two drugs to combat seizures, an antacid, a migraine medicine, and an antibiotic, but that he hadn't taken any of these that night.

Leaving aside Spector's hallucinations, Cooley responded by denying any police misconduct and insisting that the Tasering, which had come after Spector had refused to take his hands out of his pockets, had had "absolutely no effect" on him. And in the end, Fidler agreed, ruling that the Rodriguez statement was admissible, that Phil's statements had been made voluntarily, and that because he had refused to be interrogated, reading him his Miranda rights had become moot.

Cooley made a clean sweep in Fidler's rulings, winning as well the admissibility of the ten guns found at the Castle—including the shotgun, because of Dorothy Melvin's claim that Phil had chased her into the driveway with such a weapon. Cooley also asked to see Phil's sworn deposition in his lawsuit against Robert Shapiro, in which he had been subjected to probing questions from Shapiro's lawyer about February 3.

Even though Fidler said that there was "no smoking gun" in the deposition (Phil had admitted to being "borderline insane" at times during his life but not on February 3), Cooley's request was a useful tool for Cutler, who ate up more of the calendar contesting the motion to turn the deposition over. This issue stretched out for months, until Fidler ruled against Spector in January 2006—a month after Phil had dropped his suit against Shapiro.

By then, Fidler had set the trial date for April 24, 2006, more than three years after the shooting. A measure of how much time had passed was that Sortino, who'd spent what seemed like a lifetime on the case, was gone from it before the end of 2005, when he was appointed superior court judge by Governor Schwarzenegger. Elevated to take his place as lead prosecutor was Sortino's co-counsel, Deputy District Attorney Patrick Dixon. He, too, would have to play the waiting game, when Fidler postponed the trial yet again until September 2006 because Cutler had another trial to attend to back in New York in April.

Given the elliptical path to this now all-but-forgotten celebrity trial of the century, the question had become which century that would be.

Such was the paralysis of this case that Phil had plenty of time for two other court cases. One was an inevitable wrongful death civil suit filed by Lana Clarkson's mother on February 2, 2005. This was something she hadn't wanted to do until the murder trial was over, lest it interfere with the gravity of the latter, but she had been forced to because the state's statute of limitations for such a suit would have run out the next day (the third anniversary of her daughter's death). Asking for unspecified damages, Donna Clarkson, in a preview of the DA's arguments, maintained that the murder had occurred after Spector had "grabbed, hit, fought with, and restrained" Lana, preventing her from leaving his house.

In response to the suit, a disgusted and imperious Cutler issued a statement that borrowed from Phil's contempt for the Clarkson family. "He's not criminally responsible, and he's not civilly responsible, either," he said. "But I'm not surprised they filed a suit for money. That seems to be de rigueur nowadays." In Cutler's obvious desire for potential jurors to buy into the suggestion that the Clarkson family, hideously, wanted only to make a killing from Lana's tragic death, it escaped him that making the suggestion was hideous in itself.

The other case saw Phil filing his own civil lawsuit, on September 4, 2005, after he had burned another bridge—and another personal assistant—by firing Michelle Blaine. Unlike his first firing of Janice Savala, it wasn't over a computer or television but rather over $425,000 he alleged Blaine had embezzled out of his personal pension plan using the access she had had to his bank account through checks and debit cards. Phil claimed that she had called it a "loan" when he had confronted her about the withdrawals and had promised to pay it back—a story that Michelle's lawyers called fiction.

Hal Blaine sided with his daughter, saying of Phil, "He's full of shit. She'd never steal a dime. Why does she need his money? She has two companies of her own and just got a big grant to make movies from the Sundance Film Festival. This was about Phil needing to pay for his legal bills. She had two years left on her contract, and she'd be owed that, so his accountants told him to go and file a lawsuit. Brilliant. Go pay the lawyers more money."

The old drummer shook his head sadly. "You gotta understand what she did for him," he said. "Everybody said she was crazy to work for Phil. It was like, why would you want to do *that*? But she loved Phil, and she did a helluva job. She was the CEO, she held it all together even with all the shit the last three years. Hell, she saved him a lot more than $425,000. She saved him a half million on Shapiro alone. The first thing she did for him, he was going to England to do Starsailor and he wanted a private jet, and they were gonna charge him $125,000 for one. She told them no way, we'll get a jet elsewhere, and they gave it to her for under $100,000. She did things like that all the time. He'd be up shit's creek without her, 'cause he's helpless; he can't do anything by himself.

"She was just very upset. She loves him; she's so loyal. And then here he is trying to cut off her finances—for her whole family. Her son, Aaron, was also working for Phil, and Phil got rid of him, too, and made aspersions about him stealing money. With Phil, it's never about people's feelings. It's all about him. It's about power. When you've got all the money in the world, what else is there?"

Surprisingly, and indicative of the loyalty Phil has a way of inspiring, the ugliness didn't sever Hal's relationship with Spector. Trying hard to separate his daughter's dealings with Phil from his own, he went on, albeit somewhat sheepishly. "No, I don't hate Phil. I don't think that way about people. He never did anything to me. What happened is between Michelle and him. I have nothing to do with that."

This was the sort of blind loyalty that Phil was incapable of reciprocating. For Hal Blaine, there would be no more invitations to hang out at the Castle.

Michelle returned fire in March 2006 with a $5 million countersuit that threw some dirt back at Phil, who obviously hadn't foreseen what he could be in for when he rushed into suing her. She answered his charge by saying that he'd not only willingly loaned her money but also given her more—such as a $700,000 house. She also charged that Phil had sexually harassed her, sometimes appearing naked in front of her. He had, she said, once asked her to procure a prostitute for him and had invited her, in vain, to join him and a hooker in his hotel room.

The upshot of her charges was that his over-generosity and over-familiarity had had an objective—to keep her compliant and unhelpful to investigators and prosecutors. In time, she said, he had repeatedly proposed marriage to her, with his sole intention being to keep her off the witness stand under the mistaken belief that California law prohibits spouses from testifying against each other. This, of course, made it seem as if she might know a bit too much about Spector's vices and secrets. If so, could Phil have been any dumber when he had made the decision to fire her?

Cutler wearily and predictably rolled out the bluster against this new target. Michelle, he said, "stole this money and her final lie is now that it's hush money. It's all a lie."

The redundancy of it all was getting very old and very tired.

Which was a good description as well of Spector as he awaited a final judgment. The murder trial had been pushed back yet again, this time to January 16, 2007, to accommodate Judge Fidler's court calendar. But there were side issues still being settled. In early May 2006, Fidler okayed a defense motion to allow their forensics experts to examine and test the evidence. "We have said all along that once the evidence and facts of this case are examined, Phil Spector will be completely and fully vindicated and his good name restored," Cutler said. Spector also won a tactical pretrial victory in the Blaine case, when in August 2006 a judge ruled that Michelle had to surrender personal financial records, saying there was "probable validity" to Spector's charges. And optimistically— or perhaps tactically—he married Rachelle Marie Short on September 1, 2006, at a ceremony attended by a now shriveled retinue that included his daughter Nicole and the ever-loyal Dan and David Kessel.

By January 2007, "the First Tycoon of Teen" would be on Social Security. He would be nearly sixty years removed from Ben Spector's suicide; more than fifty years from his relocation to L.A. from the Bronx; forty years from the first denouement of his career; thirty years from his second dimout after leaving John Lennon's ears ringing from the shot he fired into the A&M ceiling; nearly twenty years from his induction into the Rock and Roll Hall of Fame.

But had he evolved in all that time?

Leslie Abramson, in one of her courthouse steps orations, had said, "Every one of us has people who would say negative things about us, and the larger celebrity you are, the more famous you are, the more of a genius you are, and the richer you are, the more people want to knock you down." Which sounds a lot like Danny Davis's dissection of the "stoning" Spector received after "River Deep—Mountain High." It probably also sounds a lot like what they'll say about Spector at his funeral, provided there's anyone left who will want to attend besides Marvin Mitchelson and possibly Nancy Sinatra.

If it was true that Phil Spector listened to the devils inside his head, the unstated corollary is that they were the only voices he *would* listen to. It wasn't his money or his fame or even his sword's-edge genius/madness that had him looking at fifteen years to life. It was the failure of this great maestro to change tempo. His beat remained the same, walking the very inner edge of damnation. The only wonder was that on his walkabout, he'd had to step over someone's corpse before somebody stepped over his. And even as his instincts fought for his name, railing against nonexistent enemies out to ruin him and selectively culling bits of obliging evidence, the truth was that he was already a condemned man—and would be so even if he could somehow pull out a victory, which wasn't a half-bad bet considering that, as he well knew, he was so much smarter than the cops and prosecutors. Even if he did, though, he'd already lost too much.

"For years I've had this dream about Phil," said Larry Levine, who'd been through too many lifetimes with Spector. "I see him doing this gig, where he goes back to England, where they really adore him, rents a big hall, and stands up there and conducts his old music. And people just flock to see him and it's awesome, it puts him back on top.

"And it would have happened just like that if he ever did it. He would have felt like he was on top of the world. I always wanted to tell him to do it, but there was just no way I could have brought it to his attention, because he was never happy enough in his life to say, 'Yeah, that would be a lark, let's go do it.' And now, that can never happen.

"If you ask me, that's the saddest thing of all: what might have been. For all he's done in music, there's so much more he could have done. He just didn't ever want to because of the pressure. And maybe on some level, he's happy now, or relieved, that he'll never have to try."

EPILOGUE

Marshall Lieb was also music supervisor for the movies *Macon County Line, Ode to Billy Joe,* and *Take This Job and Shove It.* He co-wrote the score of *The Farmer* with Hugo Montenegro.

Michael Spencer moved back to New York in 1969. He founded and became executive director of Hospital Audiences, Inc., which with government and corporate grants organizes concerts and other cultural exhibitions in hospitals, nursing homes, and prisons. He was recently elected Co-Chairman of the World Congress of Arts and Disabilities.

Kim Fowley recorded in the late seventies under various group names including the Renegades. After advertising for an all-girl punk band in L.A., he put together the group, including Joan Jett, that later became the Runaways. He has had two books of poetry published, *The Earth Is Really Flat* and *The Oblong Tiger.*

Annette Kleinbard (Carol Connors) became one of the top lyricists of motion picture and television source music in the 1970s and 1980s. She co-wrote (with Bill Conti) "Gonna Fly Now" for the movie *Rocky* and the themes of *Sophie's Choice* (with Marvin Hamlisch), *Falling in Love Again* (with Michel Legrand), and *Mr. Mom.* She was nominated for two Academy Awards and a Grammy for the theme music of *Rocky III,* and for four Emmys. She also co-wrote (with David Shire) the hit song "The Night the Lights Went Out in Georgia." As music supervisor for the movie *Tulips,* Marshall Lieb brought her in to collaborate on the score with Billy Goldenberg.

Stan Ross sold Gold Star Studios in 1984. Scheduled for demolition, the hallowed landmark of rock and roll was destroyed by a fire a few months later.

Lew Bedell continued to run Dore Records from the same office on Vine Street in Hollywood, with the label primarily featuring comedy albums, including *Mel's Hole,* by Bedell.

Don Peake won Academy Awards for scoring two short subject films, *In the Region of Ice* in 1978 and *Violet* in 1982.

Lou Chudd got out of the music business in the early seventies and made millions in steel pipe manufacturing and investment banking.

Jimmie Haskell has won three Grammys and an Emmy. He continues arranging and producing and has conducted more than twenty symphony orchestras throughout the world.

Lester Sill became president of Motown Records Publishing. He died on October 31, 1994, at age seventy-six.

Lee Hazelwood produced Nancy Sinatra's "These Boots Are Made for Walkin'" and sang duets with her on several other records in the 1960s. He released a solo LP in the seventies and then lived in seclusion for years in Sweden before moving back to Phoenix. In addition to producing Nancy Sinatra's comeback album, he wrote a book titled *The Pope's Daughter: His Fantasy Life with Nancy and Other Sinatras.*

Chuck Kaye became executive vice president of Warner-Chappell Publishing, CEO of Geffen Records, and CEO of DreamWorks Music Publishing.

Russ Titelman formed a working relationship with Lenny Waronker, the son of Liberty Records' Si Waronker, and the two of them produced James Taylor's *Gorilla* and *In the Pocket* LPs in the mid-seventies. As a staff producer for Warner Brothers, Titelman produced records by Randy Newman, Christine McVie, Chaka Khan, and Steve Winwood. He won a Grammy in 1986 for Winwood's *Back in the High Life* album and two more Grammys for producing Eric Clapton's *Unplugged* album. He also co-produced Brian Wilson's solo debut, *Brian Wilson.*

Annette Merar Spector returned to L.A. and in 1976 married spiritualist Richard Tapper and had a child. After their divorce, she moved to the San Fernando Valley and studied religion and philosophy. Of her painful marriage to Spector, she said in 1989, "Living in the shadow of this man is very hard. I always wanted to be gifted, to be something special. And because of him, I feel I'm not."

Warren Entner followed his stint with Spector's Three by becoming an original member of the Grass Roots. He was executive producer of the 1983 movie *The Pirates of Penzance*. He now owns an entertainment management company in L.A.

Jerry Leiber and *Mike Stoller* remained vital producers into the early eighties. After producing Peggy Lee's *Mirrors* LP in 1975, they returned to rock, working with Procol Harem ("Pandora's Box") and Stealers Wheel ("Stuck in the Middle with You"). They released a two-record album in 1981, *Only in America,* a compilation of many of the legendary songs they produced and wrote in the fifties and sixties; at least four other greatest hits albums were released thereafter. Inducted into the Rock and Roll Hall of Fame in 1987, they won a Grammy for Lee's "Is That All There Is?" and for the cast album of the long-running Broadway show based on their songs, *Smokey Joe's Café.*

Beverly Ross went on to compose Broadway shows and own a recording studio in New York.

John Bienstock and *Fred Bienstock* kept on working out of the same Brill Building offices, as overseers of the enormous Chappell Music publishing combine, which absorbed Hill and Range Songs in the mid-1970s. Their cousins and onetime bosses, Jean and Julian Aberbach, left the music business to run a prestigious art gallery.

Doc Pomus wrote songs for Dr. John and co-wrote with Willy DeVille three songs on Mink DeVille's *Le Chat Bleu* album in 1980. He also wrote the title song of B. B. King's Grammy-winning *There Must Be a Better World Somewhere* LP in 1981. He died of cancer on March 14, 1991, at age sixty-five. A tribute album, *Till the Night Is Gone,* was released by Rhino Records in 1995.

Terry Phillips became a staff producer at Decca, writing and producing songs for the Hobbits. He later formed a label, Perception Records, which had hits that included King Harvest's "Dancing in the Moonlight."

Don Kirshner followed his bubblegum-music windfall with a new gold mine in the 1970s: the television rock concert. His late-night "In

Concert" and "Don Kirshner's Rock Concert" series—simulcast on FM radio stations nationwide and featuring a comically stiff and glazed-eyed Kirshner introducing each act—thrived into the early eighties even though rock critics savaged the shows' vacuous glossiness. Another Kirshner television project was an alternative to the Grammys, the self-congratulatory "Rock Music Awards." His label, Kirshner Records, was a big winner, fueled by the pomp rock group Kansas, but it collapsed along with the band in the mid-1980s. In 2006, he formed the Don Kirshner Company, opening the Don Kirshner Rock and Roll Hotel and Casino. He also returned to the publishing business, hoping to re-create his "Golden Ear" legend by discovering new songwriters and artists.

Ray Peterson was a top attraction on the country music circuit. He died of cancer on January 25, 2005, at age sixty-five.

Curtis Lee is in the construction business in Yuma, Arizona.

Ahmet Ertegun holds the position of Founding Chairman of Atlantic Records. He was inducted into the Rock and Roll Hall of Fame—which he founded—in 1987 and was presented a Grammy Trustees Award in 1993.

Jerry Wexler produced dozens of records with Tom Dowd in the sixties and seventies, including those made by Dr. John, José Feliciano, and Dusty Springfield. Appointed senior vice president at Warner Brothers in 1978, he continued working in the studio and produced Bob Dylan's *Saved* album and Dire Straits' *Communiqué*. He also worked with George Michael in the 1980s.

Tom Dowd produced Jerry Jeff Walker, Eric Clapton, and the first three Allman Brothers albums. He also worked with Rod Stewart, Kenny Loggins, Lynyrd Skynyrd, Yes, and Pablo Cruise. Eight months after receiving a Grammy Trustees Award, he died in Miami of respiratory cancer on October 27, 2002.

Aaron Schroeder remained in the Broadway music publishing circle, but after being sued for shady business practices, he sold off his publishing interests to United Artists. He remained active in the business as owner of Aaron Schroeder International.

Gene Pitney continued to record and tour, covering "He's a Rebel" on one album. Inducted into the Rock and Roll Hall of Fame in 2002, he suffered a heart attack after performing in Wales and died on April 5, 2006, at age sixty-five.

Gerry Goffin and *Carole King* wrote together briefly after King's massive success as a solo act in the early 1970s (her sensitive and powerful *Tapestry* LP had four Top 10 hits and sold more than 13 million copies) burned out. King's 1980 *Pearls* LP reprised some of the classic Goffin-King hits. Goffin also wrote with Barry Goldberg, and King wrote with her husband Rick Evers, who died of a heroin overdose in 1978. Goffin and King were inducted into the Rock and Roll Hall of Fame in 1990. King continues writing and touring. She composed the theme for the TV show "Gilmore Girls," in which she also has guest-starred.

Jack Nitzsche composed music for the films *9½ Weeks, Breathless, Without a Trace, Starman, The Razor's Edge,* and *The Seventh Sign.* He and singer Buffy Sainte-Marie, who co-composed the Grammy-winning "Up Where We Belong," were married for thirty years until his death.

The Crystals continued to perform on the nostalgia circuit, but with only Dee Dee Kennibrew from the original group. La La Brooks gave up singing for a modeling career; Mary Thomas became a housewife in Brooklyn. Kennibrew brought suit, unsuccessfully, against Spector in the 1970s to recover back royalties for the group.

Barry Mann and *Cynthia Weil* endured far longer than any of the other Broadway writing teams of the early sixties. Although Mann's attempt at a singing career in the 1970s was a failure, he wrote Dan Hill's "Sometimes When We Touch" (with Hill) and Dolly Parton's "Here You Come Again." Weil collaborated briefly with Carole King in the eighties, and Mann and Weil won a Grammy in 1988 for the Linda Ronstadt–James Ingram duet "Somewhere Out There," from the movie *An American Tail.*

Snuff Garrett produced six straight Top 10 hits by Gary Lewis and the Playboys in the mid-sixties and two Top 10 hits by Sonny and Cher in the early seventies. He acted as music supervisor for the TV show "B. L. Stryker" in 1989 and 1990. He is now retired and lives in Arizona.

Bobby Sheen formed a short-lived label, Salsa Picante Records, in the mid-seventies. For over a decade, he sang in a latter-day touring version of the Coasters.

Ronnie Spector continues as a quivering echo of her sex kitten days, performing her old Ronettes hits ad infinitum—when Phil hasn't prevented her legally from doing so. Besides her work with Eddie Money in the 1980s, she released her second solo album, *Unfinished Business,* in 1987. In the 1990s, she appeared in a TV concert version of *The*

Wizard of Oz and the movie *Zoo*. She gave birth to twin sons, Austin and Jason. Like Phil, she has no relationship with their adopted twin sons, Gary and Louis, nor with their "firstborn," Donté.

Larry Levine became chief engineer at Premore Studios in North Hollywood and is today semi-retired.

Darlene Love sang on the Jeff Barry–written soundtrack for the movie *The Idolmaker* and tried a Las Vegas singing career, but she has never gotten far from her Spector identification. She put together a club act backed by The Wall of Sound Orchestra and released an album, *Darlene Love Live at Hop Singh's*, which consisted mainly of her old Philles standards. She was featured in Ellie Greenwich's 1985 Broadway musical *Leader of the Pack*, doing exactly the same thing. She had a small role in the film *Hairspray*, which starred Sonny Bono, and in the Broadway flop musical *Carrie*. She also recorded an album, *Darlene Love*.

Fanita James sang backup in Tom Jones's stage show in the early 1970s.

Lou Adler managed Carole King and produced the movies *Monterey Pop* and *Brewster McCloud*. He was executive producer of *The Rocky Horror Picture Show, Up in Smoke,* and *American Me*. He remains a fixture at L.A. Lakers games, seated next to Jack Nicholson and across the court from Spector's seats.

Sonny Bono, after divorcing Cher, remarried twice; was elected mayor of Palm Springs, California, where he owned a restaurant, Bono's; and was eventually elected to the U.S. House of Representatives, an office he held until he died in a skiing accident on January 5, 1998.

Cher had no more chart hits in the seventies but made plenty of headlines as the chief consort of rock stars. She married, had a son by, and made an album with Gregg Allman. After their divorce, she dated Kiss's Gene Simmons, Les Dudek, and Rob Camilletti, twenty years her junior. While her music career waned, Cher's acting career flourished. She appeared on Broadway and in the movie version of *Come Back to the 5 & Dime Jimmy Dean, Jimmy Dean* and won rave reviews for supporting roles in *Silkwood* and *Mask*. She won the 1988 Academy Award for Best Actress in *Moonstruck*. She hit the charts again in 1987 with "I Found Someone" from her Warner Brothers album *Cher.* Her retro disco hit "Believe" won a Grammy as Best Dance Recording in 1998, beating out Céline Dion's "My Heart Will Go On" as the best-selling single of that year. Her 2003 greatest hits CD spent weeks in *Billboard's*

Top 10. She also won an Emmy in 2003 for a special on her farewell concert tour.

Ellie Greenwich fell idle after the British invasion and rise of the singer/songwriter in the late sixties. Her 1985 Broadway musical *Leader of the Pack* (written with Anne Beatts) was part autobiography and part catalogue of her old hit songs. Paul Shaffer was originally featured in the thinly veiled role of—in Greenwich's words on the playbill's acknowledgment page—"the brilliant Phil Spector." In 1991, she was inducted into the Songwriters Hall of Fame with Jeff Barry.

Jeff Barry found his niche in bubblegum music—he wrote the Archies' hit "Sugar Sugar"—and television theme songs—"The Jeffersons," and "Family Ties." He co-wrote (with Peter Allen) and produced Olivia Newton-John's 1974 hit "I Honestly Love You" and co-wrote (with Barry Mann and Cynthia Weil) the 1984 Jeffrey Osborne–Joyce Kennedy hit "The Last Time I Made Love."

Vinnie Poncia worked with superstar producer Richard Perry on records Perry produced with Ringo Starr, Harry Nilsson, and Carly Simon. Poncia also produced Melissa Manchester. He wrote the Leo Sayer hit "You Make Me Feel Like Dancing" and produced Kiss's "I Was Made for Lovin' You," which he co-wrote with Paul Stanley and Desmond Child.

Danny Davis worked for Motown and Casablanca Records and for the Gallin-Morey show-biz management firm.

Brooks Arthur engineered Van Morrison and Bruce Springsteen albums and produced Janis Ian's *Between the Lines,* Liza Minnelli's *Gently,* and Adam Sandler's comedy albums, including the "The Chanukah Song." He also produced the soundtrack albums for *The Heartbreak Kid, Shirley Valentine, The Karate Kid, Lean on Me,* and *Ordinary People.* He now owns the Brooks Arthur Company.

Bill Medley and *Bobby Hatfield* reunited briefly in 1974 and had a No. 3 hit with "Rock and Roll Heaven," a tribute to dead rock stars. Medley cut an album in 1982, *Right Here and Now* (the title track was written by Mann and Weil) and toured again with Hatfield. In 1988, Medley had a No. 12 hit, a duet with Jennifer Warnes, "(I've Had) The Time of My Life," from the movie *Dirty Dancing.* The song also won a Grammy for Best Pop Performance by a Duo or Group. The duo was inducted into the Rock and Roll Hall of Fame in 2003. Eight months later, Hatfield died, on November 5, 2003, in a Kalamazoo, Michigan, hotel of a heart attack precipitated by a cocaine overdose.

Dennis Hopper became as much of a sixties cliché as *Easy Rider,* then was rediscovered in the 1980s as a middle-aged crazy. He played a gas-snorting, leather-clad gangster in David Lynch's *Blue Velvet* and was nominated for the 1986 Academy Award for Best Supporting Actor for his middle-American father role in *Hoosiers.* Hopper was nominated for an Emmy for the 1991 HBO movies *Paris Trout* and *Doublecrossed,* playing in the latter real-life drug smuggler Barry Seal. He co-starred in the 1994 blockbuster *Speed* and has made guest appearances on the TV shows "24" and "E-Ring."

Irwin Levine and *Toni Wine* wrote the first Tony Orlando and Dawn hit, "Candida," in 1970. When Wine married music publisher Chips Moman, Levine teamed up with Larry Brown to write Dawn's No. 1 hit "Tie a Yellow Ribbon Round the Ole Oak Tree" in 1971 and collaborated on the group's follow-up hits through the mid-seventies, including "Say, Has Anybody Seen My Sweet Gypsy Rose" and "He Don't Love You (Like I Love You)." Levine and Brown owned a publishing company, Levine and Brown Music, before Levine died of kidney failure on January 22, 1997, at age fifty-eight.

Dan Kessel and *David Kessel* produced songs for their New Wave label, Martian Records, many with a distinct Phil Spector feel—such as the Wigs' cover of "To Know Him Is to Love Him" and Cheri Gage's cover of "Here It Comes (and Here I Go)." They produced an updated Ventures and Frankie Avalon–Annette Funicello Christmas song in 1981. They performed and cut records under the name of the Martians, having a minor hit with "Baby Hold On." After they pretty much dropped out of studio recording in the mid-90s, they created Kessel Bros. International, representing rock acts such as Shag and producing rock stage shows. David Kessel hosted a podcast rock and roll show. Their father, Phil Spector's mentor, Barney Kessel, died from brain cancer on May 6, 2004, at age eighty.

Céline Dion rode her "shlock pop" to immense fame and fortune as arguably the most popular singer in the world. She had three other wildly successful albums in the 1990s, *Let's Talk About Love* (featuring "My Heart Will Go On," from the movie *Titanic,* one of the decade's biggest-selling singles), *These Are Special Times,* and *All the Way.* Although her recent albums have been less successful, she plays to sold-out houses in Las Vegas and on world tours and has launched her own perfume line.

PHIL SPECTOR DISCOGRAPHY

SINGLES

LABEL AND CATALOGUE NUMBER	GROUP	TITLE (WRITER)*	CHART ENTRY DATE†	HIGHEST CHART POSITION
1958				
Doré 503	Teddy Bears	"To Know Him Is to Love Him" (Spector)/ "Don't You Worry My Little Pet" (Spector)	9/28	1
1959				
Imperial 5562	Teddy Bears	"I Don't Need You Anymore" (Spector)/ "Oh Why" (Spector)	2/16 3/9	98 91
Imperial 5581	Teddy Bears	"If Only You Knew (the Love I Have for You)" (Spector)/ "You Said Goodbye" (Spector)	—	—
Imperial 5583	Phil Harvey	"Bumbershoot" (Spector)/ "Willy Boy" (Spector)	—	—

*If Spector was *not* the producer, producer's name follows in brackets.
†Date of entry onto *Billboard*'s Hot 100 or "Bubbling Under Hot 100."

SINGLES (*continued*)

LABEL AND CATALOGUE NUMBER	GROUP	TITLE (WRITER)*	CHART ENTRY DATE†	HIGHEST CHART POSITION
Imperial 5594	Teddy Bears	"Don't Go Away" (Spector)/ "Seven Lonely Days" (E. Shuman-A. Shuman-Brown)	—	—
Doré 520	Teddy Bears	"Wonderful Lovable You" (Spector)/ "Till You're Mine" (Spector)	—	—
Trey 3001	Spector's Three	"I Really Do (Spector)/ "I Know Why" (Spector)	—	—
1960				
Trey 3005	Spector's Three	"Mr. Robin" (Spector-Venet)/ "My Heart Stood Still" (Rodgers & Hart)	—	—
Trey 3006	Kell Osborne	"The Bells of St. Mary's" (Furber-Adams)/ "That's Alright Baby" (Spector)	—	—
Dunes 2002	Ray Peterson	"Corinna, Corinna" (Parish-Chapman-Williams)/ "Be My Girl" (Spector-Sands)	11/27	9
1961				
ABC-Paramount 10181	Johnny Nash	"Some of Your Lovin' " (Spector-Phillips)/ "A World of Tears" (Spector-Phillips)	2/13	104

Label	Artist	Titles	Date	Chart
Dunes 2007	Curtis Lee	"Pretty Little Angel Eyes" (Lee-Boyce)/ "Gee How I Wish You Were Here" (Boyce)	2/3	7
Gregmark 2	Paris Sisters	"Be My Boy" (Spector-Sands)/ "I'll Be Crying Tomorrow" (Spector)	4/24	56
Atlantic 2098	Billy Storm	"When You Dance" (Jones-Kirkland)/ "Dear One" (Parris)	—	—
Atlantic 2104	Ruth Brown	"Anyone But You" (Barry)/ "It Tears Me All to Pieces" (Pomus-Shuman)	—	—
Atlantic 2107	Castle Kings	"You Can Get Him Frankenstein" (Spector-Ertegun-Adlum Jr.)/ "Loch Lomond" (public domain)	—	—
Atlantic 2112	Billy Storm	"Honey Love" (McPhatter-Wexler)/ "A Kiss from Your Lips" (Davis)	—	—
Atlantic 2115	Top Notes	"Always Late (Why Lead Me On?)" (Frizell-Crawford)/ "Twist and Shout" (Berns-Medley)	—	—
Atlantic 2119	LaVern Baker	"Hey Memphis" (Pomus-Shuman)/ "Voodoo Voodoo" (Avril-Coleman)	—	—
Goldisc 3024	Ducanes	"I'm So Happy (Tra-La-La)" (Robinson)/ "Little Did I Know" (Spector-Sands)	7/7	109
Musicor 1011	Gene Pitney	"Every Breath I Take" (Goffin-King)/ "Mr. Moon, Mr. Cupid and I" (Pitney)	8/7	42
Gregmark 6	Paris Sisters	"I Love How You Love Me" (Mann/Kolber)/ "All Through the Night" (Duncan)	9/4	5
Jamie 1197	Creations	"The Bells" (Barrows)/ "Shang Shang" (Jones-Wells)	—	—
Dunes 2008	Curtis Lee	"Under the Moon of Love" (Lee-Boyce)/ "Beverly Jean" (Boyce)	10/16	46
Philles 100	Crystals	"There's No Other (Like My Baby)" (Spector-Bates)/ "Oh Yeah, Maybe Baby" (Spector-Hunter)	11/20	20

SINGLES *(continued)*

LABEL AND CATALOGUE NUMBER	GROUP	TITLE (WRITER)*	CHART ENTRY DATE†	HIGHEST CHART POSITION
Dunes 2009	Ray Peterson	"I Could Have Loved You So Well" (Goffin-Mann)/ "Why Don't You Write Me" (Hollins)	12/18	57
Big Top 3073	Arlene Smith	"He Knows I Love Him Too Much" (Goffin-King)/ "Love, Love, Love" (McRae-Wyche-David)	—	—
Big Top 3089	Sammy Turner	"Falling" (Leiber-Stoller)/ "Raincoat in the River" (Schroeder-Kaye)	—	—
1962				
Gregmark 10	Paris Sisters	"He Knows I Love Him Too Much" (Goffin-King)/ "A Lonely Girl's Prayer" (Spector-Sands)	1/27	34
Philles 101	Joel Scott	"Here I Stand" (Motola)/ "You're My Only Love" (Motola-Page) [Both sides: Lester Sill]	—	—
Liberty 55445	Troy Shondell	"Na-Ne-No" (Dino)/ "Just Because" (Price) [This side: Snuff Garrett]	—	—
Liberty 55459	Bobby Sheen	"How Many Nights" (Miller-Carroll)/ "How Can We Ever Be Together" (Halley)	—	—
Liberty 55483	Obrey Wilson	"Hey There Mountain" (Buchanan-Miller-Ervin)/ "Say It Again" (Wilson-Beavers)	—	—

Label/No.	Artist	Title (Composer)	Date	Pos.
Philles 102	Crystals	"Uptown" (Mann-Weil)/ "What a Nice Way to Turn 17" (Kolber-Keller)	3/31	13
Philles 103	Al Hazan	"Malagüeña" (Lecuona)/ "Chopsticks" (Hazan) [Both sides: Lester Sill]	—	—
Philles 104	Steve Douglas & His Merry Men	"Lieutenant Colonel Bogey's Parade" (Sill-public domain)/ "Yes Sir That's My Baby" (Donaldson-Kahn) [Both sides: Lester Sill]	—	—
MGM 13074	Connie Francis	"Second Hand Love" (Spector-Hunter)/ "Gonna Git That Man" (Curtis)	5/12	7
Columbia 4-42678	Terry Day	"Be a Soldier" (Hilliard)/ "I Love You Betty" (Spector-Hunter)	—	(Withdrawn)
Philles 105	Crystals	"He Hit Me (and It Felt Like a Kiss)" (Goffin-King)/ "No One Ever Tells You" (Goffin-King)		
Philles 106	Crystals	"He's a Rebel" (Pitney)/ "I Love You Eddie" (Spector-Hunter)	9/8	1
Philles 107	Bob B. Soxx and the Blue Jeans	"Zip-A-Dee-Doo-Dah" (Gilbert-Wrubel)/ "Flip & Nitty" (Spector)	11/17	8
Philles 108	Alley Cats	"Puddin' 'n' Tain" (Caufield-Pipkin-Willis)/ "Feel So Good" (Caufield-Pipkin)	1/12/63	43
Philles 109	Crystals	"He's Sure the Boy I Love" (Mann-Weil)/ "Walkin' Along (La-La-La)" (Spector)	12/29	11

1963

Label/No.	Artist	Title (Composer)	Date	Pos.
Philles 110	Bob B. Soxx and the Blue Jeans	"Why Do Lovers Break Each Others' Hearts?" (Greenwich-Powers-Spector)/ "Dr. Kaplan's Office" (Spector)	2/16	38

SINGLES (*continued*)

LABEL AND CATALOGUE NUMBER	GROUP	TITLE (WRITER)*	CHART ENTRY DATE†	HIGHEST CHART POSITION
Philles 111	Darlene Love	"(Today I Met) The Boy I'm Gonna Marry" (Spector-Greenwich-Powers)/ "Playing for Keeps" (Spector-Sands)	4/6	39
Philles 112	Crystals	"Da Doo Ron Ron (When He Walked Me Home)" (Spector-Barry-Greenwich)/ "Git It" (Goland)	4/27	3
Philles 113	Bob B. Soxx and the Blue Jeans	"Not Too Young to Get Married" (Spector-Greenwich-Barry)/ "Annette" (Spector-Sands)	6/8	63
Philles 114	Darlene Love	"Wait 'Til My Bobby Gets Home" (Spector-Greenwich-Barry)/ "Take It from Me" (Spector-Sands)	7/20	26
Philles 115	Crystals	"Then He Kissed Me" (Spector-Greenwich-Barry)/ "Brother Julius" (Goland)	8/17	6
Philles 116	Ronettes	"Be My Baby" (Spector-Greenwich-Barry)/ "Tedesco & Pitman" (Spector)	8/31	2
Philles 117	Darlene Love	"A Fine, Fine Boy" (Spector-Greenwich-Barry)/ "Nino & Sonny (Big Trouble)" (Spector)	10/19	53
Philles 118	Ronettes	"Baby, I Love You" (Spector-Greenwich-Barry)/ "Miss Joan & Mr. Sam" (Spector)	12/21	24
Philles 119	Darlene Love	"Christmas (Baby Please Come Home)" (Spector-Greenwich-Barry)/ "Harry and Milt Meet Hal B." (Spector)	—	—

1964

Philles 119	Crystals	"Little Boy" (Spector-Greenwich-Barry)/ "Harry (from W. Va.) & Milt" (Spector)	2/1	92
Philles 120	Ronettes	"(The Best Part of) Breakin' Up" (Spector-Poncia-Andreoli)/ "Big Red" (Annette Spector)	4/4	39
Phil Spector 1	Veronica	"So Young" (Tyrus)/ "Larry L." (Spector)	—	—
Phil Spector 2	Veronica	"Why Don't They Let Us Fall in Love?" (Spector-Greenwich-Barry)/ "Chubby Danny D." (Spector)	—	—
Annette 1000	Bonnie Jo Mason	"I Love You Ringo" (Spector-Case-Poncia-Andreoli)/ "Beatle Blues" (A. Spector)	—	—
Annette 1001	Gene Toone & the Blazers	"You're My Baby" (Spector-Poncia-Andreoli)/ "Jose" (Spector)	—	—
Annette 1002	Harvey & Doc with the Dwellers	"Oh Baby" (Harvey)/ "Uncle Kev" (A. Spector)	—	—
Shirley 500	Treasures	"Hold Me Tight" (Lennon-McCartney)/ "Pete Meets Vinnie" (Merar)	—	—
Philles 121	Ronettes	"Do I Love You" (Spector-Poncia-Andreoli)/ "Bebe and Susu" (Spector)	6/20	34
Philles 122	Crystals	"All Grown Up" (Spector-Greenwich-Barry)/ "Irving (Jaggered Sixteenths)" (Goland)	8/1	98
Philles 123	Darlene Love	"Stumble and Fall" (Spector-Poncia-Andreoli)/ "(He's a) Quiet Guy" (Spector-Poncia-Andreoli)	(Unreleased)	
Philles 123	Ronettes	"Walking in the Rain" (Spector-Mann-Weil)/ "How Does It Feel?" (Spector-Poncia-Andreoli)	10/24	23

SINGLES (*continued*)

LABEL AND CATALOGUE NUMBER	GROUP	TITLE (WRITER)*	CHART ENTRY DATE†	HIGHEST CHART POSITION
Philles 124	Righteous Brothers	"You've Lost That Lovin' Feelin' " (Spector-Mann-Weil)/ "There's a Woman" (Medley-Hatfield-Spector)	12/2	1
Philles 125	Darlene Love	"Christmas (Baby Please Come Home)" (Spector-Greenwich-Barry)/ "Winter Wonderland" (Smith-Bernard)	—	—
1965				
Philles 126	Ronettes	"Born to Be Together" (Spector-Mann-Weil)/ "Blues for Baby" (Spector)	2/6	52
Philles 127	Righteous Brothers	"Just Once in My Life" (Spector-Goffin-King)/ "The Blues" (Medley)	4/10	9
Philles 128	Ronettes	"Is This What I Get for Loving You?" (Spector-Goffin-King)/ "Oh I Love You" (Spector)	5/29	75
Philles 129	Righteous Brothers	"Hung on You" (Spector-Goffin-King)/ "Unchained Melody" (Zaret-North)	7/17	47
Philles 130	Righteous Brothers	"Ebb Tide" (Sigman-Maxwell)/ "For Sentimental Reasons" (Watson-Best)	12/4	5
Phi-Dan 5000	Florence DeVore	"Kiss Me Now" (Sacon-Hall)/ "We're Not Old Enough" (Pinter-Susser-Cooper) [Both sides: Cooper-Susser-Silberstein]	—	—

Label/No.	Artist	A-side / B-side		
Phi-Dan 5001	Betty Willis	"Act Naturally" (Morrison-Russell)/ "Soul" (Higgins) [Both sides: Leon Russell]	—	—
Phi-Dan 5005	Bonnie & the Treasures	"Home of the Brave" (Poncia-Andreoli)/ "Our Song" (Kern) [Both sides: Jerry Riopell]	8/28	77
Phi-Dan 5006	Al DeLory	"Yesterday" (Lennon-McCartney)/ "Traffic Jam" (McRae-Shaw) [Both sides: Atlas Artists Productions]	—	—
Phi-Dan 5007	George McCannon III	"You Can't Grow Peaches on a Cherry Tree" (Levitt-Monte)/ "Seven Million People" (Miller-Greenfield)— [Both sides: Anders-Poncia]	—	—
Phi-Dan 5008	Lovelights	"(When) I Get Scared" (Poncia-Andreoli-Pomuz)/ "Malady" (Mathis) [Both sides: Anders-Poncia]	—	—
Phi-Dan 5009	Ikettes	"Whatcha Gonna Do" (Turner)/ "Down Down" (Turner) [Both sides: Ike Turner]	—	—
Phi-Dan 5010	Sugar Plums	"Lovers Wonderland" (Crocker)/ "Sugar Plum Blues" (Fraser) [Both sides: Botkin-Garfield]	—	—
1966				
Philles 131	Ike and Tina Turner	"River Deep—Mountain High" (Spector-Greenwich-Barry)/ "I'll Keep You Happy" (Spector)	5/29	88
Philles 132	Righteous Brothers	"White Cliffs of Dover" (Black-Miller)/ "She's Mine, All Mine" (Hatfield)	—	—

SINGLES (*continued*)

LABEL AND CATALOGUE NUMBER	GROUP	TITLE (WRITER)*	CHART ENTRY DATE†	HIGHEST CHART POSITION
Philles 133	Ronettes	"I Can Hear Music" (Spector-Greenwich-Barry) [This side: Jeff Barry]/ "When I Saw You" (Spector)	10/29	100
Philles 134	Ike and Tina Turner	"A Man Is a Man Is a Man" (Antell)/ "Two to Tango" (Peretti-Creatore) [Both sides: Bob Crewe]	(Unreleased in U.S.)	
1967				
Philles 135	Ike and Tina Turner	"I'll Never Need More Than This" (Spector-Greenwich-Barry)/ "Cashbox Blues (Whoops, We Printed the Wrong Story Again)" (Spector)	(Unreleased in U.S.)	
Philles 136	Ike and Tina Turner	"A Love Like Yours (Don't Come Knockin' Every Day)" (Holland-Dozier-Holland)/ "I Idolize You" (I. Turner)	(Unreleased in U.S.)	
1969				
A&M 1039	Checkmates Ltd.	"Love Is All I Have to Give" (Spector-Stevens)/ "Never Should Have Tried" (Baugh-Stevens)	4/5	65
A&M 1040	Ronettes	"You Came, You Saw, You Conquered" (Spector-Wine-Levine)/ "Oh I Love You" (Spector)	4/5	108

A&M 1053	Sonny Charles and the Checkmates Ltd.	"Black Pearl" (Spector-Wine-Levine)/ "Lazy Susan" (Harvey Trees)	5/10	13
A&M 1118	Ike and Tina Turner	"River Deep—Mountain High" (Spector-Greenwich-Barry)/ "I'll Keep You Happy" (Spector)	—	—
A&M 1127	Sonny Charles and the Checkmates Ltd.	"Proud Mary" (Fogerty)/ "Do You Love Your Baby" (Stevens)	10/18	69
A&M 1170	Ike and Tina Turner	"A Love Like Yours (Don't Come Knockin' Every Day)" (Holland-Dozier-Holland)/ "Save the Last Dance for Me" (Pomus-Shuman)	—	—

1970

Apple 1818	John Lennon & Plastic Ono Band	"Instant Karma" (Lennon)/ "Who Has Seen the Wind?" (Ono)	2/28	3
Apple 2995	George Harrison	"My Sweet Lord" (Harrison)/ "Isn't It a Pity" (Harrison)	11/28	1
Atco 6780	Derek & the Dominoes	"Tell the Truth" (Clapton-Whitlock)/ "Roll It Over" (Clapton-Whitlock)	(Unreleased)	

1971

Apple 1827	John Lennon & Plastic Ono Band	"Mother" (Lennon)/ "Oh Why?" (Lennon)	1/9	31
Apple 1828	George Harrison	"What Is Life?" (Harrison)/ "Apple Scruffs" (Harrison)	2/27	9
Apple 1830	John Lennon & Plastic Ono Band	"Power to the People" (Lennon)/ "Touch Me" (Lennon)	4/3	11

SINGLES (*continued*)

LABEL AND CATALOGUE NUMBER	GROUP	TITLE (WRITER)*	CHART ENTRY DATE†	HIGHEST CHART POSITION
Apple 1832	Ronnie Spector	"Try Some, Buy Some" (Harrison)/ "Tandoori Chicken" (Harrison-Spector)	—	—
Apple 1835	John Lennon & the Plastic Ono Band	"God Save Us" (Lennon) [This side: Spector-Lennon-Ono-Evans]/ "Do the Oz" (Lennon) [This side: Lennon-Ono-Spector]	—	—
Apple 1836	George Harrison	"Bangladesh" (Harrison)/ "Deep Blue" (Harrison)	8/14	21 95
Apple 1840	John Lennon	"Imagine" (Lennon)/ "It's So Hard" (Harrison)	10/23	3
Apple 1843	John Lennon and Yoko Ono	"Happy Xmas (War Is Over)" (Lennon-Ono)/ "Listen the Snow Is Falling" (Ono)	—	—
1972				
Apple 1848	John Lennon and Yoko Ono	"Woman Is the Nigger of the World" (Lennon-Ono)/ "Sisters O Sisters" (Ono)	6/3	77

1974

Warner-Spector 0400	Cher	"A Woman's Story" (Spector-Tempo-Stevens)/ "Baby, I Love You" (Spector-Greenwich-Barry)	—
Warner-Spector 0401	Darlene Love	"Christmas (Baby Please Come Home)" (Spector-Greenwich-Barry)/ "Winter Wonderland" (Smith-Bernard)	—
Warner-Spector 0402	Cher/Nilsson	"A Love Like Yours (Don't Come Knockin' Every Day)" (Holland-Dozier-Holland)/ "(Just Enough to Keep Me) Hangin' On" (Mize-Allen)	—
Warner-Spector/ Big Tree 0403	Dion	"Make the Woman Love Me" (Mann-Weil)/ "Running Close Behind You" (Tuohy-DiMucci)	—

1975

Apple 1881	John Lennon	"Stand By Me" (King-Leiber-Stoller) [This side: Spector]/ "Move Over Mrs. L" (Lennon) [This side: John Lennon]	—
Warner-Spector 0405	Calhoon	"(Do You Wanna) Dance, Dance, Dance" (Calhoon)/ "Rain 2000" (Loseth-Robinson) [Both sides: Walter Kahn]	—

SINGLES *(continued)*

LABEL AND CATALOGUE NUMBER	GROUP	TITLE (WRITER)*	CHART ENTRY DATE †	HIGHEST CHART POSITION
Warner-Spector 0406	Jerri Bo Keno	"Here It Comes (and Here I Go)" (Spector-Barry)/ "I Don't Know Why" (Spector)	—	—
Warner-Spector 0407	Calhoon	"Soul Man" (Hayes-Porter)/ "Soul Man Pt. 2" (Hayes-Porter) [Both sides: Walter Kahn]	—	—
1976				
Warner-Spector 0408	Danny Potter	"Standing in the Sunshine" (Potter) [This side: Harry Hinde]/ "Red Bluff" (Potter) [This side: Timberlane Productions]		
Warner-Spector 0409	Ronnie Spector	"Paradise" (Spector-Nilsson)/ "When I Saw You" (Spector)	—	—
1977				
Warner-Spector 0410	Darlene Love	"Lord, If You're a Woman" (Mann-Weil)/ "Stumble and Fall" (Spector-Poncia-Andreoli)	—	—

1979

Sire 1051	Ramones	"Rock 'n' Roll High School" (Ramones)/ "Do You Wanna Dance (Live)" (Freeman)	—

1980

Sire 49182	Ramones	"Baby I Love You" (Spector-Greenwich-Barry)/ "High Risk Insurance" (Ramones)	—
Sire 49261	Ramones	"Do You Remember Rock 'n' Roll Radio" (Ramones)/ "Let's Go" (Ramones)	—

ALBUMS

LABEL AND CATALOGUE NUMBER	GROUP	TITLE	CHART ENTRY DATE	HIGHEST CHART POSITION

1959

Imperial 9067	Teddy Bears	*The Teddy Bears Sing!* Tracks: "Oh Why"; "Unchained Melody"; "My Foolish Heart"; "You Said Goodbye"; "True Love"; "Little Things Mean Alot"; "I Don't Need You Anymore"; "Tammy"; "Long Ago and Far Away"; "Don't Go Away"; "If I Give My Heart to You"; "Seven Lonely Days"	—	

1962

Philles 4000	Crystals	*Twist Uptown.* Tracks: "Uptown"; "Another Country—Another World"; "Frankenstein Twist"; "Oh Yeah, Maybe Baby"; "Please	—	

LABEL AND CATALOGUE NUMBER	GROUP	TITLE	CHART ENTRY DATE	HIGHEST CHART POSITION
		Hurt Me"; "There's No Other (Like My Baby)"; "On Broadway"; "What a Nice Way to Turn 17"; "No One Ever Tells You"; "Gee Whiz (Look at His Eyes)"; "I Love You Eddie"		
1963				
Philles 4001	Crystals	*He's a Rebel.* Tracks: "He's a Rebel"; "Uptown"; "Another Country—Another World"; "Frankenstein Twist"; "Oh Yeah, Maybe Baby"; "He's Sure the Boy I Love"; "There's No Other (Like My Baby)"; "On Broadway"; "What a Nice Way to Turn 17"; "No One Ever Tells You"; "He Hit Me (and It Felt Like a Kiss)"; "I Love You Eddie"	3/16	131
Philles 4002	Bob B. Soxx and the Blue Jeans	*Zip-A-Dee-Doo-Dah.* Tracks: "Zip-A-Dee-Doo-Dah"; "Why Do Lovers Break Each Others' Hearts?"; "Let the Good Times Roll"; "My Heart Beat a Little Bit Faster"; "Jimmy Baby"; "Baby (I Love You)"; "The White Cliffs of Dover"; "This Land Is Your Land"; "Dear (Here Comes My Baby)"; "I Shook the World"; "Everything's Gonna Be All Right"; "Dr. Kaplan's Office"	—	—
Philles 4003	Crystals	*The Crystals Sing the Greatest Hits Vol. 1.* Tracks: "Da Doo Ron Ron"; "On Broadway"; "He's a Rebel"; "Hot Pastrami"; "There's No Other (Like My Baby)"; "The Wah Watusi"; "Mashed Potato Time"; "He's Sure the Boy I Love"; "Uptown"; "The Twist"; "Gee Whiz (Look at His Eyes)"; "Look in My Eyes"	—	—

Philles 4004	Various Artists	*Philles Records Presents Today's Hits.* Tracks: (Crystals) "Then He Kissed Me"; "Da Doo Ron Ron"; "Oh Yeah, Maybe Baby"; (Bob B. Soxx and the Blue Jeans) "Zip-A-Dee-Doo Dah"; "Why Do Lovers Break Each Others' Hearts?"; "Not Too Young to Get Married"; (Ronettes) "Be My Baby"; (Darlene Love) "Wait 'Til My Bobby Gets Home"; "(Today I Met) The Boy I'm Gonna Marry"; "My Heart Beat a Little Bit Faster"; "Playing for Keeps"; (Alley Cats) "Puddin' 'n' Tain"	—	—
Philles 4005	Various Artists	*A Christmas Gift for You.* Tracks: (Darlene Love) "White Christmas"; "(It's a) Marshmallow World"; "Winter Wonderland"; "Christmas (Baby Please Come Home)"; (Ronettes) "Frosty the Snowman"; "Sleigh Ride"; "I Saw Mommy Kissing Santa Claus"; (Bob B. Soxx and the Blue Jeans) "The Bells of St. Mary's"; "Here Comes Santa Claus"; (Crystals) "Santa Claus Is Coming to Town"; "Rudolph the Red-Nosed Reindeer"; "Parade of the Wooden Soldiers"; (Phil Spector and Artists) "Silent Night"	—	—
1964				
Philles 4006	Ronettes	*Presenting the Fabulous Ronettes Featuring Veronica.* Tracks: "Walking in the Rain"; "Do I Love You"; "So Young"; "(The Best of) Breakin' Up"; "I Wonder"; "What'd I Say"; "Be My Baby"; "You Baby"; "Baby I Love You"; "How Does It Feel?"; "When I Saw You"; "Chapel of Love"	12/26	96
1965				
Philles 4007	Righteous Brothers	*You've Lost That Lovin' Feelin'.* Tracks: "You've Lost That Lovin' Feelin' "; "Ko Ko Mo"; "Ol' Man River"; "Look at Me"; "What'd I	1/23	4

ALBUMS (*continued*)

LABEL AND CATALOGUE NUMBER	GROUP	TITLE	CHART ENTRY DATE	HIGHEST CHART POSITION
		Say"; "The Angels Listened In"; "Sick and Tired"; "Summertime"; "Over and Over"; "Soul City"; "There's a Woman"		
Philles 4008	Righteous Brothers	*Just Once in My Life.* Tracks: "Just Once in My Life"; "Big Boy Pete"; "Unchained Melody"; "You Are My Sunshine"; "The Great Pretender"; "Sticks and Stones"; "See That Girl"; "Oo-Poo-Pah-Doo"; "You'll Never Walk Alone"; "Guess Who?"; "The Blues"	5/29	9
Philles 4009	Righteous Brothers	*Back to Back.* Tracks: "Ebb Tide"; "Hung on You"; "For Sentimental Reasons"; "The White Cliffs of Dover"; "God Bless the Child"; "Hallelujah I Love Her So"; "Loving You"; "Without a Doubt"; "Late Late Night"; "Hot Tamales"; "She's Mine All Mine"; "Hot Tamales" [First four: Phil Spector; Last eight: Bill Medley]	12/25	16
Philles 4010	Lenny Bruce	*Lenny Bruce Is Out Again*	—	—
1966				
Philles 4011	Ike and Tina Turner	*River Deep—Mountain High.* Tracks: "River Deep—Mountain High"; "I Idolize You"; "A Love Like Yours (Don't Come Knockin' Every Day)"; "A Fool in Love"; "Make 'Em Wait"; "Hold on Baby"; "Save the Last Dance for Me"; "Oh Baby! (Things Ain't What They Used to Be)"; "Every Day I Have to Cry"; "Such a Fool for You"; "It's Gonna Work Out Fine"; "You're So Fine"	(Unreleased in U.S.)	

1969

Ike and Tina Turner	A&M 4178	*River Deep—Mountain High*. (Tracks as above but with "I'll Never Need More Than This" replacing "You're So Fine.")	9/27	102
Checkmates Ltd. Featuring Sonny Charles	A&M 4183	*Love Is All We Have to Give*. Tracks: "Proud Mary"; "Spanish Harlem"; "Black Pearl"; "I Keep Forgettin'"; "Love Is All I Have to Give"; "The Hair Anthology Suite"	10/18	178

1970

Beatles	Apple 34001	*Let It Be*. Tracks: "Two of Us"; "Dig a Pony"; "Across the Universe"; "I Me Mine"; "Dig It"; "Let It Be"; "Maggie May"; "I've Got a Feeling"; "One After 909"; "The Long and Winding Road"; "For You Blue"; "Get Back"	5/20	1
George Harrison	Apple 639	*All Things Must Pass*. Tracks: "I'd Have You Anytime"; "My Sweet Lord"; "Wah Wah"; "Isn't It a Pity"; "What Is Life"; "If Not for You"; "Behind That Locked Door"; "Let It Down"; "Run of the Mill"; "Beware of Darkness"; "Apple Scruffs"; "Ballad of Sir Frankie Crisp (Let It Roll)"; "Awaiting on You All"; "All Things Must Pass"; "I Dig Love"; "Art of Dying"; "Isn't It a Pity"; "Hear Me Lord"; "Out of the Blue"; "It's Johnny's Birthday"; "Plug Me In"; "I Remember Jeep"; "Thanks for the Pepperoni"	12/19	1
John Lennon	Apple 3372	*John Lennon/Plastic Ono Band*. Tracks: "Mother"; "Hold on John"; "I Found Out"; "Working Class Hero"; "Isolation"; "Remember"; "Love"; "Well Well Well"; "Look at Me"; "My Mummy's Dead"	12/26	6

ALBUMS (*continued*)

LABEL AND CATALOGUE NUMBER	GROUP	TITLE	CHART ENTRY DATE	HIGHEST CHART POSITION
1971				
Apple 3379	John Lennon	*Imagine*. Tracks: "Imagine"; "Crippled Inside"; "Jealous Guy"; "It's So Hard"; "I Don't Wanna Be a Soldier Mama I Don't Wanna Die"; "Gimme Some Truth"; "Oh My Love"; "How Do You Sleep?"; "How?"; "Oh Yoko!"	9/18	1
Apple 3385	George Harrison and Various Artists	*The Concert for Bangladesh*. Tracks: "Bangla Dhun"; "Wah-Wah"; "My Sweet Lord"; "Awaiting On You All"; "That's the Way God Planned It"; "It Don't Come Easy"; "Beware of Darkness"; "While My Guitar Gently Weeps"; "Jumpin' Jack Flash"; "Young Blood"; "Here Comes the Sun"; "A Hard Rain's Gonna Fall"; "It Takes Alot to Laugh, It Takes a Train to Cry"; "Blowin' in the Wind"; "Mr. Tambourine Man"; "Just Like a Woman"; "Something"; "Bangladesh"	1/8/72	2
1972				
Apple 3392	John Lennon	*Sometime in New York City*. Tracks: Record One: "The Luck of the Irish"; "Attica State"; "New York City"; "John Sinclair"; "Born in a Prison"; "Sunday Bloody Sunday"; "Sisters O Sisters"; "Angela"; "Woman Is the Nigger of the World"; "We're All Water"; Record Two—Live Jam with the Mothers of Invention: "Don't Worry, Kyoko"; "Jam Rag"; "Scumbag"	7/1	48

1975

Warner-Spector SP 9101	Lenny Bruce	*The Law, the Language and Lenny Bruce.*	—
Adam VIII 8018	John Lennon	*John Lennon Sings the Great Rock 'n' Roll Hits (Roots).* Tracks: "Stand By Me"; "Sweet Little Sixteen"; "Angel Baby"; "You Can't Catch Me"; "Bony Maronie"; "Be My Baby"; "Just Because"; "Be-Bop-A-Lula"; "Ain't That a Shame"; "Rip It Up"; "Do You Wanna Dance"; "Peggy Sue"; "Bring It on Home to Me"; "Slippin' and Slidin'"; "Ya-Ya" [First seven: Phil Spector; Last eight: John Lennon]	—
Apple 3419	John Lennon	*Rock 'n' Roll.* Tracks: "Stand By Me"; "Sweet Little Sixteen"; "You Can't Catch Me"; "Bony Maronie"; "Just Because"; "Be-Bop-A-Lula"; Medley: "Ready Teddy"/ "Rip It Up"; "Ain't That a Shame"; "Do You Wanna Dance"; "Slippin' and Slidin'"; "Peggy Sue"; Medley: "Bring It on Home to Me"/"Send Me Some Lovin'"; "Ya-Ya" [First five: Phil Spector; Last eight: John Lennon]	—
Polydor 2307002 (G. B.)	Dion	*Born To Be With You.* Tracks: "Born to Be with You"; "Make the Woman Love Me"; "Your Own Backyard"; "(He's Got) The Whole World in His Hands"; "Only You Know"; "New York City Song"; "In and Out of the Shadows"; "Good Lovin' Man"	(Released only in England)
Phil Spector Int. 007 (G. B.)	Various Artists	*Yesterday's Hits Today.* (Reissue of Philles 4004.)	(Released only in England)

ALBUMS (continued)

LABEL AND CATALOGUE NUMBER	GROUP	TITLE	CHART ENTRY DATE	HIGHEST CHART POSITION
1976				
Warner-Spector SP 9103	Various Artists	*A Christmas Gift For You.* (Reissue of Philles 4005.)	—	—
Phil Spector Int. 008 (G. B.)	Various Artists	*Rare Masters, Volume 1.*	(Released only in England)	
Phil Spector Int. 009 (G. B.)	Various Artists	*Rare Masters, Volume 2.*	(Released only in England)	
Phil Spector Int. 012 (G. B.)	Various Artists	*Echoes of the Sixties: Phil Spector's Top Twenty.* Tracks: "River Deep—Mountain High"; "Then He Kissed Me"; "Be My Baby"; "Why Do Lovers Break Each Other's Hearts?"; "Proud Mary"; "(To-day I Met) The Boy I'm Gonna Marry"; "Zip-A-Dee-Doo-Dah"; "(The Best Part of) Breaking Up"; "You've Lost That Lovin' Feelin'"; "Da Doo Ron Ron"; "He's a Rebel"; "Not Too Young to Get Married"; "Uptown"; "Unchained Melody"; "Walking in the Rain"; "There's No Other (Like My Baby)"; "He's Sure the Boy I Love"; "Ebb Tide"; "Wait 'Til My Bobby Gets Home"; "Baby I Love You"	(Released only in England)	

1977

Warner-Spector SP 9104	Various Artists	*Phil Spector's Greatest Hits* (Double LP). Tracks: "Be My Baby"; "Da Doo Ron Ron"; "You've Lost That Lovin' Feelin' "; "Then He Kissed Me"; "Baby I Love You"; "Walking in the Rain"; "He's a Rebel"; "Uptown"; "Zip-A-Dee-Doo-Dah"; "Not Too Young to Get Married"; "(Today I Met) The Boy I'm Gonna Marry"; Wait 'Til My Bobby Gets Home"; "To Know Him Is to Love Him"; "Pretty Little Angel Eyes"; "I Love How You Love Me"; "Every Breath I Take"; "Under the Moon of Love"; "He's Sure the Boy I Love"; "Spanish Harlem"; "Unchained Melody"; "River Deep—Mountain High"; "Just Once in My Life"; "Black Pearl"; "Ebb Tide"	—	—

1978

Warner Bros. 3125	Leonard Cohen	*Death of a Ladies' Man.* Tracks: "Death of a Ladies' Man"; "True Love Leaves No Traces"; "Iodine"; "Paper-Thin Hotel"; "Memories"; "Don't Go Home"; "Fingerprints"; "I Left a Woman Waiting"	—	—

1979

Sire 6067	Ramones	*End of the Century.* Tracks: "Do You Remember Rock 'n' Roll Radio?"; "I'm Affected"; "Danny Says"; "Chinese Rock"; "The Return of Jackie and Judy"; "Let's Go"; "Baby I Love You"; "I Can't Make It on Time"; "This Ain't Havana"; "Rock 'n' Roll High School"; "All the Way"; "High Risk Insurance"	2/23/80	44

LABEL AND CATALOGUE NUMBER	GROUP	TITLE	CHART ENTRY DATE	HIGHEST CHART POSITION
Phil Spector Int. 015 (G. B.)	Various Artists	*Phil Spector 74/79.* Tracks: (Dion) "Make the Woman Love Me"; "Born to Be with You"; "Baby Let's Stick Together"; (Cher) "A Woman's Story"; "Baby I Love You"; (Nilsson-Cher) "A Love Like Yours (Don't Come Knocking Every Day)"; (Jerri Bo Keno) "Here It Comes (And Here I Go)"; (Darlene Love) "I Love Him Like I Love My Very Life"; "Lord, If You're a Woman"; (Kim Fowley) "Give It to Me"	(Released only in England)	

1986

| Capitol SJ 12533 | John Lennon | *Menlove Ave.* (Compiled from the Spector-Lennon 1973 tapes.) Tracks: "Angel Baby"; "Since My Baby Left Me"; "To Know Her Is to Love Her"; "Steel and Glass"; "Scared"; "Old Dirt Road"; "Nobody Loves You (When You're Down and Out)"; "Bless You" [First eight: Spector]; "Here We Go Again" [Spector-Lennon]; "Rock 'n' Roll People" [Lennon] | — | — |

Discography Additions to the Da Capo Edition

SINGLES

LABEL AND CATALOGUE NUMBER	GROUP	TITLE (WRITER)	CHART ENTRY DATE	HIGHEST CHART POSITION
1990				
Verve/ Forecast 871882	Righteous Brothers	"Unchained Melody"	8/90	1 a/c, 13 pop
2003				
Capitol 0724359000701 (5" CD Single)	Starsailor	"Silence Is Easy"; "Could You Be Mine?"; "She Understands"		

ALBUMS

LABEL AND CATALOGUE NUMBER	GROUP	TITLE (WRITER)	CHART ENTRY DATE	HIGHEST CHART POSITION
1990				
Curb 77381	Righteous Brothers	*Unchained Melody: Best of the Righteous Brother* (includes the original Philles singles "Unchained Melody"; "You've Lost That Lovin' Feelin'"; "Ebb Tide"; "Just Once in My Life")	11/90	161
1991				
ABKCO 71181 (4-CD Box Set)	Various Artists	*Back To Mono 1958-1969* Tracks: (Disc 1) "To Know Him Is To Love Him"; "Corrina, Corrina"; "Spanish Harlem"; "Pretty Little Angel Eyes"; "Every Breath I Take"; "I Love How You Love Me"; "Under The Moon Of Love"; "There's No Other Like My Baby"; "Uptown"; "He Hit Me (And It Felt Like A Kiss)"; "He's A Rebel"; "Zip-A-Dee-Doo-Dah"; "Puddin' N' Tain"; "He's Sure The Boy I Love"; "Why Do Lovers Break Each Other's Hearts"; "(Today I Met) The Boy I'm Gonna Marry"; "Da Doo Ron Ron"; "Heartbreaker"; "Why Don't They Let Us Fall In Love"; "Chapel Of Love"; "Not Too Young To Get Married"; "Wait Til My Bobby Gets Home"; "All Grown Up" (Disc 2) "Be My Baby"; "Then He Kissed Me"; "A Fine, Fine Boy"; "Baby, I Love You"; "I Wonder"; "Girls Can Tell"; "Little Boy"; "Hold Me Tight"; "(The Best Part Of) Breakin' Up"; "Soldier Baby Of Mine"; "Strange Love"; "Stumble And Fall"; "When I Saw You"; "So Young"; "Do I Love You?"; "Keep On Dancing"; "You, Baby"; "Woman In Love (With		

You)"; "Walking In The Rain" (Disc 3) "You've Lost That Lovin' Feelin'"; "Born To Be Together"; "Just Once In My Life"; "Unchained Melody"; "Is This What I Get For Loving You?"; "Long Way To Be Happy"; "(I Love You) For Sentimental Reasons"; "Ebb Tide"; "This Could Be The Night"; "Paradise"; "River Deep—Mountain High"; "I'll Never Need More Than This"; "A Love Like Yours (Don't Come Knockin' Every Day)"; "Save The Last Dance For Me"; "I Wish I Never Saw The Sunshine"; "You Came, You Saw, You Conquered"; "Black Pearl"; "Love Is All I Have To Give" (Disc 4) "White Christmas"; "Frosty The Snowman"; "The Bells of St. Mary"; "Santa Claus Is Coming to Town"; "Sleigh Ride"; "Marshmallow World"; "I Saw Mommy Kissing Santa Claus"; "Rudolph the Red-Nosed Reindeer"; "Winter Wonderland"; "Parade of the Wooden Soldiers"; "Christmas (Baby Please Come Home)"; "Here Comes Santa Claus"; "Silent Night"

2000

PS001   Various Artists

Phil Spector's Flips and Rarities Tracks: "I Idolize You" (Ike & Tina Turner); "Black Pearl" (Sonny Charles & The Checkmates); "Dream For Sale" (Gene Pitney); "Some of Your Loving" (Johnny Nash); "World of Tears" (Johnny Nash); "When You Dance" (Billy Storm); "Spanish Harlem" (Santo & Johnny); "Mr. Robin" (Spector's Three); "Some of Your Lovin'" (Emil O'Connor); "I Love You Betty" (Yerry Day); "That's Alright Baby" (Gary Crosby); "Yes I Love You" (Paris Sisters); "That's What Girls Are For" (Timothy Hay & Wanderobo); "Where Can You Be?" (Tony & Joe); "Raincoat In a River" (Sammy Turner); "To Know Him Is To Love Him" (Lesley Gore); "Be My Girl" (Ray Peterson); "Unchained Melody" (Blackwells); "Oh! Why" (Teddy Bears); "Home of the Brave" (Bonnie & The Treasures); "Why Can't a Boy and Girl Just Stay In Love" (April Stevens); "Why Don't They Let Us Fall In Love" (Veronica); "The Screw (Let's Dance)" (Crystals); *(continues)*

ALBUMS (*continued*)

LABEL AND CATALOGUE NUMBER	GROUP	TITLE (WRITER)	CHART ENTRY DATE	HIGHEST CHART POSITION
		Phil Spector's Flips and Rarities (continued): "Bumbershoot" (Phil Harvey); "(I'm a) Woman In Love" (Ronettes); "He's a Quiet Guy" (Darlene Love); "Here It Comes (And Here I Go)" (Jerri Bo Keno); "Puddin 'n Tain" (Alleycats); "Dream For Sale" (Joey Paige); "I'm So Happy (Tra-La-La)" (Ducanes)		

2003

LABEL AND CATALOGUE NUMBER	GROUP	TITLE (WRITER)	CHART ENTRY DATE	HIGHEST CHART POSITION
Capitol 90007 (US), EMI 5900072 (UK)	Starsailor	*Silence Is Easy.* Spector-produced tracks: #4 "Silence Is Easy"; #8 "White Dove"		

INDEX

⊙

⊙